For Colette, Eric, and Christine
la Seine constante du bouquiniste

Contents

Preface

The United States Constitution mirrors its framers' ambivalence toward democracy in their balancing popular government with restraints upon majority rule. Overriding this arrangement with respect to the several state electoral systems were the constitutional amending process and such flexible provisions as the Times, Places, and Manner Clause and the Necessary and Proper Clause. These provisions, the constitutional amendments and federal statutes passed under them, and judicial review and interpretation have provided avenues for change. The change has been in the direction of greater democratization. An increasingly unitary American electorate has come to be defined by more uniform standards, many of which have been built into federal law. Over the last century, Americans have come to rely on federal reform routes to strengthen representative government, to protect and make effective the right to vote, and to extend the population base of the franchise. In this development, the Supreme Court has assumed important functions as an agency of accommodation.

The Supreme Court and its relation to the electoral process is a necessarily complex subject. Both the Constitution and the Court have changed over time. From the Twelfth through the Twenty-fifth Amendments, the electoral process has been the subject of more constitutional alterations than any other combination of topics. Where the Supreme Court is concerned, the changes that have taken place in the views of its members in cases from 1870 to 1970 are enormous, especially with regard to voting rights and electoral process litigation.

An analysis of judicially wrought shifts in American electoral law and practices cannot rely wholly on the politically neutral language of the law, which tends to obscure the reality of politics and the give-and-take of powerful groups and interests dedicated to changing the law. To understand the emergence of an increasingly nationalized electoral system one must explore political as well as legal lines. In legal terms, the core of the matter is the successful reliance on the Constitution by voting rights litigants who have won landmark rulings affecting national, state, and local electoral practices. In recent years this has been reflected in the shift of election law contests in federal courts from a light caseload of criminal prosecutions for fraudulent practices and interference with voter registration to a preponderance of civil suits. I have viewed the public record of civil litigation in the voting rights field in broadly political terms as constructive discontent. The cadence of social and political change in the United States may be heard in civil suit after civil suit, whereby plaintiffs have attempted to bring the electoral process into rough harmony with shifting balances of power in society. Racial discrimination cases, reapportionment, and congressional districting suits, did not by themselves change the balance of power in the United States. Rather, in advance of legislative recognition, judicial rulings on these topics gave legal expression to prior shifts in the political resources of racial minorities and urban majorities. Had it been otherwise, southern filibusters and the "Dirksen Amendment" would have prevailed.

Political rights contests in federal courts have covered many types of problems. They include challenges to state prerequisites for printing a candidate's name on the ballot, suits alleging unfair bureaucratic barriers to the effective use of absentee ballots, appeals of Federal Communications Commission rulings on political broadcasting, and states-rights claims on behalf of counties and states affected by the Voting Rights Act of 1965. More voluminous than candidate-initiated suits have been cases brought by voters alleging racial discrimination and malapportionment. Litigation in these areas has multiplied greatly in recent years. For better or worse, the number of such suits reflects an increasing dependence by the effectively disfranchised and politically disaffected on federal courts rather than on other government branches or on political parties for solutions to political and social problems. The variety of litigious efforts to bring adjustments in the electoral process may be perplexing but should not be surprising, given the American penchant for transforming political problems into legal causes of action.

My most challenging problem has been how to focus on the salient trends in very disparate developments. No solution is without difficulties since there can be no natural subdivision of composite election functions. With this in mind, I made an effort to write each chapter as a unit capable of standing on its own. The result favors coherence and full coverage but at the cost of some overlapping treatment. At the same time, the task was to treat as a whole related topics which other scholars have analyzed separately. The problem is not unlike that faced in attempting to report isolated Commerce Clause cases against the background of an economy expanding into an interstate affair and gradually becoming subject to ever-larger federal supervision. But whereas the inevitable laws of the market place have come to make the states nearly irrelevant in economic regulation, the overall trend in electoral process cases has been a search for ways to revitalize the responsiveness of state and local governments to expanded and changing constituencies. The alternative—and the Court has prepared the way for it—would be for Congress to show the same willingness to regulate the electoral system that it has shown regarding the economic structure. Until the legislative process replaces the litigation process, it is clear that charting fundamental legal changes in the political system from the adversary proceedings of appellate review will remain a difficult problem.

Chapter 1 is a process-oriented and political introduction to the entire field of elections-related litigation. It includes an analysis of politics by litigation, a picture of individual litigants in action, and a discussion of sources of support and legal strategies. Chapters 2 through 11 are topically and historically differentiated. The order of topics is suggested by the sequence with which the Supreme Court has given constitutional life to various aspects of the electoral process: voting rights for U.S. representatives, Negro enfranchisement, legislative apportionment, congressional districting, and regulations affecting presidential elections. Chapter 2 supplies a substantive primer on the constitutionally based right to vote, given its earliest vitality in the 1880s by the Supreme Court in congressional election cases. An

understanding of the constitutional source of the right is of fundamental importance for the practical reason that no litigious challenges
to election laws and practices have been more successful than those
couched in the language of voters' rights. The third through the sixth
chapters follow essentially chronological order in tracing racial discrimination and voting cases in the late nineteenth century (Chapter 3), the early twentieth century (Chapter 4), federal legislation
at mid-century (Chapter 5), and Supreme Court rulings of the 1960s
(Chapter 6). Chapters 7 and 8 give an account of the one-person,
one-vote rulings of the 1960s. Chapters 9 and 10 separately concern
Supreme Court litigation relating to congressional districting and
presidential elections. The discussion in these two chapters on federal elections ranges over a wide period of time. Nevertheless, because the Supreme Court did not render significant and definitive
rulings in either area until 1968, it was appropriate to place the material toward the end of the study. The concluding chapter reviews
the courtroom events which have recently set the direction under
Chief Justice Warren's Court for a larger share of federal responsibility for the entire electoral process. Chapter 11 defines the "nationalization of the electoral process" within the framework of federal
policy-making. The role of the Supreme Court is analyzed insofar
as it has articulated (though it has not wholly initiated) a trend running counter to earlier traditions of decentralized control of the franchise and electoral administration by the states. If the judges are not
the close observers of "th iliction returns" that Mr. Dooley long ago
suggested they were, they have certainly become close observers of
the election process.

This book has benefited by the contributions of information, assistance, and support of many people, and a number of acknowledgments
are due. Of course, I reserve responsibility for any errors in the
presentation. For their encouragement of my writing, appreciation is
extended to Professors Don C. Piper of the University of Maryland
and George W. Spicer of the University of Virginia. Valuable assistance and generous interviewing time have been given by many government officials and staff members in the Department of Justice, the
Civil Rights Commission, the Office of Hearing Examiners, House
and Senate Judiciary Committees of the United States Congress, and
the Administrative Office of the United States Courts. Of the law
firms where data was sought, the following deserve special thanks:
Peticolas, Luscombe, and Stephens located in El Paso, Texas; Rhyne
and Rhyne (Washington, D.C.); and Wasserman and Carliner of

Washington, D.C. Also supplying useful unpublished information were Morris B. Abram of Brandeis University, William Boyd of the National Muncipal League, Mrs. Ann Ginger of the Meiklejohn Library in Berkeley, Jack Greenberg of the NAACP Legal Defense and Education Fund, Jerry Hutton of the Legislative Reference Service, Burke Marshall and Charles Ryan, both associated with the Lawyers Committee for Civil Rights Under Law, Neal Peirce and Joseph Foote, both with the Center for Political Research, Mrs. Margaret Price at the Potomac Institute, Professor Jerome Shuman with Howard University Law School, Professor Samuel Krislov of the University of Minnesota, and Melvin Wulf of the American Civil Liberties Union. Paul Manchey and Daniel Pflum, graduate students at the University of Maryland, and Raymond Keeney, a law student at George Washington University, each assisted in research reflected in this book. Thanks are due to the *Harvard Journal on Legislation* for the editors' permission to reprint portions of my work in the final chapter of this book. Mr. John Gallman of the Johns Hopkins Press lent the right proportions of moral and material support. Mrs. K. Lorraine Reichart earned my gratitude by her skillful typing of the manuscript. Finally, but by no means lastly, I must express my warm appreciation to my wife Colette for the inspiration necessary to give my work significance, to my parents who encouraged this enterprise, and to my children, Eric and Christine, for the decorative doodles which graced an early draft of this book.

Bethesda, Maryland   R. P. C.

The Supreme Court
and the Electoral Process

1 Litigation in
the electoral process

Like running for public and political office, presenting a litigious challenge to an election law or practice engages very few Americans, and like running for office, filing an electoral suit must offer at least a gambling man's chance of success. This book is a record of most of the successes and a few of the failures of a small but increasing number of citizens who participate in politics by seeking to change in the courts the formal or informal rules of the democratic process. Mixing politics and litigation is hardly a twentieth-century innovation in the United States. But in recent years, the appellate docket of cases involving election laws has increased greatly in volume and in national significance. In the quarter century between 1944 and 1969, the Supreme Court has ruled on 100 political rights, districting, and electoral process cases—more than the entire output of the preceding century in this area of constitutional politics.

Elections are institutional procedures for choosing officeholders. In a larger sense, they are also exercises in mass communication. The web of federal and state voting statutes, woven on the framework constructed in 1787 and altered occasionally by constitutional reform, delineates the network through which the voice of the people can be heard. Like any communication system, election machinery requires recurrent overhaul to prevent the colloquy between voter and representative becoming muffled. Lines of accountability fade in and out in an electoral system in which, to some extent, every election is within the jurisdiction of both federal and state governments. When significant groups are excluded from effective franchise rights and officeholders thereby become deaf to their social needs, litigation may function similarly to voting—as a form of political expression. In 1963, Justice Brennan acknowledged this point: "Groups which find themselves unable to achieve their objectives through the ballot frequently turn to the courts."[1] Even when the litigants and their legal staff supporters anticipate defeat in the courts, the resulting valuable publicity may act as a catalyst for a larger program of electoral reform.

The ballot and the bench, then, provide the technique and the forum for political expression. The ballot is the most direct link between the electorate and the officials they select. The bench provides a grievance panel for those who claim that they do not have access to that link. In the courts they have a public sounding board for those political and social needs which can be translated into legal questions. Of course, it is generally the major political parties which conduct and may control the flow of political communication in a government of federally divided and separated powers. In pluralized American society, interest groups also perform a communication function. Their success will depend in part upon their finding a receptive point in the governmental structure. Private organizations, particularly those without a commanding voice in party councils, sometimes articulate their demands through the labyrinthine channels of the judicial process. The airing of group complaints in this form may involve a highly specialized kind of communications feedback in which grievances are expressed in terms of political or civil rights complaints. In this perspective, voting rights claims, even though formulated in terms of alleged individual rights, may be seen as a function of intergroup conflict within the political system. No matter how innocent of tangible interest group backing the litigant in a civil suit may be, however, vir-

---

1. *NAACP* v. *Button*, 371 U.S. 415 at 429 (1963). The case involved the overruling on First and Fourteenth Amendment grounds of a complex statutory attempt by Virginia to curtail the litigious activities of the NAACP.

tually every voting case decided on constitutional grounds will have an impact upon other citizens.

As a first step in analyzing the role of the Supreme Court in the electoral process, it is appropriate here to concentrate on the political context in which judicial decision-making takes place. In this chapter, several questions are asked about public law litigation and about the parties who come before the Court—their causes and contests. Pressing a lawsuit in defense of ballot rights, in a country where the record of voter turnout is often meagre, suggests an unusual dedication on the part of the litigant. He is involved in a unique form of political participation. Who litigates and why? Who helps the litigants? What is contested and how? The answers to these questions focus respectively on litigants and their interests, on lawyers and supporting organizations, and on legal strategy and procedures.

LITIGANTS AS POLITICAL PARTICIPANTS

If you ask a political scientist who votes and why, he will refer you to a vast literature of voting behavior studies which have been nowhere so thorough in their investigations as in the United States. The findings of these empirical inquiries testify to the complexity of human motivation, but generally they conclude that education, age, and increased economic status go hand-in-hand with such civic activities as the casting of a ballot. Ten percent fewer women go to the polls than men. Usually the most important determining factor is whether a person identifies himself with one of the major political parties. The greater the feeling of identification, the stronger is the motivation to register and vote.[2] If you ask a lawyer who litigates and why, he will reply with a smile and a professional shrug of the shoulders—a reaction suited to the novelty of the question and the intricacy of any well-founded reply. He can give you virtually no answers comparable to those of the political scientist with his voting correlations to race, residence, education, age, income, marital status, sex, ethnic affiliation, occupation, geographical mobility, etc. Legal research along these lines is only beginning to be done, even though the juris-

2. See, e.g., Robert Lane, *Political Life* (Glencoe, Illinois: The Free Press, 1959); Lester Milbrath, *Political Participation* (Chicago: Rand McNally, 1965); Angus Campbell, Philip Converse, Warren Miller, and Donald Stokes, *Elections and the Political Order* (New York: John Wiley, 1966).

prudence expert Karl Llewellyn long ago invited students of the law to make use of the behavioral scientist's techniques of inquiry.[3]

Anthony Downs has given voting behavior studies a useful perspective. In his *An Economic Theory of Democracy*, he assumes that "every rational man decides to vote just as he makes all other decisions: if the returns outweigh the costs, he votes, if not he abstains."[4] A similar formula may be assumed to apply to litigation, with the recognition that the necessary skills and costs in terms of time, inconvenience, and money are considerable. Seldom does the isolated individual have the resources and persistence to litigate in response to frustration at the polls. *Terry* v. *Adams*, the Texas "white primary" case involving the Jaybird formula, was unusual for a voting rights case of broad consequences because the litigants could attract no formal group support. (See Chapter 4.) Thurgood Marshall, then director of the NAACP Legal Defense Fund, commented in 1962 that the aid of the Fund was requested by John Terry, but "we could not participate in that case, because the plaintiff . . . was well able to finance it himself. . . . I knew he could, I suggested he could, and he did."[5] Some apportionment litigation has likewise been devoid of organized sponsorship or financial support. In 1962, the Supreme Court ruled in the famous case of *Baker* v. *Carr* that federal courts could properly hear challenges to state legislative malapportionment.[6] (See Chapter 7.) The decision made predictable victories attractive to scattered voters, even when organizations could not be found to share the costs. (One freshly minted attorney filed a malapportionment complaint soon after he passed his state bar examination. He made a professional debut as his own client and acquired a political name for himself in the process.)

Electoral process litigants acting as private parties tend to fall into one of three categories: activists, the alienated, and the organized. Many suits are prepared by political activists, often urban or suburban residents who invest some or a good deal of their time in civic affairs

3. Karl Llewellyn, *The Bramble Bush* (New York: Oceana Publications, 1951). See Stuart Nagel, *The Legal Process from a Behavioral Perspective* (Homewood, Illinois: The Dorsey Press, 1969).

4. Anthony Downs, *An Economic Theory of Democracy* (New York: Harper and Row, 1957), p. 260. Cf. Richard Rose and Henry Mossawir, "Voting and Elections: A Functional Analysis," 15 *Political Studies* 173–201 (June 1967).

5. Marshall Testimony, *NAACP* v. *Gray, Transcript of Record*, U.S. Sup. Ct. Oct. Term, 1962, p. 354. (Hereinafter referred to as *Gray Record*. Decided under the title of *NAACP* v. *Button*, 371 U.S. 415 [1963]).

6. *Baker* v. *Carr*, 369 U.S. 186 (1962).

and community activities. They are often in or on the periphery of politics, candidates, or potential candidates. The alienated litigant— the party outsider—has been particularly associated with districting and apportionment cases. According to William Boyd, the professional monitor of apportionment cases for the National Municipal League, the more typical litigants "were not the party insiders who often had successful working relations with rural legislators." Though the characterization would be difficult to document, Boyd expressed the opinion that in a "great many cases," the litigant was himself a lawyer who was frustrated at the statutory output of his legislature and at least equally frustrated with the party framework of existing local politics. Boyd commented, "I think the profile: young, liberal, Democratic Party maverick, ethnic-religious minority group member, and associate of the city bar acting on his own time and funds would describe a large proportion of these litigants."[7]

The clients in a constitutional case more often than not have the backing of an organized group. Although they are of course interested in winning their law suit, they are even more interested in vindicating the principle upon which their claim is based. Generally the litigants are persons who view their courtroom activities in terms of its impact upon the special class, ethnic, geographical, or partisan interests with which they are affiliated and from which they derive organized support. When the principle involved is broad in nature, the expense of litigation (time, money, and inconvenience) may be spread widely. The litigants' cause may be strengthened and legal action made less expensive when plaintiffs are permitted by procedural rules to institute a "class action."[8] Legal benefits may go beyond the circle of those sharing litigation costs, because the allegations touching on a common right, if proved, call for a remedy benefiting all who are "similarly situated"—black voters trying to register without hindrance, urban citizens asking a fair count for their ballots, etc. "Class actions" help the political scientist to identify the group basis and political implications of the suit. Curiosity on these points is not easily satisfied, however.

When a case does not arise as a "class action" and when no *amici curiae* briefs have been filed, the court record may well give only a one-dimensional picture of a plaintiff acting purely on his own. The

7. Interview with William Boyd, editor, *National Civic Review*, June 9, 1968.
8. Federal Rules of Civil Procedure, Rule 23. Such suits are particularly well adapted to claims resting on Fourteenth Amendment Equal Protection grounds.

published accounts of the case of *Carrington* v. *Rash*, for example, give this impression.[9] Focusing on this civil action in some detail will clarify the political framework of an electoral process suit.

The trial transcript and Opinion of the Court describe the plaintiff, Sergeant Herbert Carrington, as an Army careerist, family man, taxpayer, homeowner, and resident of El Paso, Texas. A poll tax receipt for which he paid $1.75 read: "For voting in the year 1964." It also showed information appearing to confirm Carrington's eligibility to vote in Texas: he was thirty-five years old, a two-year resident of El Paso County, and a United States citizen. The facts which interested the Supreme Court also showed that Sergeant Carrington had expressed a wish to vote in the spring Republican primary. A letter to this effect was written to Alan Rash, County Chairman of the Republican Party Executive Committee. In his reply, Rash expressed regret over state policy, but Attorney General Waggoner Carr's interpretation of the Texas Constitution was that "no person who entered the service as a resident of another state may acquire a voting residence in Texas while he is in the service." The fact that Carrington had enlisted in the Army as a resident of Alabama years earlier stood as a suffrage disability in Texas, even though he had since become a Texas resident. Sergeant Carrington sought a *mandamus* order against Rash in a petition originally lodged with the state Supreme Court. Seven of the court's nine members replied that Rash's understanding of the law was correct and that Texas could reasonably seek to protect state and local politics from the influence of military voting strength. In anticipation of a lively run-off primary two months away, Carrington's lawyer next sought expeditious treatment in appealing to the Supreme Court of the United States. Review followed along with a decision favorable to the petitioner. Only Justice Harlan dissented from Potter Stewart's Opinion, which reasoned that Texas may indeed require that all military personnel enrolled to vote be *bona fide* residents of the community. "But if they are in fact residents, with the intention of making Texas their home indefinitely, they, as all other qualified residents, have a right to an equal opportunity for political representation." Justice Stewart concluded: "By forbidding a soldier ever to controvert the presumption of nonresidence, the Texas Constitution imposes an invidious discrimination in violation of the Fourteenth Amendment."

9. *Carrington* v. *Rash*, 380 U.S. 89 (1965); cf. *Carrington* v. *Rash*, 378 S.W.2d 304 (1965).

So much for the public record. And an important public record it is, for it asserts Fourteenth Amendment limitations on the traditional authority of the states to set voting qualifications. But the record is nearly devoid of illuminating clues concerning the "litigation politics" behind the important ruling: no *amici* briefs indicating group support; no telltale attorneys' names or roster "of counsel," such as the NAACP's Arthur Springarn or the ACLU's Melvin Wulf; no Justice Department intervention; and no revelation of the sources of the litigant's financial support.

The history of the servicemen's dispute with Texas was brief. Until 1963, military personnel and their dependents had been permitted as a practical matter to vote in Texas if they showed a local residence of two years. When this loophole was administratively closed, aggravated members of the armed forces were quick to organize throughout the state to change the law. In El Paso for example, the Military Taxpayers' Association established an active group under the leadership of Sergeant and Mrs. Niglio. They were instrumental in securing the legal advice of Wayne Windle, a young downtown attorney, and plans were discussed for litigation. Niglio's commanding officer, in effect, ordered him not to proceed with any legal action in his own name. For that reason, Sergeant Carrington, a member of the association, was selected to be the named party in the litigation which the group mapped out under Windle's sympathetic guidance. Association members were advised of the approximate costs involved in proceeding to the United States Supreme Court, and with this information, they decided to file suit. When the need for an appeal to Washington became necessary because of the state's ruling in Austin, the Military Taxpayers' Association began the difficult task of fund-raising to meet expenses. Their resources were quite limited, and with the welcomed encouragement of the Justice Department, Sergeant Carrington was able to proceed "as a pauper." In effect, following this standard procedure shifted the burden of paying for the printing of the briefs to the federal government. Since there were no facts in dispute and very little law in point, the briefs were short and the legal fees did not exceed $1500. The representative from the 16th Congressional District was interested in the suit, and he supplied lodging in Washington for Carrington's legal counsel. Before the application for writ of *mandamus* was filed in the Texas Supreme Court, El Paso Republican officials consented to cooperate in establishing the facts related to the dispute. Local Democratic officials were no less eager to help. They offered to supply a brief *amicus curiae*. It was refused, however, for fear of the delay its preparation might cause. Nevertheless, after the association attorney filed for a writ of *certiorari* with the United States Supreme Court, he asked for a supporting brief from the Department of Justice. The Solicitor General declined the request, however, and indicated that he thought the association's cause would prevail without the help of the Justice Department, as indeed it did.

PLEADERS, SUPPORTERS, AND RESEARCHERS

Legal Counsel and Organized Support

Since 1937, the Department of Justice has been committed to the defense of civil and political rights. Since its inception in 1957, the Civil Rights Division of the Department (replacing the 20-year-old Civil Rights Section) has invested the major portion of its activities in enforcing the right to vote against racial discrimination. The same commitment is shared by the Civil Rights Commission, which has been exercising its fact-finding functions since 1957.[10] The increasing budget of both organizations demonstrates the federal government's commitment to protect constitutional rights. In 1968, the division had a staff of 105 attorneys and 111 clerical workers, while the commission staff numbered 138. A five-year survey made of the division in 1965 showed that the number of matters received annually remained at the 3,000 plus level, with a general trend upward. Within this category covering civil rights disputes of every description, the Attorney General's Report for fiscal 1965 noted a discernible trend toward an increase of civil matters (60 percent in 1965) and a corresponding decrease in criminal matters received (60 percent in 1960).

Table 1–1 indicates the growing budgets of the Civil Rights Commission and the Civil Rights Division as well as the number of voting rights suits sponsored by the Justice Department. In 1965, Assistant Attorney General Doar of the Civil Rights Division reported that the workload of his staff continued "to consist primarily of voting matters." The stepped up volume of the division's activities in the field of civil rights is reflected not only in the number of suits for which it took full responsibility—arguing and charting legal tactics—but also in its increased participation in private suits by supplying *amici curiae* briefs. Where a voting case involves a charge of racial discrimination,

10. See Foster Rhea Dulles, *The Civil Rights Commission: 1957-1965* (East Lansing, Michigan: Michigan State University Press, 1968); Luther A. Huston, The Department of Justice (New York: Frederick Praeger, 1967).

Table 1–1   *Appropriations of the Civil Rights Commission
and Division and Volume of Justice Department
Civil and Political Rights Suits**

YEAR	NUMBER OF SUITS	CIVIL RIGHTS DIVISION: ANNUAL APPROPRIATIONS	CIVIL RIGHTS COMMISSION: ANNUAL APPROPRIATIONS
1958	7	$ 185,000	$ 200,000
1959	3	483,000	750,000
1960	12	468,000	780,000
1961	13	627,000	850,000
1962	29	778,000	888,000
1963	53	970,000	950,000
1964	34	1,230,000	985,000
1965	40	1,697,000	985,000
1966	60	2,467,000	1,925,000
1967	106	2,545,000	2,500,000
1968	120	2,566,000	2,650,000

* Figures were supplied by the respective budgets and accounts offices.

the division normally takes on the task of shepherding the contest into the federal court system. But in reapportionment litigation, the division's involvement has been restricted to submitting *amici curiae* briefs in selected cases. Its most notable success was *Baker* v. *Carr*, in which the *amicus* brief prepared by the Appellate and Research Section of the division was substantially adopted by the Opinion of the Court.

Self-help has characterized the score of lawyers who have acted at their own expense as litigants in reapportionment cases. Very few law firms have distinguished themselves as reapportionment specialists. Because of other commitments and the limits placed on interstate practice by bar associations, skilled reapportionment lawyers such as Alfred Scanlon in Maryland and Theodore Sachs in Michigan have not become involved in reapportionment litigation in other states. Specialization is confined to one or two appellate firms such as Rhyne and Rhyne of Washington, D.C. Acting as the legal representative for plaintiffs in Tennessee, Illinois, and Alabama apportionment appeals, Rhyne and Rhyne is one of the few firms to have interstate clients in the field. It does more appellate state and municipal law work than any other firm.

Organized groups made up of eligible voters have acted as plaintiffs in a handful of reapportionment and districting cases. The Maryland Committee for Fair Representation and the League of Municipalities in Nebraska are examples. Where apportionment complaints are concerned, potential plaintiffs have sometimes had difficulty in affiliating with others or securing organizational support. Finding legal representation, however, is generally an easy matter. By way of contrast, the cost of privately conducted Fifteenth Amendment suits, in terms of courage and perseverance, is high for southern Negroes. They are acutely dependent upon the Justice Department. Seldom experienced in litigation procedures, Negro voters and political candidates who suffer discrimination can expect a sympathetic ear from few attorneys. Such minority group litigants need help in initiating, financing, and conducting their courtroom contests. Of the 212,408 American lawyers enumerated by the 1960 census, only between 2000 and 2500 are Negroes. Two-thirds of these have involved themselves at one time or another (mostly in the 1960s) in unpaid civil rights work with plaintiffs or defendants, according to Professor Jerome Shuman of Howard University Law School.[11] Various bar associations—white, black, and integrated—have published statements supporting members who do such volunteer work and who defend unpopular causes.

Even with a Justice Department docket of voting rights cases that sporadically surpasses the number of complaints registered privately by civil suits, the need for assistance from non-government attorneys remains perennial. Their work in the area of constitutionally protected rights has increased sharply. Before 1963, fewer than 50 law firms were concerned with as many as a dozen civil and political rights cases per year. Some, of course, were deeply involved in such specialization. They include the NAACP Legal Defense and Educational Fund, Inc., the NAACP, the American Civil Liberties Union, the Emergency Civil Liberties Committee, the Committee to Assist Southern Lawyers of the National Lawyers Guild, and the Commission on Law and Social Action of the American Jewish Congress. The organizational roster continues to expand. For example, The Lawyers Constitutional Defense Committee with headquarters in New York retains a busy office in Jackson, Mississippi. The Law Students Civil Rights Research Council has attracted volunteer help to Southern states. Affiliated with the American Bar Association is the Lawyers Committee for Civil Rights under Law, now one of the largest "law offices" in Mississippi. The Lawyers Committee (or "President's Committee" as it is usually called since it was summoned into existence by President Kennedy in 1963) is prepared to give professional counsel, whether to arrested demonstrators, harassed registra-

11. Letter to the author from Professor Jerome Shuman, dated June 26, 1968.

tion workers, or Negro candidates and poll watchers. After 1965, its budget grew rapidly: $80,000 (1965), $300,000 (1966), $500,000 (1967), $800,000 (1968), and $1,000,000 (1969). In addition to providing free legal staffing for civil rights cases, it also pays lawyers' fees to those rare Mississippi attorneys such as Lackey Rowe who are willing to help Negro defendants.[12] The obstacles laid in the path of such work are many. One Negro LCDC volunteer attorney, Donald Jelinek, was jailed for practicing law without a license in Alabama. The Negro farmers whom the New York lawyer attempted to represent complained that county agents were responsible for preventing them from voting (although federal law permitted them to vote) in the annual agricultural quota elections of the Agricultural Stabilization and Conservation Service. Jelinek subsequently addressed a convention of the National Lawyers' Guild in New York and proposed that the Guild, "armed with threatened litigation, lobby with the federal government, to eliminate these abuses."[13]

With 20 full-time attorneys and a budget of $2,500,000 in 1968, the NAACP Legal Defense and Educational Fund Inc. (LDF) is the largest and also the oldest organization professionally concerned with civil rights litigation on behalf of Negroes. Since 1940, when they separated from the NAACP, the LDF has virtually operated a specialized law firm under the successive leadership of Thurgood Marshall (now Justice Marshall) and Jack Greenberg. Marshall once explained the group's aims in these terms:

The basic aims, purposes, of the Legal Defense are to render legal assistance and legal aid to Negro people whose rights are being denied them, particularly rights guaranteed by the Constitution of the United States; to carry on an educational program giving facts on the situation; to do research, legal and scientific, in the field of race relations; and to disseminate that information and to do legal research and to publish that legal research. That is about the sum and substance of what we do.[14]

The fund is not made up of would-be plaintiffs comparable to a citizen's committee for reapportionment. It is composed of legal specialists such as Fred Wallace, Norman Amaker, and Melvyn Zarr, all

12. See John Hounold, "The Bourgeois Bar and the Mississippi Movement," 52 *American Bar Association Journal* 228 (Mar. 1966).
13. Donald Jelinek, "Federal Regulatory Agencies and the Southern Negro," 26 *The Guild Practitioner* 18 at 24 (Winter 1964).
14. Marshall Testimony, *Gray Record*, p. 349.

of whom have worked extensively on voting cases. The LDF is not an association *of* litigants, but with the legal, financial, and research assistance it can offer, and with its legal internship program and roster of 250 "cooperating attorneys," it is clearly a formidible association *for* litigation. In 1963, Justice Brennan said of the NAACP: "Association for litigation may be the most effective form of political association" open to voteless Negroes. In Brennan's estimate, such courtroom sparring fulfills two distinct functions, litigation and education.[15]

The Information Explosion

The educational side of the work of such organizations as the LDF is reflected in gathering the data necessary to litigate intelligently and to develop effective public relations. In 1966, "non-legal research and public information" accounted for six percent of the LDF's budget. The strain on staff researchers has been relieved by the bank of voting data amassed by the Civil Rights Commission and privately by the Government Affairs Institute (*America Votes* series) and the Southern Regional Council (regular press releases and studies on southern Negro voting). The 1970 census will facilitate Fifteenth Amendment litigation by being the first census to give an account of voting and registration information by race and national origin. In its own data-gathering work, the LDF has been able to rely on volunteer or contracted research by political scientists, sociologists, and anthropologists. So many of these professional people have given generously of their time that Thurgood Marshall, as director counsel of the LDF in 1962, was prompted to comment: "I don't think anybody else could corral [so] many scientists, lawyers and law professors [to] join in giving their legal assistance. . . ." This collection even included one white southern attorney who insisted on anonymity because he was also counsel for the late Senator Bilbo of Mississippi.[16]

Several organizations have shown continuous interest in supplying reliable information to civil rights lawyers. The Duke University Law School, through its journal *Law and Contemporary Problems*, has sponsored several symposia on the electoral process, voting rights, and reapportionment. The Vanderbilt Law School until 1968 published the *Race Relations Law Reporter*, an indispensable research tool which chronicled civil rights developments as well as election law cases touching on constitutional issues.

15. *NAACP* v. *Button*, 371 U.S. 415 at 431 (1963).
16. Marshall Testimony, *Gray Record*, p. 391.

Having a much wider readership through its nationally distributed statistical reports and fact sheets for newspapers is the Southern Regional Council and its affiliated Voter Education Project under the direction of Vernon Jordan. The SRC press releases and publications on Negro voting date back to 1943. They provide the only reliable source for such information before the founding of the Civil Rights Commission. The SRC is primarily a clearinghouse dedicated to the goal of informing public opinion "so that legislation and judicial rulings may be translated into justice for the individual in his everyday life." Since 1966 VEP has sponsored hundreds of local voter education programs and candidate workshops. "Get out the vote" activities have been supplemented by programs of advising voters and candidates about their legal rights and duties, often in conjunction with NAACP lawyers. VEP voting statistics have been cited in court rulings, and its officers have been called upon as expert witnesses. The past director of the SRC, Harold Flemming, was acting on his own when he joined Bernard South in the unsuccessful 1950 challenge to the Georgia county unit system in *South* v. *Peters*. (See Chapter 9.)

Bar associations perform a limited clearinghouse service for their members. The Civil Rights Committee of the National Bar Association (mostly Negro in membership) regularly reports on political and civil rights developments. The American Bar Association publishes an annual review of franchise cases, reapportionment rulings, and civil liberties decisions as written up by its Standing Committee on the Bill of Rights. More elaborate are the tabs kept on civil rights and civil liberties litigation by the National Lawyers Guild. Its *Civil Liberties Docket*, founded in 1955, provides a brief description of most cases pending in state and federal courts in which constitutional rights questions have been raised by one party. A statistical study of 2600 cases reported between 1955 and 1962 showed racial discrimination in voting efforts was the seventh-most-litigated civil right during those years.[17] In 1965, the editor of the reporting service discontinued counting "urban discrimination" cases because their number had become so great as to "make it impossible for the *Docket* to continue to list or describe them. . . ." Readers were referred to the publications of the National Municipal League for information on reapportionment developments. Since 1962, the League has published state and

17. The study reported 59 such cases. School desegregation cases were repeatedly the most numerous. See "Statistical Study of Constitutional Litigation," Appendix, in Ann Ginger, "Litigation as a Form of Political Action," 9 *Wayne Law Review* 458, 476–81 (1963).

federal court decisions in this field in out-sized volumes which had added up to a library of over 30 volumes by 1970.

The transmission of election law information by law reviews should be noted, not only because they give lawyers preparing arguments the necessary staples of case analysis but also because they sometimes advance innovations in constitutional theory. Law review articles may acquire significance beyond their intrinsic merit when they are cited in judicial opinions, thereby alerting lawyers and scholars to the kind of research that judges think is significant. Opportunities abound in such a popular field as civil and political rights law for lawyers or judges to choose articles congenial to their particular perspective. Law reviews serve to report and interpret law, assess its relation to society at-large, help courts weigh non-legal information in a judicial way, and explore new directions for legal change.[18]

Many private organizations have contributed special publications to the information explosion in various phases of election law. Among them are The American Political Science Association, The Brookings Institution, The Institute for Social Science Research, the American Enterprise Institute, the Governmental Affairs Institute, and the National Institute of Municipal Law Officers (all of Washington, D.C.); the Council of State Governments and the Public Administration Service (of Chicago); and the Twentieth Century Fund (of New York). A lawyer may be interested in the monographs and works of such organizations for reasons which differ from those of the political scientist. Not only is the information they give useful in preparing litigation but the authors of such works make "expert witnesses." Exclusionary rules of evidence are strict when proceeding before a jury, but districting and electoral process cases (unlike criminal proceedings under the Civil Rights Acts) are not heard by juries. There is little difficulty in arranging for expert testimony by computer specialists, systems engineers, political scientists, and demographers.

A group may seek to express its interest in a case by petitioning a court to permit the filing of a brief *amicus curiae*.[19] Participating in litigation in this form entails the expression of opinion or the reporting of germane information by a "friend of the court" acting as a kind of interested spectator of the contest between plaintiff and defendant. The arguments and data so supplied to the court provide several in-

18. See Chester Newland, "Legal Periodicals and the U.S. Supreme Court," 3 *Midwest Journal of Political Science* 58 (Feb. 1959).

19. See Samuel Krislov, "The *Amicus* Brief: From Friendship to Advocacy," 72 *Yale Law Journal* 694 (1963).

formational services, not all of which are precisely legal in their import. First, the *amicus* brief may pass along to judges the benefits of pertinent social science research. This functional aspect of the *amicus* brief may be the broadest in scope, but it is not necessarily the most important in terms of its impact on the decision. Historical, demographic, and other technical information are revelant though not conclusive, even where broad issues are at stake. Such material may allow the judges to come to their decision fully aware of the social consequences that one or another ruling might have. The brief may also be enhanced by the interpretive skills of a notable scholar such as Leo Pfeffer (civil liberties) or Robert McKay (reapportionment). Second, the *amicus* brief may function as a kind of intergovernmental bridge, clarifying for the case at hand the interest and views of the Justice Department (as in many reapportionment cases before the Supreme Court), the states (as in many Fifteenth Amendment suits), or others (Puerto Rico submitted a brief in an English literacy case).

Finally, *amici* briefs may serve the plainly political function of identifying the organizational combatants: the bench is given a battle-map showing the basis of potential group support or opposition.[20] The test case for the Voting Rights Act of 1965—*South Carolina* v. *Katzenbach*—was most dramatic in this regard. (See Chapter 6.) Separate *amici* briefs with oral arguments were presented by Georgia, Louisiana, Mississippi, and Virginia. Alabama spoke with a divided voice. Its oral argument was presented by a Wallace spokesman who was assigned by the governor to supplement the moderate approach of State Attorney General Richmond Flowers (at that time a gubernatorial candidate with Negro voting support). On the other side of the case, Illinois and New Jersey submitted separate briefs. The Massachusetts brief was supported by various officials of 17 other states and was accompanied by the polished oral argument of Archibald Cox, one time Solicitor General of the United States. This landmark contest stimulated more *amici* briefs than any other voting rights case, in part because the Supreme Court specifically invited the states to put their views on record.

Ordinarily the possibility of lobbying before the Supreme Court is limited. Since 1949, Supreme Court Rule 42 has served to protect the balance of adversaries by requiring that *amici* briefs have the consent of all parties before they can be admitted. Failing this, the potential

20. See the six-function analysis by Lucius Barker, "Third Parties in Litigation," 29 *Journal of Politics* 41 (1967).

"friend of the court" may petition the bench to submit a brief, but Rule 42 warns that, unless the request is made well in advance of Supreme Court proceedings, "such motions are not favored."[21] The carefully timed application must set out the petitioner's interest in the case, convince the Court that its presentation of facts or legal arguments will not repeat those expected from other parties, and generally meet the heavy burden of justifying an increase in the judges' reading assignment. These restrictions, however, do not apply to the submitting of briefs by federal or state governments. Thus in voting rights cases between 1958 and 1968, municipal, state and federal governments have lodged nearly twice as many *amici* briefs as have private individuals or organized groups. In voting cases, the Justice Department often receives requests from federal courts to submit such briefs at every level. Table 1–2 reports on 69 *amici* briefs in 48 voting rights cases and related contests (decided between 1958 and 1968) for which Supreme Court opinions were written.

Table 1–2   *Distribution of* Amici *Briefs in Electoral Cases Decided by the U.S. Supreme Court, 1958–68**

	UNITED STATES	STATES & MUNICIPAL	PRIVATE PERSONS & ORGANIZATIONS	TOTAL	NONE
Reapportionment and Districting	14	15	13	42	12
Race-related or 15th Amendment	3	8	2	13	4
Miscellaneous Electoral Process	1	4	9	14	4
TOTAL	18	27	24	69	—

* The table makes use of cases from volumes 2 to 20, second series, of the Lawyers Edition of Supreme Court decisions. The appendix to each volume conveniently reports on all briefs, counsels and *amici*.

The table, of course, is not a complete index of interests expressed and efforts expended. For example, the table on briefs should be read in light of the fact that, in cases touching on race, the Justice Department usually serves as party plaintiff under the Civil Rights Acts. Finally, a look at the table suggests that the continuous submission of

21. Rule 42, "Revised Rules of the Supreme Court," 42 *Federal Rules Decisions* 81 at 113 (1967).

briefs by the Justice Department in districting cases reflects in documentary form a clear federal concern for the republican form of state governments and for the quality of federal representation. It remains to be noted that the table gives a somewhat deflated indication of the interest of municipal governments in reapportionment cases. Officials from urban areas have sometimes preferred to avoid the *amicus* position of being once removed from litigation and have sought—and were permitted—to intervene directly as parties plaintiff.

TECHNIQUES AND STRATEGY

Private organizations with a deep interest in politico-legal problems may participate directly as sponsors of litigation. By financing or staffing a suit or by supplying litigants, the group can influence legal strategy decisions.[22] Of course the first steps on the road to court are often taken by individuals who create an unpredictable volume of demand for legal assistance. Thus organizations such as the Legal Defense Fund or the American Civil Liberties Union cannot completely map out litigation commitments in advance. Their boards of directors do, however, set down guidelines for the allocation of resources and leave no doubt as to where their sympathies lie. The LDF always has more applications for aid than it can provide, and the volume of demand has risen steadily. A policy of selectiveness rather than the quantity of applications explains reductions in the number of persons assisted by the LDF. Some 4,200 individuals were defended or represented in 1963, 10,400 in 1964, 17,000 in 1965, 14,000 in 1966, and 13,000 in 1967. Selectivity allows the group to control the policy directions of its lawyers and researchers.

Rights are defended with writs; and (to paraphrase Roscoe Pound's quip) lawyers are in the writ business. Barratry prohibitions and legal ethics discourage the soliciting of such "business." Thus the matter of how the lawyer-client relation is created is a sensitive area. Professional limitations are, however, about as consequential as courtship customs in which the general fact prevails that "boy meets girl." Bar associations routinely provide referral services to litigants in search of legal specialists. Mutual interests may also bring lawyers to potential voting rights clients. Like other American professional people, at-

22. See Richard C. Cortner, "Strategies and Tactics of Litigants in Constitutional Cases," 17 *Journal of Public Law* 287 (1968).

torneys enjoy the recreation of conventions, and at conferences of groups such as the National Municipal League and the National Institute of Municipal Law Officers, informal conversations circulate the names of apportionment lawyers and technical consultants. A conference on redistricting jointly sponsored by the American Law Institute and the American Bar Association in 1965 brought together legislators, litigants, lawyers, and political scientists to hear panel discussions ranging from the problems of pleadings to the IBM programming of legislative districts.

In the area of race relations, law firms such as Collins, Douglas and Elie of New Orleans gain a word-of-mouth reputation passed along from civil rights meetings, pulpits, and elsewhere. In Richmond, the firms of Martin, Hill and Robinson, and more recently Tucker and Marsh, are widely known for their civil rights victories and for their cooperation with the Virginia NAACP Conference of Branches, active in both voter registration and civil rights litigation. Reflecting on the experience of the NAACP in Virginia, Roy Wilkins in 1962 described the initial lawyer-client contact in terms which dispelled suspicions of "champerty":[23]

We do not go out into the general population and solicit a man by saying, 'Don't you want to challenge such and such a law?' . . . I think . . . it is a matter of record that we have said publicly, on many occasions, that such and such a law we believed to be unconstitutional and unfair . . . , and if anyone . . . steps forward and says he wishes to challenge such a law, we will agree to assist him providing the case passes all of the requirements. But for actually going out and buttonholing people and saying, 'Will you come in and help us test this?' we don't do that.[24]

The requirements that Wilkins mentioned include the general one that a potential case should involve evidence of racial discrimination. Over and above that, the LDF takes no cases unless requested to do so by the party or his lawyer. Although it may pay *per diem* fees of from $50 to $100 to attorneys, and although travel and printing costs for a case litigated up to the Supreme Court may on occasion reach a level

23. *Black's Law Dictionary* (4th ed.; St. Paul: West Publishing Company, 1957) defines "champerty" as: "A bargain by a stranger with a party to a suit, by which such third person undertakes to carry on the litigation at his own cost and risk, in consideration of receiving, if successful, a part of the proceeds or subject sought to be recovered." "Barratry" is defined as: "The offense of frequently exciting and stirring up quarrels and suits, either at law or otherwise."

24. Wilkins Testimony, *Gray Record*, p. 295.

of from $50,000 to $100,000, the LDF is not always in full control of strategy.[25] As Wilkins explained, "I have sat in on . . . conferences . . . on strategy in which [legal aids] said, 'Well, before we can go any further, we will have to find out what the plaintiff wants to do.' "[26] For its part, a sponsoring organization has some say as to what it wants to do. It can always withdraw financial and staff aid from plaintiff or defendant, and as an aspect of its services, strategy advice is expected.

A change in legislative policy might induce a group to drop sponsorship of certain court tests when the grievance in question is remedied in Congress or elsewhere. LDF voting rights litigation has been diminished by Justice Department responsibilities in the same field. In 1965, Jack Greenberg of the fund made the decision not to appeal an adverse ruling in *Lampkin* v. *Connors* only after success for the Voting Rights Act appeared assured.[27] Resources were diverted elsewhere when the plan was discarded to seek a Supreme Court appeal by *certiorari*. The 25 southern voters whom Greenberg represented were said by the district court not to have "standing" to seek enforcement of Section 2 of the Fourteenth Amendment. (See Chapter 3.) The constitutional provision, never before successfully used, would deny congressional seats to states in proportion to their responsibility for racial discrimination in voting. However, had the Voting Rights Act not appeared on the national stage in 1965, the LDF was in the wings awaiting the hoped-for cue from the Supreme Court to appeal the Section 2 suit.

Besides the Legal and Defense Fund, the other main organization which provides legal counsel at both the trial and appellate levels is the American Civil Liberties Union. Like the LDF, the ACLU often directly staffs and finances litigation. The legal problems which the Washington, D.C. office of the Civil Liberties Union faced in a suit in 1966 involved most of the strategy ingredients of pressing a political rights suit: assembling the litigants, getting the necessary data, controlling the planning process, coordinating with other groups, and

25. *Thurgood Marshall* estimated that litigation in the 1954 school desegregation cases incurred costs in the neighborhood of $200,000; *Gray Record*, p. 354. A few private foundations, such as the Phelps-Stoke Fund and the Marshall Field Fund have made grants, without strategy strings attached, to litigants in particular test cases. In the Delaware reapportionment case of *Nolan* v. *Rhodes*, the successful plaintiff sought reimbursement of litigation expenses from the newly reapportioned and presumably grateful state legislation; 378 U.S. 556 (1964).

26. Wilkins Testimony, *Gray Record*, p. 302.

27. *Lampkin* v. *Connors*, 239 F. Supp. 757 (1965).

getting into the right court with the right arguments at the right time. Mostly these were the problems of David Carliner, forty-nine-year-old lawyer and past president of the National Capital Area ACLU. As a native and resident of the District of Columbia, Carliner has shared the fate of Washingtonians who are not permitted to vote for their own municipal government. Since 1878, Congress has governed the city through a kind of "Rube Goldberg contraption" of obscurely interconnected appointive commissions and committees. In 1965, Carliner suggested to the 25 directors of his board that *Baker v. Carr* (with its jurisdictional grant to federal courts) made feasible a legal challenge of non-representation for Washington residents. A half-year of historical homework by an ACLU volunteer pointed to the conclusions that town democracy was America's first commitment to popular government and that "the delegates to the Constitutional Convention never had the slightest idea of depriving the District of responsible local self-government." Against the constitutional grant of Article I, Section 18 (giving to Congress the power "to exercise exclusive legislation" over the District), Carliner developed the argument that voting rights, being fundamental, could not be disparaged under the Ninth Amendment. The Tenth Amendment was said to preserve the franchise of Maryland and Virginia residents who were assimilated into the ten-mile square capital. Another ACLU attorney contended that municipal voting was abolished by Congress in 1878 with "the express purpose of disfranchising the Negro citizens of the District"—a law of contemporary poignancy for over 60 percent of the Washington population. This set of arguments was circulated among 75 ACLU-associated attorneys. Friendly criticism mixed pessimism with the observation that the Fifteenth Amendment argument was "particularly thin." Accordingly, further research showed that more whites than Negroes in the District have moved from other states in which they are able to vote by absentee ballot. Also, white District citizens are free to move to Maryland or Virginia suburbs where they can vote for local officials, but Negroes are generally forced by suburban housing discrimination to remain in the District.

Controlling legal strategy was never out of the ACLU's hands because Carliner chose to be a litigant himself. This decision was made partly because one potential plaintiff named Washington proved not to be a native-born resident, which dashed the early hope of entitling the case "Washington v. Board of Commissioners." Public relations criteria combined with technical requirements and politics to shape strategy. The American Civil Liberties Union kept its eyes not only on the federal courts but on Congress as well. As long as "home rule" bills had a chance in the 89th Congress, filing the prepared suit was postponed on advice of friendly congressmen that pendency of the suit might serve some colleagues to rationalize a "nay" vote. When congressmen found other reasons to kill municipal elections for Washington, Carliner chose the eve of election day, 1966, to go to court.

This choice of timing made the best of what had become a bad situation. Unknown to the ACLU, Julius Hobson, a local civil rights leader, had filed a complaint with others against Commissioner Tobriner and his associates on the Board of Commissioners. The Hobson plaintiffs claimed that they suffered irreparable injury because Washington authorities exercised police and taxing powers delegated by Congress without being responsive to the popularity expressed view of the plaintiffs and other residents.

Both Carliner and Hobson were anxious to present their respective complaints to a specially convened three-judge court because such courts—unlike single-judge courts—may enjoin enforcement of a federal law if and when it is found to be unconstitutional.[28] The first step, however, is to petition a federal district judge to convene such an enlarged court and to do so on the demonstrated grounds that the claims of unconstitutionality are substantial. When Judge Jones told Carliner that a decision on his request would be delayed until after appeal in Hobson's suit had been exhausted, dramatic irony beset the common cause. Hobson's quickly drafted request was accompanied by no legal memoranda comparable to the elaborate scholarly work prepared by those associated with Carliner. The ACLU assumed that Hobson's thinly researched brief in part explained Judge Gasch's dismissal of Hobson's request. His application for a three-judge court to void the statutes setting up the Board of Commissioners was denied.[29] Judge Jones said that he would take Judge Gasch's ruling into account. He also noted that a petition to the Appeals Court for an order requiring Judge Gasch to convene the special tribunal to hear the complaint on its merits was unavailing. Only one step remained. On February 14, 1967, the Supreme Court of the United States denied Hobson's petition for review of *certiorari*.[30] This rapid series of judicial events undercut Carliner's own request and on March 20, Judge Jones denied the ACLU's petition for a three-judge bench.[31] A

---

28. 28 U.S.C. 2282-4. A direct appeal to the Supreme Court as a matter of right may follow the decision of such a court according to 28 U.S.C. 1253.

29. *Hobson* v. *Tobriner*, 255 F. Supp. 296 (1966). The relevant statute is Act of June 11, 1878, 20 Stat. 1024.

30. *Hobson* v. *Gasch*, 386 U.S. 914 (1966), *cert. denied*.

31. *Carliner* v. *Board of Commissioners*, 265 F. Supp. 736 (1967).

lack of coordination between civil rights and civil liberties groups dissipated legal resources, effectively scuttled the prospect of getting a hearing on the merits of the voting complaint, and checkmated review by the Supreme Court.

The uncoordinated efforts of Carliner and Hobson appeared to end in failure. In fact, they enjoyed a combined victory when the reason for their contest became moot because of changed circumstances. On February 27, 1967, President Johnson announced a plan for the reorganization of the District of Columbia government. The calendar of preparing the plan antedated litigation. The Executive action (which required no formal approval by Congress) was described as an interim measure until full home rule could be achieved. Acceded to by Congress and rapidly put into effect, the reorganization plan called for abolition of the ninety-year-old commission. The three-man panel was replaced with a single Commissioner (comparable to a mayor) and a nine-member council. The positions involved are necessarily appointive because only Congress could grant full self-government to District citizens. Nevertheless, the presidential nominations (including Walter Washington as Commissioner and other Negroes as Councilmen) reflected sensitivity to local organizations. The assumption was widely held that such appointments would be "informed" by mock elections and that full and effective voting rights would follow.

The District of Columbia suffrage suits, with their apparently fortuitous outcome, illustrate the functional utility of litigation in the electoral process. Even without favorable judicial treatment, the suit that is well timed and well chosen will effectively spotlight a public grievance. Whether so achieved by indirection or by responsive judicial remedies, the goal of electoral litigation is to effect a binding adjustment in the democratic control mechanism of voting. Individuals and groups which invest time, money, and skills in courtroom contests over the electoral process see the stakes of their disputes in political terms. Involved are important but often marginal gains or losses in the hiring-and-firing process of balloting for public officials. In the following chapters of this book, the record of such cases will be analyzed, with special reference to Supreme Court decisions—old and new. To take this direction, the frame of reference must shift from the "how to do it" matters of contemporary litigation to the "how it began" issues of historical development.

2 The right to vote in congressional elections

Any effort to discuss the Supreme Court and the electoral process is inherently a complex undertaking. The prime variables chosen for consideration—the Constitution and the Supreme Court—have changed. The transformation that has taken place in the Court's thinking and the underlying assumptions of its members between cases of the 1870s and the 1960s is so great that in reviewing voting rights and electoral process litigation, the reader may feel like an archaeologist cutting through several strata in which judicial artifacts reveal a confusing pattern of political, ideological, and cultural change. This confusion is clear even in such an apparently simple matter as judicial consideration of congressional responsibility for congressional elections. Does each state have free rein to define suffrage qualifications and to organize the election of federal legislators? The answer in the negative has been two centuries in the making. In the first instance, the men who drafted our fundamental law were hard put to deal with the question and to define the complex relationship among voters, state legislatures, and national authority. Disagreement about patterning the distribution of power is also evident in the subtle changes that the United States Supreme Court has made in constitutional doctrine relating to the right to vote in congressional elections. Congress itself has been unable to introduce rationality (in terms of clearcut and uniform standards) into a constitutional scheme rendered ambiguous by its built-in federalism and by the unexpected advent of party politics.

CONSTITUTIONAL BACKGROUND

The House of Representatives

At the Constitutional Convention of 1787, the delegates differed widely among themselves about voting qualifications for congressmen. How were the framers to avoid discriminating against any class of property owners when they were uncertain that their plan would be ratified by the states? Oliver Ellsworth of Connecticut reflected the emotional tone of the issue causing deadlock within his state delegation. The matter of suffrage, he said, was "a tender point." Clearly in this one topic the framers faced the three subjects about which they felt most strongly: the federal nature of the union, protection of property, and democratic participation. How would the three values of diversity, individualism, and equality be balanced in the test? The balance was struck in favor of compromise: the diversity inherent in a federal system. Ellsworth's politic consideration that the suffrage "was strongly guarded by most of the state constitutions" won the day. At the same time, a commitment was affirmed that, notwithstanding the property and tax qualifications required of voters by the states, the House of Representatives should be structured as "the grand depository of the democratic principle of the government."[1] The measure that finally emerged from committee, a part of the so-called "Connecticut Compromise," was unanimously adopted as Article I, Section 2, Clause 1 of the completed Constitution:

The House of Representatives shall be composed of members chosen every second year by the people of the several States, and the electors in each State shall have the qualifications requisite for electors of the most numerous branch of the State legislature.

1. Max Farrand (ed.), *The Records of the Federal Convention* (New Haven: Yale University Press, 1911), I, p. 48. See also Joel Paschal, "The House of Representatives: 'Grand Depository of the Democratic Principle'?" 17 *Law and Contemporary Problems* 276–89 (Spring 1952).

Perhaps the most telling commentary on that section is to be found in *The Federalist*, Number 52. There the author (probably Madison) provided two important clues to the understanding of Convention sentiment. He recognized that voter qualifications varied from state to state. The most nearly uniform policy among the states confined the exercise of franchise to landholders. Perhaps the most exceptional provision was New Hampshire's requirement that a poll tax be payed —specifically termed a "qualification" prerequisite to voting.[2] The author explained that, as a practical matter, it was virtually impossible to obtain agreement among the delegates on a uniform rule of voter qualifications. In principle, the framers of the Constitution nevertheless assumed that the choice of congressmen would rest with the people. The hope was that the branch of the federal government "which ought to be dependent on the people alone" should not be rendered "too dependent on the state governments." *The Federalist* concluded that *the suffrage right enjoyed by the people under state law was among the* "rights secured to them by the federal Constitution."[3]

Popular Election of Senators
The question of the constitution of the United States Senate was one of the most difficult and time-consuming to come before the Constitutional Convention. The decision went to those who maintained that a sufficient concession had been made to popular representation in the lower house. Prevailing sentiment supported the idea that the sovereignty of the states should be recognized in the method adopted for the selection of senators. In consequence, the opening paragraph of Article I, Section 3, reads: "The Senate of the United States shall be composed of two Senators from each State chosen by the legislature thereof, for six years; each Senator shall have one vote."

Few of the framers of the Constitution put great faith in majority rule. An exception was James Wilson who urged that senators be chosen democratically. Wilson stated his belief at the Philadelphia convention that "the majority of the people wherever found ought in all questions to govern the minority."[4] He went on to prophesy that frontier states would lead the way in implementing some measure of

2. For an authoritative review of state constitutional and (in the cases of Rhode Island and Connecticut) charter suffrage qualifications in 1787, see *Minor v. Happersett*, 21 Wall. 162, 172–73 (1875).

3. Alexander Hamilton, James Madison, John Jay, *The Federalist*, Number 52 (New York: The Modern Library, n.d.), p. 342.

4. Farrand, *The Federal Convention*, I, p. 342.

popular control over senators. Indeed Wilson was proved correct in subsequent decades. Frontier and western states applied the popular principle to the choice of senators as the nineteenth century progressed.[5] A by-product of party conflict and a result of frontier populism, the idea grew into a movement which culminated in 1913 with the adoption of the Seventeenth Amendment, which provides that "the electors in each State shall have the qualifications requisite for electors of the most numerous branch of the State legislature."

The Times, Places, and Manner Clause

The framers who assembled in Philadelphia provided for the federal regulation of congressional elections. The fourth section of Article I specifies that "the times, places, and manner of holding elections for Senators and Representatives shall be prescribed in each State by the legislature thereof; but the Congress may at any time by law make or alter such regulation, except as to the place of choosing Senators." When the Committee on Style of the Constitutional Convention made its report, the concluding words of the clause—"except as to the places of choosing Senators"—were added without dissent. At the Richmond meeting of the Virginia Ratifying Convention, James Monroe asked for an explanation of the exception. Madison replied that if Congress could fix the place of selecting the senators, it could compel the state legislatures to elect them "in a different place from that of their usual session, which would produce some inconvenience."[6]

In replying to Monroe, Madison stated further that the federal government should retain some veto over state regulation of congressional elections. To make his point, he drew attention to an example of inequitable representation in a state legislature. He said in explanation:

Some states might regulate the elections on principles of equality, and others might regulate them otherwise. This diversity would be obviously

---

5. John Haynes, *Popular Election of United States Senators* ("The Johns Hopkins Studies in Historical and Political Science," vol. XI; Baltimore: The Johns Hopkins Press, 1893), p. 547. On several occasions before the enactment of the Seventeenth Amendment, senatorial seats remained vacant because of deadlocks in the state legislatures. In many states, regulations required a concurrent vote of the two houses to elect one senator because the two chambers could not agree upon a candidate. To remedy frequent embarrassments of this sort, Congress enacted a law in 1866 specifying a vote-count rule designed to overcome a deadlock. The constitutionality of the law was said to be anchored in the "Times, Places, and Manner Clause." 14 Stat. 243–44 (1866).

6. Jonathan Elliot, *Debates in the Several States Conventions and the Adoption of the Federal Constitution* (Philadelphia: J. B. Lippincott Co., 1888), III, p. 366.

unjust. Elections are regulated now unequally in some States, particularly South Carolina, with respect to Charleston, which is represented by thirty members. Should the people of any state by any means be deprived of the right of suffrage, it was judged proper that it should be remedied by the general government.[7]

If the allusion by the Father of the Constitution to the Charleston example has any force, it is in the emphasis on the constitutional basis for remedy "by the general government" when the state either regulates federal elections on an inequitable basis or fails to regulate them at all. Insofar as Article I allows Congress "to make or alter" the regulation of its elections, it is given supervisory power to insure legal and fair balloting and to safeguard the franchise from fraud and violence. Even more, the Times, Places, and Manner Clause is generally conceded to give Congress plenary jurisdiction over the election of representatives and senators. Not so generally conceded is the question of whether this "plenary power" is subject to judicial review. The record indicates that only one participant in the debates relating to the formation of the Constitution addressed himself to this point. At the North Carolina ratifying convention, Delegate John Steele responded to the expressed fear that a Congress dominated by seaboard interests could use the clause as a basis for ensuring the election of a disproportionate share of coastal as opposed to inland representatives. Steele said that Congress "most probably" would "lay the State[s] off into districts." But if the national legislature on this score were to "make laws inconsistent with the Constitution, independent judges will not uphold them, nor will the people obey them."[8]

CHANGING COURT DOCTRINE

From the days of the Founding Fathers to the Reconstruction Era, Congress relied on the state courts to vindicate essential rights arising under the Constitution and federal laws. The only exception was stipulated in the Judiciary Act of 1789 which provided in Section 25 for Supreme Court review when a claim of federal right was denied by a state court. But that policy was completely changed after the

7. This was out of a representative assembly composed of 200 and occurred at the time of a westward population shift. Rufus King also confirmed the excessive Charleston representation; *ibid.*, II, p. 50–51; see Farrand, *The Federal Convention*, III, pp. 267–68.

8. Elliot, *Debates in the Several States*, IV, p. 71.

Civil War when nationalism dominated congressional views and brought with it increased powers for the federal judiciary. In 1871, Congress subjected to suit "every person who, under color of any statute" deprives another "of any rights, privileges or immunities secured by the Constitution and laws of the United States."[9] District courts were given "original jurisdiction" of actions to "redress the deprivation, under the color of any state law . . . of any right . . . secured by the Constitution. . . ."[10] Moreover, in 1875, Congress granted federal district courts "original cognizance concurrent with the courts of the several States, of all suits of a civil nature . . . arising under the Constitution or laws of the United States. . . ."[11] By these and other statutes, Congress gave the federal courts a new set of responsibilities which had lain dormant in the Constitution since 1789. As Justice Frankfurter has noted, post-Civil War federal courts "ceased to be restrictive tribunals of fair dealing between citizens of different states and became the primary and powerful reliances for vindicating every right given by the Constitution."[12] Rights guaranteed by the Constitution expanded after the Civil War with the Fourteenth and Fifteenth Amendments and federal statutes adding new promises to old. Electing representatives was an acknowledged right of the people under Article I. The Fourteenth Amendment adopted in 1868 went further to safeguard the privileges and immunities of citizens against state infringement, while the Fifteenth Amendment forbade racial discrimination in voting. Fresh language in the Constitution, combined with new responsibilities for the federal courts, resulted in some judicial faltering. A key problem in the late nineteenth century was whether the right to vote in congressional elections was secured by the Constitution. (The related and more complex problem of federal rights in state elections is taken up in Chapter 3.) In several lower federal court cases of the 1870s, congressional elections were seen in an ante-bellum light: they were exclusively administered and regulated by the states.[13] At the Supreme

9. 42 *United States Code* 1983 (1964 ed.).

10. 28 U.S.C. 1343 (3).

11. 18 Stat. 335 (1875).

12. Felix Frankfurter and James Landis, *The Business of the Supreme Court: A Study in the Federal Judicial System* (New York: Macmillan and Co., 1927), p. 65.

13. *United States* v. *Crosby*, 25 Fed. Cas. 703, No. 14,893 (1871); *United States* v. *Anthony*, 24 Fed. Cas. 829, No. 14,459 (1873); See Richard Claude, "Constitutional Voting Rights and Early Supreme Court Doctrine," 51 *Journal of Negro History* 114 (1966).

Court level, the view of the subject underwent several refinements after it was first considered in 1875. The conservative Court of that era was acutely sensitive to its function of defining the balance between state and federal power.

The issue of the constitutional basis for voting in a congressional election reached the Supreme Court in a test case developed by Francis Minor, a St. Louis lawyer whose wife was the president of the Missouri Woman Suffrage Association.[14] Minor contended that the right of suffrage was a right accorded to all adult citizens under the newly adopted Fourteenth Amendment (1868). It had declared who shall be citizens of the United States: "All persons born or naturalized in the United States and subject to the jurisdiction thereof." Formulating the constitutional view accepted by the National Woman Suffrage Association in 1870, Minor noted that the states were barred by the new amendment from abridging the "privileges and immunities" of United States citizens. He concluded that the states could not thereafter deny the vote to women. They were citizens, and the right to vote for a congressman was a right anchored in the federal Constitution. In Missouri, suffrage was limited by state law to male citizens, and consequently, Happersett, the election registrar, refused to list Mrs. Minor as a lawful voter. Susan Anthony's disciple sued Happersett on the ground that she was denied by a state official the privileges and immunities of citizens guaranteed by the Fourteenth Amendment.

In the Court Opinion in *Minor* v. *Happersett*, Chief Justice Waite correctly reiterated the fact that neither Article I nor the Fourteenth Amendment of the Constitution defines the privileges and immunities of citizens of the United States. It would be difficult to draw a list of such rights with any finality, he conceded, although in 1868 the same bench had ruled that the right to "pass freely from state to state" is a right of national citizenship.[15] But as far as suffrage is concerned, the Chief Justice emphasized, one thing is certain: suffrage has never been coextensive with citizenship. In the context of this line of reason-

14. *Minor* v. *Happersett*, 21 Wall. 162 (1875).

15. *Crandall* v. *Nevada*, a tax case, is important for its emphasis on the right to travel (6 Wall. 35 [1868]). The declaration is particularly interesting in the light of the interstate character of present day voter-registration drives and in the light of the hypothesis advanced by Harold Gosnell that "mobility is closely related to the existence of independent employment, rapid communication, general education, or any of the other changes presaging a liberalized franchise." Harold Gosnell, *Democracy, the Threshold of Freedom* (New York: Ronald Press, 1948), p. 21.

ing, the Court concluded that "the Constitution does not confer the right to vote on anyone." Waite paid special deference to the traditional authority of the states to define voter qualifications—an authority which the Court said identified the source of the right to vote, even in federal elections. Narrowly understood, Waite seemed to be saying nothing more than that the United States does not have voters of its own constitutional creation. But Waite's view has frequently been broadly interpreted to mean that the source of the right to vote rests exclusively with the states.

Dicta from *Minor* v. *Happersett* continue to be quoted in briefs designed to rebut legal claims invoking a federally based voting right against state infringement. However, Chief Justice Waite's simple assertion that the right to vote "comes from the states" has not been permitted to stand unmodified in view of changing federal commitments and policy. The point became that the states might confer or deny the right at will (except, for example, as limited by the ban on race and sex distinctions of the Fifteenth and Nineteenth Amendments). But when the right was given, the claim to exercise it freely in the election of federal officers automatically encompassed a right under the national government. It has boiled down to a distinction between getting permission to vote (from the state in the first instance) and the right of actually voting (then protected by the federal government). Indeed, Chief Justice Waite agreed to this clarification in *Ex parte Yarbrough*, a ruling of 1884 in which the Supreme Court affirmed the conviction under federal law of Georgia Klansmen who had conspired to prevent a black voter from casting his ballot for a congressman. Justice Miller, who wrote the Court Opinion, interpreted the Constitution as adopting the qualifications to vote for members of Congress that prevail in the states where the voting is to be done. The right is not conferred "on any person or class of persons by the Constitution *alone*." Acknowledging that the *Minor* case had created some confusion, Miller wrote in *Yarbrough:* "It is not true therefore that electors for members of Congress owe their right to vote to the state law . . . exclusively." Waite concurred with this modification of his reasoning in the *Minor* case probably because the word "exclusively" appeared to harmonize with his previous dictum.

In *Ex parte Yarbrough*, Justice Miller ruled that Congress has power under Article I of the Constitution to punish election law violations and to protect congressional elections from violence, corruption, or fraud. Such practices impair federal voting rights. Justice Miller concluded that a Reconstruction statute of 1870 was applicable to the racially inspired interference by private individuals with voters participating in a federal election. The statute read in part: "If two or more persons conspire to injure, oppress, threaten, or intimidate any citizen in the free exercise or enjoyment of any right or privilege secured to him by the Constitution or laws of the United States . . . they shall be fined not more than $5,000 or imprisoned not more than ten years, or both." This same Conspiracy Law has been codified in the *Judicial Code of Federal Law*, prefixed by the assertion that the right of those qualified to vote is a "right of citizens of the United States."[16] (See Chapter 3.)

In 1915, the Supreme Court construed the provision to forbid the false counting of ballots in a senatorial election. In *United States* v. *Mosley*, the Court reasoned that once the right to vote has been granted, certain other rights arise, e.g., the right to have one's vote counted honestly.[17] That federal law may hold out its protecting hand to voters in congressional elections was no longer in doubt. Said Justice Holmes, "We regard it as . . . unquestionable that the right to have one's vote counted is as open to protection by Congress as the right to put a ballot in a box." The Court held that in spite of post-Reconstruction congressional repeal of specific prohibitions against fraudulent vote-counting, the false count involved in this case was covered by the provisions of the Conspiracy Law. Mosley's trial revealed that the fraud he perpetrated was of rather large proportions. The election officers involved were convicted for omitting from their ballot count the entire vote of eleven precincts in an Oklahoma congressional election.[18]

The Conspiracy Law met its most difficult test involving congres-

16. 18 U.S.C. 241; see Chapter 5. Jurisdictional disputes in applying Section 241 to election cases were settled in *Wiley* v. *Sinkler*, 179 U.S. 58 (1900) and *Swafford* v. *Templeton*, 193 U.S. 621 (1904).

17. *United States* v. *Mosley*, 238 U.S. 383 (1915). *United States* v. *Aczel*, 219 F. 917 (1915), ruled that the statute applied in senatorial elections no less than in those for representatives.

18. Three years later, the Conspiracy Law was construed narrowly in two cases. In *United States* v. *Gradwell*, the indictment charged the defendants with conspiracy to injure and oppress three candidates for senatorial nomination by bribing a thousand nonqualified persons to vote for an opposing candidate. Federal law, said the Court, did not protect the candidates from the defendant's action in a state-sponsored primary election; 243 U.S. 476 (1917). *United States* v. *Bathgate* also involved, not the right of a discrete voter to a bribe-free election, but the claim of a candidate to the same benefit. The defendants before the Court had been accused of bribing voters in a general election at which federal offices were to be filled; 246 U.S. 220 (1918).

sional elections in *United States* v. *Classic,* decided by the Supreme Court in 1941.[19] The result was a significant victory for the new Civil Rights Section of the Criminal Division of the Justice Department. Created under the New Deal reformer Attorney General Frank Murphy, the unit was ordered to "direct, supervise and conduct prosecutions of the provisions of the Constitution or Acts of Congress guaranteeing civil rights to individuals."[20] Government lawyers vigorously prepared for the case under Attorney General Robert Jackson.[21] Involved was a prosecution against Patrick Classic and other defendants who were members of a New Orleans-based "reform" group. Overzealous to thwart the Huey Long machine, they altered and falsely counted certified ballots cast in a congressional primary.

The achievement of the Civil Rights Section in winning *United States* v. *Classic* comes into focus when one recognizes the weak legal ammunition government lawyers could bring to bear on the question of whether federal protection of the right to vote extended to state-sanctioned congressional primary elections. The government's brief could cite little favorable precedent. Harmful to the federal cause were *Grovey* v. *Townsend* and *United States* v. *Newberry.* In Grovey's case, the Supreme Court had ruled that political parties were at liberty to define the conditions of party membership that had to be met by voters at primaries, saying who could vote to nominate candidates and that such action was the private affair of the party involved, even though the state accepted the primary results.[22] Involved in the *Newberry* case was the Federal Corrupt Practices Act of 1910 which limited by criminal penalties the amount of money which might be spent in congressional elections campaigns.[23] Congress had aimed its volley at machine politics by requiring that all

19. *United States* v. *Classic,* 313 U.S. 299 (1941).

20. Ironically for the government's case, by the time the review of Classic's prosecution appeared on the Court's docket, Attorney General Murphy was himself appointed by President Roosevelt as a member of the Supreme Court. But in that forum he sided with a minority of justices (led by Justice Douglas, with whom Justice Black also joined), who expressed the dissenting view that the prosecution was defective because the Conspiracy Law did not specify sufficiently that Classic's actions were forbidden.

21. Cf. Justice Jackson's subsequent doubts about the ruling in *Classic,* expressed after he joined the Supreme Court and dissented in *Screws* v. *United States,* associating himself with Justice Robert's dissent; 325 U.S. 91 (1945). Jackson did not take part in the *Classic* briefing.

22. *Grovey* v. *Townsend,* 295 U.S. 45 (1935).

23. *United States* v. *Newberry,* 256 U.S. 232 (1921).

interstate political committees keep finances above board. They were to report on the source of campaign contributions in excess of $100 and expenditures exceeding $10. Truman Newberry of Michigan was convicted of violating the regulation in his successful campaign for the Senate against Henry Ford in 1918. The conviction, however, was set aside by a four-judge plurality of the Supreme Court, agreeing that congressional power did not extend to making rules for primary elections.

With adverse precedents dating from the preceding 20 years, the government brief submitted in the *Classic* case rested its argument on "first principles."[24] Department lawyers argued that the right of a voter in a Louisiana congressional primary election to have his ballot counted as cast is a right secured by constitutional Article I, Section 2, calling for the choice of representatives "by the people," and Section 4, the Times, Places, and Manner Clause. The government brief further asserted that the scheme alleged on the part of *Classic* and others to deprive citizens of voting rights violated the Conspiracy Law. Finally, invoking a related statute only twice used in reported cases previous to the creation of the Civil Rights Section of the Justice Department, the government concluded that as election commissioners, Classic and his cronies had abridged voting rights and violated the Fourteenth Amendment in defiance of the *Criminal Code* provision forbidding willful actions "under color of any law" that deprive citizens of privileges and immunities protected by the Constitution. (See Chapter 3.)

This simple but forceful line of argument was designed in part and presented by Herbert Wechsler. He had been Justice Stone's law clerk in 1932–33, and it was Stone who wrote the Opinion of the Court in *United States* v. *Classic*. Wechsler was effective in alerting the bench to the broad implications of the case. Reviewing the rulings and rationales of the relevant judicial precedents, Justice Stone said privately that they had provided little meaningful guidance. Indeed, Stone thought it best completely to ignore *Grovey* v. *Townsend*. In a conversation with the great Madison scholar, Irving Brant, the Justice is reported to have said: "When the *Classic* case came to us, I made a thorough study of the [constitutional] clauses dealing with federal elections and came to the conclusion that the purpose was to give the Federal Government power over the whole electoral proc-

24. Brief for the United States, pp. 15–35, *United States* v. *Classic*, 313 U.S. 299 (1941).

ess."[25] Justice Stone in *Classic*, like Justice Miller in *Yarbrough*, took advantage of the ambiguity and inconclusiveness of precedent to strengthen the right to vote and in the process to enlarge federal supervision of elections.

Two questions were formally presented to Stone's Court: whether the voters' rights and congressional power extended to primary elections, and whether Congress intended in its Conspiracy Law to exercise its power over any part of the pre-election, primary process. In a letter to Justice Douglas, whose view of the case differed from Stone's, Stone explained that he saw both questions in the context not just of the traditional view of the right to vote but of the right to vote in a meaningful way. He told Douglas: "The Constitution guarantees the right to participate in the choice of representatives, and it isn't important whether the effort to participate would or would not be successful. But in order to invoke the constitutional protection and to bring the case within the statute (the Conspiracy Law), participation in the primary must be a participation in the choice."[26] Stone explained that he was satisfied that, in guaranteeing the right to vote, the Constitution was guaranteeing to qualified voters the right to participate in the pre-election procedure.

United States v. *Classic* was Justice Stone's last signed Opinion before he was nominated to the Chief Justiceship by President Roosevelt on June 12, 1941. In Stone's ruling of May 26, the Supreme Court for the first time held that congressional power can reach behind the final election to the primary. The decision laid the groundwork for a new view of what constituted state involvement in elections, a view less mechanical than that in *Grovey* v. *Townsend* and an approach having significant application in cases involving racial discrimination in party primaries. (See Chapter 4.) In *Classic*, Stone began his analysis from the broad perspective of an enlarged right under the Constitution. He relied on Article I to specify that "the right to participate in the choice of representatives for Congress . . . includes . . . the right of the elector to have his ballot counted at the primary." By equating the elective right with the "right to choose" a political representative, he also invoked a broader phase: "the right to participate."

25. Quoted by Alpheus T. Mason, *Harlan Fiske Stone, Pillar of the Law* (New York: Viking Press, 1956), p. 589, from the Irving Brant memorandum of a talk with Justice Stone, March, 1944. See Herbert Wechsler, "Toward Neutral Principles of Constitutional Law," 73 *Harvard Law Review* 1-35 (Nov. 1959).

26. Mason, *Harlan Fiske Stone*, p. 587.

Certainly Stone was underwriting the principle stated by Alexander Hamilton in 1777 that public officials be "chosen really and not nominally by the people."[27] The fact that the framers of the Constitution and nineteenth-century statutory drafters were not familiar with primary elections was, Stone said, "of little significance."[28]

Reading the last epitaph to the much quoted doctrine of *Minor* v. *Happersett* about voting being derived from the states, Stone wrote in *Classic:*

While, in a loose sense, the right to vote for Representatives in Congress is sometimes spoken of as a right derived from the States, this statement is true only in the sense that the States are authorized by the Constitution to legislate on the subject as provided by section 2 of article I, to the extent that Congress has not restricted State action by the exercise of its powers to regulate elections under section 4 and its more general power under article I, section 8, 'to make all laws which shall be necessary and proper for carrying into execution the foregoing powers.'

United States v. *Classic* is an important doctrinal watershed in constitutional law. Looking to the past, it dealt the final *coup de grâce* to the "state derivation doctrine." Facing the future, it prophesied a flexible approach to the regulation of party primaries, an approach which finally resulted in the formal overruling of *Grovey* v. *Townsend* in 1944.[29] After the *Classic* ruling, party primaries could no longer be regarded as purely private affairs nor could the parties holding them be thought to be unconcerned with public responsibilities. Of principal importance to the one-party South where primaries were conclusive, the ruling presaged a new era of competitive politics where "lily white" partisanship had been the rule. Further, the decision may have caused the dissenting justices second thoughts in later years. As Francis Biddle, who was Solicitor General from 1940 to 1941, has noted:

The vote stood four to three, and it is interesting to note that the three dissenters were Douglas, Black and Murphy, who were usually the Court's

27. Alexander Hamilton to Gouverneur Morris, May 10, 1777, in *Works of Alexander Hamilton*, ed. Henry Cabot Lodge (New York: G. P. Putnam's Sons, 1885–1886), IX, pp. 71–72.

28. The same reasoning applied in *United States* v. *Saylor*, also involving the Conspiracy Law and with similar results applying against those responsible for ballot-box stuffing in a Kentucky senatorial contest; 322 U.S. 185 (1944).

29. *Smith* v. *Allwright* and the white primary cases are discussed in Chapter 4.

most uncompromisingly 'liberal' voices. They were apparently fearful of the extension of federal power to police state elections.[30]

No doubt, Stone's application of the Necessary and Proper Clause and his reliance on the Conspiracy Law to sustain a prosecution of offenders against state and federal law could be called upon later to legitimize further tendencies toward congressional regulation of federal elections.

CONGRESSIONAL RESPONSIBILITIES

In a speech subtly inviting congressional response, Justice Miller expounded on the right to vote in federal elections. He concluded by observing that since the Supreme Court had specified that voting in congressional elections had a constitutional grounding, there was a corresponding obligation on the part of Congress to protect the right by appropriate legislation.[31] Congressional concern for the elections of its members takes several forms. In order to shelter the integrity of the electors' ballots, Congress is invested by Article I of the Constitution with three distinguishable functions, which are examined below: the delegation function, the judicial function, and the legislative function. Where federal elections are concerned, Congress may pass the buck, pass judgment, or pass laws.

The Delegation Function

Congress may give state election officials enforcement authority or designate the agents empowered to enforce and administer federal election laws. The authority of the federal legislature to regulate the times, places, and manner of congressional elections is shared with the legislatures of the states (subject to change by Congress). That complicated arrangement of dual responsibility was illustrated in *Ex parte Siebold,* in which the Supreme Court upheld the conviction of state election supervisors who had stuffed the ballot boxes in a congressional election in Baltimore. Also at issue was an 1871 statute

30. Francis Biddle, *In Brief Authority* (Garden City: Doubleday, 1962), pp. 159–60. In *Classic,* Justice Douglas dissented, emphasizing the lack of "specificity" of the Conspiracy Law, which he and Justices Black and Murphy thought should generally not be extended to primary elections.

31. Samuel Freeman Miller, *Lectures on the Constitution* (New York: Banks and Brothers, 1893), p. 661 ff.

making it a *federal* crime for election officers to violate duties under *state* law. Mr. Justice Bradley upheld the conviction, condemned the vote-tampering, and explained: "There is nothing in the nature of federal-state relations to exclude the cooperation of both in the matter of elections of representatives. . . . The authority of the national government being paramount, collisions can only occur from unfounded jealousy of such authority."[32]

And collisions there were. Ballot-pilfering was a sufficiently popular nineteenth-century crime among state officials to make Siebold's line of defense a repeated performance in congressional election cases. In 1888, an Indiana election inspector found the results of a federal election distasteful, and he persuaded the ballot-counter to destroy some of the bad news. Before the Supreme Court, Inspector Coy's attorneys argued that the defendant's political gaming was punishable under state law and required no federal referee. Echoing the line Justice Bradley had earlier set, Justice Miller replied that, when congressional elections are involved, officials such as Coy play both a state and federal role. In denying Coy a writ of *habeas corpus*, Miller asserted that Congress "has plenary and paramount jurisdiction over congressional elections." It could, as it did, adopt state law on fraud as its own, and these regulations could be enforced properly by separate federal sanctions.[33]

The Judicial Function

The integrity of voters' ballots may be protected by a sanction mentioned in Article I, Section 5, of the Constitution. "Each House shall be the judge of the elections, returns and qualifications of its own members." To the process of judging the elections and returns of respective members, each house of Congress brings the authority

32. *Ex parte Siebold,* 100 U.S. 371 (1880). *Ex parte Clarke* was argued at the same time as Siebold's case. Again, Justice Bradley spoke for the Court and voiced a nationalist position. In *Clarke,* he held that Congress had power to pass the law under which a state election official in Cincinnati was convicted for refusing to deliver a federal ballot box to the county clerk. Justice Field, in dissent, registered his objection to the punishment of a state officer under aegis of federal law; 100 U.S. 399 (1880). Justice Bradley spoke for a majority of the Court in *United States* v. *Gale* in 1883. In that case he upheld the conviction of several state election officials of Florida indicted for stuffing a ballot box with tickets marked for the congressional candidate they preferred. Their position as agents of the state did not save them from the operation of federal law; 109 U.S. 62 (1883).

33. *In re Coy,* 127 U.S. 731 (1888).

to subpoena witnesses, require sworn testimony, or take possession of ballots and tallysheets.[34] The suggestion has occasionally been voiced (among representatives and senators who have served on election committees) that the decision of contested cases should be referred in the first instance to the Court of Appeals for the District of Columbia. The idea has never garnered significant support. Election squabbles continue to be settled by the elected.

A lively contest over Mississippi congressional seats was decided by the House of Representatives in 1965. The Mississippi Freedom Democratic Party challenged the 1964 election of five representatives from that state on the ground that blacks, comprising nearly half of the state's population, had been systematically denied the right to vote or to run candidates. The difficulties in filing for candidacy encountered by Mrs. Victoria Gray of William Colmer's Fifth District were illustrative. The State Board of Election Commissioners rejected her petition to appear on the ballot, asserting that few of the signatures on her behalf were properly certified. She explained that the circuit clerk refused to certify the others because, according to him, the petitioners were not qualified electors. "We asked him what he meant by that," Mrs. Gray testified.

Was he saying that the other people . . . whose signatures were here were not registered voters? Oh, no, he wasn't saying [that] . . . but he was saying that many of them had not paid their poll taxes. We then pointed out to him the 24th amendment. It was a Federal election and we didn't think the tax applied. He said that so far as he was concerned the Mississippi laws were the ones by which he judged and Federal law had nothing to do with it . . . when dealing with those signatures.[35]

Fatal to the cause of the black candidates was the fact that, although the administration of state law was questionable and although the

34. Statutes specify the mechanics for such procedures. See 2 U.S.C. 201 *et seq.* See also George Galloway, *History of the House of Representatives* (Washington, D.C.: Government Printing Office, 1962), pp. 28–29. The Supreme Court has ruled that, with the express constitutional authority to inquire into the election of its members, the Senate necessarily has power to summon witnesses and compel testimony for that purpose. Any delay in seating amounts to no violation of Article V which specifies that "no State, without its consent, shall be deprived of its equal suffrage in the Senate." *Barry* v. *United States ex rel. Cunningham,* 279 U.S. 597 (1929). The judicial function of the House was first examined by the Supreme Court in the case of *In re Loney,* 134 U.S. 372 (1890).

35. U.S. Congress, House, Subcommittee on Elections of the Committee on House Administration, "Contested Elections in the First, Second, Third, Fourth, and Fifth Districts of Mississippi," 89th Cong., 1st sess., 1965, p. 51.

Freedom Democratic Party held "mock elections" for three of the seats involved, the would-be representatives were not *bona fide* candidates in the legally sanctioned general election. The result was, in terms of the federal law governing contested elections, that the Freedom Democratic challengers who did not qualify as candidates in the state election failed by that fact to qualify as contestants before the House Subcommittee on Elections. In any event, that is the way a majority of the members of the House of Representatives saw the matter, voting 228 to 143 to seat the incumbent Mississippi congressmen.

The authority of the House of Representatives to exclude members-elect was given its most important review by the Supreme Court in *Powell* v. *McCormack*.[36] In November, 1966, Adam Clayton Powell was elected from the 18th Congressional District of New York to serve in the 90th Congress. However, pursuant to a House resolution, he was not permitted to take his seat. Powell (and some of the voters of his district) contested the congressional ostracism claiming that the House could exclude him only if it found that he failed to meet the specific requirements of Article I, Section 2 of the Constitution. That provision states that "no Person shall be a Representative who shall not have attained to the Age of twenty-five Years, and been seven Years a Citizen of the United States, and who shall not, when elected, be an Inhabitant of that State in which he shall be chosen." The House found that Powell met the age, citizenship, and residence requirements. Nevertheless, House Resolution 278, adopted by a vote of 307 to 116, provided that Powell be "excluded from membership in the 90th Congress," allegedly for misappropriating public funds and for incurring the contempt of New York courts.[37] Lawyers for the controversial New Yorker conceded that Article I, Section 5 grants the House authority to *expel* a *sitting* member "with the Concurrence of two thirds" and that the House may expel a member for any reason whatsoever. But the Harlem leader was excluded rather than expelled. Chief Justice Warren for seven members of the Supreme Court ruled that "the Constitution leaves the House without authority to *exclude* any person, duly elected by his constituents, who meets all the requirements for membership prescribed . . ." in the Age, Citizenship, and Residence Clause. The Chief Justice concentrated at length on historical precedents and the intent of

36. *Powell* v. *McCormack*, 395 U.S. 486 (1969): cf. 266 F. Supp. 354 (D.C.D.C. 1967); 129 U.S. App. D.C. 354, 395 F. 2d 577 (C.A.D.C. Cir. 1968).
37. 113 *Cong. Rec.* 1918 (daily ed., Mar. 1, 1967).

the constitutional framers who generally distinguished "between the power to expel and the power to exclude." In his last electoral process opinion before retirement, Chief Justice Warren asserted in 1969: "A fundamental principle of our representative democracy is, in Hamilton's words, 'that the people should choose whom they please to govern them.' As Madison pointed out at the Convention, this principle is undermined as much by limiting whom the people can select as by limiting the franchise itself."[38] Since Powell's suit was filed against House Speaker John McCormack, Warren found it necessary to deal with Article I, Section 6 which provides: "For any Speech or Debate in either House, they [Senators and Representatives] shall not be questioned in any other place." The Speech, or Debate, Clause performs an important function in representative government, the Chief Justice concluded. "It insures that legislators are free to represent the interests of their constituents without fear that they will be later called to task in the courts for that representation." Accordingly, such House employees (named in Powell's suit) as the Sergeant-at-arms and the Clerk, became the defendants, and the Court dismissed the action against named congressmen.

Justice Douglas, in concurrence, wrote that at the root of Congressman Powell's case was "the basic integrity of the electoral process." He conceded that if the Court were reviewing an expulsion case no justifiable controversy would likely be presented, the vote of the House being two-thirds or more. "Policing the conduct of members, a recurring problem in the Senate and House as well, is quite different from the initial decision whether an elected official should be seated. It well might be easier to bar admission than to expel one already seated." Justice Stewart's dissent stressed the mootness of the contest over Powell's seat in the 90th Congress. In 1969, the House admitted Representative Powell to membership in the 91st Congress. Stewart thought that the only live aspect of the case—Powell's claim to back salary—could be decided by the Court of Claims, thereby relieving the Supreme Court of any need to embark on the delicate task of reaching fundamental constitutional issues.

38. The full ruling of the Supreme Court had several facets. First, the case was not mooted by Powell's seating in the 91st Congress; second, although the suit was dismissed against the respondent Congressmen, it was sustained against their agents; third, the denial of membership involved could not be treated as an expulsion; fourth, the Supreme Court had jurisdiction over the subject matter of the controversy; and fifth, the case was justiciable and not covered by the "political questions doctrine."

The Legislative Function

On the positive side of its authority, Congress possesses a wide range of potent though traditionally little-used powers to regulate the electoral process, especially where federal elections are concerned. Such legislation falls historically and topically into about five categories involving districting, the timing of elections, Reconstruction Acts, corrupt practices legislation, and modern civil rights laws. The earliest series of federal laws, beginning with an enactment of 1842, relates to congressional control over the election districts for the House of Representatives. In that year a requirement was established that the House legislators should be elected by districts when a state became entitled to more than one representative in Congress.[39] Federal standards for drawing the necessary district boundaries were repealed in 1929. Since then, the topic of congressional districting has surpassed most other election law problems bedeviling Federal-State and Court-Congress relations. (See Chapter 9.) In regard to the scheduling of elections, Congress invokes its constitutional authority in the Times, Places, and Manner Clause to require that elections for representatives should be held on the Tuesday after the first Monday in November. Implementation began in 1876.[40]

The Reconstruction Acts, for a period of 24 years, asserted extensive regulation of federal elections. The Republican effort to nationalize election regulation and protection of voting rights was facilitated by the Fourteenth and Fifteenth Amendments. It was also permitted in congressional elections by the continuum of regulatory authority between state and federal government outlined in the Times, Places, and Manner Clause. As will be seen (Chapters 3 and 4), some aspects of the laws to protect black voters were whittled away by a hostile Supreme Court, and other portions of the Republican program were repealed by a Democratic Congress intent on reconciliation with the South of the 1890s.

In spite of this congressional retreat, the seeds of later Populist and Progressive federal statutory and court efforts to preserve federal elections from fraud and corruption were the Conspiracy Law and a companion Enforcement Law, both easily interpreted to deal with corruption in elections by state officials. Growing from these slender roots, a new period in the history of federal control over national elections began in 1907. In that year, a Republican Congress enacted

---

39. 5 U.S. Stat. 481 (1842); repealed in part by 9 Stat. 428, 432–33 (1859).
40. 2 U.S.C. 7.

the Populist-Progressive–inspired Tillman Act, prohibiting national banks and corporations from making contributions in federal elections. After 1907, the regulation of campaign practices and finances provided the major focus of congressional investigation and proposed legislative reforms in federal elections.[41] The Corrupt Practices Act, Hatch Act prohibitions touching on the political activity of federal employees,[42] and Taft-Hartley prohibitions against money contributions by national banks, corporations, and some types of financial activities of labor unions[43] add up to what must be viewed as a modest patchwork of poorly enforced reforms. Federal laws governing campaign financing especially have not kept pace with contemporary techniques and are widely recognized to be in need of revision.[44]

Finally, a significant rebirth of congressional concern for voting rights commenced in 1957.[45] The Civil Rights Acts from that year until 1968 will be discussed in Chapters 5 and 6 of this book.

As a participant in the process of making public policy work in American society, the United States Supreme Court has passed upon virtually every major statute which Congress has written into law. Along the way, the Court has developed a two-part relationship to congressional control over federal elections. As the ultimate interpreter of the law, the Court has shown that it operates both as an arbiter and as a policy-maker. As an arbiter of federal activities under the Constitution and of national-state responsibilities, the Court has identified and clarified the functions of Congress in federal elections. As a participant in the policy-making process, the Court exercises limited discretion in interpreting the law. In providing lesser courts

41. 2 U.S.C. 241–56.

42. 5 U.S.C. 118. In interpreting the Hatch Act, the Supreme Court has insisted that the law does not deprive qualified voters who are federal employees of their right to cast ballots in federal elections. Yet the right of such civil servants to participate actively in election politics may reasonably be restricted by Congress, which is responsible in part for the efficiency of government workers. The holding to this effect seems to provide a significant qualification to the broad dictum of *Classic* which identified the right to participate in the process of political choice from beginning to end. *United Public Workers* v. *Mitchell*, 330 U.S. 75 (1947).

43. 18 U.S.C. 602.

44. See, for example, U.S. Congress, Senate, Subcommittee on Privileges and Elections, *Hearings on Proposed Improvements in Federal Election Law*, 90th Cong., 1st sess., 1967 and U.S. Congress, Senate, *Hearings on S.1474 to Create a Bipartisan Commission to Study Federal Laws Limiting Political Activity by Officers and Employees of Government*, 89th Cong., 1st sess., 1965.

45. 42 U.S.C. 1971 *et seq.*

with authoritative guidance in applying the law, the Supreme Court has occasionally acted as a restraining force. The "nay saying" capability of the high Court was evidenced in *United States* v. *Newberry,* in which it interpreted the Corrupt Practices Act as inapplicable in primary elections. Taking a restrictive approach in judicial review or statutory construction is not necessarily the most important power of the bench, however. The short-lived *Newberry* ruling was replaced by *United States* v. *Classic.* The decision there illustrates the fact that the Supreme Court may not only sustain legislation but also that in so doing it may write a rationalization of importance as an historical document reflecting the politics and commitment of its day.

That the Supreme Court's role in protecting voting rights and clarifying congressional responsibilities in federal elections should shift with changes of personnel can partly be laid at the feet of the constitutional framers. They knowingly inserted into congressional election law a conflict between federal authority and local control. Chief Justice Waite in 1875 was the first spokesman for his bench to give significant judicial consideration to constitutional voting rights. At a time when Congress was anxious to shield voters' rights from debasement, it was Waite's view that the privilege of voting for congressmen was, in terms of the Constitution, no right at all. At least that appeared to be the position of the federal bench until Justice Miller in 1884 transformed the suffrage exercised in congressional elections into a right secured and guaranteed by the Constitution and, consequently, a right which Congress may protect. Taking a fresh look at the Constitution and federal statutes, Justice Harlan Fiske Stone, beginning in 1941, offered a third and more expansive perspective on voting rights. Since that time, the franchise has been considered in a new light: interpretation of the law relating to the right must be concerned with the realities of individual choice, not merely with legal forms. The integrity of voting rights depends on the integrity of the electoral process, and government responsibility may protect the operations of popular choice from first step to last.

3   The civil war
amendments and statutes

Before the Civil War, the federal government could claim very little supervisory authority over state interference with individual liberties. Article I had identified elections of representatives "by the People" as a constitutionally anchored federal responsibility. In the realm of personal freedoms, the original Constitution of 1787 restricted federal and state action by forbidding, in Article I, Section 10, the enactment of *ex post facto* laws and bills of attainder. Also, Article IV in its second section borrowed a provision from the old Articles of Confederation in stipulating that the citizens of each state should be entitled to all the privileges and immunities of citizens in the several states. That clause had been interpreted as early as 1823 in *Corfield* v. *Coryell*, which ruled on the power of states to deny to nonresidents the use of public property.[1] In that case the Jeffersonian Republican, Justice Bushrod Washington, invoked the language of natural rights theory to identify, among others, the elec-

1. *Corfield* v. *Coryell*, 6 Fed. Cas. 546 (1823).

tive franchise as a right by its nature "fundamental"—one of those privileges and immunities of national citizenship which stem from the United States Constitution.

THE CIVIL WAR AMENDMENTS

As the Civil War drew to a close, debate on the topic of Negro citizenship and suffrage began in earnest, and the first steps were taken to enlarge federal responsibilities for both federal and state elections. Passed and adopted in 1865, the Thirteenth Amendment outlawed slavery and invalidated the original basis for congressional representation which counted a slave as three-fifths of a man. In the hope that the privileges described by Justice Washington might be enjoyed by the newly freed black, the Republican Congress in the Civil Rights Act of 1866 declared that persons of African descent in the United States were citizens.[2] Later, the Reconstruction Act of 1867 went so far as specifically to require the franchise for twenty-one-year-old Negro males in states under military control. To secure their efforts from attack by the courts or repeal by some future Democratic congressional majority, as well as to develop new reserves of supporting partisans, the Republicans in Congress sought to elevate the principles of the Civil Rights Act to the status of constitutional amendment:[3] the Fourteenth Amendment, which was adopted in 1868. Its significance for the Negro was that he was acknowledged as a whole person and that he was accorded full citizenship. Historically the Due Process and Equal Protection Clauses have been the only portions of that Amendment to be employed effectively in safeguarding black suffrage. The year after the Fourteenth Amendment went into effect, the Fifteenth Amendment was approved by Congress and then adopted in 1870. It provided that the right to vote could not be denied by the United States or any state "on account of race, color, or previous condition of servitude."

The Fourteenth Amendment
The first and most important section of the Fourteenth Amendment was drafted by an abolitionist from the Western Reserve, Representative Bingham. His final draft of the first section reads:

2. 14 Stat. 27–30; Act of Ap. 9, 1866.
3. 15 Stat. 72–74; Acts of Je. 22–25, 1868.

All persons born or naturalized in the United States, and subject to the jurisdiction thereof, are citizens of the United States, and of the State wherein they reside. No State shall make or enforce any law which shall abridge the privileges or immunities of citizens of the United States; nor shall any State deprive any person of life, liberty, or property without due process of law; nor deny to any person within its jurisdiction the equal protection of the laws.

The three Civil War Amendments were the first constitutional provisions to make specific reference to their enforcement. Section 5 of the Fourteenth Amendment reads: "The Congress shall have power to enforce by appropriate legislation, the provisions of this article." Whether Bingham and his followers intended by the first and fifth sections of the Fourteenth Amendment to nationalize all civil rights by making the original Privileges and Immunities Clause and the Bill of Rights[4] effective against the states is a question which remains in dispute.[5] The congressional record in this regard is not clear. Nevertheless, to affirm the relevance of the Fourteenth Amendment to the right to vote is to underline this historical fact: of all the movements influencing the Amendment which developed prior to the first session of the Thirty-ninth Congress, that for Negro suffrage was most outstanding.[6] It should be noted at the outset that considerable controversy surrounds the historical background of the Fourteenth Amendment, particularly the meaning of the Privileges and Immunities, the Equal Protection of the Laws, and the Due Process Clauses. Each will be briefly discussed below as they were formulated and have been interpreted to refer to voting rights.

The Privileges and Immunities Clause. A strong Senate advocate of the proposed Fourteenth Amendment advised those seeking to understand the meaning of the new Privileges and Immunities Clause to return to Justice Washington's illumination of that phrase as it ap-

4. *Barron* v. *Baltimore* (7 Pet. 243 [1833]) had limited the effect of the Bill of Rights to the federal government. The *Dred Scott* decision (19 How. 393 [1857]) eliminated the possibility that the Privileges and Immunities Clause could apply to the Negro because he was there said not to be a citizen.

5. William W. Crosskey, *Politics and the Constitution* (Chicago: University of Chicago Press, 1953), II, pp. 1056–1118. Professor Crosskey concluded that Bingham intended to reverse *Barron* v. *Baltimore* by making the Bill of Rights effective against the states. Cf. Charles Fairman, "Does the Fourteenth Amendment Incorporate the Bill of Rights?" 2 *Stanford Law Review* 5–173 (1949).

6. Joseph P. James, *The Framing of the Fourteenth Amendment* (Urbana: University of Illinois Press, 1956), p. 33.

peared in the original Constitution.[7] According to Washington's dictum in *Corfield* v. *Coryell*, the Constitution conferred on the citizen of each state "a general citizenship" which "communicates all the privileges and immunities which the citizens of the same States would be entitled to under like circumstances." Among the attributes of federal citizenship, according to Justice Washington in the *Corfield* case, was the constitutionally secured right of "elective franchise as regulated by the laws or constitution of the state in which it is established." In the congressional debates preceding the Fourteenth Amendment, Representative Shellabarger of Ohio asserted that it was "universally agreed" that those privileges and immunities which Washington enumerated as "fundamental" cannot be "taken away from any citizen of the United States by the laws of any State, neither from its own citizens nor from those coming in from another State."[8] As a consequence of acquiring citizenship, Negroes would presumably enjoy the privileges and immunities which Justice Washington had defined.

Whatever the framers of the Fourteenth Amendment intended its scope to be, their Privileges and Immunities Clause was severely crippled by the Supreme Court in the *Slaughterhouse Cases* of 1873.[9] The five justices in the majority agreed that the pervading purpose of the Thirteenth and Fourteenth Amendments was the "freedom of the slave race" and the protection "of the newly-made freeman and citizens from the oppressions of those who had formerly exercised unlimited dominion over him. . . ." The real damage to the potential force of the provision was done where Justice Miller drew a sharp distinction between the privileges and immunities that were derived from state citizenship and those that were derived from United States citizenship. The case involved a privilege which 1,000 New Orleans butchers claimed was newly guaranteed by the Fourteenth Amendment—the privileges of engaging in business. This civil liberty, allegedly infringed by a Louisiana slaughterhouse monopoly, fell in the category of rights protected by the states, according to

7. *Congressional Globe*, Senate, 39th Cong., 1st sess., p. 2545 (1865–66). The clause of the original Constitution has remained little used in voting cases. However, in *Blake* v. *McClung* the Supreme Court said by way of dictum that the privileges and immunities guaranteed in Article IV do not preclude a state from requiring a specified period of residence "before a citizen of another State who becomes a resident" may "exercise the right of suffrage." 172 U.S. 239, 256 (1898).

8. *Congressional Globe*, House, 39th Cong., 1st sess., July 16, 1866, *Appendix*, p. 293.

9. *Slaughterhouse Cases*, 16 Wall. 36 (1873).

the Court. In illustrating the rights which may be safeguarded by the federal government, Justice Miller specified those secured by the Thirteenth Amendment and incidentally conceded as well the right to vote in federal elections secured by the original Constitution and indirectly protected by the Fifteenth Amendment. Opportunities to so apply the Clause, however, have been generally declined by the federal judiciary, and as a result an attack upon the constitutionality of a statute is a feeble assault indeed if it relies on the almost forgotten Privileges and Immunities Clause.[10]

The Equal Protection Clause. A close reading of the dictum in *Corfield* v. *Coryell* reveals early recognition of the fact that the constitutional right to vote does not arise until after the franchise is conferred by the state. Representative Bingham and his followers noted this in drafting the Fourteenth Amendment and sought, among other things, to influence the authority of the state to confer suffrage by means of the Equal Protection Clause (though this intention was denied by some).[11] By requiring that no state shall "deny to any person within its jurisdiction the equal protection of the laws," the amendment would supposedly require an equitable application of suffrage and election statutes. Radical critics complained, however, that the proposal did not clearly say that, if a state grants the right to vote to adult male residents, the state law encompassing this measure would apply equally to qualified white and Negro male adults. The internal logic which Bingham imparted to his amendment seemed to require that the *Corfield* rendering of the rights of citizens was to be supplemented by a provision destroying, however equivocally, the power of the states to enact unfairly discriminatory laws. After quoting from the *Corfield* case, Senator Howard, who had been instrumental in guiding the resolution through the Senate, explained: "The great object of the first section of this amendment is . . . to restrain the power of the States and compel them at all times to respect these great fundamental guarantees." Referring specifically to the Equal Protection Clause, Howard conceded that the politics of Senate and House consideration of the new amendment had required a backing

---

10. See *Colgate* v. *Harvey* where Justice Stone cited 44 cases in which state laws were contested on the basis of the clause but with no success; 296 U.S. 404 at 445–46, 2n (1935).

11. W. W. Van Alstyne, "Fourteenth Amendment, the 'Right' to Vote, and the Understanding of the Thirty-ninth Congress," *Supreme Court Review* 33–86 (1965).

away from constitutional language that would directly give the vote to adult male blacks and whites. Nor was it claimed that the ambiguous language of the Equal Protection Clause would have that effect. The clause held out the promise, nevertheless, of "abolish[ing] all class legislation in the States, and does away with the injustice of subjecting one caste of persons to a code not applicable to another."[12] Giving a contemporary reading to this point of view, the Court Opinion in the Virginia Poll Tax Case of 1966 concluded: "Our cases demonstrate that the Equal Protection Clause of the Fourteenth Amendment restrains the States from fixing voter qualifications which invidiously discriminate."[13] Elsewhere Justice Douglas—speaking for six members of the Court in the same case—echoed the language of Bushrod Washington in speaking of voting as a "fundamental" right, "preservative of other basic civil and political rights."

The Due Process Clause. The Fifth Amendment, in a provision borrowed from the early state constitutions, says that no person may be deprived of life, liberty, or property without the due process of law. The Fourteenth Amendment made the same provision applicable to the states. Senator Howard explained that the new Due Process Clause should ensure enforcement of the rights of citizenship by equalizing opportunities of citizens to use the law enforcement machinery of the state in defense of rights. Congressman Bingham said that the clause had the meaning customarily understood by judges, namely, that procedural fairness is required of the courts, particularly in criminal cases.[14] Although the Due Process Clause has taken on various substantive aspects for the Supreme Court, its most obvious importance for voting cases appears when such cases involve criminal proceedings. Also, should any state default in the fair application of voting and election law, the Due Process Clause stands as a guarantee that all persons shall have access to the courts and the due process of state and federal legal machinery to restore an abridged privilege or deprived right.

12. See Howard's speech interpreting Committee intent in the *Congressional Globe*, Senate, 39th Cong., 1st sess., May 23, 1866, p. 2766; and Benjamin Kendrick (ed.), *The Journal of the Joint Committee of Fifteen on Reconstruction* (New York: Columbia University Press, 1914), pp. 55–61.

13. *Harper* v. *Virginia*, 383 U.S. 663 (1966).

14. *Congressional Globe*, 39th Cong., 1st sess., pp. 1088–90 (1866); and *Bank of Columbia* v. *Okely*, 4 Wheat. 235, 244 (1819); *Murray* v. *Hoboken Land and Improvement Co.*, 18 How. 272 (1855).

The Voting Sanction

The second section of the Fourteenth Amendment embodied what its Republican framers expected would be a potent weapon—a congressional sanction on behalf of voting rights. Chiefly the handiwork of Representative James Blaine, the provision for reducing a state's congressional representation in proportion that it denies the right to vote has remained unused.[15] (Thus if one quarter of a state's population were composed of disfranchised blacks, that state's congressional delegation could be reduced by one-fourth.) That the stillborn scheme was aimed primarily at the South was attested by Representative Nicholson of Delaware. "It is presumed that the desire for as full representation as can be obtained will compel the states having within their limits a large Negro population to confer upon them the elective franchise."[16] More explicit with respect to the anticipated racial and sectional political consequences of Section 2 was Congressman Farnsworth of Illinois. He testified that under the new amendment, Negroes in the South "shall not be used to swell their rebel masters into giants and dwarf the . . . patriotic men of the free states into Tom Thumbs."[17] His point of view was that southern states should not be allowed to profit by their 32 votes in Congress (calculated by including the full Negro population) so long as they denied voting rights to the same Negroes.

The penalty of denying House seats to states discriminating against Negro voters—a clumsy substitute for an outright grant of Negro suffrage—was not drafted as a self-executing program. Thaddeus Stevens of Pennsylvania said that Congress must enact a workable statutory program that would enable the House to ascertain the basis of representation and would specify procedures for disqualify-

15. Section 2. "Representatives shall be apportioned among the several States according to their respective numbers, counting the whole number of persons in each State, excluding Indians not taxed. But when the right to vote at any election for the choice of electors for President and Vice President of the United States, Representatives in Congress, the Executive and Judicial officers of a State, or the members of the Legislature thereof, is denied to any of the male inhabitants of such State, being twenty-one years of age, and citizens of the United States, or in any way abridged, except for participation in rebellion, or other crime, the basis of representation therein shall be reduced in the proportion which the number of such male citizens shall bear to the whole number of male citizens twenty-one years of age in such State."

16. *Congressional Globe* 39th Cong., 1st sess., 2459 (1865–66).

17. *Ibid.*, 435. See also Horace Flack, *The Adoption of the Fourteenth Amendment* ("The Johns Hopkins Studies in Historical and Political Science," vol. XXVI; Baltimore: The Johns Hopkins Press, 1908).

ing the appropriate number of Representatives from the offending states. With the withdrawal of federal troops from the South in 1876, congressional efforts to implement the voting sanction of Section 2 subsided.

Litigious attempts to enforce Section 2 have been unavailing. Such challenges in federal courts have been dismissed by resort to the dictum from *Minor* v. *Happersett* that "the privilege of voting is not derived from the United States but is conferred by the state." Judges have also insisted on enabling legislation if federal courts are to become involved in applying the sanction.[18] The judicial "hands off" approach was illustrated in 1965. Arguing on behalf of 25 plaintiffs in an effort to reduce southern congressional representation, Jack Greenberg of the NAACP Legal Defense Fund fought a losing skirmish. He attempted to show the over-representation of southern states at the expense of voteless blacks from the area and correspondingly the extent to which the inflated southern strength in Congress diluted voting rights in the North where discrimination was not the rule. The district court dismissed the request for a judicial order requiring the Bureau of Census to gather the voting statistics necessary to implement Section 2. In *Lampkin* v. *Connors*[19] the tribunal sidestepped Greenberg's contentions by denying that the plaintiffs were in any position to sue: the amount of the voting impairment was so "speculative and remote" that the plaintiffs failed to show to the court's satisfaction a deprivation suffered. Section 2 of the Fourteenth Amendent is frequently called the "dead letter section." For a full century neither in Court nor in Congress has it been accorded the benefit of a state funeral. Nevertheless, a workable and efficient Voting Rights Act of 1965 may well be its most fitting memorial.

The Fifteenth Amendment
The Reconstruction Act of 1867 supplemented the above-mentioned voting sanction with a drastic expedient. The act provided that the representation of the southern states recently in rebellion should not be recognized until each of them had ratified the Fourteenth Amendment and had established universal adult manhood suffrage to include Negroes.[20] Congressional Republicans generally rec-

18. *Saunders* v. *Wilkins*, 152 F.2d 235 (4th Cir., 1945); 328 U.S. 840 (1946), *cert. denied; United States* v. *Sharrow*, 309 F.2d 77 (2d Cir. 1962); 372 U.S. 949 (1963), *cert. denied.*
19. *Lampkin* v. *Connors*, 239 F. Supp. 757 (D.D.C. 1965).
20. 15 Stat. 72–74; Act of Je. 22–25 (1868).

ognized this as a temporary tactic. They knew that as soon as the southern states became free to do so, they would probably repeal the federally dictated voting qualifications. Another constitutional amendment was called for to cover the possibility of a state reneging on liberal election laws and to benefit the potential Negro voter in the North as Section 2 of the Fourteenth Amendment was anticipated to advance Negro suffrage in the South.

In 1869, House and Senate Judiciary Committees prepared to submit reports concerning a universal suffrage amendment to the Constitution which would lodge in the federal government the complete power to regulate voting. The two chambers disagreed over several committee and floor proposals, including one to forbid the imposition of literacy and property tests. Over three hundred pages of protracted discussion[21] reveal that the more liberal Senate was forced, largely by Democratic gains in the House, to abandon the universal suffrage amendment in favor of a resolution similar to the final form of the Fifteenth Amendment. In its original version, the proposal was framed to protect the right to vote as well as the right to hold office against racial discrimination (in 1869, Georgia, Mississippi, and South Carolina each had one Negro representative in Congress). The office-holding provision was dropped in conference committee at the insistence of the more conservative House. As a result, the constitutional provision, as it reads today, was agreed upon by the two chambers.[22] A reading of the congressional debates suggests that the resulting resolution was sought by those with a concern for the extension of democracy, as well as by those who anticipated further entrenchment in office as a consequence of Negro enfranchisement. Reconstruction and the Fourteenth Amendment had, after all, resulted in recruiting some Republican representatives from the South, and Congressman Boutwell of Massachusetts estimated that the Fifteenth Amendment could yield similar political dividends in Northern and border states, where he calculated 146,000 Negro citizens would be new voters.

21. *Congressional Globe*, 40th Cong., 2d sess., p. 2211; *ibid.*, 3d sess., pp. 985, 1427, and *Appendix*, p. 130. On the Fifteenth Amendment, see William Gillette, *The Right to Vote* (Baltimore: The Johns Hopkins Press, 1965).

22. *Senate Journal*, 40th Cong., 3d sess., p. 361; *House Journal, ibid.*, p. 449. The Fifteenth Amendment reads: "Section 1. The right of citizens of the United States to vote shall not be denied or abridged by the United States or by any State on account of race, color, or previous condition of servitude. Section 2. The Congress shall have power to enforce this section by appropriate legislation."

THE FATE OF THE EARLY CIVIL RIGHTS LAWS

By 1870, congressional Republicans were alarmed by the way in which the Ku Klux Klan and other similar extra-legal bodies were by violence and intimidation preventing Negroes from voting. Between 1869 and 1875, several federal statutes were enacted which had as their purpose the protection of Negro voting rights against interference by state officials or private individuals. Because the Fourteenth and Fifteenth Amendments were directed at outlawing discrimination by state action in *any election*, federal statutes could presumably apply only to *state officials* who discriminated (on racial grounds) under "color of law," i.e., under state authority. On the other hand, to reach the actions of *private individuals*, the early Civil Rights Acts could find justification in Article I, Section 4 (empowering Congress to regulate *federal elections* for senators and representatives) and in the implied power of the government to safeguard its own elections. Because of this complex arrangement, there has long appeared to be a constitutional gap permitting discrimination by private persons in state elections. This penumbral area, marked by an absence of federal regulation, was highlighted in a way that cast a far-reaching shadow (especially over private interference on account of race) in the Circuit and Supreme Court decisions and events surrounding the case of *United States* v. *Cruickshank*.[23]

The *Cruickshank* case stemmed from a bloody riot in Louisiana in 1873, which resulted in the massacre of sixty Negroes who were the victims of an intrastate conflict for local political control. Violence and intimidation, white Louisianians were beginning to recognize, could be used effectively to prevent Negroes from voting and to overturn state Reconstruction governments. In dismissing the federal indictment against over one hundred defendants, Supreme Court Justice Joseph Bradley, riding the federal circuit, explained that the power of Congress to legislate for the enforcement of voting rights "does not extend to the passage of laws for the suppression of ordinary crime within the States." Such crimes are supposedly covered solely by state law. Congress can legislate only to prevent official discrimination by the states (or by the United States) but not to prevent private discrimination in state elections, unless the racial motive is painstakingly proved. This distinction was also envisioned by some of the framers of the early Civil Rights Acts, but the distinction

23. *United States* v. *Cruickshank*, 25 Fed. Cas. 707 (1874).

was not always nicely drawn in federal statutes of the time—a reflection of an absence of congressional consensus on the point.

Federal Criminal Law

Two months after the Fifteenth Amendment was ratified, Congress enacted what a legislative majority (voting along sectional and party lines) conceived to be an "appropriate" enforcement act. It concentrated on criminal sanctions designed "to enforce the right of citizens of the United States to vote in the several States of this Union, and for other purposes." The federal statute can be divided into two portions which reflect an important distinction between criminal prosecution of private individuals and criminal proceedings involving state officials. (The same distinction was carried into civil remedies which are discussed at the end of this chapter.)

Criminal Provisions Applying to Individuals. The Enforcement Act of 1870 outlawed "force, bribery, threats and intimidation" of voters (or those engaged in the free exercise of any right or privilege secured by federal law) and made it a misdemeanor to deprive a citizen of "employment or occupation" in order to control his vote.[24] In a section directed against the Ku Klux Klan, the law made it a crime for two or more conspirators or disguised groups to "go upon the public highways or upon the premises of another" with intent to interfere with constitutional liberties (including the right to vote in federal elections). Senator Pool, the sponsor of the bill, noted that it was enacted in pursuance of the Fifteenth Amendment. He conceded that the language of the amendment was directed only against action "by the United States or by any State." He argued that states could be responsible for violations of voting rights by their deliberate or negligent inaction. Federal law should fill the void where state criminal laws were ineffective. "If a State shall not enforce its laws by which private individuals shall be prevented by force from contravening the rights of the citizen under the amendment," Pool said, "it is in my judgment the duty of the United States Government to supply that omission, and by its own laws and by its own courts to go into the States for the purpose of giving the amendment vitality there."[25]

Unfortunately for Senator Pool's purpose, the Supreme Court restricted the utility of the new statute in two 1876 rulings. In *United States* v. *Cruikshank* and *United States* v. *Reese*, the Court ruled that

---

24. 16 Stat. 140 (1870).
25. *Congressional Globe*, 41st Cong., 2d sess., p. 3612 (1870).

legislation under the Civil War Amendments applies only to the states and their agents but generally not to private individuals who might seek to prevent equal voting by all races.[26] The argument supporting Chief Justice Waite's opinion in both cases was that the Fourteenth Amendment forbids states only—not private individuals—to deny citizens' rights protected by the Constitution, and that "the Fifteenth Amendment does not confer the right of suffrage upon any one." Only the right "of exemption from the prohibited discrimination comes from the United States." Once the Court said this, it was no difficult matter for southern state legislatures to exclude black voting simply by enacting statutes which did not, in their actual wording, reveal that they were discriminatory. For federal officials concerned with such litigation, the lesson seemed clear: for successful prosecutions under the Fourteenth and Fifteenth Amendments, they must show that the defendants were acting under the authority of the state, since the amendments under which the Enforcement Act was passed were addressed to the states. Where the Fifteenth Amendment is invoked, discrimination on the grounds of race must be shown if federal law is to have any effect on private interference. Any broader interpretation of the law, Chief Justice Waite's rulings said, would fundamentally change the "distinct" separation of federal and state governments.[27] For the United States to take on the task of protecting black citizens from white citizens would encroach on the jurisdiction of the states to regulate their own residents. Consequently, anti-Negro violence could be punished only by the states with their apathetic or anti-Negro administrations. The effect of the *Cruickshank* and *Reese* cases was to mutilate the Enforcement Act of 1870 and Senator Pool's understanding of it, especially with respect to its anti-Ku Klux Klan provisions.[28] The impact of the rulings is also notable. Between 1870

26. *United States* v. *Reese*, 92 U.S. 214 (1876); *United States* v. *Cruickshank*, 92 U.S. 542 (1876).

27. See *Note*, "The Strange Career of 'State Action' under the Fifteenth Amendment," 74 *Yale Law Journal* 1448 (July 1965).

28. Another voting measure of the Act of 1870 was held invalid in *James* v. *Bowman*, 190 U.S. 127 (1903). The provision in question penalized any person who prevented, hindered, or intimidated another through specified techniques from exercising the right of suffrage. The *Reese, Cruickshank*, and *Yarbrough* rulings had conceded that where racial motivation was shown (as it seldom was) private acts could be prosecuted. *Bowman* went further in finding objectionable the fact that the law under review encompassed the actions of private individuals in state as well as federal elections. There was a fatal absence of any allegation of state action. Nor did the complaining Negroes who charged a bribery attempt allege that the acts were done on account of race.

and 1894, nearly 7400 cases were tried, mostly in the South. In addition, hundreds of offenders who were never brought to trial were arrested. In the five years preceding the *Reese* and *Cruickshank* cases of 1876, federal courts handled an average of 708 cases annually. After the Supreme Court rulings, prosecutions fell to below 200 per year, with few convictions. The last significant contingents of federal troops were withdrawn from the southern states in 1878, and in that year, only 25 cases were heard in the area.[29] In 1894, congressional Democrats repealed the bulk of the remaining civil rights statutes.[30] What remains has been codified in Sections 241 and 242 of the *United States Code*.[31]

Section 241, or the Conspiracy Law, protects citizens only. According to its terms, it is directed at the actions of two or more private individuals who willfully conspire to "injure, oppress, threaten, or intimidate any citizen in the free exercise or enjoyment of any right secured to him by the Constitution or laws of the United States." The far-reaching shadow of the *Cruickshank* and *Reese* cases may be gauged by the fact that before 1966 the lower federal courts frequently held that in prosecutions of private individuals under Section 241, the only conspiracies which may be punished are those directed against rights which "arise from the relationship of the individual and the federal government." Important examples include the right to vote in federal elections and the right to vote, free of racial discrimination, in any election. Court-tested claims that fall in this category of federal rights protected against private interference also include the rights to be secure from unauthorized violence while in federal custody, to inform on violations of federal law, etc.

A restrictive judicial view of the rights protected by the Conspiracy Law is by no means the only difficulty in applying the statute. Another problem, first noted in *Cruickshank* and *Reese*, has to do with proving racially inspired motives from overt acts. Even when the defendants have committed an act of racial violence, this by itself may be inadequate to allow the jury to conclude that the purpose of the

29. Everette Swinney, "Enforcing the Fifteenth Amendment, 1870–1877," 28 *Journal of Southern History* 202, 209 (May 1962). For a discussion of the difficulties met in three such criminal prosecutions during the 1950s and early 1960s, see the letter from Assistant Attorney General Burke Marshall to Senator Sam Ervin, U.S. Congress, Senate, *Judiciary Subcommittee Hearings on S. 480*, 87th Cong., 2d sess., 1962, pp. 522–23.

30. 28 Stat. 36–37 (1894); and 35 Stat. 1153 (1909).

31. 18 U.S.C. 241, 242; a *scienter* clause was added in 1909; 35 Stat. 1092.

conspiracy was to deny constitutional rights. Additional evidence bearing on the motives of the defendants may be necessary.

Criminal Law Applying to State Officers. Difficult technical problems arise under Section 242 of the *United States Code* (Title 18), incorporating portions of the Enforcement Act of 1870. Then as now, the law applies to action taken by state authorities acting "under color of law," i.e., with the apparent support of state authority. The section makes it a misdemeanor for anyone assigned to the administration of an election, or for any state official, willfully to deprive any person of his "rights, privileges or immunities secured or protected by the Constitution or laws of the United States." The same provision proscribes intentionally discriminatory application of election laws by officials in both federal and state elections. Lawyers concerned with this provision must be especially alert to the rights referred to by the statute because, to convict, the jury must be persuaded that the defendant acted, not just out of malice or ill-temper, but with the "specific intent" to deprive the victim of a recognized constitutional right "in open defiance or in reckless disregard of a constitutional requirement which has been made specific and definite."[32] That is, the prosecutor has the difficult task of proving that the victim's constitutional right was known, or should have been known to the officer, and that he acted in spite of this knowledge. The rights referred to in this regulation have been interpreted to include not only the right to vote in federal elections but also the right of qualified persons to vote in any election free from racial distinctions imposed under the authority of state action.

It should be mentioned here that the "color of law" phrase of Section 242 may even reach private actions, when they involve, for example, discriminatory practices related to official policy. Thus a private person who acts together with a state officer to discriminate on racial grounds against a qualified voter is guilty of a conspiracy to commit an offense against the United States[33] and of aiding and abetting the commission of a crime.[34] On occasion the courts have found that the influence of some private groups may be so great in discriminatory election practices that private individuals who are involved may be treated as if they were acting under governmental aegis and were therefore subject to constitutional restraint.[35]

32. *Screws* v. *United States*, 325 U.S. 91, 105 (1945).
33. 18 U.S.C. 371.
34. 18 U.S.C. 2(a).
35. For example, see *Terry* v. *Adams*, 345 U.S. 461 (1953).

The problem of federal responsibilities in pressing criminal prosecutions under Sections 241 and 242 has been brought to the forefront of civil rights difficulties in the light of the race-related contests and pressures of the 1960s. In this contemporary background, complex legal technicalities have taken on life-and-death significance. Illustrative are the notorious events that took place on June 21, 1965, in Neshoba County, Mississippi. On that hot and steamy day typical of the Delta area, deputy sheriff Cecil Price detained three civil rights workers active in local voter education and related work. Price released the three—James Chaney, Andrew Goodman, and Michael Schwerner—after nightfall from the county jail in Philadelphia, Mississippi and then followed them by car out of town. Again intercepting the biracial trio, Price ordered them into a county-owned automobile and drove them to a remote rural area where the party was met by two other policemen and fifteen private individuals. The civil rights workers were apparently killed by the group. The bodies were carried from the rendevous point to an earthen dam where they were buried.

This brutal slaughter yielded an important test case of the scope of the Conspiracy Law and Section 242 for the United States Supreme Court which reviewed a federal indictment of the eighteen conspirators. The principal charge against each member of the group was not murder—the responsibility of Mississippi to punish—but conspiracy to despoil the victims of their Fourteenth Amendment right "not to be deprived of life or liberty without due process of law by persons acting under color of state law." In the federal district court, Judge Harold Cox dismissed the indictment counts against the private individuals where they were said to be acting "under color of law" or with the support of state authority. In *United States v. Price*,[36] Justice Fortas, for all members of the Supreme Court in 1966, reversed the lower court decision and ruled that "to act 'under color' of law does not require that the accused be an officer of the State. It is enough that he is a willful participant in joint activity with the State or its agents." Indictments under both Sections 241 and 242 were sustained in Justice Fortas' skillful opinion by the comment that the protective power of the Fourteenth Amendment must be understood in the light of its post-Civil War history. It was written in response to rising private terrorism against the Negro's newly won rights. Fortas ex-

36. *United States v. Price*, 383 U.S. 787 (1966).

plained that "it would be strange indeed were this Court to revert to a construction of the Fourteenth Amendment which would once again narrow its historical purpose—which remains vital and pertinent to today's problems."

One need not go back to the *Cruickshank* or *Reese* cases for examples of such narrow or crippling limitations. In a forced confession case of 1951, Justice Frankfurter had taken a restricted view of the Fourteenth Amendment's purpose by arguing in the name of four justices that the Conspiracy Law does not apply to the due process guarantee against the states.[37] Of course much has happened in the saga of American race relations and civil rights since 1951. Justice Fortas acknowledged in 1966 the sweep of public policy changes since 1951. He said that "the federal role in the establishment and vindication of fundamental rights—such as the freedom to travel, nondiscriminatory access to public areas and . . . educational facilities—was neither as pervasive nor intense as it is today." Social change requires legal change.

United States v. *Guest*,[38] which was decided on the same day as *United States* v. *Price*, emphasized the timeliness of up-dating the old enforcement laws. This case was concerned with six private citizens who were accused of the shotgun slaying of Lemuel Penn, a Washington, D.C. Negro educator. He was killed while traveling on a Georgia highway after a tour of duty with his Army Reserve unit. The shooting took place only one week after the Civil Rights Act of 1964, with its public accommodations section, became law. Indictments in federal court accused the six individuals involved with conspiracy to interfere with the freedom of Negroes in the Athens, Georgia area to use public accommodations and with the right to travel freely. At issue for the Supreme Court was the applicability of the Conspiracy Law to the free travel guarantee (identified as a constitutional right a century earlier) and the newly secured rights to public accommodations under the Equal Protection Clause.

Particularly in question for the high bench was a traditionally nettlesome problem. There was an apparent absence of any link between state action and the activity of the private individuals accused of depriving Penn of federal rights. In response, Justice Stewart explained in the Court Opinion that the "involvement of the State need

37. *United States* v. *Williams*, 341 U.S. 70 (1951).
38. *United States* v. *Guest*, 383 U.S. 745 (1966).

not be either exclusive or direct." He thought it sufficient to note that
one of the alleged techniques for accomplishing the conspiracy was
"causing the arrest of Negroes by means of false reports that such
Negroes had committed criminal acts."

In a separate concurring Opinion, Justices Clark, Black, and Fortas
volunteered their belief that Congress was empowered to enforce
Fourteenth Amendment rights and to punish all offending conspiracies
"with or without state action." This view was thought to be implicit in paragraph 5 of the Fourteenth Amendment, which reads:
"The Congress shall have the power to enforce this article by appropriate legislation." Justice Brennan, Chief Justice Warren, and
Justice Douglas also registered their Opinion that "although the Fourteenth Amendment itself, according to established doctrine, 'speaks
to the State or to those acting under color of its authority,' legislation
protecting rights created by that Amendment, such as the right to
equal utilization of state facilities, need not be confined to punishing
conspiracies in which state officers participate." Brennan's Opinion
hinted that conspiracy by private individuals might not be reached by
judicial interpretation of the Fourteenth Amendment alone. Here the
need to show state action would apply. Yet, if the Amendment were
buttressed with supporting legislation under the Enforcement Clause
of the Fourteenth Amendment, "*all* conspiracies to interfere with the
exercise of a right secured by the Constitution" might be prosecuted.
In short, the concurrences served Congress with a significant gratis
advisory opinion that the state action limit is not binding under the
Enabling Clause of Section 5 of the Fourteenth Amendment.[39] On this
and other points, Justice Harlan dissented.

In consequence of the two separately written concurring Opinions,
six justices were put on record saying that they would feel bound to
sustain any appropriate law aimed at punishing private individuals
who use violence to deny persons their Fourteenth Amendment rights
—thereby presumably laying to rest some of the cautions and caveats
of the *obiter dicta* in *United States* v. *Cruickshank*. The supporting
Opinion written by Justice Brennan virtually invited Congress to
specify the federal rights to be protected against private interference
and, in the process, to prevent the Conspiracy Law's "being void for
vagueness." Within hours, Justice Department officials were at work

39. Cf. the dissent of Justices Black, Harlan, and White in *Bell* v. *Maryland*,
78 U.S. 226, at 318 (1964).

drafting a law tailored to the prescription of the concurring opinions in *Guest* and addressed to the problems raised by the *Price* case. The result was the Civil Rights Protection Act proposed by President Johnson on April 28, 1966. The bill, coupled with housing legislation, was defeated in both 1966 and 1967. The tragic assassination of Reverend Martin Luther King, Jr. supplied the final stimulus for enactment of the Civil Rights Act of 1968.[40]

The new legislation improves upon Sections 241 and 242 in several ways. It sets penalties for any individual, whether privately, officially, singly, or in a group, who injures, intimidates, or interferes with any person attempting to exercise specified civil or political rights. Protected are the right to vote, to participate in any program of the United States or an activity receiving federal aid, to apply for or enjoy federal employment, or to serve as a juror in a federal court. Also forbidden is any *racially motivated* attempt to interfere with a person's right to vote, to attend public schools, and to take part in state or local government programs, as well as his right to state or private employment, to union membership, to state jury service, to travel, or to the use of public accommodations such as a hotel, restaurant, or theater. Graduated penalties are specified in amendments to Sections 241 and 242 which permit the courts to make flexible responses (fines up to $10,000 and/or imprisonment up to ten years) to differing degrees of interference or intimidation. If death results from such interference, the Civil Rights Act of 1968 authorizes a life imprisonment penalty. According to President Johnson, the penalties specified by the century-old statutes were "clearly inadequate."[41]

Federal Civil Remedies

The Reconstruction criminal laws discussed above were enacted in response to vigilante violence in southern states. In another statute of 1871, Congress acted with similar intent but focused on civil remedies. In provisions which survive today, federal courts were authorized to hear civil actions for most of the wrongs made criminal in the Enforcement Act of 1870. Those portions of the Law of Civil Remedies still in use correspond closely to surviving federal criminal law. Just as criminal Sections 241 and 242 apply respectively to private individuals and state officials, so Sections 1985 and 1983 (Title 42, *United*

40. Public Law 90–284, April 11, 1968; the section on federally protected activities is codified as 18 U.S.C. 245.
41. *New York Times*, April 29, 1966, p. 18.

States Code) apply to civil suits involving complaints of private interference (1985) and state action (1983).[42]

Section 1985 provides that if two or more persons conspire to interfere with public officers who are performing their duties, or if they obstruct justice, or deprive another of his rights and privileges, e.g., by intimidation enhanced through disguise, such offenders may be sued. This law is specific in its application to the right to vote. It allows damage suits against conspirators (such as Klansmen) who intimidate or threaten citizens engaged in peacefully supporting presidential electors or candidates for Congress. The statute has demonstrated its utility in post-Reconstruction years. Thus in *O'Sullivan* v. *Felix*, Justice McKenna concluded for a unanimous Supreme Court in 1914 that the injuries inflicted upon a Louisiana state senator who was assaulted by a group of hoodlums trying to prevent his voting in a federal election "are to be redressed by a civil suit."[43] Overlooking this case, commentators have frequently viewed with pessimism the utility of Section 1985. The common argument is that "an action under *any* of the civil rights statutes must allege acts done 'under color of state law.' " The *O'Sullivan* case notwithstanding, Section 1985 has generally enjoyed legal vitality where an element of state action is implicated with the activities of private individuals.[44]

Under the Law of Civil Remedies dealing in express terms with state action (Section 1983), Negroes and others whose voting rights suffer at the hands of public officials may sue for monetary damages and equitable relief, which of course includes court restraining orders or injunctions. No jury trial is specified, and the operation of the statute does not mandate a showing of "willfull intent," as criminal conspiracy prohibitions do.[45] An example of a case arising under Section 1983 is *Anderson* v. *Martin*, decided by the Supreme Court in

42. 42 U.S.C. 1985, 1983. Between 1866 and 1875, Congress enacted 11 civil rights statutes. Most of them are conveniently given in Appendix I of Robert K. Carr, *Federal Protection of Civil Rights* (Ithaca: Cornell University Press, 1947). Cf. Morroe Berger, *Equality by Statute* (rev. ed.; Garden City: Doubleday and Co., 1967), chaps. 1 and 2.

43. *O'Sullivan* v. *Felix*, 233 U.S. 318 (1914).

44. E.g., *Collins* v. *Hardyman*, 341 U.S. 651 (1951); cf. *United States* v. *Harris*, 106 U.S. 629 (1883).

45. The jury provision of the Civil Rights Act of 1875 survives and is relevant to voting. Prohibited is a planned pattern of racial discrimination in the selection of jury members, a potentially fortunate situation in criminal prosecutions in voting rights cases which normally require a jury verdict of guilty; 18 U.S.C. 243 (1964).

1964.[46] The Negro plaintiffs were primary election candidates for the East Baton Rouge School Board. They successfully sued the State Election Board for unconstitutionally identifying, according to state law, the race of the candidates on the official ballots. The Supreme Court was unanimous in voiding the offending Louisiana statute. Justice Clark's Opinion noted that the state law at issue set no restrictions on voting or running for office, but by using the state-printed ballot to identify the race of the candidate, the state was said to furnish a vehicle for racial prejudice. "By directing the citizens' attention to the single consideration of race or color, the State indicates that the candidate's race or color is an important—perhaps paramount consideration. . . ." In the light of sensitive public opinion on this matter, the statute was judged to have a repressive effect on state-conducted electoral processes in violation of the Equal Protection Clause of the Fourteenth Amendment.

Table 3–1 summarizes Supreme Court litigation involving the criminal and civil sections of the old Enforcement and Civil Rights Acts. Section 241, the Conspiracy Law, and Section 1983 have been frequently appealed to the Supreme Court where they have been shaped into partly effective instruments to fight private and public wrongs against citizens' and voters' rights. But comparison of the "Total Cases" and "Claims Upheld" columns in the table suggest that the overall record of success has not been impressive for those who sought the protection of the old statutes. The difficulties in criminal cases are compounded by the unlikelihood of securing a jury conviction. Thus between 1959 and 1964, the Justice Department relied on Sections 241 and 242 in a total of 119 prosecutions, but they convicted only 13 individuals.[47] The chief utility of Sections 1985 and 1983 is that they supply the legal bases for "causes of action"—the necessary authorizations to use federal courts to sue in privately instituted political and civil rights cases. In recent years, Section 1983 has also proved valuable to plaintiffs trying to gain entrance to the bench in order to challenge state legislative apportionment and districting schemes.

Problems involved in pursuing a suit fruitfully under the archaic statutes have stemmed from a variety of difficulties, chiefly involving legal confusion and money. It might fairly be inferred from the ex-

46. *Anderson* v. *Martin*, 375 U.S. 394 (1964). In *Pierson* v. *Ray* the Supreme Court held that judges were immune from suit under Section 1983; 386 U.S. 547 (1967).

47. U.S. Congress, Senate, Judiciary Committee, *Voting Rights Hearings*, (Part I), 89th Cong., 1st sess., 1965, pp. 105–109.

Table 3–1 Supreme Court Litigation under the Civil War Statutes 18 USC 241, 242 and 42 USC 1983, 1985 (to 1965)*

	STATES				TOTAL CASES 1870–1965	FED. INT.	AMICI	S.C. SPLIT VOTE	VOTING RIGHTS CASES	OTHER CIVIL RIGHTS	CLAIMED RIGHT UPHELD
	Ala. Ga. La. Miss.	Fla. N.C. S.C. Va.	Ark. Okla. Tex. Tenn.	Others							
Criminal 241 (private)	13	4	9	14	42	23	13	23	17	25	18
242 (official)	5	3	2	3	13	8	5	11	5	8	6
Civil 1985 (private)	1	0	2	4	7	3	5	7	3	5	3
1983 (official)	14	7	4	19	44	7	19	29	13	31	21

* In the table, the term "Fed. Int.," or federal interest, refers to cases argued before the Supreme Court by the Attorney General or a member of his staff. "Amici" denotes one or more *amicus curiae* briefs (particularly used after 1930) submitted by interested parties. The "Split Vote" column shows the number of cases that were not unanimously decided by the Supreme Court. A comparison of this column with the "Total Cases" column yields an index of Court consensus. "Other Civil Rights" refers to cases that turn on the alleged deprivation of rights such as free speech, press, assembly, petition, due process, public accommodations, etc. The last column indicates the number of cases in which the Supreme Court may be interpreted to have acted favorably toward the civil liberty or civil right claimed to have been deprived. On the left, the term "private" refers to statutes aimed at the actions of any person including private individuals. The term "official" makes reference to statutes in which an allegation of official action, or acts under "color of law," is required.

istence of this vintage set of laws that the remedies they promise presuppose clearly defined rights. But confusion has been recurrent in state and lower federal courts about whether the right to vote in federal elections and the right to be free of racial discrimination in any election are in fact rights guaranteed by the United States Constitution. The table shows that unanimous Supreme Court decisions interpreting these statutes have been rare. Another problem in relying on the old statutory remedies is that their usage generally requires expensive legal guidance. Not until *Baker* v. *Carr*, with its progeny of state legislative apportionment and congressional districting litigation, have white, middle-class voters felt a need to resort to civil suits to secure their political rights. As the table suggests, most of the civil and criminal suits were related to racial disputes originating in the South. Rare has been the southern Negro who, being refused the vote, could afford the legal fees necessary to secure his claimed right. Indispensible for such plaintiffs have been financial and legal-staff aid and the *amici* briefs (reported in the table) put at their disposal by various groups. These include the NAACP, the separate NAACP Legal Defense and Educational Fund, the American Civil Liberties Union, the Lawyers Constitutional Defense Committee, and others (discussed in Chapter 1).

The federal government has occasionally provided assistance. Recorded in the table is the frequency with which the Justice Department has entered political and civil rights cases to demonstrate a federal interest and to present the Supreme Court with the Administration point of view. Participation by the Attorney General and Solicitor General in such suits has helped to make Justice Department officials aware of the need for revising both civil and criminal remedies. Short of that, however, federal government lawyers have found the early civil rights statutes useful to challenge discriminatory practices in the states. For this purpose, the nineteenth-century laws come to life when combined with other provisions of the *United States Code* which authorize a petition for judicial restraint orders against the enforcement of unconstitutional laws or policies.[48] So used, these vestigial safeguards pointed the way toward fashioning the remedies developed in the 1957 Civil Rights Act and in subsequent voting and civil rights statutes of the 1960s. (See Chapters 5 and 6.)

---

48. E.g., jurisdiction in *Anderson* v. *Martin* was invoked under 28 U.S.C. 1331, 1343(3) and 42 U.S.C. 1971(a), 1983.

4 State restrictions on black voting

Following the Civil War, the South was forced to accept the North's definition of federalism in terms of democracy. Events after the enactment of the Fourteenth and Fifteenth Amendments nevertheless suggest that the effort to universalize suffrage elicited a legal counter-revolution to make the vote meaningless. The gradual displacement of southern Negro political influence after Reconstruction was first effected by economic and political methods, including violence.[1] Later, legal devices and devious electoral procedures were developed to ensure by state law that blacks would be frozen out of the political process.

Legal methods designed to disfranchise the Negro were legion. A long list of misdemeanors, punishable by loss of franchise, took some suffrage toll among both blacks and whites in Mississippi and elsewhere during the period of southern constitution-making (1890–

1. V. O. Key, Jr., *Southern Politics in State and Nation* (New York: Vintage Books, 1949); cf. C. Vann Woodward, *Origins of the New South, 1877–1913* (Baton Rouge: Louisiana State University Press, 1951).

1910).[2] Lengthy residence requirements in southern states, as elsewhere, have continued to result in some voter disqualification.[3] This chapter, however, is primarily concerned with the four historically most-litigated state restrictions on black voting. First, several states established the "white primary"—particularly effective in one-party states—as a practical method of electing representatives and public officials. Second, state literacy, character, and performance qualifications have often been required as prerequisites to casting a ballot. While literacy tests ostensibly applied to all voters, they have been made inapplicable to illiterate Caucasians by such expedients as discriminatory administration, the "grandfather clause," and the exemption of all those who have paid property taxes. Third, a poll tax was imposed by some states. The difficulty created by assessing a tax on those who wished to vote was frequently compounded by the requirement that all prior levies must have been paid before one could vote. To these three common methods may be added the tactic of state-imposed geographical rearrangements, or racially discriminatory gerrymandering, designed in some instances to exclude Negroes from the process of self-government. The reception which each of these four categories of political rights restrictions has met in the Supreme Court is the subject of the discussion in the four subsections below.

THE WHITE PRIMARY

When the United States Supreme Court was first called upon to deal with the exclusion of blacks from participation in a primary election, its members displayed vacillation and indecision. The earliest relevant case did not actually involve Negro voting, but it did supply the Court's initial answer to the question of whether the federal government possessed any regulatory authority over primary elections. In *Newberry* v. *United States*,[4] Mr. Justice McReynolds spoke for four members of the Court when he accepted the arguments at bar presented by Charles Evans Hughes that the congressional power to regulate the manner of holding elections did not encompass primary elections. For McReynolds, it followed that the provisions of the Corrupt Practices Act of 1910 did not apply to the $100,000 senatorial

2. *Ratliff* v. *Beale*, 20 So. 865 (1896).
3. W. Ross Yates, "The Functions of Residence Requirements for Voting," 15 *Western Political Quarterly* 425 (Sept. 1962).
4. *Newberry* v. *United States*, 256 U.S. 232 (1921).

campaign of Truman Newberry in Michigan and were in fact unconstitutional if applied to primaries. The reasoning of the Court Opinion (that federal regulations applied only to the "final choice" of senatorial candidates) was shrouded in doubt by Chief Justice White and others, whose concurring Opinion attacked McReynold's basic assumption. White explained that he would not have joined the majority had the Corrupt Practices Act been passed *after* the adoption of the Seventeenth Amendment, which provided for the direct election of senators. That the nominating primary is beyond the power of Congress to control was, in White's view, "suicidal" and erroneous.

The Texas legislature, presuming to benefit by the doubt, passed a law in 1923 which bluntly stated that "in no event shall a Negro be eligible to participate in a Democratic party primary election held in the State of Texas." This state action was challenged on Fourteenth and Fifteenth Amendment grounds in a suit for damages against Herndon, a Texas election official. In *Nixon* v. *Herndon*, the Supreme Court, speaking through Justice Holmes, found it unnecessary even to consider the Fifteenth Amendment contention in 1927.[5] It was enough that Holmes could hardly imagine "a more direct and obvious infringement" of the Equal Protection Clause of the Fourteenth Amendment.

To evade this decision, the Texas legislature promptly repealed the invalidated statute and authorized the state Executive Committee of the Democratic Party to establish their own qualifications for members permitted to vote and otherwise participate. Barred by his color from taking part in the Democratic primary (in Texas the final election was a mere formal flourish), the same Dr. Nixon again brought a "Section 1983" suit against election officials for damages. Lawyers for the election judges argued that the equality required by the Fourteenth Amendment, potent in *Nixon* v. *Herndon*, was unavailing in this case,[6] because private individuals, not the state, had done the discriminating. The latter distinction was, in their minds, sufficiently sharp to put the action of the party Executive Committee on a par with the operations of the membership committee of "a golf club or . . . a Masonic Lodge." Justice Cardozo wrote the Court Opinion in the *Second Nixon Case*. Joined by four of his associates on the bench, Cardozo said that the committee had acted under the authority of the state legislature; it had acted not only as a representative of the Democratic Party but as a delegate of the state. The committee's dis-

5. *Nixon* v. *Herndon*, 273 U.S. 536 (1927).
6. *Nixon* v. *Condon*, 286 U.S. 73 (1932).

criminatory policy consequently amounted to a denial of the equal protection of the laws of the state and was void under the Fourteenth Amendment.

Grovey v. *Townsend*[7] in 1935 presented an issue to the Supreme Court that was but slightly different. Grovey, a Negro, was refused a primary election absentee ballot on the authority of a resolution enacted by a Democratic Party convention. This informal party motion (involving no clear-cut state authorization) excluded Negro voting in the primary. Confronting this scheme, the Supreme Court retreated from the direction of the *Nixon* cases. The nine justices scrutinized the legal nature of political parties in Texas and noted a Texas court ruling that political parties "are voluntary associations for political action, and are not the creatures of the state."[8] It was for a unanimous tribunal that Justice Roberts announced that the rules governing party membership as laid down by the political convention were significantly different from the "whites only" policy of the Executive Committee ruled upon in *Nixon* v. *Condon*. What was involved in this new test, Roberts insisted, was a private association and not an official organ of the state. He advanced the theory that to deny a vote in a primary was a mere refusal of party membership with which "the state need have no concern." Observing that no statute authorized the party's action (therefore the Fourteenth Amendment was held not to apply) and reasoning that primaries were comparable to the elections in private clubs (therefore the Fifteenth Amendment was inapplicable), the Supreme Court sustained the party ban against Negro voters.

In 1941, in *United States* v. *Classic*, the same bench upheld the operation of the Conspiracy Law and other regulations for pre-federal election primaries.[9] No racial discrimination was involved in the *Classic* case, but its facts served to instruct the Court on the significance of primaries in the one-party South. The case concerned the federal prosecution of several New Orleans primary election officials for fraud. The Supreme Court provided two tests to determine whether such officers could be held accountable for the proper ballot count in primary elections. Such a contest for federal office is subject to federal control when it is an "integral part" of the election machinery by law and when it "effectively controls the choice" of the federal election.

7. *Grovey* v. *Townsend*, 295 U.S. 73 (1932).
8. *Bell* v. *Hill*, 74 S.W.2d 113 (1934).
9. *United States* v. *Classic*, 313 U.S. 299 (1941).

Three years later in the landmark case of *Smith* v. *Allwright*,[10] the Supreme Court resolved the inconsistency between the *Grovey* and *Classic* cases and overturned the legal doctrines upon which southern states had relied for continued use of the white primary. Lonnie Smith, a Negro, sued a Texas election official for $5,000 for refusing to give him a ballot in a primary election for nomination of House and Senate Democratic candidates. At the Supreme Court level, Smith's claim was supported by legal staff assistance and *amici curiae* briefs of the National Association for the Advancement of Colored People, the American Civil Liberties Union, the Committee on Constitutional Liberties, the National Lawyers Guild, and the Workers' Defense League. In reviewing the case, Justice Reed argued for the Court that the Texas primary was by law an integral part of the machinery for choosing officials. Consequently, it came under federal regulation according to the first test provided in the *Classic* case. State law authorized the procedure by which the party certified its nominees for inclusion in the general election ballot. "The party takes its character as a state agency from the duties imposed upon it by state statutes," the Court said. Texas law directed the selection of all party officers in a variety of ways including a network of financial regulations. To Reed, party electoral duties do not become matters of private law simply because they are performed by the party. Announcing that the electoral process is essentially a "state function," the Opinion of the Court concluded:

The United States is a constitutional democracy. Its organic law grants to all citizens a right to participate in the choice of elected officials without restriction by any State because of race. This grant to the people of the opportunity for choice is not to be nullified by a State through casting its electoral process in a form which permits a private organization to practice racial discrimination in the election. Constitutional rights would be of little value if they could thus indirectly be denied.

The conclusion was inescapable that racial discrimination by the party was endorsed and enforced by the state. In taking the stand that the action violated the Fifteenth Amendment, the Court felt obliged to avoid ambiguity in its holding and therefore forthrightly overruled *Grovey* v. *Townsend* over the bitter dissent of its author, Justice Roberts.

As a partial measure of the importance of *Smith* v. *Allwright*, it

10. *Smith* v. *Allwright*, 321 U.S. 649 (1944).

should be noted that between 1940 and 1947 Negro registration throughout the South quadrupled to nearly 600,000.[11] In Texas the Democratic legislature made no effort to circumvent the decision because by 1945 the state party liberal and conservative factions had come so to distrust each other that neither was willing to risk removing all legal control over the conduct of primaries and vesting control solely in the party.[12] That experiment was left to South Carolina.

Hoping that the second test announced in *Classic* (equating the elections that control the choice of federal officers with federal elections) was mere *dictum*, the South Carolina legislature in 1944 repealed all state laws regarding political primaries, including the statutory prohibition against fraud. The warrant of permission, which was virtually granted by the state to local Democrats, allowed the party to masquerade its racial discrimination as the act of a private club. This tactic was exposed in *Elmore* v. *Rice*.[13] Private clubs, Judge Waring asserted, relying on the "state function" theory of *Smith* v. *Allwright*, "do not vote and elect a President of the United States, and the Senators and members of the House of Representatives . . . ; and under the law of our land, all citizens are entitled to a voice in such elections." The judge also quoted from an address by President Truman in 1947 which suggested a change in public policy: "There is much that state and local governments can do in providing positive safeguards for civil rights. But we cannot, any longer, await the growth of a will to action in the slowest state or the most backward community." The President concluded, "Our national Government must show the way." Against this background, Judge Waring suggested: "It is time South Carolina rejoined the Union." The South Carolina case, under the title of *Rice* v. *Elmore*, went no higher than the federal Court of Appeals.[14] There Judge Parker was uncompromising in declaring that "no election machinery can be upheld if its purpose or effect is to deny to the Negro on account of race or color any effective voice in the government of his country or the state or community wherein he lives."

South Carolina parried by permitting qualified Negroes to vote in the Democratic primary if they first took an oath to support racial

11. D. S. Strong, "Rise of Negro Voting in Texas," 42 *American Political Science Review* 510 (June 1948).

12. W. E. Benton, *Suffrage and Elections* (Dallas: The Arnold Foundation, 1960), p. 13.

13. *Elmore* v. *Rice*, 72 F. Supp. 516 (1947); 333 U.S. 875 (1948) *cert. denied*.

14. *Rice* v. *Elmore*, 165 F.2d 387 (1948).

segregation. Furthermore, Negroes were still barred from membership in the party. For the Appeals Court in *Baskin* v. *Brown*,[15] Judge Parker sustained the injunction which had been issued to restrain the enforcement of these rules. He did this on the authority of the principle announced in *Rice* v. *Elmore;* he also subscribed to the sentiment of the lower court that the oath was invalid because it disregarded the rights of American citizens to exercise their own views and opinions in the choice of representatives in their national government. At the lower court level, the judge was led to exclaim: "To carry this to its logical conclusion, it is wondered why the State Convention did not require an oath that all parties enrolling or voting should elect them in perpetuity and with satisfactory emoluments."

Finally, a stratagem similar to the private clubs of South Carolina was put to use in Texas but without any explicit state authorization. The Jaybird Association proclaimed itself a private club and submitted political candidates (as it had since 1899) to a nominating contest in a white primary in Fort Bend County. The victorious local candidates were then named by the local Democratic Party as its candidates in the final election. The technique of relying on a racially exclusive private caucus for selecting candidates was held violative of the Fifteenth Amendment in *Terry* v. *Adams*.[16] Justice Black announced the decision of the Court and in his Opinion emphasized the similarity of the facts of the case to those in *Rice* v. *Elmore*. His reasoning stressed again that no election machinery could be sustained which had as its purpose denying, in violation of the Fifteenth Amendment, the right to vote to Negroes. By 1960, the illegal status of the white primary election had become so well defined that, after a brief skirmish in a federal district court, schemes for a white primary in Fayette County, Tennessee, were abandoned.[17]

STATE LITERACY TESTS

When the constitutionality of state literacy tests came before the United States Supreme Court, it did not equivocate or change course

15. *Baskin* v. *Brown*, 417 F.2d 391 (1949).

16. *Terry* v. *Adams*, 345 U.S. 461 (1953).

17. *United States* v. *Fayette County Democratic Executive Committee*, W. D. Tenn. No. 3835 (1960); appeal unreported after settlement by negotiation. See Burke Marshall, *Federalism and Civil Rights* (New York: Columbia University Press, 1964), p. 27.

as it had in the white primary cases. Since *Williams* v. *Mississippi*,[18] decided in 1898, the validity of literacy tests has been upheld whenever established by a state law and administered without prejudice. At the turn of the century, Mississippi statutes required qualified voters to be able either to read any portion of the United States Constitution or to give a "reasonable interpretation" of any constitutional provision to the registrar. Qualified voters made up the group from which jurors were selected, and it was an all white jury which indicted Williams, a Mississippi Negro, for murder.

The literacy test, Williams' attorneys argued on appeal, was discriminatory and violated the equal protection of the laws guaranteed by the Fourteenth Amendment. To this indirect challenge of suffrage rights, Justice McKenna found for the Supreme Court that neither in the state constitution nor in its statutes was there evidence that equal protection of the laws in regard to voting had been denied. Significantly he added, "Nor is there any sufficient allegation of an evil and discriminatory administration of them." This statement suggests that, had the case been more skillfully presented by Williams' lawyers, the result might have been different. His counsel did point out that the Mississippi constitutional convention was composed of 134 members, of whom only one was a Negro, and that the "disfranchising constitution" was not submitted for voter approval. These were lamentable facts, but for McKenna's Court they were not presented in the form of "direct and definite" allegations tractable to judicial remedy. Williams' lawyers did not take the pains to split a significant hair by showing, as Justice McKenna noted, that "the actual administration [of state voting and jury laws] was not evil, only that evil was possible under them."

The Alabama "disfranchising constitution" was also subjected to a broadside attack before the Supreme Court, and once again there was a judicial hint that the case was poorly presented, asking as it did for relief characterized by the Supreme Court as "impossible to give" and close to "maintain[ing] a bill for a mere declaration in the air." In 1903, an Alabama Negro charged that the mandatory literacy test and other requirements of his state's newly enacted constitution formed a conspiracy to disfranchise Negroes as a group. Justice Holmes refused, on technical grounds, to accept federal court jurisdiction in *Giles* v. *Harris*[19] and maintained that a violation of the

18. *Williams* v. *Mississippi*, 170 U.S. 213 (1898).
19. *Giles* v. *Harris*, 189 U.S. 475 (1903).

Fourteenth and Fifteenth Amendments had not been demonstrated. Against the separate dissents of Justices Brewer and Harlan, Holmes said that the Court was powerless to compel election officers to place Giles' name on the voting lists. There was a note of irony in Holmes' advice that Giles look to the people of his state or to Congress for relief.

The Supreme Court next considered state literacy tests when it reviewed the notorious Oklahoma "grandfather clause" in 1915. The Attorney General of the United States argued in *Guinn* v. *United States*[20] that the state constitutional provision violated the Fifteenth Amendment because it imposed a literacy examination for voting but at the same time exempted from the test persons whose ancestors had been entitled to vote in 1866. On the other hand, Oklahoma argued on the authority of *United States* v. *Reese* that the Fifteenth Amendment did not confer the right of suffrage on Negroes but merely prohibited denial of suffrage on racial grounds. All of his colleagues supported Justice White in holding that the clause, in effect, perpetuated "the very conditions which the Amendment was intended to destroy." The defiant Oklahoma legislature's immediate response was to enact a statute making registration a prerequisite to voting. The regulation permitted only a twelve-day registration period but exempted from the registration law those who had voted before the decision in the *Guinn* case. The result of this frivolous attempt to disfranchise blacks perpetually, said the Supreme Court in *Lane* v. *Wilson*,[21] was that those persons and their lineal descendants qualified to vote in 1914 by virtue of the unconstitutional "grandfather clause" were indeed entitled to vote. Yet Negroes kept from registering and voting by the clause would never attain balloting rights unless they applied between April 30th and May 12th. Justice Frankfurter found the statute in violation of the Fifteenth Amendment, a safeguard, he said sharply, "which nullified sophisticated as well as simple-minded modes of discrimination."

The State of Alabama sought to frustrate the preceding series of Supreme Court decisions by the continued discriminatory use of the so-called "Boswell Amendment." The formula of this amendment permitted registration only by persons who could "understand and explain" any article of the United States Constitution. This vague standard obviously allowed registrars to accept or reject whomever

20. *Guinn* v. *United States*, 238 U.S. 347 (1915).
21. *Lane* v. *Wilson*, 307 U.S. 263 (1939).

they wished. In *Davis* v. *Schnell*[22] a Federal District Court invalidated the law, noting that, as enforced in one county where 36 percent of the population was black, 2,800 whites were registered and only 104 Negroes. The Court was convinced that the Alabama law had been shown to be an arbitrary grant of power to election officials who, evidence demonstrated, administered the literacy test in terms of race and thus in a manner violative of the Fifteenth Amendment. "The fact that the Boswell Amendment made no mention of race or color does not save it from being unconstitutional," the District Court concluded.

In more recent years, the Supreme Court has reiterated its traditional determination that literacy tests, fairly authorized and fairly administered, need not be unconstitutional. In 1952, North Carolina required by statute that prospective voters must be able to read and write any section of the state constitution in order to qualify for the franchise. An exception was made for those freed under a pre-existing "grandfather clause." In 1957 that exception and the provision that the literacy test must be passed "to the satisfaction of the registrar" were eliminated from North Carolina statutes but not from the state constitution. In order to test the validity of the state organic law and statutes, three Negro women, who were otherwise qualified to vote, refused to take the literacy test on the ground that the provision was discriminatory. The state Supreme Court conceded that the inoperative "grandfather clause" might be unconstitutional, but the statute which provided for a demonstration of literacy disregarded the clause. Since the reading and writing test applied alike to all persons who wished to register to vote, and since no racial discrimination was charged, the statute did not offend the federal Constitution. In *Lassiter* v. *Northampton County Board of Elections*,[23] Justice Douglas sustained the state court holding and ruled that the literacy test before the tribunal was not, on its face, in violation of the Fourteenth, Fifteenth, or Seventeenth Amendments. Douglas concluded that such a test could be required by a state to ensure an independent and intelligent electorate. Whether or not the state should do so, he concluded, was a policy question, the wisdom of which the Court was powerless to judge by constitutional standards.

The doctrinal significance of the literacy test cases is that together

22. *Davis* v. *Schnell*, 81 F. Supp. 872 (S.D. Ala. 1949), *aff'd.*, 336 U.S. 933 (1949).
23. *Lassiter* v. *Northampton County Board of Elections*, 360 U.S. 45 (1959).

they reaffirm that the Fourteenth Amendment stands as no barrier to a state policy calling for a literate electorate. A showing of racially unfair administration of such electoral provisions, however, brings the prohibitions of the Fourteenth and Fifteenth Amendments into operation. Doing the homework (on discriminatory administration) which lawyers from *Williams* to *Lassiter* had failed to do, the Southern Regional Council in 1957 and the Civil Rights Commission in 1961 reported that the legal weapon most widely and most successfully used to discourage Negro registration was the literacy or interpretation test.[24] In the *Lassiter* case, for example, no attempt was made to demonstrate racially unfair administrative practices. However, in its 1961 report on voting, the Civil Rights Commission concluded that the North Carolina law upheld in *Lassiter* was frequently used to bar blacks but to admit whites to the vote.[25] The Commission called upon Congress to provide a remedy. In so doing it virtually recognized that supplying the vote to Negroes disenfranchised by literacy requirements had progressed about as far as it could in the courts. More dramatic and adequate remedies would have to come from Congress. (See Chapters 5 and 6.)

THE POLL TAX

All of the state constitutions of 1787 required that a voter be a taxpayer. At the time, however, only New Hampshire required a poll tax payment. During its first wave of post-Revolutionary popularity in the United States, the poll tax requirement for voting was actually an inducement to expanded suffrage because it frequently replaced land-holding, property, or other more burdensome taxing requirements. Thus the prerequisite was heralded as a democratic advance. Since Reconstruction days, however, there has been ample reason to believe that the poll tax remained as a weapon for white supremacy. For example, the Virginia Constitutional Convention of 1902 established the tax, according to one spokesman for the state, "to discriminate to the very extremity of permissible action under the limitations

24. Margaret Price, *The Negro Voter in the South* (Atlanta: Southern Regional Council, 1957), p. 7; Margaret Price, *The Negro and the Ballot in the South* (Atlanta: Southern Regional Council, 1960), p. 21; United States Commission on Civil Rights, *Voting* (Washington, D.C.: Government Printing Office, 1961), p. 137.

25. Commission on Civil Rights, *Voting*, pp. 33-34.

of the Federal Constitution, with a view to the elimination of every Negro voter who can be gotten rid of, legally, without materially impairing the numerical strength of the white electorate."[26]

Not until 1936 was any federal effort made to eliminate the poll tax. The prospects for a federal remedy by legislation were overshadowed in 1937 by the Supreme Court's ruling in *Breedlove* v. *Suttles*.[27] Justice Butler argued that the assessment, even though linked to voting, was a ligitimate revenue measure. The case arose from the challenge of a Georgia citizen who was excluded from voting in a federal and state election for failing to pay the tax. The nation's highest Court ruled that the Georgia tax requirement (which exempted women) did not violate the Nineteenth Amendment by abridging the right of male citizens to vote on account of their sex. More important, the tax was judged to be no violation of the requirement for equal protection of the laws. Nor did Justice Butler consider the tax to be, on its face, a racially discriminatory measure.[28] His conclusion was based on the observation that the requirement applied equally to Negro and white voters. Butler dismissed the objection to the assessment as a tax on a federally guaranteed right on two dubious grounds. First, he said that "the privilege of voting is not derived from the United States." This assertion is, of course, erroneous as applied to federal elections. Second, Butler argued that the poll tax constitutes an independent revenue measure and that payment as a voting condition was merely an effective method of collection.

The *Breedlove* case grew out of the complex fabric of Georgia electoral law and involved the exercise of the vote in both federal and state elections. Opponents of the poll tax in some quarters harbored the hope that a simpler case, a more carefully chosen one, might yield a different result. In an appearance in 1941 before a Senate subcommittee on behalf of an anti-poll tax bill which he introduced, Senator Claude Pepper of Florida pointed to a case recently decided in a federal appeals court as "an ideal test of the constitutional ques-

26. Statement of E. Carter Glass II, *Virginia Constitutional Convention, Proceedings and Debates*, 307607 (1901–2).

27. *Breedlove* v. *Suttles*, 302 U.S. 27 (1937).

28. See also *Butler* v. *Thompson*, 97 F. Supp. 17 (E.D. Va., 1951), *aff'd* 341 U.S. 937 (1951) (Mr. Justice Douglas dissenting). The plaintiff, a Virginia Negro who refused to pay her poll tax, sued the registrar for refusing to add her name to the voting list. A three-judge federal court concluded that the evidence submitted did not support the contention that the tax was administered in a way to handicap Negroes.

tion, since the election was restricted to that of a congressional Representative."[29] The patron of the bill criticized the decision of a federal court of appeals in *Pirtle* v. *Brown*[30] upholding the constitutionality of the poll tax. Senator Pepper stated that a *writ of certiorari* from the Supreme Court would be sought and predicted that it would be granted and the decision reversed. The writ, however, was denied, and the holding of the federal court was allowed to stand: the exaction of a poll tax by a state is not a violation of the Privileges and Immunities Clause of the Fourteenth Amendment.

Senator Pepper's hope for judicial invalidation of the poll tax was disappointed, and his efforts to rally congressional support for electoral reform were likewise frustrated. The Senate Judiciary Subcommittee before which he testified did, however, issue an important report concluding that the poll tax laws in southern states were "motivated entirely and exclusively by a desire to exclude the Negro from voting."[31]

The turning point in poll tax reform came on August 27, 1962, when the House approved a constitutional amendment, already accepted by the Senate, barring the requirement of the tax in federal elections and primaries. The constitutional amendment route to reform was taken rather than resort to federal legislation for several reasons. Representative Emanuel Celler, Chairman of the House Committee on the Judiciary, indicated that the reasons were political and constitutional. First, southern congressmen indicated that they would be especially offended by the implication (of statutory enforcement of the Fifteenth Amendment) that poll taxes applied unequally to the races. In political terms, the constitutional amendment route was the only one which would not incur a filibuster. Second, *Breedlove* v. *Suttles* stood for the proposition that the tax by itself did not offend the Fourteenth or Fifteenth Amendments. Further, the Civil Rights Commission agreed in 1961 that, on the whole, the poll tax was no longer a major deterrent to Negro voting, other impediments having taken its place.[32] Without undisputed proof linking the tax to racial discrimination in voting (prohibited by the Fourteenth and Fifteenth Amendments), and with insufficient evidence that the poll tax threat-

29. Quoted in U.S. Congress, Senate, *Hearings before the Senate Judiciary Subcommittee on S.J. 25*, 83d Cong., 2d sess., 1954, p. 45.
30. *Pirtle* v. *Brown*, 118 F.2d 218 (6th Cir.); 314 U.S. 621 (1941) *cert. denied.*
31. Senate Judiciary Committee, *S. Rep. No. 1662*, 77th Cong., 2d sess., 1942, p. 7.
32. Commission on Civil Rights, *Voting*, pp. 152–54.

ened the integrity of all federal elections[33] (over which Congress has authority according to the *Yarbrough* and *Classic* cases), ending the poll tax for federal elections could only rest upon the authority of the Times, Places, and Manner Clause. But Article I, Section 4, only relates to congressional elections. Chairman Celler concluded for his committee that, since the proposal included elections involving the choice of presidential and vice-presidential electors and since the Constitution does not require that the presidential electors be chosen by popular election, "the approach must be by constitutional amendment."[34] Since Congress was thought not to have power under Article II to regulate either voting qualifications for, or the manner of electing, presidential electors, including such regulation in the poll tax measure seemed to require the invulnerable sanction of a constitutional amendment. Adopted on January 23, 1964, the Twenty-fourth Amendment reads:

Section 1. The right of citizens of the United States to vote in any primary or other election for President or Vice President, for electors for President or Vice President, or for Senator or Representative in Congress shall not be denied or abridged by the United States or any State by reason of failure to pay any poll tax or other tax.

A rough indication of the impact of the Poll Tax Amendment is suggested in Table 4–1. The states listed on the left enforced their poll tax requirements in the 1960 presidential election. At the same time, the five poll tax states were among the seven states in the country with the lowest voter participation. The Twenty-fourth Amendment went into effect in time for the 1964 presidential election. At that time, the listed states were among the ten (nationwide) with the highest percentage gains of actual voters, as shown on the right of the table.

The first opportunity for the Supreme Court to consider a case arising under the Twenty-fourth Amendment was in *Harman* v. *Forssenius*, decided in 1965.[35] Months before the Poll Tax Amendment was ratified, Governor Albertis Harrison summoned the Vir-

33. Cf. Frederic D. Ogden, *The Poll Tax in the South* (Tuscaloosa: University of Alabama Press, 1958), pp. 77–110.

34. 108 U.S., *Cong. Rec.* 16604, 87th Cong., 2d sess., (Aug. 27, 1962). See U.S. Congress, House, *Report of the House Judiciary Subcommittee No. 5 on S. J. Res. 29*, 87th Cong., 2d sess. 1962.

35. *Harman* v. *Forssenius*, 380 U.S. 528 (1965).

Table 4-1   *Voting in Poll Tax States before and
after Adoption of the 24th Amendment**

STATE	POTENTIAL VOTE, 1964	ACTUAL PRESIDENTIAL VOTE	PERCENTAGES 1964	1960	NATION-WIDE RANKING OF VOTER GAINS
Alabama	1,915,000	689,817	36.0	30.6	7th highest
Arkansas	1,124,000	560,426	49.9	40.9	2d highest
Mississippi	1,243,000	409,146	32.9	25.3	6th highest
Texas	5,922,000	2,626,811	44.4	41.4	10th highest
Virginia	2,541,000	1,042,267	41.0	33.0	3d highest

* The potential vote is given in Census Bureau estimates of September 8,
1964, as reported in Research Division of the Republican National Committee,
The 1964 Election (Washington, D.C., 1965), pp. 62–63. The rank of change
refers to the percentage rank of actual voting increase between 1960 and 1964
among all 50 states.

ginia legislature in anticipation of the new federal ban. Accepting the
governor's recommendations, Virginia abolished its poll tax as an absolute requirement for voting in federal elections. In the name of
keeping the state electorate "smaller but smarter," the legislature sub-
stituted for its poll tax a provision whereby the federal voter could
qualify either by paying the customary levy or by filing a certificate
of residence in each election year. Such re-registration was to be
accomplished six months before the polling date. Those paying the
voting tax were not asked for such evidence of residence, while those
who opted for a free vote were required to provide a notarized or
witnessed certificate of residence. No statutory changes were made
with regard to the $1.50 annual poll tax prescribed for voting in state
elections. A suit attacking the legislation before a three-judge federal
court succeeded in securing the holding that the statute violated the
popular voting requirements of Article I, Section 2, concerning representatives, and the Seventeenth Amendment, concerning direct election of senators.

Virginia officials appealed to the United States Supreme Court,
where Chief Justice Warren reviewed the law solely on the basis of
the Twenty-fourth Amendment. On appeal, the Chief Justice noted
that the federal district court accepted jurisdiction before the state
courts were afforded the opportunity to construe the new statutes.
Given the importance and immediacy of the problem, the Supreme
Court concluded that the procedure of the district court was unim-
peachable. Time considerations justified the federal court's prompt
hearing: the district panel accepted the case two months before the

registration deadline and eight months before the general election of
1964. The Chief Justice insisted that the question before the Court
was not whether Virginia might abolish the poll tax and require state
or federal voters to file annually a certificate of residence. Rather the
bench's problem was whether the state could constitutionally con-
front the federal voter with the requirement that he either pay the
tax or re-register annually. The Chief Justice, expressing the view
of eight members of the Court, noted that the re-registration rule
for nontaxpayers plainly involved a cumbersome procedure. Virginia
lawyers tactically blundered in sharply contrasting the registration
alternative to the "simple" poll tax system. The Court felt constrained
to hold that the requirement (imposed upon the voter who refused
to pay the poll tax) constituted an abridgement of his right to vote.
The Chief Justice announced that "any material requirement imposed
on the federal voter solely because of his refusal to waive the constitutional immunity [to be free of voting taxes] subverts the effectiveness
of the Twenty-fourth Amendment and must fall under its ban." Para-
phrasing *Lane* v. *Wilson*, in which the bench had earlier referred
to the Fifteenth Amendment, the Forssenius Court explained: "The
Twenty-fourth Amendment 'nullifies sophisticated as well as simple-
minded modes' of impairing the rights guaranteed."

In 1966, the Supreme Court dealt the poll tax a final *coup de grâce*
by voiding it in state and local elections. *Harper* v. *Virginia State
Board of Elections* was the vehicle.[36] The litigation was privately initiated by several commonwealth residents with the help of the American Civil Liberties Union and the support of an *amicus* brief from
the Justice Department. Justice Douglas, who wrote the Opinion of
the Court, used sweeping language not only to void the Virginia tax
but also more broadly to say by way of clarification that, in granting
the franchise to the electorate, the states must draw *no* lines which
are inconsistent with the Equal Protection Clause of the Fourteenth
Amendment. Douglas wrote: "To introduce wealth or payment of
a fee as a measure of a voter's qualifications is to introduce a capricious or irrelevant factor." The degree of the discrimination is not

---

36. *Harper* v. *Virginia State Board of Elections*, 383 U.S. 663 (1966). By the
time the case was decided by the Supreme Court, federal district courts in separate actions under Section 10 of the Voting Rights Act of 1965, had already
invalidated the Texas and Alabama state poll taxes. *United States* v. *Alabama*, 252
F. Supp. 95 (1966); *United States* v. *Texas*, 252 F. Supp. 234 (1966); *United
States* v. *Mississippi*, 11 *Race Relations Law Reporter* 837 (M.D. Miss., 1966);
United States v. *Virginia*, 11 *Race Relations Law Reporter* 853 (E.D. Va., 1966).

determinative. Douglas said: "In this context—that is, as a condition of obtaining a ballot—the requirement of fee paying causes an 'invidious' discrimination. . . . *Breedlove* v. *Suttles* sanctioned use [of the poll tax] as a 'prerequisite to voting.' To that extent the *Breedlove* case is overruled." Since 1937, that decision had been paramount in other suits challenging poll tax requirements. But Douglas asserted that "notions of what constitutes equal treatment for purposes of the Equal Protection Clause *do* change." The Court's view of the right to vote was that it was "too precious, too fundamental" to be burdened by the condition of fee-paying.

Two dissenting opinions were written in the Virginia state poll tax case. Justice Black objected to the ruling on the jurisprudential ground that it objectionably smacked of "natural law formulas designed to write into the Constitution the notions of what a majority of the Court think is good governmental policy" and insufficiently took into account the intent of the framers of the Constitution. Justice Stewart agreed with Justice Harlan's dissenting opinion, the thrust of which was that Douglas' explanation for voiding the poll tax was "wholly inadequate" to explain why the payment of a poll tax was an "irrational or invidious" and therefore forbidden distinction made in state law between those who could vote and those who could not. The Equal Protection Clause, the dissenters admonished their brothers on the bench, does not "impose upon America an ideology or unrestrained egalitarianism."

RACIALLY DISCRIMINATORY GERRYMANDERING

As white primaries, unfair literacy tests, and poll taxes lapse into past chapters of history, the racial gerrymander has come into prominence in both northern and southern states. Alabama set the pattern in 1957, when state constitutional provisions were enacted allowing the legislature to abolish entire counties with the intent, according to state Senator Englehart, Executive Secretary of the Alabama White Citizens' Council, of dispersing Negro votes into adjoining counties.

Pursuant to the Englehart Amendment, Alabama passed a law redefining the boundaries of the city of Tuskegee in a jigsaw puzzle pattern which effectively excluded blacks and included whites in the city. Several Negro residents affected by the remapping operation asked the federal district court for a judgment recognizing the statute as unconstitutional. They also sought a court order to restrain officers from enforcing the state act which had changed the shape of Tuskegee from a square to a tortured twenty-eight sided figure. Allegedly this grotesque design excluded from the city all but four or five of the four hundred qualified Negro voters, while not removing a single white resident. Professor Gomillion of Tuskegee Institute and others affected charged that they were denied the due process and equal protection of the laws. In addition, they complained that they were deprived of the right to vote in municipal elections on account of race and therefore in violation of the Fifteenth Amendment.

The legal contest arising out of this situation was heard by the United States Supreme Court under the title of *Gomillion* v. *Lightfoot*.[37] There it was held that the power of the states to control the boundaries of its political subdivisions is subject to constitutional limitation. Justice Frankfurter proclaimed: "While in form this is merely an act redefining metes and bounds, if the allegations are established, the inescapable human event of this essay in geometry and geography is to despoil colored citizens, and only colored citizens, of their theretofore enjoyed voting rights." The author of the Court Opinion did not, however, shed much light on the question of whether the Fourteenth Amendment was applicable to the Tuskegee gerrymander. The earlier case of *Colegrove* v. *Green*[38] was cited by Justice Frankfurter as holding that districting constitutes a "political question" beyond the power of the courts, even when the equal protection of the laws is concerned. Why was that case not controlling here? Frankfurter's answer was confusing. He reasoned that the "affirmative legislative action" singling out a readily isolated segment of a racial minority "lift[ed]" this controversy out of the so-called 'political' arena and into the conventional sphere of constitutional litigation." This situation, Frankfurter thought, was distinguishable from the facts involved in *Colegrove* where "the appellants complained only of a dilution of the strength of their votes as a result of legislative inaction over a course of many years." (See Chapter 9.)

If there was a salient distinction to be made between *Colegrove* and *Gomillion*, Justice Whittaker's concurring opinion lent it no emphasis. For Whittaker, the fencing of Negro citizens out of one political division and into another might well leave them in possession of the vote guaranteed by the Fifteenth Amendment, but more to the point, it obviously established an unlawful racial segregation of citi-

37. *Gomillion* v. *Lightfoot*, 364 U.S. 339 (1960).
38. *Colegrove* v. *Green*, 328 U.S. 549 (1946).

zens in violation of the Equal Protection Clause of the Fourteenth Amendment. Justice Whittaker concurred with the result of the Court's review of jurisdiction of the Tuskegee question. However, he presaged the later reapportionment case of *Baker* v. *Carr*[39] by preferring to rest the Court's claim to jurisdiction over the geographical rearrangement on the Equal Protection Clause of the Fourteenth Amendment. When the Supreme Court sent the Alabama gerrymander back to the district court for further consideration at that level, the challenged statute was voided, and city officials were ordered not to enforce the racially inspired political division.

Lawsuit efforts to challenge districting lines or the boundaries of political subdivisions on Fifteenth Amendment grounds are seldom as clear-cut as the Tuskegee example suggests. The requirements of the Fifteenth Amendment were easy to apply in that case because the facts were a simple matter of "black and white." But consider a more sophisticated problem. In 1962, several Manhattan voters brought suit contesting their congressional districting as offensive to the Fourteenth and Fifteenth Amendments. They charged that the New York law governing the matter laid down "irrational, discriminatory and unequal Congressional Districts in the County of New York" which segregated "eligible voters by race and origin." In *Wright* v. *Rockefeller*,[40] a three-judge federal court found that the 17th, 18th, 19th, and 20th districts satisfied the constitutional requirement of "substantial population equality." Unquestionably, however, Congressman John Lindsay's 17th "blue-stocking" district largely excluded "nonwhite citizens and citizens of Puerto Rican origin." A majority of two judges found that the new districts resulting from the 1962 statute did not indicate an intent to deprive voters of their constitutional rights on the basis of race or color. Judge Feinberg pointed out that "since non-whites and Puerto Ricans in Manhattan lived in certain concentrated areas, many combinations of possible congressional district lines, no matter how innocently or rationally drawn, would also result in comparable figures." Thus, where virtual apartheid is involved, as in Tuskegee, the Fifteenth Amendment patently offers a remedy. It apparently does not, however, impose a standard of "racial balance," as the New York case suggests.[41]

39. *Baker* v. *Carr*, 369 U.S. 186 (1962).
40. *Wright* v. *Rockefeller*, 211 F. Supp. 460 (1962); 376 U.S. 52 (1964).
41. In 1965, a federal district court voided an Alabama reapportionment act as a racial gerrymander where legislative intent was proved. *Sims* v. *Baggett*, 247 F. Supp. 96 (1965).

Urbanization of the Negro has had a positive effect on his interest in voting and political organization. Efforts to thwart that development were curtailed by the timely decision in *Gomillion*. In the decade between 1947 and 1957, progress was made in fields of discrimination other than voting, and in that period the number of Negro voters doubled to a total of 1,238,000. By 1962, that number was increased by one third. The Supreme Court's greatest contribution toward getting Negroes on the ballot rolls and facilitating their voting has rested historically on the Court's invalidation of discriminatory state statutes and state constitutional provisions. "Grandfather clauses," white primaries, poll taxes, racially discriminatory gerrymandering—these have been the sometimes ingenious, sometimes graceless, parries and thrusts of southern states in their continuous fencing match with the Supreme Court from the turn of the century to the 1960s. Throughout, the initiative in selecting disfranchising tactics remained with the states. The Court's chief defensive weapon was its ability to formulate its decisions in terms of broad principle. It was a federal appeals court which cast its net most widely in *Rice* v. *Elmore*, in which it said that no state election machinery can be upheld where the purpose or effect is to deny to the Negro in any election the effective exercise of the vote because of race or color. Less sweeping in its effect on voter participation is the judicial negating of discriminatory administration practices, effective only on an *ad hoc* basis. To meet the challenge of racially discriminatory state administrative practices, Congress is better equipped. It can effectively take the policy initiative by laying down objective standards for fair administration. This task and the fashioning of other statutory remedies was begun in 1957.

5 The development of new federal remedies

Between 1933 and 1955, southern congressmen had done yeomen's service in fending off legislative attacks on lynching, the poll tax, and racially unfair employment practices. In Senate filibusters and congressional committees they argued at length against these measures, frequently relying on the proposition that, as an outnumbered group, they were victimized by northerners unable to understand southern problems and by politicians motivated by a desire for votes from minority groups—especially from the blacks who were migrating in large numbers to northern cities. In policy areas such as equal employment and fair housing, the southerners were not the underdogs they claimed to be. In these fields, northern congressmen were familiar with hometown discrimination and could seldom depend on clear constituency support. The argument for beginning with the ballot in broadening legislative constituencies and opening the door to civil rights has been that it provides Negroes with the essential key: once they have the right to vote, they will possess a powerful instrument (if combined with organization) against other forms of discrimination. This philosophy was at the political core of the Civil Rights Acts of 1957 and 1960, which deal primarily with the franchise.

Linked to this politically inspired point of view is the more legal-istic assertion that established constitutional rights require federal protection against proved state denials—an assertion reflected in the litany of Supreme Court cases from *Guinn* v. *United States* to *Terry* v. *Adams*. Indeed Attorney General Brownell, whose Department of Justice lawyers drafted the Civil Rights Act of 1957, argued insis-tently in Eisenhower cabinet meetings that, if the Constitution guar-anteed rights to the citizen, it was the government's responsibility to protect those rights.[1] Federal avowals of such rights were everywhere on public record, but a federal commitment to protection would be a new step. In 1957, the accumulated rulings supporting American Negro legal claims and the increasing political resources of Negro groups—proved voting strength and leadership—created the oppor-tunity for a meaningful legislative step, under bipartisan sponsorship, toward black inclusion in the political system. The potential threat of the new federal laws was immediately acknowledged, if not over-estimated, by southern legislators who were accustomed to losing battles in the courts but unsure of themselves in facing the first hos-tile federal legislation since Reconstruction.

The architects of the voting rights legislation proceeded in the pragmatic American tradition of incrementally building public policy on experience. Congress followed Justice Department suggestions in 1957, 1960, and 1964 in choosing to place enforcement responsibility on the courts with their history of settling voting disputes and their formal procedures and opportunities for counter-arguments, rather than on more direct but untested administrative remedies. This chap-ter will focus on various aspects of these three laws and will briefly discuss the related establishment and operation of the Civil Rights Commission and of the Civil Rights Division of the Department of Justice.

THE CIVIL RIGHTS ACT OF 1957

Legislative Background

A study made by the *Congressional Quarterly* in 1956 indicated that potential Negro voters exercised a balance of power in 61 con-

1. J. W. Anderson, *Eisenhower, Brownell and the Congress* (Tuscaloosa: University of Alabama Press, 1964), p. 28 and *passim*.

gressional districts in 21 northern and western states.[2] The results of the 1956 election, including a 15 percent increase from 1952 of Negroes voting for President Eisenhower, convinced many leaders of both parties that Negroes were becoming politically significant. Senator Hubert Humphrey put the point bluntly when he said in 1956 that the Democrats "are digging their own graves by inaction in the field of civil rights." At the national level this was especially true in view of the influx of Negroes into the industrial states of New York, Pennsylvania, New Jersey, Ohio, Michigan, Illinois, and California. Together, these urbanized states contribute 212 of the 268 electoral votes required for a presidential election victory. In 1956, of all major groups in the nation's population, the one that shifted most to the Eisenhower-Nixon ticket was the traditionally Democratic northern Negro.[3]

To a Congress sensitized to civil rights issues by changing constituencies, by the Supreme Court's school desegregation decision of 1954, and by the role of the United States in world affairs, President Eisenhower presented a civil rights program of relatively broad scope. The Administration proposed that the Attorney General be allowed to file civil suits for court orders forbidding the deprivation of *any* civil right. Defeated in the Senate, this sweeping suggestion gave way to a bill focusing on voting rights. The core of the measure as enacted is to be found in Title IV of the 1957 Civil Rights Act which made significant additions to the old Section 1971 (Title 42) of the *United States Code*, a statutory version of the Fifteenth Amendment. In place of expensive suits brought by individuals, the 1957 act allows suits for equitable relief to be brought by the Attorney General.[4] Intimidation and threats or coercion abetting racial discrimination against voters in federal elections are prohibited. The act made it possible for Justice Department lawyers to seek preventive relief (a permanent or temporary injunction) which would call a halt to the activities of any person who is engaged in, or is "about to engage in," the outlawed discriminatory practices. Thus the Attorney General has instituted suits in situations such as the refusal to renew the con-

2. "Fact Sheet on Negro Voting," *Congressional Quarterly*, April 30, 1956.

3. H. L. Moon, "The Negro Vote in the Presidential Election of 1956," 26 *Journal of Negro Education* 219–20 (Summer 1957).

4. A comprehensive discussion of federal court cases between 1959 and 1965 is given by Donald S. Strong, *Negroes, Ballots, and Judges* (Tuscaloosa: University of Alabama Press, 1968).

tract of a Negro teacher who testified for the Government in a voting case[5] and the use of other types of private reprisals and economic coercion.[6] The practice of using state criminal processes to intimidate registrants has been successfully litigated,[7] and the arresting of voter registration workers on baseless charges has been challenged.[8] The provisions of the 1957 Civil Rights Act are careful to state that a person cited for contempt of a court order forbidding such practices is guaranteed counsel if he cannot afford his own lawyer. Regardless of whether other remedies (e.g., state court suits) have been exhausted, federal district courts were assigned jurisdiction in contests arising under the act.

Other highlights of the Civil Rights Act of 1957 included, in Title I, the creation of an executive Civil Rights Commission composed of six members chosen from both political parties. Detailed rules of procedure were also established. In the provision concerning the Justice Department, Title II authorized the President to appoint one additional Assistant Attorney General to head a Civil Rights Division. Title III of the statute expanded the jurisdiction of the district courts: their power to hear suits for damages or to secure equitable relief under any federal civil rights law was established. This provision was balanced by Title V which restricted the courts, in taking action against those who flouted or disobeyed the voting rights laws, by requiring jury trials under certain conditions.

Related Supreme Court Cases

In September 1958, in its first complaint under the statute of the preceding year, the United States sought to enjoin several Georgia election registrars from continuing racially discriminatory practices. In Terrell County, where only 48 out of 5,036 Negroes of voting age were registered, four Negro teachers were disqualified for their alleged inability to read. The teachers charged that the election of-

---

5. *United States* v. *Board of Education of Green County*, 332 F.2d 40 (1964). An excellent analysis of federal court law and politics is given by Charles V. Hamilton, "Southern Judges and Negro Voting Rights: The Judicial Approach to the Solution of Controversial Social Problems," 1965 *Wisconsin Law Review* 72–103.

6. E.g., *United States* v. *Bruce*, 353 F.2d 474 (1965).

7. E.g., *United States* v. *Wood*, 295 F.2d 772 (1961).

8. E.g., *United States* v. *Dallas County*, 229 F. Supp. 1014 (1964).

ficials delayed the handling of Negro applications, arbitrarily refused to register others, and applied more stringent standards to Negroes than to white applicants. When their complaints reached the first plateau of federal courts, Title IV of the Civil Rights Act was held to be unconstitutional in *United States* v. *Raines*[9] on the ground that the legislation was so broadly worded as to punish private individuals for interfering with voting rights.

The question of whether the act applied to private persons other than state officials was not even relevant to the case, Justice Brennan ruled when the case reached the Supreme Court. He admonished the lower court that the delicate power of voiding an act of Congress is not to be exercised with reference to hypothetical cases. What was involved here, he pointed out, was the action of election registrars. In addition to reaffirming the rule of practice that bars anticipating constitutional questions in the courts, Justice Brennan left ajar the door to possible prosecutions of private individuals. In addressing himself to the lower court's model, *United States* v. *Reese* (in which Congress was lectured that it must restrict its Fifteenth Amendment enforcement legislation to state acts of racial discrimination), Brennan stated that because that decision pursued a different line of reasoning, "we cannot follow it here." In *United States* v. *Raines*, the Supreme Court held Title IV to be valid as applied to discriminatory treatment of Negroes by state registration officials.

Another case, decided by the Supreme Court the same day as *Raines*, involved private individuals linked to state authority. *United States* v. *Thomas*,[10] a *per curiam* decision, affirmed a lower bench's holding that Title IV was constitutional as applied to members of White Citizens' Councils in Louisiana who had conspired with state officials to purge registered Negroes from the voting lists.[11] The election registrars in a Louisiana parish had sought to cancel the suffrage of practically all Negro voters residing there by applying presumably valid disqualification standards to them but not to whites. The widespread disfranchisement in Washington Parish was the result of challenges made by members of the White Citizens' Council. The District Court, in granting injunctive relief to the 1,377 registered Negro voters, pointed out that all of the defendant "white citizens" were

9. *United States* v. *Raines*, 172 F. Supp. 552 (M.D. Ga. 1959); 362 U.S. 17 (1960).

10. *United States* v. *Thomas*, 362 U.S. 58 (1960).

11. Heard in the Federal Court of Appeals under the title of *United States* v. *McElveen*, 177 F. Supp. 355 (E.D. La. 1959); 180 F. Supp. 10 (E.D. Las. 1960).

engaged in supervising the state election process; consequently, their deprivation of voters' rights amounted to state action. The *Thomas* decision stands for the proposition that discriminatory conduct by a registrar occurs when he allows others to avail themselves of state machinery in order to implement a disfranchisement scheme based on race.

THE CIVIL RIGHTS COMMISSION AND DIVISION

The Civil Rights Act of 1957 provided for the establishment of a Commission on Civil Rights as an independent agency within the executive department. The group was empowered only to investigate, study, appraise, and make recommendations. Aside from its authority to issue court-enforced subpoenas in connection with its fact-finding investigations, it was to have no enforcing powers. For law enforcement, the Civil Rights Act raised the Civil Rights Section of the Department of Justice to the division level under a new Assistant Attorney General.

The Civil Rights Commission

According to the statute of 1957, the newly created Commission on Civil Rights was directed by Congress to perform three functions. (1) The commission investigates allegations, submitted in writing and under oath or affirmation, that certain citizens are being deprived of the right to vote by reason of color, race, religion, or national origin. (2) The commission collects information and reports on legal developments which constitute a denial of the equal protection of the laws under the Constitution. (3) The commission is authorized to evaluate the laws and policies of the federal government with respect to equal protection of the laws required by the Fourteenth Amendment. Although in its first two years of operation, voting rights consumed more man-hours of commission work than any other single area of civil rights, the commission is not charged with reviewing other aspects of the electoral process untouched by discrimination.[12]

12. See U.S. Congress, Senate, Judiciary Subcommittee on Constitutional Rights, *Literacy Tests and Voter Requirements in Federal and State Elections,* Erwin Griswold Testimony (Hearings on S. 480, S. 2750, and S. 2979), 87th Cong., 2d sess., 1962. In 1964, the unit was empowered to explore vote-fraud practices.

The Civil Rights Commission has published a number of reports having a bearing on denials of voting rights.[13] In its first comprehensive report made to the President and Congress in 1959, the Civil Rights Commission made five voting rights recommendations which contained the key issues of the congressional debate over civil rights in 1960. The commission urged:

1. That the Bureau of the Census make a compilation of registration and voting statistics, including a count of individuals by race, color and national origin, who are registered and have voted since the recent decennial census.
2. That Congress enact a law requiring that voting records be preserved for five years, and be subject to public inspection.
3. That Congress enact an amendment to existing civil rights laws regarding the evasion by state officers of registration responsibilities.
4. That the Commission be permitted to go directly to the appropriate United States District Court for an order to enforce its subpoenas, instead of having to get the Justice Department to do it "as at present."
5. That the President be authorized to appoint federal registrars to administer state voting laws in places where it is felt that discrimination warrants.[14]

Three of the commissioners also proposed a constitutional amendment guaranteeing voting rights and permitting states to set no qualifications for voting except those concerning "age or length of residence requirements uniformly applied to all persons within the state, or legal confinement at the time of registration or election."[15]

In 1961, the Civil Rights Commission issued a one volume report entitled *Voting*, which pointed out that there were reasonable grounds to believe that substantial numbers of Negro citizens had been denied the right to vote on grounds of race or color in about 100 counties in eight southern states.[16] On the basis of its new findings, the majority of the commission members agreed that five important steps should

13. *Report of the United States Commission on Civil Rights, 1959*, Part I, Voting; *Voting* (1961); *Voting in Mississippi* (1965); *The Voting Rights Act, the First Months* (1965); *The Voting Rights Act of 1965* (1965). Related publications include: *Freedom to the Free, 1863 Century of Emancipation 1963* (1963); *Law Enforcement, A Report on Equal Protection in the South* (1965); *Political Participation* (1968). In 1968 the Commission began publication of the quarterly *Civil Rights Digest*.
14. Commission on Civil Rights, *Report*, 1959, pp. 134–41.
15. *Ibid.*, p. 144.
16. Alabama, Florida, Georgia, Louisiana, Mississippi, North Carolina, South Carolina, and Tennessee. Commission on Civil Rights, *Voting*, p. 135.

be taken to safeguard the right to vote. (1) In contrast to the suggestion for a constitutional amendment made by three commissioners in 1959, the panel in 1961 urged that Congress enact legislation providing that all citizens shall have the right to vote in federal and state elections, except those unable to meet reasonable age or length of residence requirements, those legally confined at the time of registration or election, or those convicted of a felony. (2) Congress was asked to enact a "literacy test law" providing for the satisfaction of state educational, interpretation, and literacy tests by proof of at least six grades of formal education. (3) Interference by private persons with the right to vote should be prohibited, the commission said, by outlawing "any arbitrary action or (where there is a duty to act) arbitrary inaction, which deprives or threatens to deprive any person of the right to register, vote, and have that vote counted in any Federal election."[17] (4) After the commission had reviewed the facts of the *Gomillion* case and other instances of inequitable apportionment, it recommended that Congress require that federal and state voting districts, where they are established by the state, should be "substantially equal in population." Further, Congress should clarify the federal courts' jurisdiction of suits to enforce federal legal and constitutional requirements with regard to such electoral districts. (5) Finally, Congress was requested to direct the Bureau of the Budget to compile nationwide voting statistics. Such information would include a "count of persons of voting age in every State and territory by race, color, and national origin, who are registered to vote," and the extent to which such persons have voted since 1960.

In general, the commission concluded that in 1961 the promise of the Constitution had not been fulfilled to the extent that the franchise was denied entirely to some because of race and diluted for many others because of the gerrymander and malapportionment. According to the 1961 report, "disfranchisement on racial grounds in some areas exaggerates the inequalities produced by malapportionment, and each inequity makes the other more difficult of solution."

The commission's operations during its first three years of existence were almost as controversial as its recommendations. The fact-finding procedures used by the group came under some criticism, chiefly from southern congressmen in whose states most of the hearings by the rights unit were then held. Senator Talmadge provocatively expressed his reservations about the bipartisan group's activities. Ac-

17. Commission on Civil Rights, *Voting*, pp. 141–42.

cording to the Georgia senator, the commission is "armed with unheard-of investigatory procedures" and operates as though it were "given a roving commission to conduct investigations and issue compulsory process to harass, accuse and try State election officials."[18]

In 1960, the Supreme Court upheld the rules governing the investigatory procedures of the commission against a claim that they violated the Due Process Clause of the Fifth Amendment by "denying witnesses a fair hearing." The case was entitled *Hanna* v. *Larche*.[19] By early 1959, the Civil Rights Commission had received 67 complaints of voting rights' denials from western Louisiana. Interviews conducted by individual staff members and letters to the state attorney general proved of little use to the commission in verifying the accusations. Told that four sworn complaints against her administrative practices had been sent to Washington, Mrs. Lannie Linton, registrar of Claiborne Parish, asked the commission for copies of the affidavits so that she could press perjury charges. The Civil Rights Commission insisted on protecting the identity of the complainants and announced that hearings would be held in Shreveport. Insisting that irreparable harm faced them because of the commission's refusal to reveal the names of those who had made accusations, the Louisiana registrars and private persons summoned to the hearings successfully sought a federal order barring the public inquiry. Because the rules of procedure governing the conduct of the federal parleys made no provision for advance notice, confrontation with accusers, or cross examination, the white Louisianians involved claimed that the 1957 Civil Rights Act deprived them of the due process of the law required by the Fifth Amendment. Building on this contention, they asserted that the statute was not "appropriate legislation" under the Fifteenth Amendment—a point that Chief Justice Warren denied when the case was reviewed by the Supreme Court. His ruling also rejected the due process argument. Warren noted that suggestions for "more protective rules" of procedure were considered and voted down by Congress. The Chief Justice reasoned that the requirements of due process vary with the type of proceeding. The Supreme Court held that under the Administrative Procedures Act, the methods of the commission did not deprive witnesses of their rights within the due process of the

18. Senate Judiciary Subcommittee, *Literacy Tests*, 87th Cong., 2d sess., 1962, p. 93.

19. *Hanna* v. *Larche*, 363 U.S. 420 (1960). A discussion of the case in the larger setting of the Commission's activities in 1960 is given in Dulles, *Civil Rights Commission*, pp. 90–91.

law because its activities, under the chairmanship of Dr. Hanna, were neither proscriptive nor adjudicatory. The commission does not take any affirmative action that will affect an individual's legal rights, according to the Opinion of the Court. Rather it gathers facts which may subsequently be used as the basis for legislative or executive action.

Justices Douglas and Black filed a dissent in *Hanna* v. *Larche*. Their point of view was that, in the process of widening the enforcement of the franchise right, the spectre of conflict with other rights had become apparent in this case. Conceding that voting rights had properly enjoyed "new meaning in recent years," the dissenters concluded: "Yet important as these civil rights are, it will not do to sacrifice other civil rights in order to protect them." The Opinion written by Douglas showed special concern that if charges made to the commission against the registrars were true, they were criminally responsible under Section 242 (Title 18) of the *United States Code*. That there may be a link between commission inquiries and criminal prosecutions was revealed in a different context by a member of the commission. Testifying before a Senate subcommittee, Dean Erwin Griswold said, "If the investigations which we are authorized to make disclose criminal or illegal action, it would be our duty to refer them to the Department of Justice. We have no power to prosecute, and of course do not undertake to do so."[20] The rules of procedure governing the commission's operation take into account the possibility that uncovered facts might tend to incriminate an individual. When this appears to be the case, the commission conducts hearings in executive session. Anyone giving testimony may, if he wishes, be accompanied by his own counsel and may request that further light be shed on his activities by calling other witnesses. With these and other safeguards shaping the conduct of commission inquiries, there would be no need to bring into operation the more stringent requirements of the Fifth Amendment unless a criminal trial were to grow out of commission hearings.

The Civil Rights Division of the Justice Department
Basing his views on almost 20 years of Department of Justice experience, Attorney General Brownell, in 1956, called for new civil remedies in defense of constitutional rights. He expressed disappoint-

20. Senate Judiciary Subcommittee, *Literacy Tests*, 87th Cong., 2d sess., 1962, p. 157.

ment about inadequate voting protection in federal statutes dating back to the Reconstruction period. Although he acknowledged to an economy-minded Administration that new laws would call for increasing the budget and staff of Justice Department specialists in civil rights, he argued successfully for expanding the Civil Rights Section of the Criminal Division into a full-fledged Civil Rights Division within the Department of Justice.[21]

Although its budget increased from $185,000 in 1958 to $468,000 in 1960 the new division came under considerable criticism from several quarters for not filing more suits and acting with greater vigor.[22] Assistant Attorney General Rogers replied in 1960 that Department policy had been affected by two considerations. First, insufficient evidence had been collected to sustain more suits because of a lack of federal law (before 1960) authorizing access to voting records during an investigation. Second, the department wished to act with caution by carefully choosing its strongest cases from the beginning, knowing that the scope and constitutionality of new congressional enactments would be tested in these suits.[23] A third explanation for what initially appeared to be Justice Department timidity in voting rights cases was advanced by Assistant Attorney General Burke Marshall in 1961. He explained that department policy was to forestall legal action under existing voting laws until state and local authorities were given full notice and ample "opportunity to avoid recourse to litigation by corrective measures at the state and local level."[24] Unquestionably, political sensitivity to the charge of unkept promises and administrative difficulties and disappointment with the effectiveness of the 1957 statute were major factors in the passage of the Civil Rights Act of 1960.

THE CIVIL RIGHTS ACTS OF 1960 AND 1964

Speaking before the Senate in 1960, Senator Joseph Clark commented that the number of persons who "had been given their voting rights" under the terms of the Civil Rights Act of 1957 was "small

21. U.S. Congress, House, *H.R. Rep. No. 2187*, 84th Cong., 2d sess., 1956, p. 13.
22. See *Congressional Quarterly Supplement*, May 6, 1960, p. 758.
23. 39 *Congressional Digest* 20, 22 (Jan. 1960).
24. Department of Justice, *Annual Report of the Attorney General* (Washington, D.C.: Government Printing Office, 1961), p. 167.

indeed."[25] The Civil Rights Act of 1960 was, like the 1957 law, basically designed to help Negroes vote. And like its statutory antecedent, the Civil Rights Act of 1960 was secured with bipartisan cooperation. A sampling of congressional support by both parties in the House of Representatives is illustrated below. Table 5–1 (making use of Guttman scaling) shows the voting rights attitudes of members of the House in 1957 and 1960. Calculations are based for each year on a composite tabulation of five separate roll calls taken on each bill. Both bills were based on Administration proposals, and in both instances, the resulting legislation was generated by a marriage of convenience between nonsouthern Democrats and Republicans.

Table 5–1   *House of Representatives Attitudes on the 1957 and 1960 Civil Rights Bills**

	FAVORABLE		MODERATE†		UNFAVORABLE		TOTALS	
	1957	1960	1957	1960	1957	1960	1957	1960
Southern Democrats	4	8	0	8	106	93	110	109
Non-Southern Dems.	118	163	1	3	1	1	120	167
Republicans	169	127	9	8	21	18	199	153
TOTALS	291	298	10	19	128	112	429	429

* Behind the 1957 attitude scores are the votes on: (1) the motion to recommit the bill; (2) the motion to end debate on the resolution amending the Senate jury-trial amendment; (3) the motion for the House to concur in the Senate amendments; (4) the passage of the bill as amended in the House; (5) House Resolution 259, providing for the consideration of H.R. 6127. Behind the 1960 scores are votes on (1) the resolution for the House to concur in the Senate amendments; (2) passage of the McColloch-Celler Amendment; (3) the motion to recommit; (4) the passage of the bill as amended; (5) the passage of the resolution authorizing the House to consider H.R. 8601, the Civil Rights Bill of 1960.
† Refers to those whose votes were favorable on some motions and unfavorable on others.

In contrast to the 1957 Civil Rights Act, the statute of 1960 made it clear that the Attorney General could proceed not only against named officials but also against a state if for any reason the registrars resign and are not replaced. The need for this change was dictated by experience. The embarrassing fact that upon the resignations of registrars, the Justice Department was left with no suable party was brought out in the case of *United States* v. *Alabama.*[26] The case

25. 106 *Cong. Rec.* 6113 (Jan. 18, 1960).
26. *United States* v. *Alabama*, 177 F. Supp. 720 (1959) upon passage of the 1960 act: remanded 362 U.S. 602 *per curiam* (1960).

stemmed from Macon County, Alabama (83 percent Negro), where legal gaming with Negro voting rights was made notorious in *Gomillion* v. *Lightfoot*. Of the 3,398 Negroes who had been rejected by county election officials, the least among them had 12 years of formal education, and six others held master's degrees.[27] When an effort was made to enjoin the registrars to discontinue their discriminatory practices, they resigned. A federal district court held that the ex-board members were no longer the proper subjects for injunction, and the State of Alabama was not a "person" subject to suit within the meaning of the 1957 Civil Rights Act.

Within months after the district court decision was affirmed by a federal court of appeals, the Civil Rights Act of 1960 was enacted, and it contained two provisions pertinent to the dispute in Macon County. First, in instances of voting discrimination, the state was to be considered a legal, suable entity in case the registrars should resign. Second, in the absence of registrars, the federal court could appoint voting referees who were empowered to register voters. (For four years Macon County was without voting registrars.) The new law held out to civic-minded Negroes a promising instrument by which to realize their political rights. In reviewing the court of appeals decision, the Supreme Court noted the recent enactment of the Civil Rights Act of 1960. In view of the technique it gave to litigants to hold their states responsible for voting denials, the nine-man bench sent the case back to the district court with instructions to resume the suit against the State of Alabama. Soon after, the district court decreed that the members of the Macon County Board of Registrars were to end their discriminatory tests, that they were to assemble regularly, and that they were to handle Negro applications as expeditiously as they had those of others. The applicants were to know within 20 days whether they would be registered. The court called for a monthly progress report from the board of registrars, and a consent decree was granted authorizing 54 specific Negroes to be put on the voting polls.[28] Subsequently, the Supreme Court affirmed the power of federal judges to require the registration of specific applicants.

Title I of the Civil Rights Act of 1960 establishes a penalty of $1000 or one year in prison for any person who obstructs or interferes with any order issued by a federal court. Injunctions to prevent

27. See Joseph Brittain, "Some Reflections on Negro Suffrage in Alabama," 47 *Journal of Negro History* 127 (Apr. 1961).
28. *Alabama* v. *United States*, 371 U.S. 37 (1962), affirming 304 F.2d 583 (C.A. 5th Cir.).

such obstructions were also authorized. Another provision empowered the Civil Rights Commission, which was extended for two years in 1959, to administer oaths and take sworn testimony. The third Title early proved important for voting rights cases. It requires that election records, poll tax documents, and registration papers for federal general and primary elections must be preserved for 22 months. Upon written application, these documents must be turned over to representatives of the Attorney General.[29] In 1963, the Attorney General reported that as much as half of the Civil Rights Division staff was involved in the task of analyzing, especially by data-processing techniques, registration records of various counties for courtroom use. Examination of such records reached a high in 1964, by which time the records of 82 counties had been examined. In 1965, the Attorney General was able to report that litigation to secure local registration documents was "phasing out and its need will be even more limited with the added tool of the Voting Rights Act of 1965."[30]

The most heatedly debated portion of the 1960 law, Title IV placed responsibility for guaranteeing voting rights on the federal courts, which may be aided by "voting referees"—special court-appointed officers with duties comparable to a registrar. It provides that, after a suit is filed by the Attorney General on behalf of one or more voters whose franchise right has allegedly been deprived because of race, the Government may then ask the court to evaluate the nature of the deprivation. If the district court determines that the persons concerned were cheated of their voting rights pursuant to a "pattern or practice" of racial discrimination, they may avail themselves of a new remedy: the services of voting referees. The district courts are empowered to review the applications (within ten days of filing) of others in the same area making similar complaints. The statute envisages the use of the referees to advise the court concerning its decision in regard to each applicant.[31] Enhanced by the spectre of contempt proceedings, the act permits the court to direct the appropriate state official by a "consent decree" to permit the qualified

29. The provision has been court-tested in several cases including *Crum Dinkens* v. *The Attorney General of the United States*, 285 F.2d 430; 366 U.S. 913 (1961) *cert. denied*. See also *Kennedy* v. *Bruce*, 298 F.2d 860 (1962).

30. Department of Justice, *Annual Report of the Attorney General of the United States, 1965* (Washington, D.C.: Government Printing Office, 1965), p. 170.

31. In *United States* v. *Mayton*, a detailed Opinion describes the duties and responsibilities of voting referees: 335 F.2d 153 (1964).

complainants to vote. Late applications, filed less than 20 days before the election, may be approved by the court for provisional voting. In 1965, Attorney General Katzenbach explained that it was his department's policy to bring "pattern or practice" suits on a "voting district" basis, rather than to attempt to show a scheme of discrimination throughout an entire state with the necessity of getting referees appointed in every district.[32] The Attorney General explained the difficulties of pleading a "pattern or practice" suit:

> To show a pattern and practice of discrimination, you have to show one of two things, either that Negroes who were clearly qualified were denied the rights or you have to show that Negroes who were as well qualified as whites were denied their rights. And so you have to examine. In the first place, you have to identify the race of the particular applicants within the county, and then you have to try to figure out what standard and practice was being used by that registrar, if any, and then . . . the courts require us to show that Negroes who possess the same or superior qualifications to the white applicants were rejected. So we have to look at both.[33]

The Attorney General concluded by noting that, as of early 1965, a pattern of discrimination had been found by courts in 19 instances, but that voting referees were appointed only in Perry and Dallas Counties, Alabama. In several cases in scattered states, the judges themselves acted as "federal registrars."[34]

The 1960 Civil Rights Act declares that state officials must be notified of any "consent decree" or court order declaring a person to be a qualified voter. The state officers are bound, under the law, to permit the person to vote; disobedience would be subject to contempt of court proceedings. At this point, a provision of the 1957 act may come into play. This voting law, as amended in 1960, gives the judge in a contempt case the discretion to decide whether the defendants shall be tried with or without a jury. If the judge tried the case without jury, and if he imposed a fine of more than $300 or a jail term of more than 45 days, the defendant would then have the right to retrial with a jury.[35] A jury trial in criminal contempt cases is not required by the Constitution. This statutory jury trial provision, a concession to

32. U.S. Congress, Senate, Judiciary Committee, *Voting Rights, Hearings on S.1564*, 89th Cong., 1st sess., 1965, p. 114.
33. *Ibid.*, p. 118.
34. *Ibid.*, p. 128.
35. See *United States* v. *Barnett*, 376 U.S. 681 (1964).

southern congressmen, operates to minimize judicial penalties or to require that a jury, i.e., made up of 12 southerners, impose the stiffer penalties.

On the eve of the passage of the 1964 Civil Rights Act, the Attorney General announced that his department's handling of voting complaints had multiplied sharply, but most of these cases turned on the forbidden practices section of the 1957 act. By mid-1964, a total of 61 suits had been filed (compared with 41 at the end of the previous fiscal year and only 12 between 1958 and June of 1960). Of these 61 cases, 45 concerned racial discrimination and 16 involved voter intimidation, all falling under the prohibitions stemming from 1957. Thus the court restraining order, grounded on the regulatory scheme set up in 1957, remained the tool most often used by the Justice Department before 1965.

In 1965, the chief grievance voiced by the department concerning the 1960 statute related to the time-consuming background research required before the two-step process of challenging a "pattern or practice" of voting discrimination could be initiated and then court- or referee-administered registration be secured. Actually, two such suits were pending with the Fifth Circuit Court of Appeals when the Voting Rights Act of 1965 was enacted. Since the areas involved came under the voting examiner program of the new law, the Justice Department withdrew the request for referees and so ended all reliance on the "pattern or practice" suits described in 1960.

Even though such litigation has been eclipsed by improved remedial instruments, the "pattern or practice" technique for ferreting out large-scale discrimination did have an enduring effect in underscoring the need for complete data. Title VIII of the 1960 law requires the Census Bureau to secure registration and voting statistics by race and national origin in areas recommended for that purpose by the Civil Rights Commission. Such information is to be gathered on a nationwide basis beginning in 1970 with the decennial census of that year. The 1964 act also extended the life of the Civil Rights Commission to 1968. The commission's first request under the act was that the Census Bureau collect voting information by race in Alabama, Louisiana, and Mississippi, the states in which the Justice Department has been most active.

The Civil Rights Act of 1964 broke new ground by guaranteeing to all persons freedom from discrimination in places of public accommodations. This requirement is the feature most frequently associated with the civil rights innovations of the 1964 law. Nevertheless, the same statute made notable contributions to the safeguarding of voting rights as well, and these legal improvements were drafted in the spirit of the 1957 and 1960 acts. By Title I, local officials, in determining whether persons are qualified to vote, are barred from applying standards or procedures different from those used for others in the same political subdivision. Election officers are also forbidden to disqualify applicants for errors or omissions which are immaterial to their substantive qualifications for voting. To reduce whimsical discriminations in the administration of literacy tests (and to make proof of discrimination easier) the tests where used are required to be in writing and a copy must be made available to the applicant, prior to the test, if he requests it. Also, if the literacy of a would-be voter is disputed, he can rely on the 1964 act provision that persons who have completed the sixth grade in an accredited English-speaking school are presumed to be literate. The result is that in any proceeding under the law, local officials are put in the position of having to justify the rejection of an applicant with six grades of schooling.

The remaining regulations on voting under the Civil Rights Act of 1964 are aimed at the law's delay. The provision for expediting voting cases brought by the United States cannot make hostile district court judges act quickly, but it can minimize delay and expose judges who deliberately retard the judicial process.[36] The law of 1964 authorizes the Attorney General, when he files a "pattern or practice" suit, to request the convening of a three-judge federal court to hear it and to require that such cases be expedited. The judgment of such a three-man panel is directly appealable to the Supreme Court—a provision helpful in dealing with federal district court judgments which do not comport with the spirit of federal civil rights legislation. For example, by 1965, Judge Harold Cox of the Southern District of Mississippi had been reversed on eight out of nine of the voting cases in which he took a decisive part. Judge Daniel H. Thomas (Southern District, Alabama) was reversed in all six of his election rulings during the same period, and Judge Claude Clayton (Northern District, Mississippi) was re-

36. See the excellent article by one of the most conscientious (and until his retirement in 1968, one of the busiest) judges in the voting field, Chief Judge Elbert P. Tuttle of the United States Court of Appeals for the Fifth Circuit: "Equality and the Vote," 41 *New York University Law Review* 245–66 (Apr. 1966). The Fifth Circuit includes Alabama, Georgia, Florida, Louisiana, Mississippi, and Texas. Between 1961 and 1965 its nine judges reviewed a score of voting cases with the following results: Judge Rives: 11 cases, 9 decided favorably to the voting rights claim; comparably, Judge Tuttle: 8/8; Wisdom, 7/7; Brown: 5/5; Jones: 4/3; Cameron: 3/3; Gewin: 3/2; Hutcheson: 2/2; Bell: 2/2.

versed on both of his voting rights opinions by the Fifth Circuit Court of Appeals. The appellate process is inherently time-consuming, and the delays involved sometimes work real civil rights deprivations. The Justice Department calculated that the expediting requirements and improvements directed at judicial dilatory tactics by the 1964 Civil Rights Act would reduce the time for litigation from an average of 16 or 17 months to about half a year. The workload of the Civil Rights Division, however, was consequently intensified because a thorough preparation of each case had to be accomplished in a shorter time.

In March of 1964, Assistant Attorney General for Civil Rights, Burke Marshall, expressed his faith in litigation as the tool with which to secure Negroes the vote. In a series of lectures at Columbia University, he argued that the obstacles could be overcome by men, money, and time. The process, however, was arduous, he conceded. "It is as if the Government had to sue every citizen to make him pay his income tax, and had to prove over and over in every case that the tax was constitutional."[37] Speaking on behalf of the Leadership Conference on Civil Rights, Roy Wilkins took issue with Marshall's view by expressing sharp disappointment with the operation of federal voting laws in the courts. He said:

In 1960 Congress strengthened the 1957 voting rights law. Only last year Congress tried again to make the 1957 law more effective [in the 1964 Act]. All three laws put together have not done the job of making the Fifteenth Amendment a living document. In too many areas of the Nation, Negroes are still being registered one by one and only after long litigation. We must transform this retail litigation method of registration into a wholesale administration procedure registering all who seek to exercise their democratic birthright.[38]

Wilkins acknowledged that only two weeks earlier the Supreme Court had made significant "inroads against voting discrimination" in Louisiana and Mississippi. He was referring to two cases, *United States* v. *Louisiana* and *United States* v. *Mississippi*.[39] Their significance rested on the fact that the decisions virtually authorized the government to seek to invalidate voting discrimination against Negroes on a mass basis instead of proceeding against each individual

37. *New York Times*, Mar. 29, 1964, p. 32.
38. Senate Judiciary Committee, *Voting Rights*, (Part II), Statement of Roy Wilkins, 89th Cong., 1st sess., 1965, p. 1005.
39. *United States* v. *Louisiana*, 380 U.S. 145 (1965) and *United States* v. *Mississippi*, 380 U.S. 128 (1965).

abuse. The two cases illustrate the efforts of the Department of Justice to break away from the pattern of legal attacks on the acts of individual voting registrars and challenge more broadly the state constitutional provisions and laws under which the registrars acted.

In the Louisiana case the Court sustained the decision of a three-judge bench holding unconstitutional the requirements of Louisiana law which obliged voting registrants to read and interpret any section of the federal or state constitutions. In his Opinion of the Court, Justice Black noted that Louisiana had relied on a "grandfather clause" in 1898, and an interpretation-of-the-constitution test in 1921, successfully to reduce the number of Negro voters from a 44 percent share of the electorate in 1898 to about one percent in 1944. By that time disfranchisement was reinforced by a "white primary," with the result that requiring applicants to "give a reasonable interpretation" of state or federal constitutional provisions fell into disuse. After the "white primary" was outlawed by *Smith* v. *Allwright* in 1944, many registrars continued to ignore the interpretation test, thereby permitting Negro registration to grow from two-tenths of one percent to 15 percent of the Louisiana electorate by 1956. Justice Black said in *United States* v. *Louisiana* that after the school desegregation cases, White Citizens' Councils with the support of the state legislature "set up programs, which parish voting registrars were required to attend, to instruct the registrars on how to promote white political control." Subsequently political participation was successfully stifled by the wholesale challenging of Negroes' names on the voting rolls and by the use of a 1960 state requirement that one who registers must "be able to understand" and reasonably interpret state and federal constitutions "when read to him by the registrar." Justice Black said, "This is not a test but a trap, sufficient to stop even the most brilliant man on his way to the voting booth." The Court sustained the decision of the lower bench, voiding the provisions of the state "interpretation test."

In the Mississippi case, the Supreme Court reversed a federal court ruling dismissing the Government's suit because it failed to state a claim on which relief could be granted. At the Supreme Court level (with the aid of a 133-page history of restrictions on Negro voting in Mississippi prepared by the American Civil Liberties Union), the Justice Department questioned a series of Mississippi voting laws. In sum, it was alleged, the laws amounted to a pattern and practice of discrimination. Mississippi's reply relied heavily on the proposition that, even though in 1960 and 1964 Congress had authorized the Government to make a state a defendant in voting rights cases, the national legislature had no constitutional power to do so. Again for a full Court, Justice Black responded that the Fifteenth Amendment "in plain and unambiguous language provides that no 'State' shall deny or abridge the right of citizens to vote because of their color." Admonishing the district court for throwing the case out, Justice Black exclaimed that the allegations of the federal complaint "were too serious, the right to vote in this country is too precious, and the necessity of settling grievances peacefully in the courts is too important, for this complaint to have been dismissed."

Also rejected by the lower court were Justice Department challenges to Mississippi voter qualifications set in 1954. The Delta State that year required applicants for the ballot: (1) to read and copy any section of the Mississippi constitution; (2) to give a reasonable interpretation of the provision to the registrar; and (3) to demonstrate "a reasonable understanding of the duties and obligations of citizenship under a constitutional form of government." Giving registrars an additional arbitrary tool useful in rejecting applicants, a state law of 1960 said that those wishing to register successfully "shall be of good moral character." In response to the Civil Rights Act of 1960, the Mississippi legislature authorized the destruction of voting records. A state statute of 1962 further multiplied the difficulties of those wishing to vote by requiring that they fill out application forms "properly and responsively" and by forbidding registrars to tell an applicant why he failed the test. The Supreme Court held that the complaint's assertion of "a common purpose running through the State's legal and administrative history . . . to adopt whatever expedient seemed necessary to establish white political supremacy . . ." was sufficient to justify relief. The case was remanded to the federal district court. In June 1965, Mississippi revised its registration requirements and eliminated the discriminatory provisions attacked in the suit.

United States v. *Louisiana* and *United States* v. *Mississippi* were decided on March 8, 1965. The Attorney General's *Annual Report* for that year described the cases as having "far-reaching significance in the voting area."[40] Yet only ten days after the rulings were announced, Attorney General Katzenbach appeared before a congressional committee to complain that the cases and statutes composing

---

40. Department of Justice, *Annual Report of the Attorney General, 1965,* p. 171.

federal law on voting rights were inadequate to make good the promise of the Fifteenth Amendment. Giving figures to compare the gains made between 1958 and 1964, he noted that black registration in Alabama had increased by 5.2 percent to a total of only one-fifth of those eligible. In Mississippi, only 6.4 percent of qualified Negroes were registered in 1964 compared with 4.4 percent in 1953. In Louisiana, the number of eligible Negroes who were actually registered remained unchanged at 31.8 percent between 1956 and 1964. Particularly in these three states, Katzenbach said that "the three present statutes have had only minimal effect." The Attorney General concluded that the disappointing figures represented nothing less than "the inadequacy of the judicial process to deal effectively and expeditiously with a problem so deep-seated and so complex."[41]

Of course, the Attorney General could have given other statistics to suggest the notable increase of Negro voting strength in several southern states, especially during the period from 1957 to 1964. But his statement appropriately focused on the "hard core" states of Alabama, Louisiana, and Mississippi where Justice Department lawyers then invested most of their time with only the most discouraging results. Table 5–2 tells a story of real progress between 1956 and 1964 in states such as Florida, Tennessee, and Texas. In these and other states, many of the gains can be attributed to voluntary compliance with the new legislation. But the three statutes passed between 1957 and 1964 held out no promise for hope in such areas of "last ditch" resistance as Alabama, Louisiana, and Mississippi where it was not uncommon for registrars to symbolize their view of state policy by wearing buttons saying "Never."

In these states and elsewhere, existing federal laws did little to change local political habits. In spite of the fact that new statutes were administered under four Attorneys General serving under three Presidents of both parties, results were meagre. Judicial and administrative remedial efforts were dammed up in a backwash of ineffectiveness, their force delayed at every pressure point. Voting suits were onerous to prepare, sometimes consuming as many as 75 full work days of plodding through registration records in preparation for trial. Litigation often proved excruciatingly drawn out, in part because of the ample opportunities for delay afforded to voting officials, hostile district court judges, and others involved in the proceedings. Delay also

41. U.S. Congress, House, Judiciary Subcommittee No. 5, *Voting Rights Hearings on H.R. 6400 before Subcommittee No. 5 of the House Committee on the Judiciary*, H.R. Rep. No. 439, 89th Cong., 1st sess., 1965, pp. 4–5.

Table 5-2   *Estimated Percentage of Voting-Age Negroes Registered in the South, 1940–64**

STATE	1940	1947	1952	1957	1960	1964
Alabama	—1	1	5	11	14	19
Arkansas	3	21	27	36	38	40
Florida	3	13	33	32	39	51
Georgia	2	20	23	27	?	27
Louisiana	—1	2	25	31	31	32
Mississippi	—1	1	4	5	6	6
North Carolina	10	14	18	24	38	37
South Carolina	—1	13	20	27	?	37
Tennessee	16	25	27	29	64	70
Texas	9	17	31	37	34	58
Virginia	5	11	20	19	23	34

* The figures for 1964 combine the statistics presented by Attorney General Katzenbach in House Judiciary Subcommittee No. 5, *Hearings on H.R. 6400*, 89th Cong., 1st sess., 1965, and by the Voter Education Project of the Southern Regional Council (Aug. 1964). Registration data for 1960 are in Commission on Civil Rights, *Voting*. For 1947, 1952, and 1956, see Price, *Negro and the Ballot*, pp. 9–10. For 1940, see Gunnar Myrdal, *An American Dilemma* (New York: Harper and Brothers, 1944), pp. 474–504.

scotched other federal protection efforts on behalf of ballot rights. For example, by the time the United States Supreme Court in *Hanna v. Larche* was able to reverse the order of a three-man district court (Judge Wisdom dissenting) enjoining Civil Rights Commission hearings in Louisiana, a full year of compulsory investigation had passed. Even when favorable decisions were at last obtained under the 1957, 1960, and 1964 laws, some of the states and registrars affected had switched with ease to discriminatory devices not covered by federal decrees. Additionally, states such as Mississippi and Alabama enacted difficult new tests designed to hold the line on existing disparities between white and Negro registration figures. In other instances, local officials defied and evaded court orders or simply closed their registration offices to freeze the voting rolls. As an antidote to such electoral maladies, "pattern or practice" suits proved to be weak medicine by the Attorney General's admission. Registration by federal officers under the 1964 act had little impact on local maladministration because of procedural complexities built into the federally designed suits. As long as recalcitrant localities pinned their hopes for resisting Negro enfranchisement on officials displaying "Never" buttons, federal court decrees by themselves could be of little avail.

6   The voting rights act of 1965

In 1903, Justice Holmes advised a group of voteless black litigants that federal courts could offer them remedies of only limited effectiveness. He told the Alabamians that, in the long run, relief from such a "great political wrong" as that alleged against the state's "disfranchising constitution" must be given within the framework of state government, "or by the legislature and political department of the government of the United States."[1] Sixty-two years later, that advice was accepted by the Reverend Martin Luther King, President of the Southern Christian Leadership Council. His campaign to secure Negro voting registration in the "black belt" counties of the South culminated in the Voting Rights Act of 1965. The law will be discussed below in terms of its passage, statutory provisions, administrative practices, and Supreme Court litigation.

Dallas County, Alabama, of which Selma is the county seat, was chosen carefully by Reverend King as the location for protesting the

1. *Giles* v. *Harris*, 189 U.S. 475, 488 (1903).

insufficiency of judicial remedies available to support Negro voting rights, particularly in Alabama, Mississippi, and Louisiana. Dallas was not a county where Negroes had failed to try to vote. Nor was it an area that was overlooked by Civil Rights Commission investigations or Justice Department scrutiny. But Dallas was a county in which qualified Negroes were not permitted to vote, litigation under the Civil Rights Acts of 1957, 1960, and 1964 notwithstanding. The principal defect lay in the judicial process itself, hence Dr. King's decision to reverse the tactic of taking conflict out of the streets and into the courts. It was in Dallas County that the first voter discrimination case was instituted by the Kennedy Administration. Yet by 1965, Attorney General Katzenbach was able to report that four years of litigation in Dallas County, including intimidation suits against Sheriff Jim Clark, his deputies, and the White Citizens' Council, had yielded the registration of only 383 Negroes out of a voting-age population of 29,500 (about one-half white), with about 65 percent of the whites registered. Delay was the typical response to federal efforts. And delay to many white southern officeholders was tantamount to victory, for every election conducted without Negro voting participation meant one more term in office for the beneficiaries of the old system.

The Dallas County "Walk for Freedom," punctuated by police use of tear gas, whips, night sticks, and ropes against the demonstrators on March 8, 1965, has become legendary for the legislative results that it generated. Republican Senator Thomas Kuchel, the Senate Minority Whip, echoed the comment of many in predicting that an "effective bipartisan right-to-vote measure will be Congress' response." Within a week, President Johnson effectively pre-empted leadership of the new voting rights struggle.

The address of the President to Congress on March 15, 1965, takes its place among the memorable documents of American history. It was delivered on a stage appropriate for the great scenes of our national life. Probably no forum in the American political process is as imposing as the ceremonial convocation of the two chambers of Congress summoned in solemn joint session to receive the recommendations of the President. In a speech marked by eloquence and a sense of urgency, the Chief Executive asked for the speedy enactment of new voting legislation, for "no law we now have on the books . . . can ensure the right to vote when local officials are determined to deny it. . . . In Selma as elsewhere we seek peace. We seek order. We seek unity. But we will not accept the peace of stifled rights, the order imposed by fear, the unity that stifles protest. For peace cannot be purchased at the price of liberty." Most poignantly, the President made the American Negro's cry for freedom his own and proclaimed: "We shall overcome."[2]

The State of the Union Message in January 1965 had earlier committed the President to "eliminate every remaining obstacle to the right and the opportunity to vote."[3] By mid-February, Senate Majority Leader Mike Mansfield and his Republican counterpart, Senator Dirksen, had begun to map plans with the Attorney General for thrashing out a new voting rights bill. During the first week in March, newspapers around the country carried such headlines as "Katzenbach Beseiged by Sit-Ins Demanding U.S. Action," "Crowd of 15,000 at Lafayette Park Protest Federal Inaction," "King Asks President for U.S. Registrars," "Violence Takes Over in Selma," and "Leaders of Both Parties in Senate Rush Drafts of Voting Rights Bill." The events behind these captions, particularly the shootings and bludgeonings of civil rights workers in Selma which resulted in three deaths, were the catalysts that hurried Johnson Administration work on a voting law proposal.

On March 17, the President's rights bill was sent to Capitol Hill. Extensive hearings were conducted by the Judiciary Committees of the Senate and House.[4] Approval of a cloture motion on May 25 obviated a fiilibuster in the Senate, which passed the voting rights bill the following day. Arrayed against a majority of 47 Democrats and 30 Republicans were 19 "nay" votes, cast by two Republicans and 17 southern Democrats. The House took a roll call vote on H.R. 6400 on July 9, following a five-week delay imposed by Chairman Howard Smith's Rules Committee. The vote was 333–85.[5] Of the 221 Democrats in favor of the House bill, 33 were from the South, while three southerners were included among the 112 Republicans voting "aye."

Both the House and Senate versions as separately passed retained the two central features of the Administration bill, elimination of discriminatory literacy tests and assignment of federal examiners. The thrust of the bill urged by the President was to prohibit literacy and

2. 111 *Cong. Rec.* 4924 (daily ed., March 15, 1965).

3. 111 *Cong. Rec.* 28 (daily ed., Jan. 4, 1965).

4. U.S. Congress, *Voting Rights Hearings on S. 1564 before the Senate Committee on the Judiciary. Sen. Rep. No. 162.* 89th Cong., 1st sess., 1965; and *Voting Rights Hearings on H.R. 6400 before Subcommittee No. 5 of the House Committee on the Judiciary. H.R. Rep. No. 439,* 89th Cong., 1st sess., 1965.

5. 111 *Cong. Rec.* 11341 (daily ed., May 26, 1965) and 111 *Cong. Rec.* 15716 (daily ed., July 9, 1965).

similar tests where fewer than 50 percent of voting age citizens were registered or voted in the presidential election of 1964. The 1964 vote, involving a 62 percent national turnout, failed to exceed that of the 63.2 percent mark of 1960, but the proportion of eligible voters casting ballots increased over 1960 in 14 states, including six of those won by Senator Goldwater. Attorney General Katzenbach explained that the 1964 date was chosen because "the national average was about 11 points higher than the 50 percent figure taken here [in the coverage formula]. Therefore, it seemed to us that there was a reasonable connection established between discrimination, a violation of the Fifteenth Amendment and that date."[6] Left unexplained, however, was the political *savoir faire* of the formula. Table 6–1 shows that in every southern state carried by Senator Goldwater (the sixth and only other state he won, Arizona, is not shown), there were enough unregistered Negroes potentially to have offset his margin of victory (on the safe assumption that voting eligible Negroes would have opted for the Johnson-Humphrey ticket).

Table 6–1   *Southern Presidential Voting Margins and Voteless Southern Negroes, 1964**

STATE	PRESIDENTIAL WINNER	WINNING MARGIN	NUMBER UNREGISTERED ADULT NEGROES
Alabama	Goldwater	213,625	370,000
Arkansas	Johnson	70,932	88,000
Florida	Johnson	42,599	170,000
Georgia	Goldwater	94,027	343,000
Louisiana	Goldwater	122,157	350,000
Mississippi	Goldwater	303,910	394,000
No. Carolina	Johnson	175,295	293,000
So. Carolina	Goldwater	93,348	227,000
Tennessee	Johnson	126,082	96,000
Texas	Johnson	704,619	275,000
Virginia	Johnson	76,704	237,000

* Adapted from figures and estimates of the Southern Regional Council, 20 *New South* 15 (Feb. 1965), p. 15.

In the final stages of the legislative process, the two chambers settled on somewhat different versions of the bill. Accordingly the proposals were sent to a conference committee, where the House-supported

6. Senate Judiciary Committee, *Voting Rights Hearings on S. 1564*, 89th Cong., 1st sess., 1965, pp. 197–98.

statutory ban on poll taxes at the state level was replaced by the Senate plan that the Attorney General should seek court action against enforcement of state and local poll taxes. Potential legal difficulties under this plan, and incidentally the cause of legislative compromise, were eased by the inclusion of a strong congressional assertion that poll taxes operated in some areas so as to deny voting rights in violation of the Fourteenth and Fifteenth Amendments. Also included in the final bill was a section (chiefly affecting Puerto Ricans in New York) excusing citizens educated in American schools conducted in a foreign language from passing English-language literacy tests. Within two days after the conference report was issued, it was accepted in the House and Senate, and the President signed the Voting Rights Act of 1965 into law on August 6.[7] As enacted, the statute is a complex scheme of stringent remedies and subsidiary cures aimed particularly at areas of the country where voting abuse has been most flagrant.

Shifting the Advantage of Time and Inertia

In the first case in which it considered the constitutionality of major sections of the Voting Rights Act, Chief Justice Warren commented for the Supreme Court in *South Carolina* v. *Katzenbach:* "After enduring nearly a century of systematic resistance to the Fifteenth Amendment, Congress might well decide to shift the advantage of time and inertia from the perpetrators of the evil to its victims."[8] The blueprint of this shift is principally found in Sections 4, 5, and 6 of the Voting Rights Act, which provide for circumventing time-consuming litigation. These provisions, in concert with others, create a series of relatively automatic and speedy remedies. To understand the statute and how and where its counterweights against discrimination are applied, some definitions of terms in the Voting Rights Act should be mastered.

Vote. The word "vote" is defined in conformity with the definition provided in the Civil Rights Act of 1960 [42 U.S.C. 1971(e)] to refer to: "all action necessary to make a vote effective including, but not limited to, registration or other action required by state law prerequisite to voting,

7. The House vote on August 3 is reported in 111 *Cong. Rec.* 18499 (daily ed.); Senate approval the following day is recorded on p. 18665; the Conference version was enacted into law, Pub. L. No. 110; 79 Stat. 437.
8. *South Carolina* v. *Katzenbach,* 383 U.S. 301 (1966).

casting a ballot, or having such ballot counted and included in the appropriate totals of votes cast with respect to candidates for public office and propositions for which votes are received in an election" [Section 11(c)].

Political Subdivision. This term, for the purposes of the act, is used to refer to the districts within which registration is conducted. A "political subdivision" is "any county or parish, except that where registration is not conducted under the supervision of a county or parish, the term shall include any other subdivision of a state which conducts registration for voting" [Section 14(c)].

Section 4(b) Areas. This phrase is a short-hand reference to the states and political subdivisions covered by the act. The coverage formula of Section 4(b) "shall apply in any State or in any political subdivision of a state which (1) the Attorney General determines maintained on November 1, 1964, any test or device, and with respect to which (2) the Director of the Census determines that less than 50 per centum of the persons of voting age residing therein were registered on November 1, 1964, or that less than 50 per centum of such persons voted in the presidential election of November, 1964."

Test or Device. The law suspends forbidden "tests or devices" in Section 4(b) areas. The phrase "test or device" shall mean any requirement that a person as a prerequisite for voting or registration for voting (1) demonstrate the ability to read, write, understand or interpret any matter, (2) demonstrate any educational achievement or his knowledge of any particular subject, (3) possess good moral character, or (4) prove his qualifications by the voucher of registered voters or members of any other class" [Section 4(c)].

The House and Senate Judiciary Committees, in considering the voting rights bill, concluded (to use the words of the House) that, where there was a coincidence of the two factors in the coverage formula (the 50 percent-or-less figure combined with the use of tests or devices), "there is a strong probability that the low registration and voting are the result of racial discrimination in the use of such tests."[9] In the 1964 election, 62 percent of the national electorate cast presidential ballots. Of the exceptional nine states where fewer than 50 percent of those eligible voted, seven maintained literacy tests (Alabama, Alaska, Georgia, Louisiana, Mississippi, South Carolina, and Virginia). Table 6–2 describes the nature of literacy and related tests in the six such states with large Negro populations. It shows the initial date of adoption of these requirements and suggests the particular stringency of requirements for voting registration in Alabama, Louisi-

9. House Judiciary Committee, *Voting Rights Hearings on H.R. 6400*, 89th Cong., 1st sess., 1965, p. 13.

ana, and Mississippi. In addition to the six states listed and Alaska, a correlation between the use of tests or devices and voting or registration at the 50 percent-minus level occurred in 1964 in scattered counties, including three counties in Arizona, one in Hawaii, one in Idaho, and 26 in North Carolina.[10] Section 4(b) of the Voting Rights Act makes the Attorney General responsible for determining which states or subdivisions maintained the forbidden voting prerequisites. The Director of the Census is charged with verifying the percent of voting age residents in such areas who were registered or voted in the 1964 presidential election.

Table 6–2   *Initial Dates of Adoption of Literacy and Related Tests in States with Large Black Populations**

STATE	READING AND/OR WRITING	APPLICATION COMPLETION	ORAL CONSTITUTIONAL INTERPRETATION	CITIZENSHIP INFORMATION EXAMINATION	GOOD MORAL CHRTR.
Ala.	1901		1964	1901	1901
Ga.	1908			1908	1908
La.	1921	1898	1921	1921	1921
Miss.	1890	1954	1890	1921	1921
So. Car.	1900		1895	1954	
Va.	1902	1902	1902		

* Adapted from House Judiciary Subcommittee No. *5, Hearings on H.R. 6400,* 89th Cong., 1st sess., 1965.

Suspension of Tests and New Voting Prerequisites

In Section 4(b) areas, a variety of potent aids are promised to voteless Negroes. The first corrective calls for the suspension of literacy and similar voting qualifications for a period of five years from the last occurrence of substantial voting discrimination. In effect this aid permits black registrants to catch up with their white fellow-citizens by freezing the standards to those, such as state-imposed age and residence requirements, which had previously applied to whites. The remedy was built on earlier judicial experience, particularly in the Fifth Judicial Circuit where registrars were ordered in equity proceedings to ignore the current state requirements for qualifications to the extent that they had not been enforced by the letter of the law against white applicants.[11] In the opinion of the majority of the Senate

10. 30 *Fed. Reg.* 9897, 14505 (1965).

11. For example, see *United States* v. *Duke,* 332 F.2d 759, 768–69 (1964), where Judge Tuttle described the equity remedy of "freezing" voter qualifications to refer to a court order to keep in effect those requirements previously used to the benefit of others, at the time that Negroes were being discriminated against.

Judiciary Committee, localities which had been allowing white illiterates to vote for years could not sincerely complain about the "dilution" of their electorates through the enrolling of illiterate Negroes.[12] When the Attorney General and the Director of the Census determine that a Section 4(b) area is using a discriminatory registration technique, suspension of "tests or devices," is automatically triggered upon announcement of the determination in the *Federal Register*. The publication date marks the time when the prohibited state requirements are set aside, and the determination thus made "shall not be reviewable in any court."

A second technique for relief is found in the fifth section of the Voting Rights Act. Following the Administration bill, Congress developed another mechanism for keeping the initiative in federal hands should Section 4(b) areas invent new traps and tricks. Any prospective voting regulation (not in effect on November 1, 1964) which is newly instituted by such a state subdivision is automatically held in abeyance.[13] Its operation is suspended pending review by federal authorities to determine whether the innovations would work in such a way as to perpetuate disfranchisement or frustrate effective use of the vote. Administrative or judicial approval is required for new locally proposed voting prerequisites. The qualifications or election practices must be approved by the Attorney General, who is given 60 days to approve or veto submitted proposals (approval is assumed if he fails to object during this period). Alternatively, or if the Attorney General does object, the state may submit its new plan to a three-judge district court for the District of Columbia, requesting a declaration that the proposal is "innocent" of racially discriminatory features. The entire procedure is hedged with the proposition that neither administrative nor judicial approval "shall bar a subsequent action to enjoin enforcement of such qualification, prerequisite, standard, practice or procedure."

Section 5 further promises an antidote to state efforts to dilute the impact of the ballot once it is effectively in Negro hands. It builds on the history of the "white primary" cases which demonstrated that the vitality of black votes could be impaired by restrictive political party rules and that political participation by black voters can be as effectively frustrated by preventing candidates sympathetic to the group from seeking office as by denying Negroes the right to vote. Ac-

12. Senate Judiciary Committee, *Voting Rights Hearings on S. 1564*, 89th Cong., 1st sess., 1965, pp. 15–16.
13. See *United States* v. *Mississippi*, 256 F. Supp. 344 (1966).

knowledging this, the Civil Rights Commission concluded in 1968 that:

States and political subdivisions in which tests are suspended are obligated by Section 5 of the Voting Rights Act to see that changes in party rules are submitted to the Attorney General for his approval or that the approval of the U.S. District Court for the District of Columbia is obtained.[14]

This construction of Section 5 notwithstanding, the commission found in 1968 that several states, including those subject to Section 5, had adopted measures to prevent Negroes from competing for office.[15] Such practices, rules, and laws take several forms: (1) abolishing the office sought by the Negro candidate; (2) extending the term of office of incumbent white officials;[16] (3) making formerly elective offices appointive;[17] (4) raising the filing fees required of candidates for party office and party nomination for public office; (5) increasing the number of signatures of registered voters required on the nominating petition for independent candidates;[18] (6) withholding from Negro candidates pertinent information about qualifying for office and other election information;[19] (7) withholding or delaying certification of the nominating petition of Negro candidates; and (8) barring office to successful Negro candidates.[20]

Where practices such as those described are relied upon for purposes of racial discrimination in a Section 4(b) area, the loss of local control of elections may be greater than anticipated. A section 4(b) area trying to abridge operation of the act must be prepared to seek a declaratory judgment from the District of Columbia District Court.

---

14. Commission on Civil Rights, *Political Participation*, Appendix II, pp. 198–99. See recommendation 6, calling for adoption of this interpretation by the Attorney General, *ibid.*, p. 184.

15. *Ibid.*, pp. 172–73.

16. See *Sellers* v. *Trussell*, 253 F. Supp. 915 (Ala., 1966).

17. See *Bunton* v. *Patterson*, (S.D.Miss., 1967) appeal consolidated with *Allen* v. *Board of Elections*, 393 U.S. 544 (1969).

18. See *Whitley* v. *Johnson*, 260 F. Supp. 630 (1966), appeal consolidated *sub nom. Whitley* v. *Williams*, with *Allen* v. *Board of Elections*.

19. See *Bynum* v. *Burns*, 379 F.2d 229 (1967).

20. *Bond* v. *Floyd*, 385 U.S. 116 (1966). The Supreme Court held unanimously that the refusal of the Georgia House of Representatives to seat Julian Bond, a duly elected representative, because of certain statements he made or subscribed to in opposition to the Vietnam War, violated Bond's right of free expression under the First Amendment, as applied to the states through the Due Process Clause of the Fourteenth Amendment.

In that forum, the state or subdivision is required to show to the satisfaction of the three-judge court that "tests or devices" have not been used during the preceding five years to abrogate the franchise on racial grounds. According to controversial provisions of Section 5, the Attorney General's cooperation is required here. If he decides that the voting requirements of the locality have not been misused for five years, he may consent to a judgment favoring the petitioning state or election district. To overcome the burden of the state's having to prove local compliance with the Fifteenth Amendment, the petitioner must show that incidents of discrimination have been few in number and have been promptly corrected, that "the *continuing effect* of such incidents has been eliminated," and that they are unlikely to recur in the future (emphasis added).[21] Certainly, examples of racially unfair selection of election officials and thinly veiled discrimination against Negro candidates testify to the "continuing effect" of Fifteenth Amendment violations. A state or subdivision which adapts to the Voting Rights Act by changing its focus from preventing Negro registration to obstructing black candidates in the electoral process may unwittingly be inviting a continued federal presence. Any Section 4(b) area which has earned a federal court decision against its discriminatory practices in the voting process, may not, for five years from the date of that decision, reinstate its tests or devices. Thus according to the stringent limitations on the "escape hatch" provision, a previous judgment (for example that against Mississippi in *United States* v. *Mississippi*[22] prevents the petitioners rebutting the presumption of discrimination. These complicated exemptions boil down to a congressional acknowledgment that the coverage formula may cast its net too widely. Accordingly, the act provides for the ending of special statutory coverage at the request of areas in which the danger of voting discrimination does not exist or has not materialized during the preceding five years.

The Examiner Program

The third remedy made available by the law of 1965 to would-be voters in areas falling within the reach of the coverage scheme is set out in Sections 6 (b), 7, 9, and 13(a). The Civil Service Commission

21. Section 4(d). This section and Sections 2, 5, 6, 7, 9, 12(d,f), and 14(b,c) were extensively discussed and held to be constitutional against state challenges in *United States* v. *Louisiana*, 265 F. Supp. 703 (1966), and *United States* v. *Mississippi*, 256 F. Supp. 344 (1966).

22. *United States* v. *Mississippi*, 380 U.S. 128 (1965).

is directed, when authorized by the Attorney General, to appoint voting examiners to list those applicants qualified to vote in all elections. This administrative remedy is tailored for those districts in which local officials have persisted in obstructing or disobeying the law. The Attorney General sets the examiner program in motion by certifying either (1) that he has received "meritorious" written complaints from at least 20 residents alleging that they have been disfranchised under color of law on account of race, or (2) that the appointment of examiners is otherwise necessary to make effective the guarantees of the Fifteenth Amendment.

Where examiners are used, the Civil Service assumes responsibility for selecting personnel (almost always from the local area), training them in the field, and contracting for office space (frequently in post offices). Examiners have generally had previous experiences as government investigators in the field offices of agencies such as the Interstate Commerce Commission, the Federal Trade Commission, etc. and are subject to Hatch Act prohibitions against partisan political activities. Their on-the-job training in custom and law covers a wide range of instruction, from reminders that applicants should be addressed courteously as "sir" or "ma'am" to the applicable voter qualifications of state law.[23] In every state immediately affected by the Voting Rights Act, the surviving state qualifications specify age, residence, an oath of affirmation, citizenship, and the absence of criminal convictions and mental disabilities. Anyone who meets the qualifications but is not registered to vote must promptly be placed on the list of eligible voters. The new registrant is supplied with a listing certificate—his pasteboard "ticket" to the voting booth—which is valid only if he were on the voter list at least 45 days prior to the election.[24]

The examiner posts his monthly listings at his office and sends a copy to state registration officials. Additionally and by law, he sends a monthly report to the state Attorney General and to the Attorney General of the United States. This statement shows the names of those listed who were previously not registered. Drawing upon these reports, the Management Systems Division of the Civil Service Commission has followed the practice of periodically enumerating voting statistics for the Justice Department and the Civil Rights Commission.

23. Sections 7(a) and 9(b).

24. Section 7(b,c). On the duty of state officers to accept federal "listing" see *Reynolds* v. *Katzenbach*, 248 F .Supp. 593 (Ala., 1965). Challenges to examiner activities were judicially thwarted in *Perez* v. *Rhiddlehoover*, 247 F. Supp. 65 (La., 1965), and in *Gray* v. *Alabama ex rel. Wallace*, 185 So.2d 123 (1966).

Cumulative statistics published for June 30, 1966, showed 126,529 applications received during the first 260 days of examining, 3,372 rejections (based on crime, insanity, failure to meet residence requirements, and prior registration), and 405 removals—a net listing of 35.2 percent of the potential nonwhite voters in 41 deep-South counties. Of course, the vast majority of those newly listed were Negroes. The most dramatic exception was in Plaquemines Parish, Louisiana, where the late Judge Leander Perez encouraged whites to compete with Negroes for the time of federal examiners and to maintain a white voting majority. The result was that by mid-year 1966, examiners there had listed 1,404 whites (17 more were added in 1967 and 111 in 1968) and 1,203 Negroes (4 more were added in 1967 and 61 in 1968). This imbalance, which favored listed whites, was unique in examiner areas. More typical for the first year of listing activities was Dallas County, Alabama, where examiners listed 69 whites (five were added in 1967 and one in 1968) and 8,892 Negroes (77 were added in 1967 and 23 in 1968). The total figures by states are provided in Table 6–3, which compares the work of the Office of Hearing Examiners in its first and busiest year with the cumulative totals for the fourth year. A comparison of the 1966 figures with subsequent years reveals that the volume of listing operations generally crested and levelled off by the end of 1966. A check of 1966 and 1969 nonwhite listings in Louisiana and Mississippi, however, shows respectively a 51.5 and 37.2 percent increase. Georgia listings, which totalled 3,402 by June 30, 1969, did not begin until 1967, when 3,329 nonwhites were listed. On June 30, 1968, 3 counties in Georgia were designated for hearing examiner jurisdiction, 2 in South Carolina, 9 in Louisiana, 12 in Alabama, and 32 in Mississippi (some of Mississippi's were so identified only for purposes of bringing in observers). By the time of the 1968 presidential election, a total of 161,443 new voters had been listed under the examiner program.

The heading "Removals" on the table requires special explanation. The examiner is required to remove a person's name from the eligible list either as a result of a successful challenge in accordance with the procedures prescribed in the act or upon some surviving state legal ground governing the loss of eligibility.[25] An applicant informed that he has been removed from the federal list because of the decision of an examiner or hearing officer (who decides appeals from the exam-

---

25. Section 7(b). Throughout the challenge period, the listed person remains eligible to vote.

Table 6–3. *Cumulative Listings by States of Examiner Program Results after the First and Fourth Years, June 30, 1966 and June 30, 1969**

| | APPLICANTS | | | | LISTED | | | | TOTAL ESTIMATED POTENTIAL | |
| | WHITES | | NONWHITES | | WHITES | | NONWHITES | | | |
	1966	1969	1966	1969	1966	1969	1966	1969	1966	1969
Ala.	5,161	5,326	61,788	63,455	5,135	5,299	59,403	61,027	149,263	152,685
La.	1,530	1,879	12,379	25,558	1,499	1,842	12,193	25,136	31,142	72,733
Miss.	66	2,669	41,012	65,130	62	2,651	40,312	64,181	140,721	163,474
So. Car.	16	16	4,577	4,678	16	16	4,537	4,638	9,248	9,248
Ga.	—	16	—	3,453	—	16	—	3,402	—	7,161
TOTAL	6,773	9,906	119,756	162,264	6,712	9,824	116,445	158,384	330,374	405,301

| | REJECTIONS | | | | REMOVALS | | NO. OF COUNTIES | | NET LISTINGS | |
| | WHITES | | NONWHITES | | | | | | | |
	1966	1969	1966	1969	1966	1969	1966	1969	1966	1969
Ala.	26	27	2,385	2,418	337	2,090	10	12	64,202	64,236
La.	31	37	186	422	7	49	5	9	13,685	26,929
Miss.	4	18	700	949	4	1,397	24	32	40,370	65,435
So. Car.	—	—	40	40	57	72	2	2	4,496	4,582
Ga.	—	—	—	51	—	30	—	3	—	3,388
TOTAL	61	82	3,311	3,880	405	3,638	41	58	122,753	164,570

* Adapted from figures supplied by courtesy of the Office of Hearing Examiners.

iner's determinations) may reapply for listing immediately. Hearing officers are generally lawyers trained in quasi-judicial procedures and supplied on request by other federal agencies such as the National Labor Relations Board. (Ordinarily they have a Civil Service rating of GS-12 or higher.) The challenge procedure under hearing officers was primarily used during the first two months of examiners' operations. During the period, about 60 percent of the successful challenges turned on failures to meet residence requirements, while the remainder were based on disqualifying crimes.[26]

Section 13 of the Voting Rights Act describes the procedures for bringing the examiner program to a close. Such federal supervision of election procedures and processes is to terminate in any political subdivision whenever the Attorney General notifies the Civil Service Commission that all persons listed have been placed on the appropriate registration rolls and that there is no longer reasonable cause to believe that the color of a man's skin will prejudice his opportunity to register to vote. Waning demand, according to the Office of Hearing Examiners, might virtually bring a program to a close, and thus local usage of federal facilities dictates the number of days that an examiner's office will remain open. During June of 1966, for example, only in Mississippi were two or three offices open on a full-time daily basis. After 1967, once-a-month openings or less were typical in most offices. It should be noted that formally ending the examiner program in a state does not necessarily lift the suspension of "tests or devices." By another procedure, the listing activities of examiners may be terminated if the affected political subdivision obtains a favorable declaratory judgment from the District Court in Washington and if the Director of the Census has found that more than half of the nonwhite residents of voting age are registered to vote. With progress that seems likely in all states affected by the Voting Rights Act, the 1970 census could spell the end of the examiner program in most Section 4(b) areas. A turning point was marked in mid-year 1967, when the Justice Department reported that the rate of Negro registration in five examiner states had increased from 28 to 52 percent.[27]

Table 6–4 reports on progress made in voter registration in southern states between 1964 and 1967. The first six states in the table are referred to as Group I. These are the states in which the fewest gains

26. Commission on Civil Rights, *Voting Rights Act, the First Months*, p. 20.
27. Department of Justice, Press Release of July 6, 1967.

in Negro registration (proportionate to statewide voting-age numbers) had been made in the previous decade. They are also the states upon which Voting Rights Act sanctions fell most heavily. "Tests or devices" were suspended on a statewide basis in each, and 60 selected counties were designated for examiners among each of the states except Virginia. The table shows the advances made in Group I states. By 1967, according to the right-hand column of the table, each of these states had acquired a higher proportion of Negroes in their

Table 6-4 *Southern Voting Registration, 1964-67*

STATE	APRIL 1, 1964 NEGRO REGISTRATION (EST.)	EXAMINER-LISTED (JE. 30, 1967)		TOTAL REGISTERED (JE. 30, 1967)		PERCENT NEGRO OF TOTAL (1967)
		WHITE	NEGRO	WHITE	NEGRO	
Ala.	104,000	5,266	62,611	1,200,000	260,000	17.8
Ga.	240,000	11	3,329	1,380,000	325,000	19.1
La.	162,866	1,593	21,971	1,125,000	270,000	19.4
Miss.	28,500	169	53,922	624,000	194,000	23.7
So. Car.	127,000	62	4,606	718,000	191,000	20.8
Va.	121,000	—	—	1,187,000	240,000	16.8
GROUP I TOTALS	738,366	7,101	146,439	6,234,000	1,480,000	AV. % 19.65
Ark.	80,000			600,000	120,000	16.7
Fla.	240,616			2,169,000	304,000	11.4
No. Car.	248,000			1,603,000	277,000	14.7
Tenn.	211,000			1,375,000	225,000	14.0
Tex.	375,000			2,600,000	400,000	13.3
GROUP II TOTALS	1,154,616			7,347,000	1,326,000	AV. % 14.0
TOTAL SOUTH	1,937,982	7,101	146,439	14,581,000	2,806,000	AV. % 16.1

* The figures in column 1 on Negro registration before the Voting Rights Act of 1965 are the estimates of the Southern Regional Council, News Release of August 4, 1964. See also Voter Education Project, *Voting Registration in the South* (Atlanta: Southern Regional Council, 1966). The examiner listings for the end of the fiscal year 1967 were supplied by courtesy of the Office of Hearing Examiners, United States Civil Service Commission. The total registration estimates as of June 30, 1967 may be found in volume I, *Voter Education News* 3 (July 1967).

respective electorates than any of the Group II states, which were less affected by the act of 1965. A comparison of the "Examiner-Listed" and "Total Registered" columns among Group I states suggests that considerable gains were made under the operation of the act, and most of these gains were made without invoking the ultimate sanction of the examiner program. Voluntary compliance with the Voting Rights Act by state administrations is roughly measurable. Discounting federal listing figures, the 1964–67 Negro registration gain in each of the Group I states indicates the levels of voluntary compliance under federal law because the resulting figure reports the Negro enrollments which took place under standard state procedures, excepting the use of "tests or devices." States where such tests were suspended generally made the largest gains in Negro registration in the South.

A ranking of all eleven states by voluntary compliance (i.e., in the order indicated by the absolute number of Negroes registered solely under state administration between 1964 and 1967) follows. Virginia was first with a gain of 118,000 Negro registrants, followed by: Mississippi +111,578; Alabama, +93,389; Louisiana, +85,163; Georgia, +81,671; Florida, +63,384; South Carolina, +59,394; Arkansas, +40,000; North Carolina, +29,000; Texas, +25,000; Tennessee, +14,000. By this measure, the front-runners are generally Group I states, demonstrating that suspension of "tests or devices" is an effective sanction, even when its results are separated from the enrollment yield of the examiner program. Nevertheless, the need for continued use of both sanctions is suggested by ranking the same states according to the extent to which each has fully registered its eligible Negro population under state administration. A ranking of southern states according to the percent of all eligible adult Negroes registered (nearly the reverse of the above listing) follows: Tennessee, 71.3 percent of eligible Negroes were registered by 1967; Texas, 63.1 percent; Florida, 62.5 percent; Arkansas, 62.3 percent; Virginia 59.3 percent; Georgia, 52.4 percent; South Carolina, 50.2 percent; North Carolina, 50 percent; Louisiana, 48.2 percent; Alabama, 41.2 percent; Mississippi, 33.2 percent.[28] According to this listing, Group I states fall behind their southern neighbors, where they would probably remain if Voting Rights Act sanctions were prematurely withdrawn.

28. The percentages rely on state Negro populations (adult) in: United States Commission on Civil Rights, "Registration and Voting Statistics" (Washington, D.C., mimeographed, 1965).

SUPREME COURT LITIGATION

It is not surprising that when South Carolina was brought within the coverage of the Voting Rights Act state officials wasted no time coming to the defense of their traditional "tests and devices," ended as of August 7, 1965. The state Attorney General acted with dispatch in filing a bill of complaints challenging parts of the new statute and asking for an injunction against their enforcement by the Federal Attorney General. The case was entitled *South Carolina* v. *Katzenbach*.[29] The state particularly called into question the coverage formula, the suspension of new voting prerequisites, and the examiner program. In view of the national importance and scope of the challenge, the Supreme Court invited all states to participate as "friends of the Court." Accordingly Alabama, Georgia, Louisiana, Mississippi, and Virginia submitted *amici curiae* briefs supporting South Carolina. Allied with the Attorney General were briefs written for California, Illinois, Massachusetts, and 17 other states.[30]

With respect to the suspension of "tests and devices," South Carolina asserted that the coverage formula prescribed in Section 4 violates the principle of the "equality of States," denies due process by employing an invalid presumption and by barring judicial review of administrative findings, constitutes a forbidden bill of attainder, and impairs the separation of powers by adjudicating guilt through legislation.

Chief Justice Warren wrote the Opinion of the Court, which held that "the sections of the Act which are properly before us are an appropriate means for carrying out Congress' constitutional responsibilities and consonant with all other provisions of the Constitution." For example, the contention based on the Due Process Clause of the Fifth Amendment was dismissed by the Chief Justice on the ground that the traditional understanding of the guarantee of a person's liberty against abridgement without due process had never been "expanded" to include the state as a "person." Likewise, the Chief Justice added, "Courts have consistently regarded the Bill of Attainder Clause of Article I and the principle of separation of powers only as protections for individual persons and private groups, those who are peculiarly vulnerable to non-judicial determinations of guilt."

29. *South Carolina* v. *Katzenbach*, 383 U.S. 301 (1966).
30. Hawaii, Indiana, Iowa, Kansas, Maine, Maryland, Michigan, Montana, New Jersey, New York, Oklahoma, Oregon, Pennsylvania, Rhode Island, Vermont, West Virginia, and Wisconsin.

Not to be detained long by these subsidiary contentions, Warren proceeded quickly to what he thought to be the salient argument presented by South Carolina. The basic question can be put simply. Has Congress exercised its powers under the Fifteenth Amendment in an appropriate manner with relation to the states? The answer must be, the Court held, that although the states have "broad powers" to determine the conditions for exercising the vote, the Fifteenth Amendment, addressed to Negro voting rights, "supersedes contrary exertions of state power" when discrimination is practiced. Section 2 of the Civil War amendment declares that "Congress shall have the power to enforce this article by appropriate legislation." What is appropriate? The basic test for the appropriateness of federal statutes under the Constitution was laid down in the permissive terms of Chief Justice John Marshall's time-honored interpretation: "Let the end be legitimate, let it be within the scope of the constitution, and all means . . . which are plainly adapted to that end, which are not prohibited, but consist with the letter and spirit of the constitution, are constitutional."[31] For the Warren Court, Marshall's *dictum* had lost none of its vigor and was sufficient to reject South Carolina's argument that Congress could enforce the Fifteenth Amendment only by legislation cast in terms that avoided specific remedies having a local focus. The argument that only the courts may fashion remedies tailored to specific local grievances was discarded by the Supreme Court. The Chief Justice explained that the term "appropriate" could not be limited by "such artificial rules."[32]

As to the doctrine of the equality of states, also invoked by South Carolina, that approach has traditionally been applied "only to the remedies for local evils which have subsequently appeared." The coverage formula fell unequally on the states, there was no doubt about that. But the Court agreed with Congress that Section 4(b) areas were an "appropriate target for the new remedies." Congress, according to Warren, "began work with reliable evidence of actual voting discrimination in a great majority of the States and political subdivisions affected by the new remedies." The phrase "great majority" refers to Alabama, Louisiana, and Mississippi, where federal

---

31. *McCulloch* v. *Maryland*, 4 Wheat. 316, 421 (1819).

32. Citing a rule that was not "artificial," Chief Justice Warren again relied on Marshall where, referring to the Commerce Clause, he said: "This power, like all others vested in Congress, is complete in itself, may be exercised to its utmost extent, and acknowledges no limitations, other than are prescribed in the constitution." *Gibbons* v. *Ogden*, 9 Wheat. 1, 196 (1824).

court cases of recent years evidenced substantial voting discrimination. The Civil Rights Commission reports could be relied upon for similar information compiled in Georgia, South Carolina, and large sections of North Carolina. Such firm bases for voting rights legislation under the Fifteenth Amendment would be difficult to assail. But what of the appropriateness of a legislative formula which extended its sweep to Alaska and to counties in states such as Arizona, Hawaii, and Idaho? The Supreme Court excused the awkwardly composed formula as it applied to the "few remaining States and political subdivisions," noting that in virtually penalizing such areas, "Congress is clearly not bound by the rules relating to statutory presumptions in criminal cases when it prescribes civil remedies against other organs of government under Section 2 of the Fifteenth Amendment." In other words, the Court was in the difficult position (where it lingered only for the space of a few brief sentences) of arguing that the coverage formula could "appropriately" extend to areas where no significant evidence of Fifteenth Amendment violations was on public record but where the operation of state law was nevertheless to be presumed "guilty" until proved "innocent." This difficulty belies the casual identification the Chief Justice made at three points in his Opinion between the words "appropriate" and "rational." Exposing this defect in the coverage formula is an academic exercise. Before the bar of the Supreme Court, South Carolina was in no position to argue Alaska's case, and Alaska, certain that she could expeditiously reinstate her "tests or devices," registered no protest—nor did Arizona, Hawaii, or Idaho.

The fact that such reinstatement required a petition lodged in a "distant" and single court in the District of Columbia also presented no difficulty to a majority of the Supreme Court. Chief Justice Warren simply retorted to South Carolina's objections along these lines, "We have discovered no suggestion that Congress exceeded constitutional bounds in imposing these limitations on litigation against the Federal Government, and the Act is no less reasonable in this respect." The burden of proof resting on the Section 4(b) area to demonstrate that it has not administered "tests or devices" with an eye to race is a bearable burden, the Court reasoned. The petitioners in any termination plea "need do no more than to submit affidavits from voting officials, asserting that they have not been guilty of racial discrimination through the use of tests and devices during the past five years, and then to refute whatever evidence to the contrary may be adduced by the Federal Government." The Court here seemed to be saying that if the statutory shoe fits, wear it—and if it does not, trying it on for size is not too much to ask.

Justice Black wrote a short, separate Opinion in *South Carolina* v. *Katzenbach* which concurred in part and dissented in part from the Opinion of the Court. Whereas the Chief Justice sustained the coverage formula of Section 4(b) on the conclusion that it was "rational in both practice and theory," Justice Black proceeded on a different tack. He was willing to sustain the suspension of tests and devices in specific localities, not because of any purported "rationality," but rather, he said, because "it is enough for me that Congress by creating this formula has merely exercised its hitherto unquestioned and undisputed power to decide when, where, and upon what conditions its laws shall go into effect." However, what bothered Justice Black was that at least one portion of the new law was, to his way of thinking, not "appropriate" legislation, in that it did not "consist with" what Chief Justice Marshall much earlier had called the "letter and the spirit of the constitution." There was no doubt in Black's mind that the federal government could "invalidate a state law once enacted and operative on the ground that it intrudes into the area of supreme federal power." Justice Black objected to the "termination" procedures applying to Section 4(b) areas because they did not conform to established federal-state relations as he saw them. Anticipating an issue more sharply raised three years later, Justice Black also concluded: "A federal law which assumes the power to compel the States to submit in advance any proposed legislation they have for approval by federal agents approaches dangerously near to wiping the States out as useful and effective units in the government of our country."

A unique provision of the Voting Rights Act relating to literacy tests (Section 4[e]) stimulated significant litigation in 1966. The amendment, sponsored by New York congressmen and based on the Fourteenth Amendment, was intended to guarantee the vote to Spanish-speaking Puerto Ricans in New York. To secure the rights of persons educated in accredited schools in United States territories in which the predominant language is other than English, it was necessary to prohibit the states from requiring such persons to pass literacy tests in English in order to vote. Thus, under the law, anyone who completes the sixth grade (or whatever grade the state requires as evidence of literacy) shall not be denied the right to vote in any election because of his inability to read or write in English.

The Puerto Rican literacy provision of the Voting Rights Act appears on its face to be limited in scope and relatively uncontroversial in its effect. Because it was virtually uncontested in Congress and because it was introduced late in the progress of the voting rights bill over the hurdles of the legislative process, little evidence in support of Section 4(e) is to be found in the hearings, reports, or debates.[33] Nevertheless, when the validity of the New York literacy test requiring a demonstrated ability to read English was considered by the Supreme Court in two cases decided in June of 1966 (*Cardona* v. *Power* and *Katzenbach* v. *Morgan*), an interesting constitutional debate resulted. A revealing range of distinguishable positions about the outer limits of state authority over voter qualifications emerged among members of the Court. At the liberal end of the nine-man bench, Justices Douglas and Fortas stood out as the "judicial activists" by supporting the broadest Equal Protection standards where "fundamental liberties" such as the right to vote are threatened. When Douglas wrote, "the heavier burden which New York has placed on the Spanish-speaking American cannot . . . be sustained . . . ," he was suggesting that under the Equal Protection Clause a state must show a need greater than mere rational policy to justify classifications for voting. In *Cardona* v. *Power*,[34] Justices Douglas and Fortas, speaking in dissent, would have invalidated the New York literacy test on Fourteenth Amendment grounds without reference to the Voting Rights Act of 1965. (The challenge to the state law was initiated by a Spanish-speaking New Yorker before the federal statute was enacted). Justice Brennan's three-paragraph Opinion of the Court remanded the case to a lower court, noting that it was probably moot in view of Section 4(e) of the Voting Act.

Justices Harlan and Stewart occupy the most conservative positions, giving maximum deference to the validity of state voter regulations—"primarily" and "essentially a matter of state concern." Justice Stewart, for example, supported Justice Harlan's dissenting Opinion in *Katzenbach* v. *Morgan*,[35] in which the constitutionality of Section 4(e) was upheld. For Harlan, applying the equal protection standard to New York's literacy test merely required a showing that the state law is "reasonably designed to serve a legitimate state in-

---

33. E.g., see 111 *Cong. Rec.* 10675–88 (May 20), 15666 (July 9), 18490–94 (Aug. 3), 18664 (Aug. 4, 1965), daily eds.; House Judiciary Committee, *Voting Rights Hearings on H.R. 6400*, 89th Cong., 1st sess., 1965, pp. 100–101, 420–21, 508–17.

34. *Cardona* v. *Power*, 384 U.S. 672 (1966).

35. *Katzenbach* v. *Morgan*, 384 U.S. 641 (1966).

terest." New York's policy of "integrating non-English speaking residents into the mainstream of American life" through its English-language literacy test satisfied the requirements of the Fourteenth Amendment for Harlan and Stewart. The middle position set out by Justice Brennan for the majority of the Court in *Katzenbach* v. *Morgan* revealed a posture of deference (informed by the Supremacy Clause of the Constitution) toward the authority of Congress to define the substantive scope of the Fourteenth Amendment where state authority over voting rights is concerned.

John and Christine Morgan were New York City registered voters who brought a suit challenging the validity of Section 4(e) of the Voting Rights Act and seeking an injunction against the Attorney General and the New York City Board of Elections from enforcing the new law. To the delight and surprise of the Morgans two members of the three-judge federal district court agreed that Congress had exceeded its constitutional powers and therefore usurped authority reserved to the states by the Tenth Amendment. The Supreme Court reversed the lower court. Mr. Justice Brennan argued that the Fourteenth Amendment is not the responsibility of the courts alone to enforce. The question as he saw it was this: "Without regard to whether the judiciary would find that the Equal Protection Clause itself nullifies New York's English literacy requirement . . . , could Congress prohibit the enforcement of the state law by legislating under Section 5 of the Fourteenth Amendment?" The answer is supplied by the *McCulloch* v. *Maryland* standard of "appropriate" legislation.

The remainder of Brennan's opinion is based on a retread of Chief Justice Marshall's famous measure of the "appropriate." "Let the end be legitimate, let it be within the scope of the Constitution . . . " Following this incantation, Brennan explained that Section 4(e) was within the scope of the Enforcement Clause because it was a "measure to secure for the Puerto Rican community residing in New York non-discriminatory treatment by government—both in the imposition of voting qualifications and the provision of administration of governmental services. . . ." Because Section 4(e) enables Spanish-speaking New Yorkers better to obtain an equal measure of civil rights and equal protection of the laws, he had little difficulty amplifying Marshall's phrase, "all means which are appropriate, which are plainly adapted to that end. . . ." Justice Brennan concluded: "It was well within congressional authority to say that this need of the Puerto Rican minority for the vote warranted federal instrusion upon any state interests served by the English literacy requirement." According to the balance of Marshall's *dictum*, appropriate legislation must not be constitutionally prohibited "but consist with the letter and spirit of the constitution." In the Opinion of seven members of the Court, no substantial failing in this regard was alleged by the New York challengers of the federal law. Brennan accordingly concluded that Section 4(e) of the Voting Rights Act is appropriate legislation to enforce The Equal Protection Clause of the Fourteenth Amendment and that, by force of the Supremacy Clause of Article VI, the state literacy requirement cannot be enforced insofar as it is inconsistent with the Voting Rights Act of 1965.

Strained and unprecedented judicial rationalizing? Yes, and more. The unexpected bonus Congress derived from its poll tax and literacy test provisions in the Voting Rights Act is that the Court has responded with important state papers explaining and justifying these programs and in the process has lodged in Congress broad powers of supervision over the electoral process. This tendency was given further impetus in 1969 when the Supreme Court in several cases took up the Voting Rights Act and gave it a broad reading.

Gaston County v. *United States* involved an effort of a Section 4(b) area to reinstate its literacy tests.[36] A declaratory judgment action was instituted before a three-judge district court in the District of Columbia. Gaston County made the necessary effort to show that for five years prior to the filing of the action no test or device was used in a racially discriminatory way. Denying the County's request, Judge Wright ruled that, irrespective of whether the literacy requirement was evenhandedly administered, it had the effect of discriminating on account of race because "Negroes of voting age in Gaston County were, as children, denied a public education equal to that provided white children." Accordingly, the court concluded that "*any* literacy test imposed upon Negroes as a precondition to voting would have the effect of abridging the right of many Negroes to vote on account of race or color," in the North Carolina locale.

Before the Supreme Court on appeal in 1969, Gaston County argued that the District Court was erroneous. The County said that as a matter of statutory construction and legislative history where the Voting Rights Act was concerned, the Court could not consider past practices of educational discrimination in determining whether its literacy test had the effect of unfairly denying the vote. Also, what-

36. *Gaston County* v. *United States*, 395 U.S. 285 (1969).

ever may have been the situation in the past, the County asserted that it had not fostered discrimination in education or voting in recent years. Justice Harlan wrote the Opinion of the Supreme Court and responded directly to these contentions. First, he declared that Judge Wright's Court had properly taken judicial notice of Gaston County's dual school system. This was consistent with the legislative history of the Voting Rights Act, in that committee reports had noted a causal relationship between unequal educational opportunities and effective use of the franchise. To this point, the Brief for the United States had offered elaborate evidence and satisfied the District Court that Gaston County Negro schools "were of inferior quality in fact as well as law." Justice Harlan asserted that the Voting Rights Act had attempted to overcome the link between inferior schooling and the deprivation of an equal chance to pass literacy tests. He ruled that, in an action to end the suspension of voting tests under the act of 1965, "it is appropriate for a court to consider whether a literacy or educational requirement has the 'effect of denying the right to vote on account of race or color' because the State . . . has maintained separate and inferior schools for its Negro residents who are now of voting age." With regard to Gaston County's recent history of equal educational opportunities, Harlan noted that "today's Negro youth" will be the beneficiaries, but this improvement "does nothing for their parents." The result of a new system of re-registration making use of an "impartially" administered literacy test "would serve only to perpetuate these inequities in a different form."

In the *Gaston County Case*, only Justice Black dissented, and he did so for the reasons he stated in *South Carolina v. Katzenbach*, regarding the procedures prescribed by the Voting Rights Act for bringing to an end the suspension of "tests or devices." In a related matter, the Supreme Court ruled in 1969 on the controversial provisions of Section 5 dealing with the suspension of new voting prerequisites as set by Virginia and Mississippi. *Allen v. Virginia Board of Elections* was the title case in four privately instituted contests involving state election regulations which NAACP Legal Defense Fund lawyers alleged were subject to federal approval.[37] Chief Justice Warren for the Supreme Court decided that private citizens may seek a three-judge court declaratory judgment that a state statute or regulation is subject to the act. Unlike state initiated litigation under the law, private litigants are not restricted to filing suit solely in the

---

37. *Allen v. Virginia State Board of Elections,* 393 U.S. 544 (1969).

District of Columbia. The central issue in *Allen* v. *Board* was whether the new state rules fell within the prohibition of the act that prevents the enforcement of "any voting qualification or prerequisite to voting, or standard, practice, or procedure with respect to voting" unless the state first seeks federal approval. The required approval procedures of Section 5 compel the submission of new election regulations to the Attorney General and/or to the District Court for the District of Columbia. These alternative procedures were not followed by Virginia and Mississippi. At issue were four state-sponsored innovations. A Virginia Board of Elections bulletin instructing election judges to aid illiterates was administratively interpreted to forbid the use of pre-printed sticking labels for a write-in candidate. Three Mississippi laws called for stricter qualifications for the inclusion of independent candidates on the ballot, a change from district to at-large voting for county supervisors, and a change of county educational superintendents from elective to appointive positions.

As diverse as these regulations were, the Chief Justice for seven members of the Court ruled that in each instance the states should have submitted the changes to the Attorney General under the terms of Section 5. The statutory requirement for consulting with Washington regarding any new "practice or procedure with respect to voting" is to be interpreted broadly where the right to vote is concerned, said Warren. He recognized that voting includes "all action necessary to make a vote effective," including changing rules for write-ins, setting new qualifications for independent candidates, and deciding how or whether a local official is to be elected. Finally, the Mississippi appellants, supported by the Solicitor General, asked the Court to set aside the affected elections and to order new ones. Speaking for five members of the Court on the question of relief, Chief Justice Warren refused to take the appellant's course: he preferred to remand the cases to the district courts with instructions to enjoin further enforcement of the enactments pending the outcome of the approval proceedings.

Justice Harlan took exception to the Court's broad view of voting regulations transcending "tests or devices" and extending even to Mississippi's change of certain elections from a districted to an at-large formula. On the three other cases, however, Harlan argued the appropriateness of granting the relief sought by the appellants. Justices Marshall and Douglas would have called for new elections in each case as requested. Justice Black, in dissent, reiterated his position in *South Carolina* v. *Katzenbach*. He insisted that requiring several southern states, Reconstruction-style, to amend their laws contingent upon federal approval violated the constitutional scheme of proper federal-state relations.

One of the new Mississippi laws reviewed in *Allen* v. *Board* changed the deadline for filing a petition as an independent candidate from 40 days before the *general* election to 60 days before the *primary* election. Shortly after the *Allen* decision, a comparable Alabama law was subject to dispute in *Hadnott* v. *Amos*.[38] The Supreme Court ruled that an Alabama statute of 1967 was subject to Section 5 of the Voting Rights Act because it increased the difficulty of filing for candidacy. The Garrett Act barred candidates from the ballot in general elections unless they filed for office by March first, either with a party designation or as independents. Before the Garrett Act, independents were exempted from the deadline, and they were able to get on the ballot after nomination by a mass meeting held in May. Justice Douglas for six members of the Court ruled that the increased barriers placed on independent candidates by the Alabama statute brought the statute under Section 5's approval procedures. Since Alabama had not cleared its new law with federal officials under the terms of the Voting Rights Act, Douglas said that state officials had acted unlawfully in disqualifying independent Negro candidates in four counties. In three counties the disqualifications applied to election victors whom Justice Douglas said should "be treated as duly elected to the offices for which they ran." Involved were candidates allied as the National Democratic Party of Alabama (NDPA, mostly black). In Greene County, the NDPA candidates for local office were left off the ballots altogether. This was done on authority of Probate Judge James Herndon. The Supreme Court declared that Herndon's omission of the NDPA candidates was the result of discriminatory application of the State Corrupt Practices Act. Herndon decided that Wallace-affiliated Democrats need not twice file information regarding nomination procedures and finance committees, while the NDPA should do so. In Greene County, Justice Douglas required a prompt new election at which the NDPA candidates should appear on the ballot. The Supreme Court ruling was given broad constitutional scope. Douglas wrote: "We deal here with Fifteenth Amendment rights which guarantee the right of people regardless of their color or political persuasion to cast their votes effectively and with First Amendment rights

38. *Hadnott* v. *Amos*, 394 U.S. 358 (1969). Justices White and Stewart dissented. Justice Black did not participate because of the involvement of a relative in the Alabama election.

which include the right to band together for the advancement of political beliefs." He concluded with a condemnation of loose discretionary authority under state election laws which cause Fifteenth and First Amendment rights to be subject "to disparate treatment."

THE JUDICIAL TRADITION, NEW REMEDIES, AND SUPPORTS

A section of the Voting Rights Act intended to toughen and multiply available judicial remedies remains to be explored. Section 3(b) of the Voting Rights Act permits a federal court to suspend any test or device when it finds, in a case brought by the Attorney General, that such prerequisites have been used to deny voting rights on account of race or color. Likewise, if a federal court agrees with the Attorney General in a suit brought by him that forbidden practices touching on race have chronically infected the registration and voting process of an area, the court may authorize the use of federal examiners. The functions and procedures used in Section 3(b) and Section 4(b) areas are the same, except that the examiner program instituted as a result of a civil suit is ended only by an order from the court which made the original authorization. During the first four years that the Voting Rights Act was in operation, the Justice Department was sufficiently satisfied with voluntary compliance with the act that examiners were not requested for any area not covered by Section 4(b). The use of examiners and suspension of tests and devices may be expected to take on greater vitality after 1970, when problem areas in the South are released from the automatic sanctions of the Voting Rights Act. Of course, sanctions such as court-ordered examiners could be used anywhere in the country where racial discrimination in voting prevails. Justice Department action along these lines might ease the southern frustration with the appearance of a regionally discriminatory federal law.

The new voting law equipped the courts with updated criminal sanctions to fight obstructions to voting rights. For example, Section 11 authorizes penalties of up to $5,000 in fines as an alternative or in addition to five years imprisonment for a conviction of vote fraud or acts to intimidate or otherwise interfere with voters or those exercising duties under the act.[39] This provision is an important supple-

39. See, e.g., *United States* v. *The Original Knights of the Ku Klux Klan,* 250 F. Supp. 330 (1965), a case involving systematic economic coercion, intimidation, and physical violence in the Bogalusa, Louisiana area.

ment to the general scheme of the law, as one NAACP Legal Defense Fund lawyer said, "because with unfair tests and devices set aside, we expect hostile election officials to fall back on intimidation or fraud tactics, such as the recording of ballots supposedly made by white persons who died, or who moved out of the county, or who simply don't exist. We hope the Justice Department will accept its responsibilities here, though in the past they have been reluctant to 'police' elections."[40] Under the law, the false vote-count prohibitions operate only against state officials, while the intimidation proscriptions apply to anyone. The $10,000 penalty for false or purchased registration is in effect only in federal elections (including the election of the resident commissioner for Puerto Rico and elections in federal territories and possessions).[41]

Special civil remedies are available to aid federal officials in any area where examiners have been appointed. If within 48 hours after the election, any eligible and listed person alleges to an examiner that he has not been permitted to vote, the examiner relays any such well-founded complaints to the Attorney General. The result may be a Justice Department suit in a federal district court with a consequent order that the person's ballot be cast and counted before final certification of the election results. This simple procedure, outlined in Section 12(c) of the Voting Rights Act, has been overlooked occasionally by zealous civil rights leaders who have been needlessly embittered by "federal inaction" as a result of fruitless telephone calls to the Justice Department in Washington. When the Attorney General acts on a complaint sent to him by an examiner, the district court is obliged to make a decision on the matter immediately after the application has been filed. Thus, the complaint procedure is swift, but it does require the orderly filing of complaints through a "chain of command" beginning with the federal examiner.

CIVIL RIGHTS GROUPS AND THE LAW

The full promise of the Voting Rights Act of 1965 to facilitate the meaningful political participation of all groups in American society can be fulfilled only with a heavy investment of private efforts, regis-

40. Interview with Gerald Smith, attorney for the NAACP Legal Defense Fund, June 3, 1967.
41. Section 14(a) of the act makes the jury trial provisions of the Civil Rights Act of 1957 applicable to criminal contempt cases arising under the law.

tration drives, and grassroots organization. In their masterful study of *Negroes and the New Southern Politics,* Donald Matthews and James Prothro end their discussion of black political organizations with the comment that the southern Negroes' greatest political asset is the vote. "They are very poor in other political resources. And in order to maximize the impact of their votes on political decision making, they must organize their votes."[42] The Matthews and Prothro study goes into a detailed analysis of the preconditions for effective organization. These include favorable white attitudes and styles of political leadership, a factional system in which the votes of Negroes may tip the electoral scales enough to make them sought after by one white group or another, a locally heterogeneous society, and a community ethos that does not glorify ante-bellum days. Matthews and Prothro conclude: "Although effective Negro political organizations require conditions that are not present in many—probably most—southern communities today, those that do exist stimulate a larger, more rational, and more concentrated Negro vote than would exist if there were no such organizations."[43]

The Voting Rights Act does not directly affect any of the preconditions found by Matthews and Prothro to facilitate political organization. The law does, nevertheless, touch marginally on organizing activities in at least four ways.

1. Under the statute, political organizing efforts can proceed more freely because harassment is subject to criminal sanctions. Section 11(b) of the Voting Rights Act provides penalties for intimidation of persons "for voting or attempting to vote," and "for urging or aiding any person to vote or attempting to vote." This law has been supplemented by a provision of the Civil Rights Act of 1968 which lays down criminal penalties for intimidation of persons engaging in "voting for elective office, or qualifying or acting as a poll watcher or any legally authorized election official, in any primary, special or general election." Although the statute of 1968, with its focus on protecting political candidates does not expressly cover campaign assistants, the law of 1965 is broad enough to cover private registration and civil rights workers involved in "urging or aiding any person to vote." Justice Department efforts remain somewhat frustrated in supplying such protection from intimidation and economic harassment because of the difficulties of proving the motive of the defen-

42. Donald R. Matthews and James W. Prothro, *Negroes and the New Southern Politics* (New York: Harcourt, Brace and World, 1966), p. 234.
43. *Ibid.,* p. 235.

dant. Department lawyers concede that the criminal sanctions against interference with private groups involved in election activities have "more bark than bite" because it remains more difficult to win verdicts from southern juries than an injunction from a district court judge (the law of 1968 does not provide for civil actions for damages or injuctive relief).

In 1968, the Civil Rights Commission concluded that the mere threat of criminal and civil sanctions embodied in the Voting Rights Act had a significant impact in deep-South states. In its report the commission said:

Since the passage of the Voting Rights Act and the assignment of Federal examiners to many counties where Negroes had experienced the greatest hardships in attempting to register, there have been fewer incidents of intimidation related to voter registration.[44]

According to Alexander Heard, there has been a rapid growth of southern Negro associations devoted to organizing and encouraging political activity.[45] The members of such groups are the chief beneficiaries of the protective features of the Voting Rights Act: they may conduct their voter registration drives without discrimination, intimidation, or economic reprisals from public officials or private individuals. Reliance on these new federal safeguards has been acknowledged by the Southern Christian Leadership Council and the Southern Regional Council. Vitally affected is the work of local groups such as the Tuskegee Civic Association and the Greenville Voter Education Project, to name only two examples among hundreds. The book *Climbing Jacob's Ladder* (1967) gives a first-hand account of the Voter Education Project (VEP) of the Southern Regional Council.[46] In 1968, VEP sponsored registration drives in 106 southern communities, often in conjunction with the local chapter of the NAACP. The significance of such activity was underscored by Matthews and Prothro in 1965:

44. Commission on Civil Rights, *Political Participation*, p. 155. See also chap. 7.

45. Alexander Heard, *A Two-Party South?* (Chapel Hill: University of North Carolina Press, 1952).

46. Pat Watters and Reese Cleghorn, *Climbing Jacob's Ladder* (New York: Harcourt, Brace and World, 1967), pp. 244–48. On the first anniversary of the Voting Rights Act, the VEP publicity and education program was associated with 100,000 registrations. The VEP reported the highest black registration figures for counties where examiner and VEP programs coincided. Next were counties with examiners, followed by counties with VEP programs only.

About 10.5 percent of the voting-age Negroes in the South belong to political organizations and associations—most commonly the NAACP. Only 2.5 percent of the whites are similarly involved. Thus we find that, at this extremely demanding level, Negroes in the South participate more than do Southern whites.[47]

2. Beyond selling six-cent memorial "Register and Vote" postage stamps, the federal government has abstained from "get out the vote" campaigns. These have customarily been the province of political parties and private groups such as the League of Women Voters. The Voting Rights Act does not depart from this tradition and leaves with such groups the responsibility to stimulate voter participation. (Yet the Voting Assistance Act of 1965 requires the Defense Department to publicize state and federal election requirements among members of the armed services.) Where Section 4(b) Areas under the Voting Rights Act are concerned, the customary "hands off" policy has created some difficulties. The chief problem grows out of the reluctance of federal listing officials to publicize their presence in a community or to encourage the previously disfranchised to vote. Thus, the Justice Department squelched the suggestion made by the Office of Hearing Examiners that notices concerning the listing program be mailed to all residents of the area. Press notices and posted announcements in or near examiner offices have been used instead. The result has been that the burden of "passing the word" in areas where federal listing is available falls chiefly on ministers and civil rights workers.[48] Where no such network is fabricated, the critical problem is whether local black leaders have received accurate information about the listing program. A communications impasse may be compounded further by the folk-practice—documented by Matthews and Prothro—that among southerners, "almost all political talk takes place within racial groups, and very little between them."[49] Of course, word of mouth communication is particularly necessary in areas of high illiteracy. One possibility for a federal solution was voted down by Congress in 1967 when it amended the Economic Opportunity Act to prohibit the use of funds or personnel (VISTA

47. Matthews and Prothro, *The New Southern Politics*, p. 52. See also, William Keech, *The Impact of Negro Voting* (Chicago: Rand McNally, 1968), Chap. 3.

48. See Fayette County Project Volunteers, *Step by Step* (New York: The Norton Library, 1965), p. 70.

49. Matthews and Prothro, *The New Southern Politics*, p. 41.

and poverty program workers) in connection with "any voter registration activity."

3. In many states, including Alabama, each candidate for public office is given the right to have election observers at every polling place. For the observers chosen by Negro candidates in the May 1966 Alabama primary election, the NAACP Legal Defense Fund drew up a mimeographed pamphlet entitled "Instructions to Poll Watchers." Many of these observers were civil rights workers. Typical of the suggestions made there was this instruction:

When the polls close, STAY THERE. There is not supposed to be a break. The inspectors are required to start counting the ballots immediately. You have a right to inspect the ballots as they are being counted. The total number of votes tallied by the inspectors should be the same as your private count of the number of Negro and white voters who have gone into the voting booths. If there is a large difference, notify your people immediately. Do not leave until you have seen the ballots all sealed up and given to the returning officer.[50]

Under Section 8 of the Voting Rights Act, the Civil Service may assign, at the request of the Attorney General, one or more persons to act as poll watchers in areas where the examiner program is in effect. The federal poll watcher and examiner programs are so wedded by the law that where a need for observers is apparent, the Attorney General may have to call for unnecessary (but legally permissible) listing procedures in order to justify the use of election observers. Table 6–5 indicates the scope of the Observer Program through 1968.

The Civil Service provides the personnel for both programs. That agency has followed a strict policy of not using civil rights workers as examiners, hearing officers, or observers. According to William C. McCutcheon who was Examiner in Charge until late 1967, the Civil Service has avoided close working relations with civil rights groups. "Unlike a party candidate's poll watcher, our observers are all subject to the Hatch Act. What's more, we have to maintain a nonpartisan reputation. That incidentally is why the Civil Service was picked for this task. To ensure nonpartisanship, we recruit observers, exam-

50. "Instructions to Poll Watchers" (New York: NAACP Legal Defense Fund, 1966, mimeographed), pp. 3–4. Voiding a local Georgia election and requiring a new contest was the relief granted where a Negro candidate's poll watcher was physically attacked by an election official. *Bell* v. *Southwell,* 376 F.2d 659 (1967).

Table 6–5   *Elections Given Observer Coverage (1965–68)**

ELECTIONS WITH FEDERAL OBSERVERS	NO. OF COUNTIES DESIGNATED FOR EXAMINERS	NO. OF COUNTIES WITH OBSERVERS	NO. OF OBSERVERS
Alabama			
1966	12 out of 67	7	357
1966	13	7	382
1966	13	7	84
1968	13	4	98
Georgia			
1966	1 out of 159	1	22
Louisiana			
1966	6 out of 64	6	195
1966	6	5	111
1966	6	5	91
1967	9	5	193
1967	9	2	58
1968	9	2	34
1968	9	1	18
1968	9	3	55
Mississippi			
1966	24 out of 82	14	205
1966	25	14	216
1967	34	27	588
1967	34	14	331
1967	34	6	139
1968	34	7	140
1968	34	7	115
1968	34	5	109
South Carolina			
1966	2 out of 46	2	102
1966	2	1	56
1968	2	2	58
1968	2	1	36

* Adapted from figures published in Department of Justice, *Annual Report of the Attorney General, 1968* (Washnigton, D.C.: Government Printing Office, 1968), p. 113.

iners and hearing officers from within the Civil Service, and thus we wouldn't use civil rights workers."[51] McCutcheon noted that clarification of the observer's role by litigation had reinforced the utility

51. Interview with William C. McCutcheon, Office of Hearing Examiners, Civil Service Commission, July 5, 1967.

of the office. Under the Voting Rights Act as construed by federal courts, election observers are permitted to enter polling places and note whether listed persons are permitted to vote and to determine whether the votes are being properly tabulated.[52] In the estimate of the Department of Justice, "the federal observer program has had a significant influence in insuring fairness in local elections." This view was based on the results of local elections in selected counties of five states where observers were used in 1966 and 1967 and where some 50 Negro candidates were elected.[53]

4. The fourth way in which the Voting Rights Act touches upon the activities of voter registration workers is not to be found in its provisions and subsections but in its spirit—a spirit of invitation and challenge. The conditions of political freedom for black voters and candidates differ considerably from one area of the South to another. But in those many localities where Negroes are unaccustomed to voting, they cannot be expected to enter political life in numbers comparable to whites without assistance and encouragement. In some southern examiner areas, minorities of Negroes take pride in displaying their newly guaranteed rights by registering with state officials rather than with federal examiners. But even among people of such spirit, back-sliding into nonparticipation may result when examiners, observers, and civil rights workers leave and when disappointing elections return the incumbents of many years.

Virtually unaided by federal power, although protected in their activities under federal laws of 1965 and 1968, civil rights groups and voter registration workers in the deep South are faced with a formidable challenge. In a perspective which overreaches the capacity of the law, it must be understood that these local Negro leaders, college students, and other helpful allies have been involved in trying to lead often illiterate, impoverished, exploited, and intimidated Negroes out of the mental environment of virtual serfdom and into the middle-class habits of civic-minded participation in the political process. Po-

52. A full discussion of federal observers is given in *United States* v. *Executive Committee of the Greene County Democratic Party*, 254 F. Supp. 543 (Ala., 1966). Judge Thomas ruled that Alabama law on the secrecy of the ballot was superseded under the Supremacy Clause of Article VI so that federal observers could view state election inspectors assisting illiterate and other voters requiring the aid of state election inspectors. Cf. *United States* v. *Louisiana*, 265 F. Supp. 703 (1966), *aff'd.* 386 U.S. 270 (1967).

53. Department of Justice, *Annual Report of the Attorney General of the United States, 1967* (Washington, D.C.: Government Printing Office, 1967), p. 179.

litical scientists refer to roughly this procedure as "political socialization."[54] But in the context of black belt counties of the deep South, what is transpiring is nothing less than revolution—and four or five statutes do not make a revolution! Even a Justice Department report conceded that administration of the Voting Rights Act accounted only fractionally for the fact that Negroes registered in Alabama, Georgia, Louisiana, Arkansas, and South Carolina increased from 1965 to 1967 by 75 percent. Attorney General Ramsey Clark said:

This result was accomplished, (1) by the voluntary compliance of many local officials; (2) by the appointment and functioning of federal examiners and observers in problem counties; and (3) by the organized efforts of Negro leaders and groups to stimulate registration.[55]

Political behavior studies consistently reveal a close correlation between low educational and socioeconomic status and low levels of political participation. Most southern blacks have low social status, relatively small incomes, and limited education received in inferior schools. These attributes, Matthews and Prothro write, "are associated with low voter turnout among all populations. The low voting rates of Negroes in the South are, to perhaps a large extent, a result of these factors rather than of direct political discrimination by the white community."[56] These factors—the socioeconomic, cultural, and psychological impediments to full political participation—are the concern of civil rights groups and Negro community leaders. They are especially needed to better literacy levels, to develop channels of political communication, to create the conditions that will raise economic achievements and expectations, and to give expression to the blacks' view of their own self-interest. This is at best a slow and painful process. It may be touched at every point by litigation—ensuring effecting balloting by illiterates,[57] enjoining harassing acts of economic coercion,[58] and guaranteeing the rights of Negro candi-

54. Herbert Hyman, *Political Socialization* (New York: Free Press of Glencoe, 1959).

55. Department of Justice, *Report of the Attorney General, 1967*, p. 178.

56. Matthews and Prothro, *The New Southern Politics*, p. 12. Empirical inquiry into nonlegal influences on Southern Negro voting behavior is the focus of the Matthews and Prothro study.

57. *Morris v. Fortson*, 261 F. Supp. 538 (1966); cf. *Allen* v. *Virginia Board of Elections*, 268 F. Supp. 218 (1967), 393 U.S. 544 (1969).

58. *Paynes v. Lee*, 377 F.2d 61 (La., 1967); cf. *United States v. Harvey*, 250 F. Supp. 219 (La., 1966), judgment for defendant.

dates to non-discriminatory application of state laws.[59] The process may be aided at strategic points by federal officials. But law and those who enforce and administer it are hardly panaceas. "Our overall record of listing is spotty," said one examiner interviewed by the author in June of 1968. He continued:

Except for the first month or so, Negroes have just not been turning out like it was predicted they would. It's not our fault; we know our job. The civil rights boys say we should go out door-to-door and drum up business. But I think its up to the Negroes to show some get-up-and-go and earn the vote by exerting the effort it takes to come here and list with us.

Of course, "get-up-and-go" is born of a tradition of self-reliance not from a history of slavery, and clichés about "drumming up business" are spawned in an upheaval of economic gain not in a stagnant background of "keeping one's place." The law may facilitate black voting in the deep South for those able to overcome the natural defenses of apathy and distrust and for those courageous enough to brave possible intimidation and economic retaliation, but generally only Negroes organized through the private efforts of civil rights groups will achieve power and the advantages that accrue to it. Only where Negro leadership and political organizations are free to develop will blacks be able to sustain a relatively high level of voter registration. On the other hand, the experience of Charles Evers in southern Mississippi shows that Negro registration drives can also shape Negro political organizations and create a leadership group. The struggle for the ballot itself generates morale, a new understanding of shared interests, patterns of cooperation, and communication— and with all of these, a set of politically oriented leaders. Even with votes and organization, southern blacks will still require time to develop skills in forming coalitions with at least some white politicians and voters. During that time, groups such as the Freedom Democratic Party of Mississippi and the NDPA of Alabama may be forced into temporary independence from traditional party loyalties, especially in the absence of close working relations between local political parties and civil rights groups and between the federal government and voter registration workers.

59. *United States* v. *Crook*, 253 F. Supp. 915 (1966); *United States* v. *Executive Committee of Democratic Party of Dallas County*, 254 F. Supp. 537 (1966); *Sellers* v. *Trussel*, 253 F. Supp. 915 (1966); *Hamer* v. *Campbell*, 358 F.2d 215 (1966).

7 Judicial review of state legislative apportionment

This chapter and the one following focus on a recent and, in some quarters, unwelcome offshoot of the Fourteenth Amendment: a hybrid new political right to fair *per capita* representation in state government. The analysis of state legislative apportionment in these chapters is designed to develop four points. (1) The success of apportionment litigation in the 1960s owes a debt to the judicial frame of mind shaped by the logic of earlier right-to-vote cases, notably those involving racial discrimination. (2) The forging of equal protection standards by the Supreme Court in 1964 benefited significantly from the variety of alternative approaches suggested by lower court decisions. (3) The Supreme Court reapportionment decisions since 1964 have been addressed, not to minority rights or even majority rights, but to a new federalized standard of equality for individual rights. (4) Supreme Court rulings of the late 1960s have shown that the Court can remedy some political inequities in the name of affirming individual voting rights. At the same time, the judiciary has not proved itself an apt forum for giving systematic consideration to the overall improvement of the fabric of representative government. The Court has acknowledged the appropriateness of legislatively inspired experimentation.

Apportionment and districting problems have been generated by the fact that twentieth-century America has moved to the city.[1] The theme of dynamic expansion dominated by a continuous pattern of urbanization clearly stands out in the human geography of the United States. In 1790, when Rufus King and James Madison complained of under-representation for "the back country," the population profile of the United States was very different from that of today, as Table 7-1 demonstrates. Material and cultural advances have attended the

Table 7-1   *U.S. Urban and Rural Population, 1790-1970**

YEAR	TOTAL POPULATION	URBAN PERCENT OF TOTAL	RURAL PERCENT OF TOTAL
1790	3,929,000	5.1	94.9
1800	5,308,000	6.1	93.9
1810	7,240,000	7.3	92.7
1820	9,638,000	7.2	92.8
1830	12,866,000	8.8	91.2
1840	17,069,000	10.8	89.2
1850	23,192,000	15.3	84.7
1860	31,443,000	19.8	80.2
1870	38,558,000	25.7	74.3
1880	50,156,000	28.2	71.8
1890	62,948,000	35.1	64.9
1900	75,995,000	39.7	60.3
1910	91,172,000	45.7	54.3
1920	105,711,000	51.2	48.8
1930	122,775,000	56.2	43.8
1940	131,669,000	56.5	43.5
1950	150,697,000	64.0	36.0
1960	178,464,000	70.0	30.0
1970	207,326,000	72.0	28.0

* "Population Projections for the United States," Series P-25, No. 359 (Washington, D.C.: Department of Commerce, 1967), Census Bureau estimate for 1970. In the *United States Summary*, P.C.(1)-1A, the bureau defines "urban" in terms of incorporated communities of 2,500 or more.

1. The literature in this field is extensive. See, e.g., Robert McKay, *Reapportionment* (New York: Twentieth Century Fund, 1965); Gordon Baker, *The Reapportionment Revolution* (New York: Random House, 1966); Royce Hanson, *The Political Thicket* (Englewood Cliffs, New Jersey: Prentice-Hall, 1966); Robert Dixon, Jr., *Democratic Representation, Reapportionment in Law and Politics* (New York: Oxford University Press, 1968).

urbanization of the United States, but a host of social, legal, and political challenges has also arisen. One of the most vexing questions has been malapportionment resulting from population shifts, which has given rise to voting districts differing greatly in the size of their electorates. Repeatedly, the result has been that the ballots of the residents of growing urban and suburban areas are compromised. One legislator is given a large constituency while another answers to fewer voters. From the constituent's viewpoint, the vote of one man may become worth many times that of another.

THE TRADITIONAL LOGIC OF VOTING RIGHTS LAW

When the state legislative apportionment case of *Baker* v. *Carr* was argued before the Supreme Court in 1961, the petitioners were supported by a strong *amicus curiae* brief from the Justice Department. The Solicitor General relied upon Justice Stone's comment that "it is proper for the Court to look closely where [a] statute affects the right to vote."[2] The right after all is fundamental "because preservative of all rights."[3] The Government brief insisted that constitutionally offensive racial discrimination against voters was akin to the geographically discriminatory Tennessee apportionment plan which made the vote of some citizens worth a fraction of the value of others. Building on this line of reasoning, the Justice Department asserted that "the right to be free from gross discrimination in the selection of a State legislature is a federal right protected by the Fourteenth Amendment."[4] The claim had a certain surface appeal, but did it have roots in the law sufficiently deep to prevail?

Tennessee passed an apportionment act in 1901. Since that time, population shifts had been so great that the number of representatives assigned to an area often bore no rational or definable relation to the number of constituents in the area. For example, the ballot of a Tennessee voter in south-central Moore County (population 2,340) was worth 23 times the value of a ballot for a state legislator in Shelby County (population 312,345, including the city of Memphis); one vote in Stewart or Chester County was worth nearly eight times a single vote in Knox County. With each county having only one

2. *Skinner* v. *Oklahoma*, 316 U.S. 535 (1942).
3. *Yick Wo* v. *Hopkins*, 118 U.S. 356 (1886).
4. *Brief for the United States as Amicus Curiae on Reargument*, Baker v. Carr, 369 U.S. 186 (1962), pp. 21–22.

spokesman in the lower house of the legislature, and with comparable inequalities affecting the upper house, legislation reflected the geographical weighting of representation. Thus Moore County enjoyed 17 times greater appropriations-per-vehicle from state motor fuel taxes than Shelby County.

The set of facts described above formed the basis for a courtroom challenge with no precedent in any federal tribunal that would assure a successful remedy. Fourteenth Amendment standards of fairness, said to be involved in state legislative apportionment, had been developed for other areas of state law such as economic regulation and racial discrimination. Under the first category, states have traditionally enjoyed wide discretion to impose reasonable classification schemes on economic and social welfare programs. In the regulation of the "police power" areas of health, wealth, and public morals, state laws are generally conceded a strong presumption of constitutionality by reviewing courts.[5] But where basic civil rights are concerned, the Fourteenth Amendment, according to traditional jurisprudence, calls for a different approach. Where state laws touch upon civil rights, the Equal Protection Clause may operate to overcome the presumption of constitutionality—that is, to demand strict judicial scrutiny of the state standards set. Rigorous defense of the statute or state policy may be required to disprove any taint of the arbitrary or the invidiously discriminatory. Thus the equal protection requirement has generally served to forbid any classification system based on race and outlaws all forms of state-supported racial discrimination.

Racial and Geographical Discrimination

If malapportionment challenges asserted on Fourteenth Amendment grounds had had no satisfactory day in court, voting rights cases involving race pointed to a relevant rule: where there is voting there should be equality. Analogies between racial and geographical discriminations by state laws were helpful to the cause of those challenging representation schemes, and because such analogies were linked by the same basic right, they were not difficult to develop. According to the brief which Solicitor General Archibald Cox presented to the Supreme Court in *Baker* v. *Carr*, there was really no substantive difference between voting rights abused on account of race and "the refusal to count at full value votes cast by hundreds of thousands of

5. See, e.g., *Florida Avocado Growers* v. *Paul*, 373 U.S. 132 (1963). Cf. *Morey* v. *Doud*, 354 U.S. 457 (1957).

Negroes and whites in certain Tennessee counties."[6] Of course, the reference to "Negroes and whites" was included in the argument, not to insert an unwarranted racial note into the complaint, but to suggest that voting classifications by geography, like unfair race distinctions in state voting laws, should be remedied by court action under the Fourteenth Amendment.

Recall that the Equal Protection Clause had served in the *Nixon Cases* to help to eliminate the white primary in Texas.[7] Furthermore, nothing in the Fourteenth Amendment suggests that its "thou shalt nots" are exhausted by discrimination by race. It is then a short step to say that invidious and irrational distinctions between residents of a state on the basis of geographical location are not insulated from the prohibitions of the Fourteenth Amendment. The *Nixon Cases* show that the Equal Protection Clause is capable of sheltering those who lack political power against arbitrary discrimination. The Tennessee voters who complained of state legislative malapportionment in *Baker v. Carr*, according to the Solicitor General, were no different in their claim than Dr. Nixon, who successfully scored racial discrimination under Texas law. The violations of the Fourteenth Amendment asserted in the Texas and the Tennessee cases involved private wrongs directly affecting the complainants and others similarly situated. The two kinds of cases, according to the argument, asserted voting rights that are constitutionally protected by the Fourteenth Amendment and are therefore enforceable in the federal courts.[8]

In the complexity of state regulations and legislative reluctance to reform prior to the Supreme Court decision in *Baker v. Carr* a pattern was evident: acreage was favored in many state legislatures at the expense of people. Pressures for reform, reflected in the increasing volume of law review articles and litigation to challenge malapportionment, crested with the high tide of urbanization in the 1950s and 1960s. In all 50 states under-representation of urban voters seriously undermined responsible state and local government, particularly by allowing legislatures to ignore the pressing urban needs.[9] Promi-

6. *Brief for the United States as Amicus Curiae* (upon first argument, 1960, *Baker* v. *Carr*), p. 10.

7. *Nixon* v. *Herndon*, 273 U.S. 536 (1927); *Nixon* v. *Condon*, 286 U.S. 73 (1932).

8. *Brief on Reargument, Baker* v. *Carr*, p. 51.

9. See Paul David and Ralph Eisenberg, *Devaluation of the Urban and Suburban Vote: A Statistical Investigation of Long-Term Trends in State Legislative Representation* (Charlottesville: University of Virginia Bureau of Public Administration, 1961), I.

nent among these urban needs were the housing, employment, and educational requirements of minority groups.[10] Civil rights and race relations difficulties during the 1950s and 1960s have demanded high priorities in national attention. In these areas the Supreme Court, particularly beginning with the *School Desegregation Cases* of 1954, has taken notable initiatives to provide legal solutions framed in terms of individual rights guaranteed by the Fourteenth Amendment. This chapter in judicial history, plus the record of judicial vindication of voting rights in cases of racial discrimination, provided malapportionment critics an arsenal of tested legal weapons and a public primed by past decisions to view the courts as defenders of individual rights.

Borrowing from civil rights developments, litigants who pressed their equal protection claims against state malapportionment did not hesitate to read into the Civil Rights Act of 1957 an answer to the traditional assertion of "no jurisdiction." The act of 1957 could be understood to state a national policy that, whatever disagreements existed about other civil rights, the right to vote should be afforded federal protection to the fullest extent and that protection should chiefly take the form of court action. The Civil Rights Act added to the *United States Code* the proposition (repetitious of Title 42, Section 1983) that federal district courts should have original jurisdiction over civil rights cases brought to secure equitable relief "for the protection of civil rights, including the right to vote."[11]

Electoral Problems and "Political Questions"

Why should the same courts that had done so much for black voting rights default in legislative apportionment cases charging violation of voting rights? Why should the Supreme Court that had ruled fraudulent vote tabulating and ballot box stuffing unconstitutional because such practices devalued votes later refuse to hear malapportionment cases involving a similar dilution of ballot value?[12] A three-judge district court reviewing *Baker* v. *Carr* in 1959 agreed that the allegations were proved that the average value of the plaintiffs' votes was worth one-tenth that of others in the state.[13] To the

10. Thus it is not surprising that groups such as the American Jewish Congress and the NAACP Legal Defense and Educational Fund combined with the American Civil Liberties Union to present an *amicus curiae* brief in *WMCA Inc.* v. *Lomenzo*, 377 U.S. 633 (1964) and a companion apportionment case, *Maryland Committee for Fair Representation* v. *Tawes*, 377 U.S. 656 (1964).

11. 28 U.S.C. 1343(4).

12. See *United States* v. *Classic*, 313 U.S. 299 (1941); *United States* v. *Saylor*, 322 U.S. 385 (1944).

13. *Baker* v. *Carr*, 179 F. Supp. 824 (M.D. Tenn., 1959).

judges this constituted an "evil" that was "serious" and one which "should be corrected without delay." The court then refused to remedy the "evil" they had found and dismissed the case. The reason for such judicial retreat was the authority of Justice Frankfurter's Opinion in *Colegrove* v. *Green*, decided in 1946.[14] To Frankfurter, the remedial course of action urged by those disfavored by popularly unequal districting could not be granted by a federal court. Such plaintiffs asked for relief as though they had suffered judicially remediable personal wrongs. The Illinois congressional districting statute questioned in *Colegrove* was said by Frankfurter to be a complaint about the scheme of representative government not a voters' rights case. His decision implied that districting and apportionment cases, no matter what the wording of the complaint involved, can rest on no federal constitutional right except one based on the "guaranty" of a republican form of government. But according to Frankfurter, Article IV, Section 4 of the Constitution, which assures the states of a "Republican form of Government," is not enforceable through the courts. Cases under that provision had traditionally been said to involve "political questions," meaning that the resolution of conflicts involving schemes of representation must come from the legislature and the executive, i.e., from the "political departments" elected by the voters. It is to them, not the courts, that the voters must look to solve the delicate and complex problems of drawing the lines of political subdivisions and parcelling out among them a predetermined number of representatives. According to a nineteenth-century precedent on which Frankfurter relied heavily, one cannot bring into question before the bar of a court the very legitimacy of a state's government, questioning the constitutionality of its entire structure, personnel, and laws. This was the upshot of *Luther* v. *Borden*, the 1848 case involving the rival claims of two governments, both of which purported to rule Rhode Island under sharply different constitutions during the Dorr Rebellion.[15]

To sidestep the "political questions" barrier, the complainants in malapportionment cases rarely went so far as to question the legitimacy of their state governments. The lesson to avoid such a broadside attack had been taught years earlier in the Fifteenth Amendment case of *Giles* v. *Harris*, in which the Negro plaintiffs tried to recover use of their voting rights by challenging the constitutionality of the entire

14. *Colegrove* v. *Green*, 382 U.S. 549 (1946).
15. *Luther* v. *Borden*, 7 How. 1 (1848).

Alabama government.[16] Justice Holmes dismissed the complaint for want of jurisdiction. The moral for voting rights litigants was that they should aim lower to score high. It was not necessary to pit the limited power of the courts against the entire apparatus of a *de facto* state government in order to vindicate individual rights.

The briefs in apportionment cases were generally narrowly framed to prevent state officials from conducting future elections in a manner that would deprive them of their full ballot rights.[17] Apportionment cases brought under the Fourteenth Amendment were therefore as different from *Luther* v. *Borden* as were the rulings resting on the Equal Protection Clause in the white primary cases. In one such case, Justice Holmes characterized an argument which sought to equate claims pertaining to electoral matters with "political questions" as "little more than a play on words."[18]

The *Colegrove* case involved congressional districting, although Justice Frankfurter's opinion there served for succeeding courts as sufficient authority to immunize state legislative apportionment from judicial inquiry. The Court Opinion in *Colegrove*—or Frankfurter's rationale that districting questions should not be decided upon by the judiciary—was cited over the next fifteen years in the Supreme Court as reliable precedent for the tribunals to refuse to hear or rule on the merits of apportionment contests.[19] For example, in *Cox* v. *Peters* in 1952, involving an attack on Georgia's county unit laws, and in *Remmey* v. *Smith*, involving a suit in the same year to compel reapportionment of the Pennsylvania legislature, the appeals were simply dismissed because they were said to lack any substantial question involving federal law. Likewise, when a challenge to the legislative apportionment of Tennessee was first appealed to the Supreme Court in *Kidd* v. *McCanless*, the challenge to the state statute of 1901 was dismissed on the authority of *Colegrove* v. *Green*.

16. *Giles* v. *Harris*, 189 U.S. 475 (1903).

17. In *Kidd* v. *McCanless*, the Supreme Court of Tennessee expressed the fear that sustaining a legal challenge to the existing apportionment act would leave Tennessee without a legislature to enact a new apportionment act; 200 Tenn. 273, 292 S.W.2d 40 (1956).

18. *Nixon* v. *Herndon*, 173 U.S. 536, 540 (1927).

19. *Cook* v. *Fortson*, 329 U.S. 675 (1946); *Truman* v. *Duckworth*, 329 U.S. 675 (1946); *Colegrove* v. *Barnett*, 330 U.S. 804 (1947); *Tedesco* v. *Board of Supervisors of Elections*, 339 U.S. 940 (1950); *Remmey* v. *Smith*, 342 U.S. 916 (1952); *Cox* v. *Peters*, 342 U.S. (1952); *Anderson* v. *Jordan*, 343 U.S. 912 (1952); *Kidd* v. *McCanless*, 352 U.S. 920 (1956); *Radford* v. *Gary*, 352 U.S. 991 (1957); *Hartsfield* v. *Sloan*, 357 U.S. 916 (1958); *Mathews* v. *Handley*, 361 U.S. 127 (1959).

In several of these cases in which the high court took a "hands off" position on state legislative apportionment, Justices Douglas and Black dissented. An important example drawing the dissenters' fire was *South* v. *Peters* in 1950, where a majority of the nine-man bench refused to hear or decide upon objections leveled against the Georgia county unit system, which projected inequalities in the legislature to state-wide and congressional primary elections.[20] Under the system, which particularly disfavored urban Negro voters, each county was allotted from two to six electoral or "unit" votes which went to the candidate receiving the most votes in the county. Although the majority of the bench had refused to see that any substantial question of federal law or rights was involved, Justice Douglas in his dissent stressed that federally protected voting rights in fact formed the cornerstone of the complaint. Where such rights are concerned, "geographical and racial discrimination are equally onerous." Joined by Justice Black, Mr. Justice Douglas concluded that an unequal voice in elections and a complete denial of participation in an election "are of the same offensive order."

Civil rights and voting rights law converged in 1959 in the Tuskegee districting case of *Gomillion* v. *Lightfoot*.[21] Justice Frankfurter drafted the Court's ruling which struck down an Alabama attempt to redraw the boundary lines of a political subdivision because the state could show no rational justification in reply to Professor Gomillion's claim of racial discrimination. Justice Frankfurter was careful to distinguish the holding from his opinion in *Colegrove* where the "political questions" doctrine was said to stand in the way of judicial scrutiny of the fairness of districting. Justice Frankfurter noted that special constitutional considerations are involved where voting rights are shown to be debased by racial discrimination. He insisted on drawing a line between districting cases invoking the Fourteenth Amendment and Negro voting cases involving the Fifteenth Amendment. Generalizations applying to race cases must not be applied out of context without regard to variant controlling facts, Frankfurter cautioned. Justice Whittaker wrote a concurring Opinion in the Tuskegee case in which he expressed the view that "the decision should be rested not on the Fifteenth, but rather on the Equal Protection Clause of the Fourteenth Amendment." Inherent in Whittaker's opin-

20. *South* v. *Peters*, 339 U.S. 276 (1950).
21. *Gomillion* v. *Lightfoot*, 364 U.S. 339 (1959).

ion was the idea that the Fourteenth Amendment protects persons from arbitrary discrimination no less than the Fifteenth does, and unfair geographical distinctions are scarcely less invidious and constitutionally offensive than discrimination based upon race. Notwithstanding Justice Frankfurter's disclaimer that the facts in the *Gomillion* case were wholly different from the considerations which controlled *Colegrove*, critics of state malapportionment took encouragement from the ruling in the Alabama districting case. Courts which could remedy racial gerrymanders should have little more difficulty in remedying the ordinary political gerrymander associated with malapportionment.

In the *Gomillion* case, it was possible to repair the damage done voting rights by falling back upon the previous law establishing Tuskegee's boundary, once enforcement of the new gerrymander was enjoined. In *Colegrove* v. *Green*, the Court could have called for elections-at-large if it had invalidated the challenged districts. Another remedial technique was illustrated by a case arising in New Jersey in 1960. The State Supreme Court held that it had the "authority and duty" to act in cases of malapportionment. After noting numerous decisions by other state tribunals in which this same responsibility was accepted, the New Jersey Supreme Court held:

> If by reason of passage of time and changing conditions the reapportionment statute no longer serves its original purpose of securing to the voter the full constitutional value of his franchise, and the legislative branch fails to take appropriate restorative action, the doors of the courts must be open to him. The law-making body cannot by inaction alter the constitutional system under which it has its own existence.

Here was a clear statement of the power of a court to act.[22] But what type of remedial action could it take? The New Jersey court stated its intention to postpone drafting any particular relief. Instead, it chose to retain jurisdiction until the legislature had been given an opportunity to reapportion under the 1960 census. Nevertheless, when the legislature failed to act, the court specified that it would frame an appropriate remedy on February 1, 1961, by 5 p.m. The governor responded by convening the legislature. At 3:13 p.m. on February 1,

22. *Asbury Park Press, Inc.* v. *Wooley*, 161 A.2d 705 at 711 (1960). See also *Magraw* v. *Donovan*, 159 F. Supp. 901; 163 F. Supp. 184; 177 F. Supp. 803 (D. Minn., 1959); and *Dyer* v. *Kazuhisa Abe*, 138 F. Supp. 220 (D. Hawaii, 1956).

the legislature, which had been called in special session, enacted a re-apportionment act. At 5 p.m. the state Supreme Court issued this statement:

> We are informed that the legislature has adopted an apportionment bill which the Governor has signed. Litigation, accordingly, appears to be moot and hence the prepared opinion will not be filed.

THE APPORTIONMENT LANDMARK OF *Baker* v. *Carr*

In 1961, New Jersey was not alone in grappling with apportionment and districting problems. State and federal courts across the country were burdened that year with an unprecedented number of cases involving such voters' suits. The question of whether the federal courts could entertain apportionment disputes raising questions of constitutional law was ripe for a definitive answer. The holding of the Supreme Court in the Tennessee apportionment case was above all timely.

Baker v. *Carr* involved a complaint on the part of 11 Tennessee voters and tax-payers that they suffered a "debasement of their votes" and were thereby denied the equal protection of the laws guaranteed to them by the Fourteenth Amendment. They asserted that their grievance resulted from the continued operation of a 1901 state statute "arbitrarily and capriciously" apportioning the seats of the General Assembly among the 95 counties of Tennessee. The injustice that they said they suffered was the consequence of legislative failure over a fifty-year period to reapportion state representation according to the requirements of the Tennessee constitution. The effect of the failure was amplified by substantial growth and redistribution of the state's population. Under federal law, the voters sued state election officials who admitted the discriminatory purpose of the 1901 statute. Upon questioning, counsel for the election officials even conceded that the appellants and others similarly situated (the majority of the state's voters) were the acknowledged victims of the apportionment. In response to this set of facts, however, the state officials contended that the issue was purely and peculiarly political in nature. Accordingly, no court should intervene, on the grounds that to do so would violate court precedent and the principle of the separation of powers.[23]

23. *Statement in Opposition to Appellants Statement of Jurisdiction* (*Baker* v. *Carr*), p. 21.

In Tennessee, the effect of population shifts and of the failure of the legislature to take account of demographic changes was to reduce by nine-tenths the average weight of the vote of those who brought suit in comparison with the value of the ballot in other areas. This situation had been permitted to develop by the legislature even though the Tennessee constitution required that the state allocate representation among the counties or districts at least every ten years according to the number of qualified voters in each such area. The 50 representatives elected by one-third of the voting population had demonstrated over the years their unwillingness to surrender their seats, the predictable result of any updated apportionment. Significantly the existing apportionment operated so that 60 percent of the voters could elect only 36 of the 99 members of the lower house,[24] and no reapportionment bill since 1901 had received more than 36 votes in that chamber. Sixty-three percent of the voters could elect only 13 of the 33 members of the state senate, and no reapportionment bill since 1901 had ever received more than 13 votes in that body. In an earlier appeal, the Tennessee Supreme Court had denied relief to voters against the same apportionment act; federal courts followed a similar course of action.[25] Urban voters could not circumvent the legislature by calling a constitutional convention because in Tennessee only the legislature could call such a convention, and the state constitution made no provision for referendum.[26] Judge Miller of the federal district court in the state conceded that the "situation is such that if there is no judicial remedy there would appear to be no practicable remedy at all."[27] By the time *Baker* v. *Carr* reached the nation's highest tribunal on appeal, all other possible avenues of relief had been exhausted.

The United States Supreme Court did not decide that the legislature apportionment of Tennessee was unconstitutional. Justice Brennan,

24. These figures rely on the method for evaluating malapportionment developed by Manning J. Dauer and Robert C. Kelsey, "Minimum Percentage of Population Needed to Elect Majority," 44 *National Municipal Review* 571–75 (Dec. 1955).

25. *Kidd* v. *McCanless*, 292 S.W.2d 40 (1956); *Baker* v. *Carr*, 179 F. Supp. 824 (M.D. Tenn. 1959).

26. Governor J. Howard Edmundson of Oklahoma submitted an *amicus curiae* brief in *Baker* v. *Carr*. He argued that referenda and initiatives are impractical alternative avenues of relief for malapportionment because of the expensiveness of the procedures, the difficulty of explaining and popularizing the complex topic of apportionment, and the lack of compromising and amendatory processes that are ordinarily fundamental parts of the legislative process.

27. *Baker* v. *Carr*, 175 F. Supp. 649 (1958).

speaking for a majority of seven justices, did not consider the merits of the voters' complaint in *Baker* v. *Carr*. What the Court did was to rule unequivocally that federal courts could exercise their judicial power over malapportionment cases. The express holding of the Supreme Court was that a voter's claim that equal protection had been denied by the allegedly discriminatory apportionment of a state legislature presented a judicially manageable claim which could be decided by a federal court. On its face, this was a modest enough assertion, but it was a necessary beginning for the birth of a new body of law. Acting as midwife in this operation, Justice Brennan concerned himself with the questions of jurisdiction, standing to sue, and justiciability, all technical problems long since settled in other types of voting rights case.

The authority of a court to exercise its judicial power in a specific case is called jurisdiction. Tennessee voting officials in *Colegrove* v. *Green* relied on the proposition that the bench lacked jurisdiction; Justice Brennan rejected that proposition as resting on a misunderstanding of the authority of that case. According to Brennan's recounting of the case, a majority of four justices in the Illinois contest "flatly held that there was jurisdiction of the subject matter." Counting Mr. Justice Rutledge's concurring Opinion with Justice Frankfurter's minority Opinion, a majority of the justices concluded that the relief sought should be denied. But Rutledge exempted himself from Frankfurter's view on jurisdiction. Counting Rutledge with the dissenters, then, a majority of the justices participating in *Colegrove* refused to find that there was any want of jurisdiction. The allegation of a violation of the Fourteenth Amendment was said to be sufficient to meet the prerequisites for jurisdiction, unless the claim is "so attenuated and unsubstantial as to be absolutely devoid of merit" or is "frivolous."[28]

In 1918, the Supreme Court said in an election law case that the right to vote is a personal right.[29] Voters who allege facts showing disadvantages to themselves as individuals have such a personal stake in the outcome of the controversy that they are entitled to a hearing and to a federal court decision on their claim. Such, according to Justice Brennan, is the gist of the matter of "standing to sue." Citing the *Classic* and *Saylor* cases, Brennan said that a citizen's right to vote free of arbitrary impairment by state action has been judicially recog-

28. The two quotations respectively are from *Newburyport Water Co.* v. *Newburyport*, 193 U.S. 561 (1904) and *Bell* v. *Hood*, 327 U.S. 678 (1946).
29. *United States* v. *Bathgate*, 246 U.S. 220 (1918).

nized as a right secured by the Constitution, "when such impairment resulted from dilution by a false tally or by refusal to count votes from arbitrarily selected precincts, . . . or by stuffing of the ballot box."[30] The personal stake of the voters in the Tennessee case stemmed from the fact that their right to vote encompassed the right to cast their ballots free of arbitrary impairment by state action and to have their votes counted as cast.

The Opinion of the Court next turned to the problem of whether the case presented was proper for judicial consideration because judicial remedial instruments were at hand—the essence of justiciability. According to Justice Brennan, the issues raised under the Guaranty of a Republican Government Clause have often presented the Supreme Court with "political questions" beyond the scope of the courts to handle but not beyond the reach of the legislature or executive. The courts purportedly could not enforce the Guaranty Clause for absence of a "federal claim" on which basis relief could be granted. But where, as with Baker's claim, the Equal Protection Clause of the Fourteenth Amendment formed the sole basis of questions allegedly political in character, the courts should not invoke the "political questions" doctrine without first making "a discriminatory inquiry into the precise facts and posture of the particular case." The majority of the high bench was thus saying that judicial retreat from "political questions" functions beneficially in a democracy when that tactic serves to place decisions where they can be responsibly decided, and it operates harmfully when it places responsibility nowhere.

The central point of Justice Douglas' concurring Opinion was to make plain the fact that federal courts have frequently intervened to safeguard voting rights. In regard to the weighting of votes through apportionment he observed that one of the traditional tests has been whether a state has made an "invidious discrimination." In view of this standard, he conceded that "universal equality is not the test; there is room for weighting." The question of whether the supposed weighting of votes in Tennessee amounted to "invidious discrimination" was the question returned to the district court for an answer. The concurring Opinions of both Justices Douglas and Clark agreed that "if the allegations in the complaint can be sustained a case for relief is established." Indeed, Justice Clark went so far as to suggest that the Court was delinquent in its obligation because it "refuses to

30. *United States* v. *Classic*, 313 U.S. 299 (1941); *United States* v. *Saylor*, 322 U.S. 385 (1944).

award relief—although the facts are undisputed—and fails to give the District Court any guidance whatever." Though the Opinion of the Court fell short of providing specific relief, Justice Clark evaluated its main thrust as "in the greatest tradition of this Court." He explained:

It is well for this Court to practice self-restraint and discipline in constitutional adjudication, but never in its history have those principles received sanction where the national rights of so many have been so clearly infringed for so long a time. National respect for the courts is more enhanced through the forthright enforcement of those rights rather than by rendering them nugatory through the interposition of subterfuges.

Justice Stewart's brief cautionary note that the Court had merely announced a decision in favor of justiciability tends to deflect attention from the broad dictum of the several Opinions which, at points, appeared to be addressed to the merits of the case. To stress the narrow character of the Court's holding, however, cannot conceal a significant threat of consensus tying the majority and concurring Opinions together. Standing behind Justice Brennan's rather abstract discourse and the concurring Opinions of Justices Douglas and Clark, one can discern a principle of necessity at work. Stated most forthrightly, the underlying and largely unexpressed premise of the majority of the Court was that the discrimination involved in malapportionment was so harmful to a democratic society that it became a judicial imperative to strike at the malady without regard to "political questions." The necessity for judicial action in this field arose from the fact, as Justice Clark said in response to Justice Frankfurter, that the voters were unable to "sear the conscience" of the legislature. Where malapportionment was concerned, the Supreme Court was indeed the court of last resort.

Justice Frankfurter's trenchant dissent, with which Justice Harlan concurred, warned the Court of the entanglements of the "political thicket" and the "mathematical quagmire." Frankfurter dwelt at length on the historical tenet that the equal weighting of votes has not been and is not now required. Perhaps the most telling point which emerges from Frankfurter's scholarly sixty-three page dissent lies in a truth which he cast in Holmesian terms. After comparing the Guaranty Clause of Article IV and the Equal Protection Clause of the Fourteenth Amendment, Frankfurter predicted that judges would have great difficulty with apportionment cases. Their hardest task would be in making decisions which could be accepted as something more than their "private views of political wisdom" about the minimum standards of representation required by the Constitution. To Frankfurter, the *Baker* Opinion amounted to a false promise: judges would disguise their political preferences in terms of inapposite constitutional requirements. He thought it an empty promise as well—a pledge of "empty rhetoric, sounding a word of promise to the ear, sure to be disappointing to the hope. . . ."

Joined by Justice Frankfurter, Justice Harlan in dissent advanced a tenuous case for the rationality of the existing Tennessee apportionment.[31] Harlan expressed certainty that the majority of the Court erroneously accepted the argument pressed at bar that if federal tribunals would assert authority in this field, Tennessee and other malapportioned states might well respond voluntarily to the judicial threat, as the New Jersey legislature had the previous year, with appropriate political action. However, Harlan lamented, "The majority has wholly failed to reckon with what the future may hold in store if this optimistic prediction is not fulfilled." Justices Harlan and Frankfurter were striking at the Court Opinion where it was most vulnerable (largely because of its silence) when they emphasized the great difficulty of formulating standards to answer an important question. That question was: to what extent does the Fourteenth Amendment permit a state to weight one person's vote more heavily than it does another's? Justice Brennan's answer seemed cavalier and inadequate to the dissenters. Brennan wrote:

Judicial standards under the Equal Protection clause are well developed and familiar, and it has been open to the courts since the enactment of the Fourteenth Amendment to determine, if on the facts of the particular case they must, that a discrimination reflects no policy, but is simply arbitrary and capricious.

FORGING RULES OF FEDERAL LAW

Few Supreme Court decisions have spurred such a rush to the court house door as did the Tennessee case. In the year following the Supreme Court's ruling of March 26, 1962, more than 50 reapportionment suits were filed or revived in 32 states. Within ten months after

31. See especially the Appendix to the Opinion of Mr. Justice Harlan, *Baker* v. *Carr*, at 340–49.

Baker v. *Carr*, 10 states called special legislative sessions, and in 14 other states courts cast doubt upon or invalidated apportionment arrangements. When the Supreme Court of the United States in 1964 finally laid down the federal guidelines that apply to state legislative apportionment, the high bench could look back upon and benefit by two years of judicial experience and problem-solving at the lower court level.

The difficulty of greatest constitutional import among the lower courts immediately after *Baker* v. *Carr* was not the matter of remedies, as was widely anticipated in 1962. Positive judicial relief has invariably been postponed by lower courts for at least one legislative session. Deadlines, guidelines, and warnings of apportionment under a court-devised plan or election-at-large have all been used. Litigants have been sometimes asked to develop specific suggestions for a new apportionment plan, and special "masters" appointed by the courts as administrative assistants occasionally receive the same assignment. In some instances, courts have declared the legislature to be impotent to transact any business other than apportionment.

In apportionment cases considered in state and federal courts between 1962 and 1964, persistent attention was focused on the question of standards. The Court Opinion in *Baker* and the concurring Opinions of Justices Douglas and Clark implied that where the equal protection of the laws is concerned, a distinction is necessary between permitted "rational classification" (discrimination justified by reasonable differences) and forbidden "invidious discrimination" (discrimination not reasonably justified and therefore "arbitrary"). In the wake of *Baker* v. *Carr*, lower courts followed their own lights for two years on the meaning of the invidious discrimination test[32] and variously construed it as requiring that an apportionment system have a rational basis.[33]

In making a judgment about whether a particular state apportionment is or is not arbitrary, the post-*Baker* cases reveal that, in the absence of specific Supreme Court guidance which was not to come until 1964, at least three broad avenues of approach were travelled by the lower courts. First, in regard to "rationality," some courts sug-

---

32. For examples see, *Toombs* v. *Fortson*, 205 F. Supp. 248 (D.C., Ga., 1962); *Sobel* v. *Adams*, 108 F. Supp. 316 (D.C., Fla., 1962) and 214 F. Supp. 811 (1963), revd. *Swann* v. *Adams*, 378 U.S. 533 (1964).

33. For examples see, *WMCA Inc.* v. *Simon*, 208 F. Supp. 368 (D.C., N.Y., 1962), revd. *WMCA Inc.* v. *Lomenzo* 377 U.S. 633 (1964); *Simon* v. *La Fayette Parish Police Jury*, 226 F. Supp. 301 (D.C., La., 1964).

gested that a state legislature patterned after the structure of the United States Congress is a legislature for which a *prima facie* case for rational classification may be presumed. The result of this policy, whether it was based on disparities of voting weights in the federal Senate or Electoral College, was to give judicial warrant to substantial inequality of representation in at least one state legislative house. Second, in regard to any numerical equality required by the Fourteenth Amendment, some courts went so far as to suggest the precise mathematical point beyond which inequality of representation became "invidious discrimination." Both of these alternatives were open to criticism in that they appeared to be too obviously arbitrary and inflexible to become serious candidates for a set of guiding principles in apportionment cases to be decided on the basis of federal standards. A third approach, one which appeared to have been widely adopted with different results by the courts, was more pragmatic. It placed primary emphasis on substantial equality, but on a case-by-case basis to allow certain "rational deviations" from such equality. Examples of each approach are discussed below.

The Federal Analogy

"Rationality" is hardly a self-defining term. Should a state legislative apportionment be presumed rational if it, like the United States Senate and House of Representatives, provides in one house for equal representation of political sub-units without regard for population and establishes representation according to population in the other house? One answer was given by a federal district court in Alabama in *Sims* v. *Frink*.[34] In order to break the "stranglehold" of the minority in the legislature, the three-judge court became the first bench actively to reapportion a state. The judges laid down the outlines of a new apportionment that was to remain in effect until the reconstituted legislature should act. The tribunal readily conceded that, under both the state and federal constitutions, neither house need be strictly apportioned on a population basis, but "representation to some extent must be established in both Houses if invidious discrimination in the legislative system is to be avoided." Counsel for the defendants in the *Sims* case argued that any requirement for equality of voting weight in both chambers ignores the historical precedent of the federal legislative system where the Senate is apportioned with reference to the

---

34. *Sims* v. *Frink*, 208 F. Supp. (D.C., Ala., 1962), *aff'd. Reynolds* v. *Sims*, 377 U.S. 533 (1964).

representation of political subdivisions. The court thought that the county did not occupy the same constitutional position in the state that the state holds in the Union. The judges rejected the "federal analogy" argument as a "most superficial examination into the history of the requirement of the federal Constitution."

On the other hand, in Maryland, the State Court of Appeals cited the "federal analogy" as sufficient authority to insist that in the state senate, "greater latitude" concerning population would be permissible. In *Maryland Committee for Fair Representation* v. *Tawes*, the tribunal refused to order senate reapportionment despite major population inequalities represented in that house.[35] The decision emphasized the proposition that it would be pointless to have two chambers if they had identical representation.

In the two years following the Tennessee case, most of the lower courts dealing with challenges to state legislative apportionment entered the unfamiliar area by careful attention to any reference to constitutional standards which could be gleaned from the majority Opinions in *Baker* v. *Carr*. Thus they inferred that to deny the equal protection of the laws, a discrimination in district population must be at least "invidious" or "arbitrary and capricious," or a "crazy quilt without rational basis," or must manifest "irrational disregard of any standard of apportionment." Within the context of these requirements, the "federal analogy" argument urged that relatively equal representation of the political subdivisions of a state, as opposed to equality of population representation, is permissible in at least one chamber. The argument concluded that both the population disparities of the federal Senate and those characteristic of the Electoral College, when implemented in one house of a state legislature, can hardly be described as failing to show a rational basis. The rejoinder, drawn from history and pointing up the fallacy of the analogy, lies in the fact that counties and other subdivisions are creatures of the state and subject to its dissolution, whereas the original thirteen states created the United States.[36]

In 1963, the United States Supreme Court issued an unmistakable hint that arguments by analogy to federal institutions tell us little

35. *Maryland Committee for Fair Representation* v. *Tawes*, 228 Md. 412 (1962), revd. 377 U.S. 656 (1964).

36. The argument is amplified in the *Brief for the United States as Amicus Curiae* (*Maryland Committee* v. *Tawes*, 1964), pp. 80–90; and Robert B. McKay, *Reapportionment and the Federal Analogy* (New York: National Municipal League, 1962).

about the requirements imposed upon the states by the Equality Clause of the Fourteenth Amendment. *Gray* v. *Sanders* did not concern state legislative apportionment.[37] The views expressed by Justice Douglas in the Opinion of the Court are so broad, however, that their relevance to the federal analogy argument seemed (for any observer willing to read between the lines) to spell doom for the legal vitality of the analogy. The Court decided that the county unit system of voting in Georgia state-wide and congressional primary elections was an unconstitutional deprivation of the right of voters to the equal protection of the laws. In ruling that all votes in a state-wide election must have equal weight, Justice Douglas returned to the argument he had advanced years earlier as a dissenter. But in 1963 he spoke for the majority of the Court when he said that for a state to count the votes of whites more heavily than Negroes or to weigh the ballots of men more heavily than women would be uncontestably void. He continued, "How then can one person be given twice or 10 times the voting power of another person in a statewide election merely because he lives in a rural area or because he lives in the smallest rural county?" Douglas concluded:

Once the geographical unit for which a representative is to be chosen is designated, all who participate in the election are to have an equal vote—whatever their race, whatever their sex, whatever their occupation, whatever their income, and wherever their home may be in that geographical unit. This is required by the equal protection clause of the Fourteenth Amendment.

37. *Gray* v. *Sanders*, 372 U.S. 368 (1963). The unit system of voting in Georgia, used only in primary elections, bore some relationship to legislative apportionment. The state constitution required that each of the eight most populous counties should have three representatives in the lower house. The 30 next most populous counties each had two legislators, and the remaining 121 counties were entitled to one representative apiece. By corresponding calculation, each county was assigned six, four, or two units in primary elections, thus giving a dominant voice to the numerous rural counties. The candidate for United States Senator or state-wide office who won majority support in the county was awarded all the county units. On the other hand, candidates for the state legislature needed only to win a plurality of popular votes to gain all the county unit votes. Under the system used in the decisive Democratic primary elections for state wide offices, the choices of candidates for governor or United States Senator were finally made in a run-off primary if no candidate received a majority of county unit votes. The glaring statistical inequity supported by the plan in 1962 permitted one unit vote in Echols county to represent only 938 people while one such vote in Fulton County (Atlanta) stood for 92,721 residents—a 99 to 1 vote-weight ratio.

Thus in *Gray* v. *Sanders*, the Supreme Court sustained a federal court's invalidation of the notorious Georgia election machinery.[38] However, the lower bench had said that a unit vote system would not violate the Equal Protection Clause "if the disparity against any county is not in excess of the disparity that exists against any state in the most recent electoral college allocation" or the variance existing "under the equal proportions formula for representation of the several states in Congress." Justice Douglas' response to the district court's reliance on the federal analogy was unequivocal. He said the "analogies to the electoral college, to districting and redistricting, and to other phases of the problems of representation in state or federal legislatures or conventions" were not pertinent. Douglas reasoned that the electoral college had been included in the Constitution "as the result of specific historical concerns," which had required as the price for state ratification of the Constitution a degree of "inherent numerical inequality." Against this eighteenth-century background, the Court observed that "passage of the Fifteenth, Seventeenth and Nineteenth Amendments show that this conception of political equality belongs to a bygone day, and should not be considered in determining what the equal protection clause of the Fourteenth Amendment requires in a state-wide election." This exposition in the *County Unit Case* was a first step toward consigning the "federal analogy" argument to legal repose. But it was necessarily a measured and rather short step, for the Court was careful to point out that in regard to the question of state or federal legislative districts of unequal size, "we intimate no opinion on the constitutional phases of that problem beyond what we said in *Baker* v. *Carr*." Justice Stewart was joined by Justice Clark in a concurring Opinion which stated: "We do not deal here with the basic ground rules implementing *Baker* v. *Carr*." Justice Harlan, in dissent, criticized the Opinion of the Court's statement that

the concept of 'we the people' under the Constitution visualizes no preferred class of voters but equality among those who meet basic qualifications. . . . The concept of political equality from the Declaration of Independence, to Lincoln's Gettysburg Address, to the Fifteenth, Seventeenth and Nineteenth Amendments can mean only one thing—one person, one vote.

To Justice Harlan, the principle of "one person, one vote" surely "flies in the face of history." He was satisfied that a slight modification of

38. *Sanders* v. *Gray*, 203 F. Supp. 158 (N.D., Ga., 1962).

the Georgia plan could bring it "within the tolerance permitted in the federal scheme." Harlan's views did not prevail, and after the Court's decision in *Gray* v. *Sanders*, it became fanciful after 1963 to attempt to detail a case for the proposition that, although appeals to federal analogies are inadequate to sustain as rational a state-wide election plan, such arguments were sufficient to sustain population inequities in district elections for legislators.

Mathematical Equality

At what point is equal representation so eroded by an apparently rational plan that apportionment may be said to be unfairly discriminatory? Of course, in an ideal state apportionment of a legislature, each district should have the same population. This would be found by dividing the population of the state by the number of representatives. Even if district lines could be drawn so as to cut across county lines, which was disfavored in most states, the ideal can hardly be attained. Is it part of the judicial function to say at what precise arithmetic point an apportionment becomes inequitable? The courts seldom spelled out their views of equal protection requirements in mathematical terms; nevertheless, the Supreme Court of Rhode Island went out on a constitutional limb in *Sweeney* v. *Notte* to specify a rule of mathematical equality. The tribunal asserted: "The dilution of the vote of a majority of electors to one fourth of that enjoyed by others is, in our opinion, so unjust as to be invidiously discriminatory."[39] Equally willing to draw the line somewhere lest it be drawn nowhere were a majority of Michigan judges in *Sholle* v. *Hare.* Invalidating the geographic formula for the state senate because it merely operated to freeze existing districts, they laid down a rule with precision. "When a legislative apportionment provides districts having more than double the population of others, the constitutional range of discretion is violated." The court conceded that "this is not to say less than such 2 to 1 ratio is constitutionally good. It is to say that peril ends and disaster occurs when that line is crossed."[40] The test was supported by reference to the statement in the dissenting Opinion of Justices Douglas and Black in *MacDougal* v. *Green.* With reference to the nomination of presidential electors, the dissenters had

39. *Sweeny* v. *Notte,* 183 A.2d 296, 301 (R.I., 1962). See Edward N. Beiser, "A Comparative Analysis of State and Federal Judicial Behavior: The Reapportionment Cases," 62 *American Political Science Review* 788 (Sept. 1968).

40. *Scholle* v. *Hare,* 367 Mich. 176, 188–89 (Mich., 1962), *cert. denied sub nom. Beadle* v. *Scholle,* 377 U.S. 990 (1964).

said that a "State law giving some citizens twice the vote of other citizens . . . would lack the equality which the Fourteenth Amendment guarantees."[41]

Finding in the Equal Protection Clause some intrinsic and absolute quantitative meaning, as did the courts in Rhode Island, Michigan, and the Supreme Court dissenters in the Illinois case, seems to lend to that provision a definition difficult to rationalize as anything but arbitrary and difficult to justify as a single standard applying to the multivariant conditions among 50 states. Judges in none of the three cases above were able to give any reason for their description of the mathematical tolerances of the Fourteenth Amendment requirement for the equal protection of the laws. Yet what is the alternative? Is it true that once a court is able to conceive a general plan of apportionment to be based on rational factors that the task of the tribunal under the Equal Protection Clause is at an end? Justice Harlan in *Baker* v. *Carr* was able to see rationality even in the Tennessee plan of 1901 as applied in 1961. There the voting weight ratios of legislative district populations extended to an average of ten to one. Obviously, to strike down an apportionment plan only because it seems to be a "crazy quilt without any rational basis" is to establish a permissive standard. Experience seemed to suggest that a strict standard be devised without resorting to a uniform rule of mathematically defined equality of voting rights.[42] At the same time, if those rights were not to be seriously diluted, a principle—if not a mathematical one, then one at least stressing quantitative factors—seemed called for to require substantial population equality among legislative districts.

Rational Deviations

The federal analogy doctrine and rules of mathematical equality precisely defined are the dogmatic polar extremes which many state and federal courts avoided in the two years following *Baker* v. *Carr*. If decisions in the middle range (between the extremes noted) share any approach to the problem of standards it is a difficult one to formulate. As might be expected, a rough pattern of consistency among many of the courts revealed adherence to the proposition that equality

41. *MacDougal* v. *Green*, 335 U.S. 281, 288 (1948). See Chapter 10.
42. Notable efforts to bring mathematical sophistication to the subject were made by Glendon Schubert and Charles Press, "Measuring Malapportionment," 58 *American Political Science Review* 302–27 (Je. 1964); and by Henry F. Kaiser, "A Measure of the Population Quality of Legislative Apportionment," 62 *American Political Science Review* 208–15 (Mar. 1968).

of popular representation is a part of any rational plan of apportionment. But is it the first part?

A suggestion addressed to that question was made by the Solicitor General of the United States when he appeared before the Supreme Court in *Baker* v. *Carr*. The Government's brief asserted that the "starting point must be *per capita* equality of representation. . . . Any serious departure from apportionment according to population . . . is subject to question, although the divergence might also be shown to have a rational justification."[43] Writing in the *American Bar Association Journal*, Solicitor General Cox amplified his point of view and said that serious departures from the standard of numerical equality should be considered "invalid unless shown to have a rational justification."[44] The key word here is "shown." It suggested a procedural device to make as certain as possible that the equality of popular representation should be the "starting point" or the first part of any rational scheme of apportionment. The technique for judging apportionment plans that was suggested in the Solicitor General's article would require that once the plaintiffs in an apportionment case proved the absence of parity in the allotment of representatives on the basis of population in either or both houses, the burden to adduce evidence of other factors rationally explaining the disproportion would then fall upon the defendants. The Solicitor General's argument in *Baker* v. *Carr* conceded that in drafting apportionment plans, "a State has wide discretion in evaluating the opposing interests and making an accommodation." But the "starting point" argument insists that, in addition to population equality, other desiderata must be "capable of the kind of rational statement and analysis which is required for constitutional adjudication." Mr. Cox's brief concluded: "If the State can point to neither rhyme nor reason for a discriminatory apportionment, save that it is an anachronism, the apportionment should be held to violate the Fourteenth Amendment."[45] In a case in which a comprehensive justification for a departure from the principle of equal representation was asserted, courts would have to go further and determine whether the justification offered was sufficient; but the larger the departure, the less adequate the justification would be. This approach is consistent with the democratic presupposition that the diffusion of political power through the suffrage should start with a

43. *Brief on Reargument, Baker* v. *Carr*, p. 26.
44. Archibald Cox, "Current Constitutional Issues," 48 *American Bar Association Journal* 712 (Aug. 1962).
45. *Brief on Reargument, Baker* v. *Carr*, pp. 28, 33.

common denominator: the individual. By recognizing a presumption in favor of numerical equality in representation, a high standard for legislative apportionment is set, and even a moderate departure from the equality standard goes far to evidence unwarranted discrimination. The consequence of this approach, with its built-in priority favoring equality, is that the constitutionality of any population disparities among districts are discounted in advance. Once persons similarly situated have been denied equality of *per capita* representation, the apportionment presumably stands condemned, unless the differentiations involved have a relevant and substantial justification. It must be relevant in terms of the objectives of the apportionment law and substantial in terms of meeting the heavy burden of proof required of those called upon by a court to defend departures from the equality principle.

The situation in Virginia after the 1962 enactment of a new apportionment was not as aggravated as the inequalities among legislative districts in most states. Nevertheless, a three-judge federal court in Richmond ruled in a two-to-one decision that the new apportionment was void. The court majority noted that the state constitution provides no ground rules for the placement of state senators and delegates. The majority then turned to the requirements of the federal Constitution. According to the court in *Mann* v. *Davis*, "the Equal Protection Clause of the Fourteenth Amendment . . . demands that apportionment accord the citizens of the State substantially equal representation." "Invidious discrimination" was evident in a malapportionment in which voting strength for senators varied in weight up to 2.67 to one, and in the Virginia House of Delegates population per delegate varied up to a ratio of 4.35 to one.[46] In view of these uncontested facts, the federal district court made it plain that the burden to provide a rational explanation for the disparities passed to the defendants, "but none was forthcoming. . . ." The explanation by the appellees that large numbers of military transients lived in Arlington, Fairfax, and Norfolk was rejected by the court as an inadequate justification for the short shrift given these areas in the legislature. According to the court, "exactitude in population is not demanded by the Equal Protection Clause. But there must be a fair approach to equality unless it be shown that other acceptable factors may make up for the differences in the numbers of people [represented per district]."

46. *Mann* v. *Davis*, 213 F. Supp. 577 (E.D. Va., 1962).

It may be said that this formula merely sweeps important questions "under the rug," for apart from the question of under-representing areas with military personnel, left wholly unidentified were the "acceptable factors" which may be incorporated into a plan of substantial equality. This objection mistakes for legerdemain the operation of the American judicial process. The lower courts, such as the one in Virginia, recognized that their decisions were subject to review by the Supreme Court, and in due time the import, if any, of the "one person, one vote" maxim for legislative apportionment would be clarified. Identification of such acceptable factors as might justifiably modify a rule of voting equality could be expected to make their weight felt in cases where they were particularly raised.

8   Voting and representation

The plethora of apportionment cases working their way up the judicial ladder after 1962 sharpened the lines of division between opposing sides on apportionment issues. The adversary system of courtroom argument and the appeals process served through successive filtrations to crystalize concrete problems into questions legally framed and ripe for Supreme Court determination. In litigation from Rhode Island to Hawaii, courts grappled with problems that once seemed text-bookish and abstract. Before the bar, they became issues of pressing and practical import. Among the questions affecting many states and raised by voting rights cases from coast to coast were the following. (1) May a state legislative apportionment plan satisfy the requirements of the Equal Protection Clause of the Fourteenth Amendment by following the representation pattern of Congress? That is, may one house be structured like the United States Senate in providing for political subdivision representation regardless of population and another like the House of Representatives according to a plan of equal constituencies? (2) How equal is equal? That is, are there identifiable mathematical limits in the representational value required for each voter in state legislative apportionment schemes? (3) What reasons, if any, may properly be advanced to justify departures from a standard of substantially equally weighted votes? (4) In the long run, the most important question mark attaches to the future fabric of representation in the United States in general. Answers to the foregoing three questions do not add up to all that can be expected of representative government. What latitude is left at the state and local levels for experimentation with various schemes of representation suited to particular conditions and changing needs?

VOTING EQUALITY AND *Per Capita* REPRESENTATION

In 1964, the Supreme Court made history by replying to the first three of these questions. In *Reynolds* v. *Sims* and its five companion cases, the national bench said through Chief Justice Warren that it intended to set out "only a few rather general considerations which appear to us to be relevant." In fact, however, the Court Opinions in the six *Reapportionment Cases* contained a formidable amount of detailed law. Announced with maximum clarity were a series of guidelines which Supreme Court majorities, differently composed from case to case, said were constitutionally necessary for the dividing of state legislative seats. Counting the memorandum decisions, cases involving legislatures in 15 states were disposed of in 1964. Full-length Opinions were provided in the six cases for which rulings were published on June 15. Chief Justice Warren emphasized the necessity to look at each case on its distinctive merits, and he followed the implications of this suggestion by writing separate Court Opinions for each of the six cases from Alabama, New York, Maryland, Virginia, Delaware, and Colorado.[1] From among the decisions in these cases a collage of interrelated guidelines emerged which were destined to have an impact on all 50 states.

One of the overriding rules spelled out in the Alabama case, which the Chief Justice chose as the principal vehicle for extended exposition, was that population must be the "starting point" and the "controlling criterion" for judgment in legislative apportionment contro-

1. *Reynolds* v. *Sims,* 377 U.S. 533; *WMCA, Inc.* v. *Lomenzo,* 377 U.S. 633; *Maryland Committee for Fair Representation* v. *Tawes,* 377 U.S. 656; *Davis* v. *Mann,* 377 U.S. 678; *Roman* v. *Sincock,* 377 U.S. 695; *Lucas* v. *Forty-fourth General Assembly of Colorado,* 377 U.S. 713 (1964).

versies. To show population discrepancies, in voting strength among districts and inequalities under the reapportionment plans examined in 1964, the complainants relied on many statistical comparisons of voter strength per representative from district to district. The *amici curiae* briefs submitted by the Justice Department consistently made such comparisons in terms of "*per capita* representation." Thus, in each of the six briefs submitted by Solicitor General Archibald Cox, the argument was advanced that "the basic standard of comparison, in applying the Equal Protection Clause, is the representation of qualified voters *per capita*."[2] Justice Harlan, impatient with the direction of some of these arguments, suggested that the resulting comparisons of voter strength and the ratios of representation *per capita* amounted to sixth grade arithmetic lacking relevance to the issues. The comment raised the fundamental question whether the Equal Protection Clause is concerned with uniform apportionment *per capita* or with some broader concept of representation, such as one systematically taking into account the diversity of interests in the community and one attentive to the variety of control mechanisms in addition to voting which the represented have over policy-makers. If the broad topic of representation is at issue, do figures showing *per capita* voter strength in one geographical district compared with another really reflect the quality, equality, or inequality of representation? Or must the focus of the Equal Protection Clause be widened to encompass other aspects of state government before one can determine whether the particular governmental system denies some voters equal protection of the law? After all, representation, defined as the relationship between the voter and his chosen spokesman in which the actions of the spokesman correspond with voter desires, is a complex process that includes the determination of who shall vote and techniques for controlling the representative after he has been elected. The Solicitor General's reply to Justice Harlan was that "state action which gives rise to hostile or capricious discrimination in the *per capita* apportionment of representatives is so related to unequal representation in the larger sense as to violate the constitutional guarantee of equal protection of the law, however fairly other aspects of the State government have been constructed."[3]

In his 1964 reapportionment decisions, Chief Justice Warren

2. *Brief for the United States as Amicus Curiae*, pp. 34–35, *Lucas v. Colorado General Assembly*, 377 U.S. 713 (1964).

3. *Brief for the United States as Amicus Curiae*, p. 17, *Roman v. Sincock*, 377 U.S. 695 (1964).

avoided use of the Solicitor General's term, *"per capita* representation" but relied on his statistical measures. Warren's assumption was that although the process of vote-weight measurements concentrated on only one aspect of representation, their simplicity should not hide the importance of what is measured: equality or inequality of voting power in the selection of the composite legislature. Unequal voting power almost surely means unequal representation. But representational systems in all of their complexity involve infinitely more than the equality or inequality of voting strength. Thus the possibility of giving the term *"per capita* representation" too much weight made it appropriate for the Court to reject its use. A remedy in its name would appear to promise greater representational reform than the *Reynolds* majority was prepared to offer in 1964. Showing that the larger dimension of representational theory was peripheral to its vision, the majority characterized the *Reapportionment Cases* as suits brought to vindicate discrete rights of individual voters rather than as contests over the forms of government. Thus in *Reynolds* v. *Sims,* the Chief Justice stated:

While the result of a court decision in a state legislative apportionment controversy may be to require the restructuring of the geographical distribution of seats in a state legislature, the judicial focus must be concentrated upon ascertaining whether there has been any discrimination against certain of the State's citizens which constitutes an impermissible impairment of their constitutionally protected right to vote.

To understand this limited perspective is the necessary first step in recognizing internal consistency in the majority position in the 1964 *Reapportionment Cases.* It helps to explain in part, for example, why the similarity of federal and state bicameral arrangements was rejected as an adequate defense for population inequalities among legislative districts. Criteria of representational rationality might justify a state's use of a "little federal" plan in its bicameral legislature, but measured voting equality under the Equal Protection Clause does not.

Inapposite Comparisons

In response to the "federal analogy" arguments pressed by four states, the Supreme Court specified that a state may not, by analogy to the federal Congress, establish one house of its legislature on a population basis and the other house on an area basis. In a statement of principle so broad as to apply to every state except Nebraska with its unicameral legislature, the Court held in *Reynolds* v. *Sims* that, "as a basic constitutional requirement, the Equal Protection Clause requires that the seats in both houses of a bicameral state legislature be apportioned substantially on a population basis." In the Virginia case of *Mann* v. *Davis*, the Court rejected a second federal analogy argument. There deviations from otherwise popularly equal districts were compared favorably by the state officials with the deviations from population equality among electoral college votes in presidential elections. According to Chief Justice Warren, the federal plan says nothing about the validity of state legislative apportionment plans because the comparison urged was irrelevant. Under-representation of some voters in a state legislature cannot be justified simply because it favors equality more than does the electoral college in the way it departs from a standard of population equality. A third federal factor held inapposite in the rulings of 1964 was dealt with in the Colorado case of *Lucas* v. *Forty-fourth General Assembly of Colorado*. The Court found "not justified" the argument that population equality among legislative districts is unnecessary because the states were originally admitted into the Union with state constitutions creating bicameral legislatures not apportioned on a population basis. The argument incorrectly assumed that, in voting upon their admission to the Union, Congress passed judgment upon and approved the republican form of governments of the new states.

The Dimensions of Equality

The Supreme Court rejected the three federal factors mentioned above because it found that, when they were relied upon, population as the controlling consideration was submerged. The Equal Protection Clause of the Fourteenth Amendment, according to the Court in *Reynolds*, "demands no less than substantially equal state legislative representation for all citizens, of all places as well as of all races." The courts must judge the validity of apportionment plans against the requirement for representation "substantially equal" in terms of voting strength and against the yardstick of "one person, one vote." Avoiding any precise mathematical definition of this criterion, the high bench acknowledged that case-by-case litigation would predictably reveal that what is marginally permissible in one state may be unsatisfactory in another. The *Reynolds* Court noted that mathematical exactness in districting is a practical impossibility. Nevertheless, while it is neither practical nor desirable to establish rigid mathematical standards for evaluating apportionment plans by constitutional rubrics, a rigorous reviewing procedure is called for. The Court said that the proper judicial course of action in apportionment cases is to determine whether, under the particular circumstances existing in the individual state, there has been a faithful adherence to a plan of population-based representation. The Supreme Court conceded that the lower courts may work out more concrete and specific standards, but members of the majority in the *Reynolds* case said, "we deem it expedient not to attempt to spell out any precise constitutional tests."

Although the tribunal thus carefully avoided any slide rule formula showing where "substantial equality" ends and unwarranted dilution of voting rights begins, it did make some noteworthy statistical comments. Against the background of the Alabama case, the Chief Justice said, "While mathematical nicety is not a constitutional requisite, a state house of representatives is not apportioned sufficiently on a population basis to be sustainable under the Equal Protection Clause where the population-per-representative disparities range from 6,731 to 42,303 and 43 percent of the state's population comprises districts which can elect a majority of the house." Speaking on the positive side in the Colorado case, the Court explained that a state legislative body with a population variance ratio of 1.7 to 1 between the most and least populous districts and with 45.1 percent of the state's population residing in the minimum number of districts represented by a bare majority of representatives, "is at least arguably apportioned substantially on a population basis." Of course, this statement does not constitute a binding statistical rule for all states. The fact remains that the task of reapportioning legislatures continues to be more difficult than if a specific mathematical ratio had been established. Such difficulty, however, is inherent in the requirement "that a State make an *honest and good faith* effort to construct districts, in both houses of its legislature, as nearly of equal population as is practicable." (Emphasis added.)

The range of population-per-district which the Court relied upon in all the decisions of 1964 provides an index directly addressed to voters' rights because it identifies the legislative district in which individual voters suffer the most grievous vote dilution and the districts where a small population enjoys the greatest relative advantage. The other measure adopted for usage by the Supreme Court and extensively relied upon by the briefs of the plaintiffs was the Dauer-Kelsey index. It discloses the minimum percentage of the state-wide electorate needed to control or elect a majority of representatives in each house. Where that figure falls much below 50 percent, a politically favored class of voters with power disproportionate to its numbers is revealed. Such a system of minority rule is presumably not a permissible objective of legislative apportionment on the ground that it evidences an arbitrary denial of the equal protection of the laws to the majority of voters.

Rational Deviations

The six *Reapportionment Cases* of 1964 covered a variegated landscape of fact situations. Thus the Court was able to deal specifically with a number of reasons advanced to justify modifications of the principle of population equality. The Court stated in *Roman v. Sincock* that some departure from the equality principle is permissible in either or both houses of a bicameral legislature, but the Constitution permits "such minor deviations only as may occur in recognizing certain factors that are free from any taint of arbitrariness or discrimination." In the *Reynolds* case, the majority had also asserted that, so long as the dilution of voting rights does not become significant, it may be feasible to use political subdivision lines to a greater extent in establishing state legislative districts than in congressional districting. Rationally according political subdivisions (such as counties) some independent representation in at least one house is justifiable as long as the basic standard of equality of population among districts is maintained. The justification for taking county lines into consideration in districting is especially substantial where much of the state's legislative activity involves the enactment of so-called local legislation directed only to the concerns of particular political subdivisions. Additionally and incidentally, the Court recognized that reliance on county lines for districting may blunt the temptation to isolate partisan or racial minorities by drawing boundaries to lessen the effectiveness of their vote. Thus reliance on county boundaries in setting up district lines, where such reliance does not impair the operation of the population equality principle, may "deter the possibilities of gerrymandering."

In the circumstances of the *Reynolds* case and the other apportionment cases decided the same day, the Court addressed itself to several state policies asserted to amount to rational justifications for limited deviations from population-based representation. Several state policies were ruled insufficient to justify population disparities between legislative districts. What follows is a list of conditional "thou shall nots" from the 1964 rulings. The general condition is that, although the factors mentioned may have some minor bearing on the decisions that go into an apportionment scheme, none of them, or no combination of them, may be invoked as rational bases justifying deviations from "substantial equality."

Balancing Urban and Rural Interests. Virginia officials argued that, although they could show no evidence of legislative intent, in retrospect they were satisfied that their state apportionment represented a rational attempt to balance urban and rural power. In *Davis* v. *Mann*, the Chief Justice replied: "Deviation from the equal-population principle in the apportionment of a state legislature is not sustainable as an attempt to balance urban and rural power in the legislature."

Recognizing Heterogeneous Characteristics. Colorado officials argued that it was appropriate that the apportionment plan reflect the varied mineral and water resources of the state distributed unevenly over an area sharply divided by rivers and mountains. The Supreme Court's reply was that "according recognition to a state's 'heterogeneous characteristics' do[es] not justify substantial deviations from the equal-population principle in the apportionment of seats in a state senate."

Protecting "Insular Minorities." The Colorado apportionment was said to protect small pockets of population cut off by mountainous terrain, bodies of water, and great distances from the Eastern Slope Region where 75 percent of the population lives. In the *Lucas* case, the Supreme Court said that the asserted necessity to protect "insular minorities" is not a principle which may be invoked so as to justify substantial deviations from equally populated districts.

Representing Sparsely Settled Areas. For the three successive Alabama plans reviewed by the Court, state officials offered no justification for discrimination among districts. They acknowledged that inequalities in both houses ran in favor of the same slightly settled counties and against the more populous. The Chief Justice ruled this to be impermissible "where the number of counties is large and many of them are sparsely populated and the number of seats in the legislative body being apportioned does not significantly exceed the number of counties."

Taking into Account the Accessibility of Constituents. In the federal government's brief for the Maryland case, the Solicitor General offered for the Court's consideration the suggestion that the principle of substantial equality may disregard those slight variations "that the practicalities of . . . the electoral process make inevitable."[4] In the

4. *Brief for the United States as Amicus Curiae,* p. 29, 11n, *Maryland Committee for Fair Representation* v. *Tawes,* 377 U.S. 656 (1964).

Reynolds case, the Court commented that arguments for allowing deviations "in order to insure effective representation for sparsely settled areas and to prevent legislative districts from becoming so large that the availability of access of citizens to their representatives is impaired are today, for the most part, unconvincing."

Securing Representation for Economic and Other Sorts of Group Interests. Colorado argued that her legislative apportionment justifiably distributed representation to take into account mining, livestock, agricultural, and other economic interests. Casting the net of generalization broadly, the Court in *Reynolds* stated that tampering with the equal population principle is not justified "by economic or other sorts of group interests, or by considerations of area alone."

Making Geographic or Topographic Considerations Affect Representation. Addressing itself to the Colorado arguments concerning the natural divisions which have historically been taken into account in mapping the state's legislative districts, the Court in *Lucas* said: "Geographical, historical, topographic, and economic considerations fail to provide adequate justification for substantial disparities from population-based representation in the allocation of state senate seats to disfavored populous areas."

Giving Effect to History or Tradition. Maryland particularly insisted on the rationality of its tradition of giving one state senator to each county irrespective of population and six senators to the city of Baltimore because of its history as a separate political subdivision. In *Maryland Committee for Fair Representation* v. *Tawes*, the Supreme Court ruled that: "Consideration of history and tradition cannot provide a sufficient justification for substantial deviations from population-based representation in both houses of a state legislature."

Giving Greater Representation to Permanent than to Temporary Residents. Although the argument did not serve to explain the dimensions of population disparities in legislative districts whereby the Virginia suburbs of Washington, D.C. and the Hampton Roads area were disfavored, Virginia explained that exclusion of military personnel from its representation base was the reasonable policy underlying its apportionment. In *Davis* v. *Mann*, the Supreme Court held that "the underrepresentation in a state's legislature of three of its more populous counties is not justifiable under the equal protection clause on the ground that it results in part from the fact that the three counties contain large numbers of military and military-related personnel."

Giving Effect to an Apportionment Plan Approved by the Elec-

torate. Colorado officials were able to make the unique plea that their senate, modelled on that of the federal government, resulted in justifiable population inequalities because the plan was approved through referendum by a majority of the voters in every Colorado county. The Supreme Court in the *Lucas* case ruled to the contrary that referendum approval "is without federal constitutional significance if the scheme adopted fails to satisfy the basic requirements of the equal protection clause."

In the case arising in Colorado, the Supreme Court also said that in determining whether a good-faith effort has been made to establish legislative districts substantially equal in population, a court must necessarily consider the apportionment scheme as a whole. Evaluating the overall plan thus means, in the case of a bicameral legislature, looking into the apportionment of both houses. Giving this scope to its view, a court may look benignly on a plan where rationally justifiable deviations from a strict population basis involve balancing a slight over-representation of one area in one house against a slight under-representation of the same area in the other house. Nevertheless, where the same area is disadvantaged in both houses, the disparities, although minor, are cumulative rather than offsetting.

In Justice Harlan's dissenting view, the majority's exercise in reiterating the equality principle by tediously rejecting the ten competing bases for representation, mentioned above, had no constitutional basis. Nor could he subscribe to any "principle of logic or practical or theoretical politics" establishing the exclusion of all these factors. Harlan's 46-page essay focused especially on historical records which led him to the conclusion that those who drafted and sponsored ratification of the Fourteenth Amendment did not intend it to give to the federal government any authority for interfering with the internal organization of state legislatures.

Justices Clark and Stewart separately distinguished their views from the majority. They thought, unlike Justice Harlan, that the Equal Protection Clause was relevant to apportionment disputes. The two justices would have preferred the Court to hold that if one state legislative house was apportioned by population, the other house could be apportioned by "rational" nonpopular criteria if the result were not a "crazy-quilt" (Clark) or the senseless product of "legislative inaction" (Stewart). Fundamental to Stewart's view was the assumption "that population factors must often to some degree be subordinated in devising a legislative apportionment plan which is to achieve the important goal of ensuring a fair, effective, and balanced representation of the region, social and economic interests within a State." By way of contrast, the majority assumed that:

Legislators represent people, not trees or acres. Legislators are elected by voters, not farms or cities or economic interests. As long as ours is a representative form of government, and our legislatures are those instruments of government elected directly by and directly representative of the people, the right to elect legislators in a free and unimpaired fashion is a bedrock of our political system. It could hardly be gainsaid that a constitutional claim had been asserted by an allegation that certain otherwise qualified voters had been entirely prohibited from voting for members of their state legislature. And, if a State should provide that the votes of citizens in one part of the State should be given two times, or five times, or 10 times the weight of votes of citizens in another part of the State, it could hardly be contended that the right to vote of those residing in the disfavored areas had not been effectively diluted.

The majority single-mindedly focused on the equality principle in electing legislators not only because it stipulates the preferred representation principle for a democracy (a point specified in the above quotation but left unargued in the Court Opinion) but because it was the necessary consequence of giving full effectuation to a basic civil right (a point fully developed). No justification, however rational, which submerged the equality principle—even including Colorado's appeal to majority will expressed by referendum—was sufficient to overcome the individual voter's claim to equal treatment under the Fourteenth Amendment. Where Justices Stewart and Clark saw rational schemes of representation at work, as in New York and Colorado, the majority saw individual rights subverted. The representational process, from the weighting of votes to the controlling of the voters' spokesmen, may be suffused with problems involving equal protection of state laws. But the majority thought that the 1964 cases raised questions only where one of the first steps in the representation process was concerned. Those questions focused on whether the right to vote for a legislative representative specified a vote that would be counted on a par with others. The rights involved, thought the majority, mandated population equality as the basis for apportionment in both houses of a bicameral state legislature. Deviations from this principle were said to be permissible only "so long as the divergences from a strict population standard are based on legitimate considerations incidental to the effectuation of a rational state policy. . . ." This statement, hardly clear in its scope or operation, invited subsequent

litigation to test how much latitude for experiment was left to legislatures in devising apportionment schemes once the requirement for
"substantial equality" was satisfied.

The Florida and Texas Cases

Just how such "legitimate considerations" would have to be invoked by the states' lawyers was well illustrated in reapportionment
suits that Florida and Texas brought to the Supreme Court for decision in 1967. On June 22, 1964, Florida's legislative scheme for
apportionment was rejected, along with schemes from eight other
states, in a brief memorandum decision from the Supreme Court.[5]
The response of the district court in Florida was to defer further
action until the conclusion of the 1965 meeting of the legislature. The
plan drawn up that session was found defective by the United States
Supreme Court in a brief unsigned ruling.[6] In response, the legislature
met for the seventh time in four years to act on the matter of its
composition. The State Attorney General circulated a memo, relying
on a district court ruling from Alabama,[7] in which he speculated that
"a percentage variance of more than 15 per cent would be difficult to
sustain as complying with 'one man-one vote.' It is therefore respect-
fully submitted that a percentage variation not exceed 15 per cent."
The legislature missed the mark in the Senate with one constituency
15.09 percent above the average, and in the House with districts
ranging from +18.28 percent above to −15.27 percent below the
average of 42,321 persons. The new reapportionment design was
promptly attacked by the redoubtable Dade County voter-litigant,
Richard Swann. In addition to presenting the court with three much
more nearly equalized districting plans for both houses, the Swann
plaintiffs asked for decisiveness from the district court. They noted
that special apportionment sessions of the legislature had cost the state
some $12,000 per day and begged the bench not to permit another
"expensive exercise in futility."

In defense of the new scheme, the State Attorney General argued
that the few examples of rural over-representation were mere "unconstitutional fragments." Swann's lawyers were quick to point to the
comment in the *Lucas* case that population disparities, though minor,
add up to cumulative disadvantage if the same areas are affected in
both houses. In the new Florida plan, over-represented districts in both

5. *Swann* v. *Adams*, 378 U.S. 553 (1964).
6. *Swann* v. *Davis*, 383 U.S. 210 *per curiam* (1966).
7. *Crawford County Bar Association* v. *Faubus*, 238 F. 290 (1965).

houses were sparsely populated. Chief Judge Jones then turned to the attorney representing the state and asked simply: "What is the defense?" The answer offered was that the districts were as equalized in population as the legislature found "practical" to make them.

The legislature . . . attempted to comply . . . with constitutional standards in the State of Florida in not changing any county unit. The political subdivisions . . . have . . . remained intact. The congressional districting was used as a criteria to arrive at the differential. And it is the manipulation of these counties by population within these districts as to why the deviations are present. . . . We feel further that the defense is that in and of itself, it is not invidiously discriminatory.[8]

To this Judge Jones commented, "It is unless explained, isn't it?"

The courtroom discussion then shifted ground, leaving behind an example of the "rational deviations" doctrine in operation. If the legislature is bound to explain fully its departures from a strict population standard, its statutory output in this area, so put on the defensive, cannot be said to enjoy a full presumption of validity. Such a presumption is customary where a legislative scheme of regulatory classifications (not touching on fundamental rights) is being judicially scrutinized with the equal protection standards of the Fourteenth Amendment. But constitutionally defined voting rights are different, where they are the subject of a scheme of classifications, because they touch upon the sensitive and important area of human rights. According to the Chief Justice in the *Reynolds* case, "any alleged infringement of the right of citizens to vote must be carefully and meticulously scrutinized."

As far as the district court was concerned in reviewing Swann's challenge to the legislature, the few departures "from the ideal are not sufficient or great enough in percentages to require an upsetting of the legislative plan."[9] With sharp dissents from Justices Stewart and Harlan, the Supreme Court in 1967 took a different view. Justice White spoke for a seven-man majority in *Swann* v. *Adams*.[10] He announced tersely: "We reverse for the failure of the State to present or the District Court to articulate acceptable reasons for the variations among the populations of the various legislative districts with respect

8. Cowart Testimony, Transcript of Record, *Swann* v. *Adams*, 385 U.S. 440 (1967), pp. 103–104.

9. *Swann* v. *Adams*, 258 F. Supp. 819 *per curiam* (1965).

10. *Swann* v. *Adams*, 385 U.S. 440 (1967).

to both the senate and house of representatives." True, Florida had asserted that its plan came "as close as practical" to complete population equality and that the state was attempting to follow congressional district lines. But the state's brief argued only that the legislature followed congressional boundaries "in most instances," while the opposing brief pointed out that this was true only of one house, and at that the congressional districts were under constitutional challenge. With respect to practicality, Justice White said: ". . . it seems quite obvious that the State could have come much closer to providing districts of equal population than it did." This was "obvious" from Swann's brief in which alternative apportionment plans, drawn up with the help of state university professors, were submitted; they whittled down inequalities among districts to an over- and under-representation variation from the average of not more than 3.35 percent. Justice White did not hesitate to point to the appellant's plan in order to "demonstrate that a closer approximation to equally populated districts was a feasible undertaking." The Supreme Court ruling in *Swann* v. *Adams* makes clear that when a district court has before it an apportionment scheme, such as Swann's with its close approximation to population equality, it may not accept the legislature's enactment with deviations five times as great without a clear and precise explanation as to its reason for rejecting the former and accepting the latter.

While *Swann* v. *Adams* was still on appeal in 1966, a federal district court in Texas was involved in issuing a ruling on a similar complaint against the state's design for apportioning the Texas House of Representatives. The voter-plaintiffs showed that population-per-representative varied from 14.84 percent over-representation to 11.64 percent under-representation. The district court upheld the plan on the ground that the legislature's work should be presumed constitutional. When this decision was appealed to the Supreme Court under the title of *Kilgarlin* v. *Hill,* six members supported reversal by *per curiam* decision.[11] The brief Opinion noted that the lower court ruling had not taken *Swann* v. *Adams* into account: "Under that case, it is quite clear that unless satisfactorily justified by the court or by evidence of record, population variances of the size and significance evident here are sufficient to invalidate an apportionment plan."

The result of Supreme Court decisions in Florida and Texas cases is that two important guidelines supporting voting equality have been

11. *Kilgarlin* v. *Hill,* 386 U.S. 120 *per curiam* (1967).

clarified. First, it is up to the state to justify all deviations from a standard of population equality if plaintiffs establish that such deviations prevail. The Supreme Court has refused to specify a mathematically defined limit, preferring to reiterate that such a determination may better be made on a state-by-state basis. But the 1967 Texas ruling suggests that avoidable deviations, even in the range of from ±10 to 15 percent from the average, are suspect and therefore need not be presumed valid. Second, if those bringing a challenge to the official apportionment plan submit their own alternative which conforms to all state constitutional requirements and contains smaller population variations, the court hearing the case is obliged to accept the alternative or to justify its failure to do so.

VOTING RIGHTS AND REPRESENTATIONAL EXPERIMENT

In his Opinion of the Court in *Swann* v. *Adams,* Justice White acknowledged that the Supreme Court thought it unnecessary to deal with certain other complaints about the legislature's plan besides unequally populated legislative districts. For example, an *amicus curiae* brief for three voters (two Republicans and one Democrat) asserted that the departure by the legislature from districts each with one representative to multi-member districts for such areas as populous Broward, Dade, and Orange Counties was invidiously discriminatory. They asserted, for example, that in some areas of proved Republican strength in and around Miami, single-member district voting would yield Republican legislators who inevitably lost elections when they were conducted on a county-wide basis. A comparable effect undercutting Negro representation was alleged to be the result of multi-member districts in urban areas where county-wide voting was required for state legislators. The *amicus* concluded that single-member districts would result in more Republican and Negro legislators, thereby giving concentrated political and racial groups an opportunity to have their voice heard in the state legislature. But as it was, the plural-member districts were said to submerge minority views. The party litigants therefore "submitted that a single-representative-per-district provides the only method which would adhere to both the Equal Protection Clause of the Fourteenth Amendment and *Reynolds* v. *Sims.*" This argument did not take into account the fact that the *Reynolds* Opinions specifically said that once the equality of vote-weighting per-representative was satisfied, legislatures could properly experiment with various representational structures. A comment about the need for "a little play in the joints" was footnoted on the same page of the *Reynolds* Opinion where Chief Justice Warren said:

Simply because the controlling criterion for apportioning representation is to be the same in both houses does not mean that there will be no difference in the composition and complexion of the two bodies. Different constituencies can be represented in the two houses. One body could be composed of single-member districts, while the other could have at least some multi-member districts. The length of terms of the legislators in the separate bodies could differ, even significantly, and the geographical size of the districts from which legislators are elected could also be made to differ. An apportionment in one house could be arranged so as to balance off minor inequities in the representation of certain areas in the other house.

The Georgia and Hawaii Cases

In spite of this clear concession to representational experiment, a suit challenging Georgia's use of multi-member senatorial units was brought before a three-judge district court soon after the *Reapportionment Cases* of 1964 were decided.[12] The district court agreed with the plaintiffs that the difference between electing senators in districts comprising a county or group of counties and in the multi-district counties amounted to invidious discrimination in violation of Amendment Fourteen.[13] The case was appealed to the United States Supreme Court where eight members disagreed with the lower court.

Justice Brennan wrote the Opinion of the Court in *Fortson v. Dorsey*.[14] He reviewed the facts of the case, noting that Atlanta's Fulton County has a population nearly seven times that of a single district constituency and for that reason elects seven senators. The complaint made rested on the assertion that this scheme is defective

12. Georgia's 54 senatorial seats were parcelled out among districts of unchallenged population equality. So far as possible, however, the districts were created along county lines. Only two districts consisted of a single county. Elsewhere, sparsely populated counties were combined in such a way as to make up 31 districts of from two to eight counties each. The remaining 21 districts went to the most populous counties (each containing from two to seven districts). But in the urban areas under the plan, voters were not to elect a senator by a district-wide vote. Rather, within the urban counties, districts served to localize the residence of the senator, but voters of his area were to join with voters of other districts of the county in electing all the assigned senators by a county-wide vote.

13. *Dorsey v. Fortson*, 228 F. Supp. 259 (1964).

14. *Fortson v. Dorsey*, 379 U.S. 433 (1965). See also *Toombs v. Fortson*, 384 U.S. 210 (1966).

because county-wide voting in multi-district counties *could* as a matter of mathematical possibility result in the nullification of the unanimous choice of the voters of a district, thereby imposing upon them a senator for whom no one in the district voted. Thus a senator in a four-district county could be elected from district D without local support but with the "foreign votes" from A, B, and C where such votes amount to a county majority. If, unlike A, B, and C, district D includes a concentration of Republican voters, it may well happen that the elected senator from D will be a Democrat beholden to A, B, and C. Justice Brennan's response to this line of argument was that the Supreme Court could not condemn the Georgia system as constitutionally void on a "highly hypothetical assertion" and because it inaccurately treated a senator from a multi-district county as the representative of only that district where he resides. In his final remarks on this score, Brennan made a concession which forecasts future litigation:

It might well be that designedly or otherwise, a multi-member constituency apportionment scheme, under the circumstances of a particular case, would operate to minimize or cancel out voting strength of racial or political elements of the voting population. When this is demonstrated it will be time enough to consider whether the system still passes constitutional muster.

Justice Brennan was again given the opportunity to comment on the need for concrete evidence to support a charge of unfairness against multi-member districts in the Hawaii case of *Burns* v. *Richardson* (1966).[15] Like the Georgia plaintiffs in *Fortson* v. *Dorsey* (1965), the Hawaii plaintiffs failed to convince the Supreme Court that, on the record of the case, multi-member districts were an Equal Protection problem. An important aspect of the complex Hawaii litigation concerned the advice of the district court to the legislature. In following a court order to reapportion and redistrict the senate, the legislature was advised that only single-member districts would be appropriate for the Island of Oahu where nearly 80 percent of the state's population live. The legislature disregarded the federal court's

15. *Burns* v. *Richardson*, 384 U.S. 73 (1966). The appellants argued that their case was distinguishable from *Fortson* v. *Dorsey* because in the Georgia suit the only challenge "was to the deprivation of equal voting weight; while in the present case, the deprivation of other elements of the right to representation on an equal basis is challenged." *Brief for John A. Burns, Governor of the State of Hawaii*, pp. 72–73, *Burns* v. *Richardson*.

cautionary memorandum and insisted on three- and four-member senatorial districts. The result was judicial condemnation for the lumping together of districts without taking any account of "community of interests, community of problems, socio-economic status, political and racial factors." Legislators were apparently guided rather by a fear of the kind of "political duel-to-the-death with a fellow and neighboring senator" that would result from single-member districts.[16] When the contest was appealed to the Supreme Court, Governor Burns of Hawaii joined with Honolulu voters as plaintiffs while Lieutenant Governor Richardson and members of the state senate were named as parties-defendant. In an important clarification of the *Fortson* principle that multimember districts are not bad *per se* under the Equal Protection Clause, Justice Brennan gave future litigants the following hints:

It may be that [an] invidious effect can more easily be shown if, in contrast to the facts in *Fortson*, districts are large in relation to the total number of legislators, if districts are not appropriately subdistricted to assure distribution of legislators that are resident over the entire district, or if such districts characterize both houses of a bicameral legislature rather than one. But the demonstration that a particular multi-member scheme effects an invidious result must appear from evidence in the record.

According to Justice Brennan, the fact that the Hawaii district boundaries were admittedly drawn so as to minimize the number of contests between incumbents from an earlier apportionment "does not in and of itself establish invidiousness." He added that there may be merit in the argument that by encouraging block voting, multi-member districts diminish the opportunity of a minority party to win seats. But such effects must be shown by evidence, and that "demonstration was not made here." This ruling may mean that a few elections would have to pass by the boards before the necessary data could be accumulated to show submergence of partisan or minority group voting strength. As presented by the Honolulu plaintiffs, however, the complaint against multi-member districts did not involve an allegation of population disparities (thereby bringing into play the *Reynolds* principles of voting equality). Rather, it raised questions about the differences in representational effectiveness between multi-member and single-member legislative districts. At least, that is the way Brennan characterized the contest. Conjecture as to the effects

16. *Holt* v. *Richardson*, 240 F. Supp. 724, 730–31 (1965).

of plural-member districting, he said, is more appropriate "to the body responsible for drawing up the districting plan." This comment was the Court's way of reconfirming the *Reynolds* principle that legislative apportionment is primarily the state's responsibility. Thus, in the absence of an indication of discriminatory effects on minority groups, the district court was said by Justice Brennan to have erred in insisting that the legislature "justify" its proposal.[17]

The Future of Representation Suits

A comparison of *Burns* v. *Richardson* and *Swann* v. *Adams* indicates that a majority of the Supreme Court has attempted to separate voter equality suits of the type involved in the 1964 *Reapportionment Cases* from other kinds of representational contests. When voter equality from district to district is shown to be compromised, it is an easy matter to challenge the state's plan. When other aspects of a representative scheme or of state electoral arrangements are challenged on Equal Protection grounds, a conventionally heavy burden of evidence and argument falls on the plaintiffs. The difference of treatment accorded to the two kinds of cases suggests that constitutional voting rights have been assigned a preferred-to-privileged position over other components of the electoral system. Casting equally weighted votes is now a matter of legal right, but insuring the impact of those votes on public policy by effective representation, or even requiring that an election be held in the first place, remains a matter of politics.

Further illustration of this point was given in the Supreme Court's ruling in *Fortson* v. *Morris* in 1966.[18] The bench was divided five to four when it decided that Georgia had the power to select a governor

17. The following justifications were offered by the legislature: (1) Single-member districts would tend to cause the senators therefrom to be concerned with localized issues and to ignore the broader issues facing the State; (2) Multi-member districts would correspondingly require the voter to focus his attention on the broad spectrum of community problems as opposed to those of more limited and local concern; (3) Historically the members of the House of Representatives had represented smaller constituencies than members of the Senate, and tradition and experience had proved the balance desirable; (4) To set up single-member districts throughout the state would compound the technical problems of drawing the boundaries; and (5) Oahu's population boom would more drastically affect single-member districts than would be the case with larger multimember districts in the area.

18. *Fortson* v. *Morris*, 385 U.S. 231 (1966).

through its legislature when no gubernatorial candidate obtained a majority in the election. The decision resulted, as expected, in the selection of the Democratic candidate, Lester Maddox, who ran second in the popular vote. Justice Black spoke for the Court majority in saying that "there is no provision of the United States Constitution or any of its amendments which either expressly or impliedly dictates the method a State must use to select its Governor." Justice Douglas, dissenting with the support of Chief Justice Warren and Justices Brennan and Fortas, asserted on the contrary that "if the legislature is used to determine the outcome of a general election, the votes cast in that election would be weighted contrary to the principle of 'one person, one vote.' "

The two Georgia cases of *Fortson* v. *Dorsey* and *Fortson* v. *Morris* and the Hawaii case of *Burns* v. *Richardson* were the first Supreme Court decisions in what promises to be (and has already become at the lower court level) a lengthy collection of challenges to representational experiment. After all, Chief Justice Warren had noted by way of dictum in *Reynolds* v. *Sims* that "the achieving of fair and effective representation for all citizens is concededly the basic aim of legislative apportionment." But is fair and effective representation a basic aim of the Equal Protection Clause of the Fourteenth Amendment? Under this head, the complex questions which may be expected to come to the Supreme Court will ask what impact if any the Equal Protection Clause has on constitutionally unexplored areas of the "political thicket." These include problems touching on every step of the representation process: (1) designating the representational base, e.g., by total population, citizens only, or voters;[19] (2) widening the voters' scope of choice, e.g., by cumulative voting;[20] (3) assigning representatives to constituencies, e.g., by elections-at-large, or by use of single, multiple, or floterial districts;[21] (4) setting the district

19. William Boyd, *Changing Patterns of Apportionment* (New York: National Municipal League, 1965). Ruth Silva, "Population Base for Apportionment of the New York Legislature," 32 *Fordham Law Review* 1 (1963).

20. George Blair, "Cumulative Voting: Patterns of Party Allegiance and Rational Choice in Illinois State Legislative Contests," 52 *American Political Science Review* 123 (1958).

21. Twiley Barker, Jr., "A Long, Long Ballot," 53 *National Civic Review* 170 (April 1964). Ruth Silva, "Compared Values of the Single- and the Multi-Member Legislative District," 17 *Western Political Quarterly* 504 and 742 (1964). John Banzhaf III, "Multi-Member Electoral Districts—Do They Violate the 'One Man, One Vote' Principle," 75 *Yale Law Journal* 1309, 1310 (1966).

boundaries, e.g., by standards of compactness and contiguity;[22] (5) taking account of sociopolitical differences in the population, e.g., by proportional representation or by drawing district lines that will reflect concentrated populations of ethnic and partisan minorities so as to facilitate their representation;[23] (6) controlling the legislator's influence, e.g., by weighted voting in the legislature commensurate to the size of his constituency.[24] The list is hardly complete. Representation, its components, functions, and definition remain in dispute.[25] Even if there were agreement on an operational definition of representation, the relation of the Federal Constitution to its working order at the state and local levels would remain in question. If the equal protection net is to be broadened from its focus on the equality of individual voting rights to minority and majority rights in the representation process, then why leave untouched questions about minority groups made voiceless by at-large elections and those work-a-day devices which restrain enthusiastic majorities: seniority rules, filibusters, parliamentary devices to keep bills off the floor, and the selec-

---

22. Ernest C. Roeck, Jr., "Measuring Compactness as a Requirement of Legislative Apportionment," 5 *Midwest Journal of Political Science* 70 (1961). James B. Weaver and Sidney W. Hess, "A Procedure for Nonpartisan Districting: Development of Computer Techniques," 73 *Yale Law Journal* 289 (1963).

23. See C. V. Laughlin, "Proportional Representation: It Can Cure Our Apportionment Ills," 49 *American Bar Association Journal* 1065 (Nov. 1963). Malcolm E. Jewell, "Minority Representation: A Political or Judicial Question," 53 *Kentucky Law Journal* 563 (Winter 1964–65). In 1964, a federal district court in South Carolina specified the operative constitutional rule that "it is the legislature's prerogative to weigh contending considerations and to make enlightened choices among several alternatives open to it with respect to schemes for cumulative and proportional voting, as long as . . . it is not arbitrarily unfair and discriminatory . . . under the Fourteenth Amendment." *Boineau* v. *Thornton*, 235 F. Supp. 175 (1964), *aff'd.* 379 U.S. 917.

24. John Banzhaf III, "Weighted Voting Doesn't Work: A Mathematical Analysis," 19 *Rutgers Law Review* 317 (1965).

25. Important contributions to the debate include: C. A. Auerbach, "Reapportionment Cases: One Person, One Vote—One Vote, One Value," *Supreme Court Review* 1 (1964). Alfred de Grazia, *Essay on Apportionment and Representative Government* (Washington, D.C.: American Enterprise Institute, 1963). Robert Dixon, Jr., "Reapportionment Perspectives: What is Fair Representation?" 51 *American Bar Association Journal* 319 (1965). C. E. Gilbert, "Operative Doctrines of Representation," 57 *American Political Science Review* 604 (1963). J. D. Lucas, "Legislative Apportionment and Representative Government: The Meaning of *Baker* v. *Carr*," 61 *Michigan Law Review* 711 (1963); Douglas Rae, *The Political Consequences of Electoral Law* (New Haven: Yale University Press, 1967).

tion of officials by appointment rather than by popular election? The impact of the Fourteenth Amendment on many of these problems may well have been keynoted by the Supreme Court in a school board representation case in 1967. There Justice Douglas said that in the absence of any demonstration that voting equality is impaired where voting is required (as it is not in such "nonlegislative" bodies as school boards), the Court "sees nothing in the Constitution to prevent experimentation."

Experimentation at the Local Level

Developments in the late 1960s suggest that although cases involving local elections bring some of the larger questions of representational effectiveness into sharp focus, the Supreme Court can deal with such problems with considerable flexibility. In two cases a unanimous Court showed a restrained approach to the question of whether the "one person, one vote" rule applied to municipal and other local agencies. For each ruling, Justice Douglas wrote a brief and cautious Opinion of the Court.

In *Sailors* v. *Kent County Board of Education*, Justice Douglas asserted that "viable local government may need many innovations, numerous combinations of old and new devices, great flexibility in municipal arrangements to meet changing urban conditions." The Court ruled that the "one person, one vote" principle had no relevancy to the selection of the county school board by delegates from local school boards. The fact that the districts of the school boards differed widely in population was not constitutionally consequential. The selection process was largely appointive, and no election was required since the officers involved are "not legislative in the classical sense." The Court upheld a procedure for choosing a school board that placed the selection with boards of component districts, even though the latter panels had equal votes and served unequal populations.[26]

In *Dusch* v. *Davis*, the apportionment of a city council was upheld, even though seven of the eleven council members who were elected at-large were required to reside in Virginia Beach (Virginia) boroughs of widely differing population sizes. In an Opinion expressing the views of all but two members of the Court (Justices Harlan and Stewart concurred in the result), Douglas said that the plan on its face was unassailable. Even "assuming for the sake of argument" that "one person, one vote" applied to municipal or county legislative agencies,

26. *Sailors* v. *Kent County Board of Education*, 387 U.S. 105 (1967).

the residence requirement which placed four councilmen in rural or tourist areas did not render the plan unconstitutional.[27]

The Court concluded that the at-large feature of the plan was sufficient to save it from constitutional attack, since each councilman *presumably* represented all of the city's voters and not just those residing in the residence district. In support of his ruling, Justice Douglas noted that the arrangement constituted an accommodation to the problems incident to consolidation of metropolitan government. He said that the scheme was such that the more populous boroughs could elect a majority and possibly all of the council, and that "different conclusions might follow" if "residence [were] only a front" and a "borough's resident on the council represented in fact only the borough." Apparently then, the circumstances leading to the adoption of at-large elections of the type involved in Virginia Beach may be significant. Flexibility is permissible with respect to government arrangements achieved through compromises incident to consolidation, e.g., where a city and county are merged into a large municipality. Of course, other circumstances could be at work. Couple unequally populated residence districts with at-large elections in locality after locality, and it is not difficult to see how complaints may arise charging ineffective representation of concentrated racial, partisan, and other minorities. In 1968, the Civil Rights Commission warned that switching to at-large elections and the consolidation of local government units could be a racially motivated "front" for an effort to divide concentrations of black voting strength.[28] In the *Dusch* case, Justice Douglas' ruling was premised on a fact situation in which racial discrimination was no part of the record. The Virginia Beach plan, he said, reflected "a detente between urban and rural communities that may be important in resolving the complex problems of the modern megapolis in relation to the city, the suburbia and the rural countryside."[29]

In 1968, the Justice Department filed an *amicus curiae* brief in the ground-breaking case of *Avery* v. *Midland County*, a local apportion-

27. *Dusch* v. *Davis*, 387 U.S. 112 (1967).

28. Commission on Civil Rights, *Political Participation*, pp. 21–39 and 171–72.

29. In *Moody* v. *Flowers*, also decided in 1967, the Supreme Court remanded Alabama and New York county apportionment suits to their respective district courts on procedural grounds. Constitutional attack on the county governing boards involved was said not to warrant the convening of a three-judge district court because laws of state wide application were not involved. 387 U.S. 97 (1967).

ment suit.[30] Submission of the federal brief in *Avery*, as in *Dusch* and *Sailors*, was said to be justified by "the public interest—and that of millions of American citizens—in fair representation at the local governmental level."[31] There was also the fact, not involved in *Avery*, that racial gerrymandering had increased at the local level by 1968. For several reasons the Justice Department urged the Supreme Court to review the constitutional question of whether the equal population principle was applicable to the Midland County Commissioners Court, the general governing body of the County. Attorney General Ramsey Clark thought that *Reynolds* v. *Sims* and the Supreme Court rulings of 1967 had stimulated a decision-making momentum in local apportionment cases which ought not to be thwarted in indecision at the Supreme Court level. Although there were contrary examples, eight top state courts and five federal benches had ruled that the Equal Protection Clause of the Fourteenth Amendment carried the "one person, one vote" principle into local government.[32]

Hank Avery's legal complaints against Midland County government dated back to 1962. Although Avery was the mayor of the City of Midland, he filed suit in his capacity as a voter and taxpayer of Midland County, acting "individually and on behalf of other persons [city residents] similarly situated." Under the Texas Constitution, county commissioners are generally elected by districts. The population of the four Midland County districts was estimated to be 67,906 (City of Midland); 852; 828; and 414 (outlying areas). A fifth member of the county government, the chairman, is elected at-large and votes only in case of a tie. In Texas, the title "Commissioners Court" is the traditional misnomer for the county government. Among other things, it administers the business affairs of the county, issues bonds, adopts the county budget, and serves as a board of equalization for

---

30. *Avery* v. *Midland County*, 390 U.S. 474 (1968).

31. *Brief for the United States as Amicus Curiae*, p. 3, *Avery* v. *Midland County*, 390 U.S. 474 (1968).

32. Pre-*Avery* cases in which state highest courts applied *Reynolds* to units of local government include: *Miller* v. *Board of Supervisors*, 63 Cal.2d 343 (1965); *Montgomery County Council* v. *Garrott*, 243 Md. 634 (1966); *Hanlon* v. *Towey*, 274 Minn. 187 (1966); *Armentrout* v. *Schooler*, 409 S.W.2d 138 (Mo., 1966); *Seaman* v. *Fedourich*, 16 N.Y.2d 94 (1965); *Bailey* v. *Jones*, 81 S.D. 617 (1966); *Wisconsin ex rel. Sonneborn* v. *Sylvester*, 26 Wis.2d (1965); *Newbold* v. *Osser*, 425 Pa. 478 (1967). Comparable results in federal courts may be seen in *Hyden* v. *Baker*, 286 F. Supp. 475 (M.D. Tenn., 1968); *Martinolich* v. *Dean*, 256 F. Supp. 612 (S.D., Miss., 1966); *Strickland* v. *Burns*, 256 F. Supp. 824 (M.D. Tenn., 1966); *Ellis* v. *Mayor of Baltimore*, 234 F. Supp. 945 (D.C., Md., 1964).

tax assessment. It also runs the local hospital, airport, courthouse, and jail. Its work is characteristically executive (it appoints numerous county officials), administrative (it draws school district boundaries), and legislative (it sets the county tax rate). It even carries on some judicial functions. Avery asserted that the commissioners' policy-making responsibilities were broad and general. He charged that because "great disparity in population and qualified voters among the Commissioners' precincts exists," those residing in the City of Midland—over 97 percent of the County's population—are inadequately represented. Their voices as citizens are "diluted" where policy-making affecting them is concerned.

For a Supreme Court divided five-to-three, Justice Byron White gave an affirmative answer to the question of whether the substantial population inequalities among Midland County districts violates the Equal Protection Clause of the Fourteenth Amendment as interpreted by *Reynolds* v. *Sims*. The Court held, first, that local government units which exercise legislative functions must give voters the chance to cast a substantially equally weighted vote. On the theory that local governing bodies act as an extension of the state legislature, White ruled:

When the State apportions its legislature, it must have, due regard for the Equal Protection Clause. Similarly, when the State delegates lawmaking power to local government and provides for the election of local officials from districts specified by statute, ordinance, or local charter, it must insure that those qualified to vote have the right to an equally effective voice in the election process.

Second, the *Avery* majority agreed that the Commissioners Court was sufficiently involved in legislative activities to mandate equalized apportionment. Concededly the numerous functions assigned to the unit make it difficult to classify neatly, e.g., as legislative as opposed to administrative. In this regard, Midland County government is representative of most of the general governing bodies of American cities, counties, towns, and villages. According to the Bureau of the Census, there were 81,304 such "local units of government" in the United States in 1967.[33] The Justice Department noted that "only about 25

33. U.S. Department of Commerce, Bureau of the Census, "Census of Governments 1967, Governmental Units in 1967," Preliminary Report, Oct. 1967 (Washington, D.C.: Government Printing Office, 1967), p. 1.

percent of these are elected in whole or in part, from districts or, while at-large, under schemes including district residence requirements."[34] The significant point for Justice White was that in Midland County, the Commissioners Court makes a "large number of decisions having a broad range of impacts on all citizens of the county." Its decisions are "long term judgments" about how the county should develop, and it legislates "immediate choices among competing needs." Was the commissioners' disproportionate concern for rural roads dictated by a division of functions between city and county governments or the result of the three-to-one voting majority enjoyed by the rural areas? White thought the latter. And he added that "a decision not to exercise a function within the court's power—a decision for example, not to build an airport or a library, or not to participate in the federal food stamp program—is just as much a decision affecting all citizens of the county as an affirmative decision."

Justice White concluded by acknowledging that multiple new problems challenge American local governments. "The Constitution does not require that a uniform straitjacket bind citizens in devising mechanisms of local government suitable for local needs and efficient in solving local problems." He indicated that the Court would not build "roadblocks in the path of innovation, experiment and development among units of local government."

The newly appointed Justice Thurgood Marshall did not participate in Mayor Avery's case. Three dissenters each wrote separate opinions. Justices Harlan, Stewart, and Fortas agreed that the Supreme Court had asserted its jurisdiction prematurely. The result desired by the majority may have developed without intervention since the Texas Supreme Court ruling was merely advisory and not a final judgment in terms of nonpopulation factors. Each dissenter took a different view of the merits of the case. Justice Harlan reconfirmed his *Reynolds* dissent and presented a carefully reasoned critique of the majority's "adventure" in political science. He thought the result neither constitutionally sanctioned nor practical. Justice Stewart briefly noted that he would join in support of Fortas' "thorough" dissent "were it not for the author's unquestioning endorsement of the doctrine of *Reynolds* v. *Sims*." Fortas invoked the *Reynolds* rationale that the Fourteenth Amendment prevents government from treating differ-

34. *Brief for the United States as Amicus Curiae*, p. 22, 31n, *Sailors* v. *Board of Education*, 387 U.S. 105 (1967).

ently people who stand in the same relation to that government. State legislative functions are comprehensive and pervasive. The same cannot be said of thousands of local government units, including the Midland County Commissioners Court which, in law and practice, Justice Fortas characterized as primarily administrative. To him, the majority's decision did not serve the *Reynolds* view of the Equal Protection Clause because "only the city population will be represented, and the rural areas will be eliminated from a voice in the county government to which they must look for essential services."

Both political and legal doctrinal reasons explain why the Supreme Court may wish, in Justice Fortas' terms, to be "careful and conservative" in interfering with state experimentation but to continue its pursuit of "rational" representation down the corridors of mathematical equality.

On the political side, Justice White acknowledged in his *Avery* Opinion that "the immense pressures" of modern-day social change fall heavily upon units of local government. In response, he thought the Supreme Court had set a cautious record in *Dusch*, *Sailors*, and *Avery*. He thought these rulings of 1967 and 1968 would frustrate neither innovation nor flexibility by too rigorous an application of the "one person, one vote" rule to local units. It was affirmatively applied only in *Avery*, and there at least two loopholes were left open. County governments such as that in Midland could be relieved of all powers over city residents and thereby remain in control of rural inhabitants. Or, popularly unequal residence districts, as in the Virginia Beach case, could be tolerated where at-large voting is employed as a concession to the politics of metropolitan consolidation.

Another factor restraining the Court from a doctrinaire position on representational experiment lies in the politics of the Supreme Court itself. The intra-Court divisions and shifting coalitions from *Reynolds* v. *Sims* to *Fortson* v. *Morris* and *Avery* v. *Midland County* show bitter disagreements among the justices expanding the guidelines of 1964 beyond a simple rule of vote-weighting equality. Only *Burns* v. *Richardson* and the narrow rulings of 1967 with their permissive results were able to secure unanimous support. However illogical or unrealistic may be a failure to acknowledge the integral link of the vote with other aspects of representational theory and practice, a cautious approach does comport with the facts of intra-Court and national politics. Chief Justice Warren displayed sensitivity to the threat of the "Dirksen Amendment" and the proposal of the

Council of State Governments to alter the 1964 rulings by constitutional amendment.[35] Holding the line was appropriate at least until the "one person, one vote" rule had become an accomplished fact in three-fourths of the states, the proportion necessary to ratify constitutional change by amendment.

On the legal side, brakes have been applied to Supreme Court innovating rulings in Equal Protection adjudications of representational schemes because, as the Court so frequently said, plaintiffs have been short on factual proof of invidious discrimination. The most activist member of the Supreme Court in voting rights cases, Justice Douglas, explained in 1967 that the subdistricting of city councilmen's seats irrespective of population differences was not barred by the Constitution in at-large elections. Yet Douglas concluded that, after some experience with the challenged plan in Virginia Beach, Virginia, "if it then operates to minimize or cancel out the voting strength of racial or political elements of the voting population, it will be time enough to consider whether the system still passes constitutional muster."[36] This was another way of saying that the Court would like to benefit from more lower court experience with such novel claims. The Justice Department observed that not until *Avery* v. *Midland* was it in agreement with a majority of the Court that a fully satisfactory vehicle had materialized for "a broad based consideration of the constitutional issues of local apportionment."[37]

Reynolds v. *Sims* and its companion rulings, even narrowly interpreted, specify requirements of such enormous nation-wide impact that a period of implementation and definition is needed, uncomplicated by other major innovations. As it is, the "one person, one vote"

35. Immediate steps to obtain a constitutional amendment after the 1964 *Reapportionment Cases* were begun in and out of Congress. On April 20, 1966, a proposed amendment failed of Senate passage for lack of a two-thirds vote, although it received a majority of votes cast. That version of the "Dirksen Amendment" would have allowed a state by referendum approval to apportion one house "on the basis of population, geography and political subdivisions in order to insure effective representation in the State's legislature of the various groups and interests making up the electorate." S.J. Res. 103 as voted on April 20, 1966: 55 yeas, 38 nays. See Elizabeth Yadlosky, "State Petitions and Memorials to Congress on the Subject of Apportionment of State Legislatures" (Library of Congress Legislative Reference Service, Feb. 1, 1968).

36. *Dusch* v. *Davis*, 387 U.S. 112, 116 (1967).

37. *Brief for the United States as Amicus Curiae*, p. 28, 45n, *Avery* v. *Midland County*, 390 U.S. 474 (1968).

principle cuts deeply into any representation structure.[38] Indeed, it specifies the major plank, and it has stimulated voluminous litigation to bring its requirements to every one of the 50 states. Justice Fortas noted this in his *Avery* dissent and urged "a reasoned, conservative, empirical approach" to the intricate problem of applying constitutional principle to the complexities of representative government. Justice Fortas called for more legislative and fewer judicial initiatives in working out the complexities of representational systems. It remains true, nevertheless, that any voter-litigant, acting as a kind of sidewalk observer of apportionment planning, is easily capable of challenging the state's architect on the equality score and laying the "hatchet" to his edifice. *Swann* v. *Adams* allows the equalizing of state legislative, congressional, and, to a lesser extent, local government districts to become a sporting matter of popular litigious kibitzing.

By contrast, the burdens of showing unconstitutional discrimination are heavier for those challenging a state's representational blueprint in which population equality is not precisely prejudiced. This was doubly illustrated by the Hawaii case of 1966 in which the Supreme Court not only took a permissive view of the use of multi-member districts but also sanctioned the state's use of registered voters rather than population as the basis for the apportionment. In *Burns* v. *Richardson*, Justice Brennan asserted that the decision to insure district equality by reference to full population figures, a citizen census, or according to the distribution of registered voters should be left in the first instance to the state. Hawaii, with its many aliens, tourists, and military transients, could decide to include or exclude any such groups. The decision, Brennan wrote, "involves choices about the nature of representation with which we have been shown no constitutionally founded reason to interfere." Part of the reason judicial interference on constitutional grounds was unwarranted in the Hawaii case lay in the demonstrated fact that voter registration figures and the permanent population census substantially corresponded to one another. A high proportion of the possible voting population was registered, and strong drives to bring out the vote resulted in participation of from 88 to 93.6 percent of all registered voters during the

38. See James K. Pollock, "Reapportionment and Fair Representation," in Howard D. Hamilton (ed.), *Reapportioning Legislatures* (Columbus, Ohio: Charles E. Merrill, 1966).

elections of 1958, 1959, 1960, and 1962. Justice Brennan's conclusion on this record deserves extended quotation.

> In these circumstances, we find no demonstrated error in the District Court's conclusion that the apportionment achieved by use of a registered voters basis substantially approximated that which would have appeared had state citizen population been the guide.
>
> We are not to be understood as deciding that the validity of the registered voters basis as a measure has been established for all time or circumstances, in Hawaii or elsewhere. The District Court was careful to disclaim any holding that it was a "perfect basis." We agree. . . . Future litigation may reveal infirmities, temporary or permanent, not established by the present record.[39]

Deciding whether a particular aspect of a scheme of representation suffers constitutional "infirmities" is a more specific task than that of establishing a "perfect" form of representative government. The former task belongs to the courts where plaintiffs must come equipped with conclusive evidence. The latter task is the legislature's where conjecture and the art of the possible must have their latitude. It is the legislature which must face the threshold assignment of defining "representation" and of identifying the populations to be represented. Even if it were agreed that an ideally representative legislature would be a microcosm of the whole people, reproduced in exact proportions, it would still be apparent that the allocation of representatives in exact proportion to the population of the several districts would not alone ensure the objective. The legislator from a single-member district, with less party pressure on him, will likely be more amenable to the needs of various interest groups; the legislator from a multi-member district will tend to be more responsible to his political party and less amenable to pressure groups. Which of these two results produces a preferable scheme of representation? If, in the case of multi-member districts, something is lost to interest group representation, something may be gained in terms of avoiding gerrymandering.

39. *Burns* v. *Richardson*, 384 U.S. 73, 96 (1966). Justice Brennan also said that the hazards of a voter basis of representation would tend to be avoided if reapportionment were more frequent than every ten years, perhaps every four or eight years corresponding to the higher levels of voting usually found in presidential election years. "Other measures, such as a system of permanent personal registration, might also contribute to the stability and accuracy of the registered voters figure as an apportionment basis."

In the 500-odd counties in the United States in the late 1960s where multi-member districts from two to four members were used, the potential for drawing lines by purely partisan criteria was blunted because county lines were determinative.[40] Even without gerrymandering, a population that was divided 60–40 on a critical issue might conceivably select a legislature having a unanimous view because the vote could divide 60–40 in every district if single-member districts are employed throughout the state. Until 1964, Illinois took account of this possibility by giving each district in its lower house three representatives. By a system of "cumulative voting," each elector had three votes which could be assigned to one candidate, be divided between two, or among all three candidates. The system usually resulted in two seats for the district's majority party and one for the minority. This encouraged a vitalized two-party system and minimized the potential for "wasted votes" inherent in almost any electoral system by opening an opportunity for minority representation not given in single-member districts. The statesman, political scientist, and state commission-member organizing the framework of government must concern themselves with "wasted votes," with the question of where to draw district lines, and with whether and how to make the legislature reflect the divisions and intensity of opinion within the individual districts. Sundry plans which comport with the equal population principle, such as proportional representation, weighted voting by legislators to reflect the unequal size of their constituencies, plural-member districts, and other devices have been directed at making representation more effective. Nothing the Supreme Court said between *Baker* v. *Carr* and *Burns* v. *Richardson* has cast doubt upon their constitutionality, although lower courts have divided on most of these issues. Whether the Fourteenth Amendment reaches such representation questions is the problem which may well identify the issues of constitutional politics before the Supreme Court in the 1970s.

---

40. Paul T. David, "One Member, vs. 2, 3, 4 or 5," 55 *National Civic Review* 77 (Feb. 1966).

9 Congressional districting

"A free ballot and a fair count" was an often quoted Republican battle cry of the early nineteenth century. In a time of restricted suffrage, it expressed the fear, not that votes were few, but that because of false counts they were unconsidered. The twentieth-century counterpart to the unconsidered vote is the less villainous, more impersonal, and highly complex development of voting dilution through inequitable districting. This chapter deals with judicial and legislative efforts to protect the quality of voting rights in congressional elections from impairment through unfair districting.

Constitutional and Statutory Requirements

Where the apportionment of congressional seats is concerned, only the House of Representatives poses problems. The Constitution expressly assigns seats in the Senate on the basis of two to each state. Periodic reallotment of the seats of representatives in proportion to state population is required by the United States Constitution. Originially a compromise measure, Article I has been altered by the Fourteenth Amendment in such a way that it presently requires that "Representatives shall be apportioned among the several states according to their respective numbers, counting the whole number of persons in each state, excluding Indians not taxed."[1] Thus the general population, as opposed to citizens or voters only, forms the basis for representation in the House.

To avoid the English example of over-representation in "rotten" or "pocket" boroughs, the Constitutional Convention adopted Randolph's proposal that "the actual enumeration shall be made within three years after the meeting of the congress of the United States, and within every subsequent term of ten years in such manner as they shall by law direct." This stipulation may be interpreted as a directive to Congress to reapportion representatives among the states in the light of the decennial census. An upper limit on the size of the House of Representatives is set by the Constitution. The ratio of representatives to persons represented should not exceed a ratio of "one to every thirty thousand." Although realistic for 1787, that figure applied to the population of 1970 would probably yield a House of about 6,000 members. The minimum limit on the membership of the same body is determined by the requirement that "each State shall have at least one Representative."

Historically there have been recurrent difficulties in determining a formula to be employed in distributing House seats among the states. A century and three quarters of discussion, debate, and experimentation have provided a variety of answers to the question: how shall the number of representatives for each state be determined in view of the changing national population? The number of seats to be apportioned among the states is shown in Table 9–1 which reflects changing statutory limits.

Given the traditional twentieth-century size limitation of 435 members, the House has struck upon a satisfactory answer to the question, "who gets what?" According to the Automatic Reapportionment Act of 1929 (as amended in 1941), the President is directed to transmit to Congress within the first week of the regular January session following each census the new allocation of congressional seats. The assignment of seats to each state is computed according to the "method of

1. See Paschal, "House of Representatives," 276–89.

Table 9-1   *Growth of the House of Representatives, 1790–1970*

YEAR	NUMBER OF REPRESENTATIVES	YEAR	NUMBER OF REPRESENTATIVES
1790	106	1880	332
1800	142	1890	357
1810	186	1900	391
1820	213	1910	435
1830	242	1920	435
1840	232	1930	435
1850	237	1950	435
1860	243	1960	437
1870	293	1970	435

equal proportions," an impartial formula.[2] Requiring this statistical approach, the present federal law has succeeded, by the impersonal character of its operation, in adjusting representation to population in the House of Representatives.

In politics as in biology, change is a rule of life; growth and division follow apace with a usual quotient of pain. As a result of the re-apportionment of 1960 following population shifts and increases of the previous decade, nine states gained 19 seats in the lower House of Congress, and 16 states lost 21 seats. The post-1960 reapportionment meant an increase in western voting power and a decrease in New England and Middle Atlantic voting strength. This change is reflected in the make-up of national presidential nominating conventions in 1964 and 1968 where congressional representation is the chief standard used to determine the size of state party delegations. Moreover, in view of the fact that the electoral college vote accorded each state is based on the sum total of its membership in the House and its two senators, there has been a resultant and parallel redistribution of presidential voting power which projected the 1960 census into the 1968 electoral college. This rebalancing of congressional and electoral college votes seems a dust-dry and altogether unremarkable abacus exercise in view of population changes during the decade of the fifties.

2. Laurence F. Schmeckebier, "The Method of Equal Proportions," 17 *Law and Contemporary Problems* 302–13 (Spring 1952), and his *Congressional Apportionment* (Washington, D.C.: Brookings Institution, 1941), pp. 21–33. For information on the relationship between the Census Bureau and representation in Congress, see U.S. Congress, House, "Congressional Apportionment—Role of the Bureau of the Census," House Report *No. 2223*, 86th Cong., 2d sess. (Washington, D.C.: Government Printing Office, 1960).

But the smooth operation of the Automatic Reapportionment Act is notable because it provides a relatively equitable and undisputed solution to an apportionment problem of broad consequences.

Apportioning congressional seats among the states is only one aspect of the process of dividing political power. The remaining and unresolved difficulty concerning congressional apportionment arises after the provisions of the automatic act have been attended to. That law requires that within 15 days following the receipt of the President's message, the Clerk of the House should inform the executives of each state of the number of members to which his state is entitled in the next Congress. Governors generally turn the problem over to state legislatures, where districts are often drawn to preserve favored bailiwicks rather than to ensure population equality among constituencies. This follows from the fact that neither the Constitution nor federal statutes in clear terms direct the states to redistrict periodically to ensure equality of representation. Unless representatives are to be chosen in their state by election-at-large, a procedure both hazardous and expensive to incumbents, the seats assigned to each state must be apportioned among election districts within the state. However, the familiar twentieth-century pattern of rural control of state legislatures, party conflicts, interest group competition, deadlocks following reapportionments, and other considerations bring politics into districting.[3] Disparities in the population of congressional districts within the states, rural-urban discrepancies, and gerrymandering are all symptomatic of state legislative efforts to align congressional representation with those interests which dominate the state legislature.

What happens if a state fails to apportion its representatives in accordance with population distribution? The question has a modern ring about it, but there is at least one ancient answer. Constitutional framers such as James Madison, Charles C. Pinckney, and Francis Dana noted examples of inequitable legislative representation and equated malapportionment with the deprivation of the right to vote.[4] Rufus King, in 1788, noted that the South Carolina congressional delegation reflected the urban bias (Charleston) of that state's legislature. Defending the power of Congress under the new Constitution to regulate such state failings, he exclaimed, "if the general govern-

---

3. The character of congressional districting disputes in state legislatures is presented in Malcolm E. Jewell (ed.), *The Politics of Reapportionment* (New York: Atherton Press, 1962), pp. 131–218.

4. Farrand, *The Federal Convention*, II, 241; Elliot, *Debates in the Several States*, IV, 303, 49–51; Farrand, *The Federal Convention*, III, 267–68.

ment cannot control in this case, how are the people secure?" Unfairness in districting may be remedied by Congress under the Times, Places, and Manner Clause.

During the Tyler Administration, when the practice of electing representatives by districts had become commonplace because of enlarged constituencies and the difficulties of running at-large, the apportionment act of 1842 laid down rules for congressional districting. Representatives "should be elected by districts composed of contiguous territory equal in number to the representatives to which said state may be entitled, no one district electing more than one representative." What followed this precedent was a mixed bag of legislative enactments. The apportionment act subsequent to the census of 1850 made no reference to districts. However, the districting requirement was used again in 1862, and ten years later the federal provision was amended to require that districts should contain "as nearly as practicable an equal number of inhabitants." The law of 1892 also left no doubt but that, if there were an increase in the quota of any state, the additional representatives could be elected at-large. These provisions were re-enacted after each census until 1901. In that year, and again in 1910, federal law laid down the district-equality rule, adding the requirement that congressional districts should be both contiguous and compact. But during the 1920s, as if to celebrate the census decade during which the nation passed the 50 percent urban mark, Congress submitted to the temptation to freeze the representational *status quo*. In preparation for the population count of 1930, Congress made little provision for apportionment, and the statute of 1929 contained no requirement for compactness, contiguity, or equality in population.[5] The apportionment act passed after the population count of 1940 likewise contained no such standards for the states to follow. The same omission in the past two decades has become notorious: there is no federal statute which presently applies to the population or form of congressional districts.

In an important special message in 1951, President Truman relayed the census information to Congress for 1950 and prescribed the number of representatives to which each state was entitled. He recom-

---

5. In 1964, Congressman Emanuel Celler commented on the statute of 1929, recalling that in that year, "the whole business was eliminated . . . to help our late Speaker Sam Rayburn in Texas and that is the real reason for the elimination [of statutory standards for districts]. There is no other reason for it." U.S. Congress, House, Judiciary Subcommittee No. 5, *Hearings on Congressional Redistricting*, 88th Cong., 2d sess., 1964, p. 12.

mended that Congress re-enact the traditional requirements for compact, contiguous, and demographically equal districts. In regard to the last standard, he urged that the federal legislature establish the limits of permissible deviation in population between districts at about 50,000 either above or below the average size of about 350,000.[6] This meant, in effect, that congressional constituencies should not deviate more than 14.2 percent from the state average. The suggestion closely paralleled recommendations made in 1950 by the Committee on Reapportionment of Congress of the American Political Science Association. Among other proposals, the committee advised Capitol Hill that the deviation in population size of congressional districts from the state average should be kept within a limit of 10 percent and should never exceed 15 percent.[7] Since 1951, Representative Emanuel Celler has recurrently but unsuccessfully introduced bills in Congress in harmony with these recommendations.[8]

Following publication of the results of the 1960 census, Congress continued to refuse any action requiring an equality of representation in the House. One consequence of congressional default in laying down any standards for districting may be illustrated by noting the contrasting make-up of the largest and smallest districts represented in the Eighty-eighth Congress. Following limited redistricting, the 20 largest districts (of predominantly urban-suburban complexion) encompassed a cumulative population of nearly 14 million, while the 20 smallest districts served four and a half million persons (mostly rural). During the year which preceded Supreme Court action calling for voting equality among congressional districts within each state, the average population among the 20 largest districts was 697,074 or 69.8 percent above the national average of 410,481, reckoning all congressional districts. In contrast, the 20 smallest districts in 1963 could claim an average population of 227,531, a figure 44.6 percent below the national average.[9]

6. U.S. Congress, *Message of the President*, H.R. Doc. No. 36, 82d Cong., 1st sess., 1951.

7. Cf. Andrew Hacker, *Congressional Districting: The Issue of Equal Representation* (Washington, D.C.: The Brookings Institution, 1964), p. 79.

8. See Emanuel Celler, "Congressional Apportionment," 17 *Law and Contemporary Problems* 268–75 (Spring 1952).

9. See the Congressional Quarterly Special Report, *Congressional Redistricting* (Washington, D.C.: Congressional Quarterly Service, 1966), p. 2. For complete data, see the *Congressional District Data Book* series for the 87th, 88th, 89th, 90th, and 91st Congresses (Washington, D.C.: Department of Commerce, Bureau of the Census, 1961, 1963, 1965, 1967, and 1969).

"Political Questions" Legally Asked: The 1932 Cases

In 1932 the Supreme Court heard several cases challenging the validity of new congressional districts resulting from the allotment of House seats after the 1930 census. Of pivotal importance in each case was the fact that Congress had allowed the traditional regulations to lapse.

The leading case, *Smiley* v. *Holm,* involved a dispute arising from the reduction of Minnesota's representation in the House of Representatives from 10 to 9 seats.[10] The legislature divided the state into the requisite number of districts but for partisan reasons the plan was vetoed by the governor. A voter brought suit to enjoin the use of the vetoed plan. The statute was described as invalid because the proposed districts were neither equal in population nor compact as specified by the old federal law of 1911. The Minnesota Supreme Court responded with some imaginative constitutional theory. The court speculated that the state legislature redistricted under a special federal constitutional power and not under its regular law-making power which was subject to veto by the governor. Further, the state court held that congressional standards for districting had expired and the asserted inequalities among the nine election areas presented a "political" and not a judicial question. On the latter point, the United States Supreme Court, in deciding the case on appeal, made no comment. Reasoning that the federal Constitution did not shield state redistricting from gubernatorial vetoes, the nation's highest bench reversed the state court ruling. Chief Justice Hughes explained that the Times, Places, and Manner Clause authorized Congress to provide a complete code for congressional elections. As it turned out, Congress chose to remain silent, and thus the state legislature was to follow its normal law-making procedures in setting up congressional elections. From the first step of the apportionment process involving a presidential report in 1930 to the last step involving Chief Justice Hughes' ruling in 1932, no less than five government units had taken a position on Minnesota's congressional delegation: the President, the Legislature, the Governor, the state Supreme Court, and the United States Supreme Court. Congress was mute. The net result of Chief Justice Hughes' having the last word on the subject was that Minnesota was left without any valid districts and the only recourse was an election-at-large.

10. *Smiley* v. *Holm,* 285 U.S. 355 (1932). The decision in that case controlled two other cases involving a reduction of seats from 16 to 13 in Missouri and an increase by two seats of the New York delegation to a total of 45; *Carroll* v. *Becker,* 285 U.S. 380 (1932), and *Koenig* v. *Flynn,* 285 U.S. 375 (1932).

In a Mississippi case decided the same year, the Supreme Court squarely faced the question of whether the Apportionment Act of 1911, with its standards for continuity, compactness, equality of population, was still in force. In *Wood* v. *Broom*, the Court sustained a state statute which allegedly gerrymandered congressional districts.[11] Wood, a Mississippi voter and candidate for Congress, complained that the state redistricting act was invalid because it failed to comply with federal standards. The Supreme Court, speaking through Chief Justice Hughes, decided that the injunctions granted by the district court to prevent operation of the state law should be dismissed. The nine justices agreed that, in enacting the 1929 apportionment law without carrying over the provisions dating from 1911, Congress had deliberately permitted the latter to expire leaving no statutory standards to which the voter could appeal. Five members of the Court did not think it necessary to discuss whether the right to vote is a legal right which equity could protect from dilution by maldistricting. Nevertheless, the way that the 1932 disputes were handled positively demonstrated that congressional districting is subject to judicial scrutiny.

Questions without Answers: The Colegrove *Case*

In 1946, the Supreme Court was asked on voting rights grounds to rule that a state's districting was without legal effect. The case of *Colegrove* v. *Green* involved an action questioning the legality of Illinois' refusal, since 1901, to redraw the lines of congressional districts, with the result that some representatives were elected by constituencies almost nine times larger than others.[12] Along with several voters, Kenneth Colegrove, a Northwestern University political scientist, argued that because the legislature had ignored changes since 1901 in the map of Illinois residents it had permitted a lack of district compactness and unequal popular representation patterns to impair full voting rights. A seven-man Supreme Court, divided four to three, dismissed the petition. The light-weight majority would not restrain the continued use of the disparate and antiquated districts even though they were alleged to violate the Equal Protection Clause of the Fourteenth Amendment and the congressional voting guarantee implicit in Article I. Justice Frankfurter spoke for three members of the four-man majority when he voiced the idea, new to the Court

11. *Wood* v. *Broom*, 287 U.S. 1 (1932).
12. *Colegrove* v. *Green*, 330 U.S. 804 (1947).

after the precedents of 1932, that legislative districting is a "political question" and "not meet for judicial determination." Frankfurter reasoned that "the Constitution has conferred upon Congress *exclusive* authority to secure fair representation by the States in the popular House." Essential to Frankfurter's Opinion was the assumption that the case involved not a private wrong to Professor Colegrove but rather a wrong suffered by the state of Illinois as a political entity. Frankfurter explained:

This is not an action to recover for damage because of the discriminatory exclusion of a plaintiff from rights enjoyed by other citizens. The basis for the suit is not a private wrong, but a wrong suffered by Illinois as a polity. In effect this is an appeal to the federal courts to reconstruct the electoral process of Illinois in order that it may be adequately represented in the councils of the Nation. Because the Illinois legislature has failed to revise its Congressional Representative districts in order to reflect great changes, during more than a generation, in the distribution of its population, we are asked to do this, as it were, for Illinois. Of course, no court can affirmatively re-map the Illinois districts so as to bring them more in conformity with the standards of fairness for a representative system.

Aside from the chaos that might result from an at-large election in the wake of judicial condemnation of the Illinois districts, Frankfurter reasoned that judicial remedies were simply beyond judicial reach. True, Article IV, Section 4 of the Constitution says that the United States "shall guarantee to each State in this Union a republican form of government." But Frankfurter insisted that no violation of this clause could properly be challenged in the courts. The Guaranty Clause, like the "performance of many duties in our governmental scheme" is left by the Constitution "to depend on the fidelity of the executive and legislative action, and ultimately on the vigilance of the people in exercising their political rights." For the Supreme Court to settle disputes like Colegrove's would bring the federal courts into "immediate and active relations with party contests" and consequently strand the judiciary in a "political thicket," Frankfurter feared. Accordingly he ordered dismissal of the complaint.

Justice Rutledge was the all-important judge in this case. He joined the three-man Frankfurter contingent to concur with the result of their holding. Rutledge made it clear that he would refrain from supplying any remedy in this particular case on the prudential grounds that the closeness of the election would not permit time for a proper remedy to be fashioned. But that such could be done, he thought clear from the ruling of 1932 in *Smiley* v. *Holm*. Rutledge, then, may be counted with the three dissenters to form a "hidden majority" which agreed that the issue presented was one which the courts could properly decide.[13] Joined by two other dissenters, Justice Black asserted that vote fraud and ballot-tampering cases such as *United States* v. *Classic* and *United States* v. *Saylor* defined a constitutional right to have one's ballot counted as cast. To the extent that the out-dated districting law reduced "the effectiveness of appellant's votes, [it] abridges their privilege as citizens to vote for Congressmen," (citing *Ex parte Yarbrough*).

Unanswered Questions: Baker v. Carr

In 1962, the Supreme Court took the first step toward repudiating the *Colegrove* ruling in the landmark Tennessee reapportionment case of *Baker* v. *Carr*.[14] True, legislative inaction with regard to apportionment for the state legislature was involved in *Baker* v. *Carr*, and accordingly, the Court faced a somewhat different situation than the congressional districting at issue in *Colegrove*. Nevertheless, the Tennessee case involved the three major courtroom supports affecting all constitutional ballot rights: the interest of the claimant, the power of federal courts, and the availability of remedies. Nothing in the *Baker* Opinion suggested that the Court could not later traverse all three of these bases in a congressional districting case properly before it.

As Justice Brennan saw it, the complaint in *Baker* v. *Carr* did not call for the Supreme Court to conjure up its version of republican government. It called for securing ballot rights under the Equal Protection Clause of the Fourteenth Amendment. Justice Frankfurter's Opinion in *Colegrove* had not faced the districting issue in this light. Thus the weight of the *Baker* ruling was distinguished from the alignment of justices in *Colegrove* because, in the earlier litigation, those who sided with Justice Frankfurter had meant no more than that equity remedies were not available to the Court. According to Bren-

13. Professor Walter Murphy writes that Justice Frank Murphy's papers show that Chief Justice Stone, Justices Black and Rutledge at first agreed that districting "isn't court business." Consequently, "the original vote on *Colegrove* was 6-1, with Murphy 'passing,' Jackson not participating and Douglas dissenting alone. Black and to some extent Rutledge later changed their minds. Stone did not live to do so." Walter Murphy, "Deeds under a Doctrine," 59 *American Political Science Review* 64–79 at 74 (Mar. 1965).

14. *Baker* v. *Carr*, 369 U.S. 186 (1962); cf. *Colegrove* v. *Barnett*, 330 U.S. 804 (1947); *South* v. *Peters*, 339 U.S. 279 (1950); *Remmey* v. *Smith*, 242 U.S. 216 (1952); *Radford* v. *Gary*, 352 U.S. 991 (1957).

nan, "no constitutional questions, including whether voters have a judicially enforceable constitutional right to vote at elections of congressmen from districts of equal population, were decided in *Colegrove*." That case should not be relied upon by courts to reject as "no law suit" a *bona fide* controversy as to whether some action called "political" exceeds constitutional authority.

In both *Colegrove* and *Baker*, an action was brought by voters challenging a state statute (which parcelled out representatives) as contrary to the requirements of the Fourteenth Amendment. In the Tennessee case, the state constitution provided that seats in both chambers of its legislature should be apportioned among districts in direct ratio to population and that the legislature should make a new apportionment every ten years. Illinois (the setting for *Colegrove*) and Tennessee (which was involved in *Baker*) had last been malapportioned in 1901. In each case, demographic shifts had made the vote from the most populous voting district a fractional franchise. The ratio was nine to one in Illinois and 19 to one in Tennessee when the weight of the ballots were compared in the most and least populous legislative districts. To the question of whether such inroads on the equal protection guarantee presented a controversy over which the courts could assume jurisdiction to prod the political logjam, the *Colegrove* Opinion had replied: "It is hostile to a democratic system to involve the judiciary in the politics of the people." To the same question in regard to state legislative apportionment, Justice Brennan in *Baker* replied: "It is ludicrous to preclude judicial relief when a mainspring of representative government is impaired."

The decision of the Supreme Court in the Tennessee case left major questions undecided. Did *Colegrove* v. *Green* retain any legal vitality with respect to congressional districting? What standards might the courts evolve in the traditional pragmatic process of adjudication? The silence of the Court Opinion in *Baker* v. *Carr* as to the precise requirements of the Constitution where fair weighting of voting rights was concerned left the impression that some Court members hoped that lower tribunals would "turn up something."[15] As might be expected, in the year following the reapportionment case, federal district court rulings patched together (out of a Supreme Court mandate with no standards) an inconsistent set of decisions on state legislative reapportionment, and (without either clear mandate or precise

15. As suggested in an interview with Morris B. Abram, legal counsel in *Gray* v. *Sanders*, April 17, 1963.

standards) the courts dealt variously with congressional districting cases. The fact that federal courts appeared to acquiesce to the state legislative *status quo* on congressional districting suggested the need for tutelage from the Supreme Court.

Answers that Raise New Questions: Wesberry v. Sanders

In Georgia a three-judge district court held that *Colegrove* v. *Green,* with its judicial "hands off" approach, remained applicable to congressional districting cases, as distinct from apportionment for state legislative elections where *Baker* v. *Carr* applied. The Georgia suit in *Wesberry* v. *Vandiver*[16] was filed by Atlanta voters from the fifth congressional district. They showed that their district population of 823,680 was 108.9 percent larger than the state average of 394,312 persons-per-district. Allegedly the failure of the state legislature to redistrict resulted in a denial of the equal protection of the laws. It was also said to be contrary to Article I, Section 2 of the Constitution which provides that members of the House of Representatives shall be elected "by the People." In dismissing the case, two judges presumed that *Baker* v. *Carr* had left *Colegrove* intact in regard to congressional districts because the case involved a "coequal political branch of the government." Judge Tuttle prominantly disassociated himself from the Court Opinion by reading the key Rutledge Opinion in *Colegrove* to mean only that the Illinois voters had failed to demonstrate their right to relief under the particular circumstances of the case.[17]

Two years (and one governor) after the action was filed, the Supreme Court reversed the district court ruling, the case having been retitled *Wesberry* v. *Sanders.*[18] Justice Black, speaking for six members of the Court, cited Judge Tuttle's dissent and agreed with him that, in debasing the weight of Atlanta and fifth district ballots in congressional elections, the state abridged constitutionally guaranteed voting rights. Accordingly, the district court had erred in dismissing the suit. Black thought the district court put misplaced confidence in Justice Frankfurter's minority Opinion in *Colegrove* in which he had said that the Times, Places, and Manner Clause gave Congress the exclusive authority to protect the right of citizens to vote for congressmen. To Black, that clause could not be read to "immunize state congressional apportionment laws which debase a citizen's right to

16. *Wesberry* v. *Vandiver,* 206 F. Supp. 276 (1962).
17. *Sanders* v. *Gray,* 203 F. Supp. 158 (1962).
18. *Wesberry* v. *Sanders,* 376 U.S. 1 (1964).

vote from the power of courts to protect the constitutional rights of individuals from legislative destruction." Implicit in Justice Black's reasoning here is the assumption that the congressional beneficiaries of unequal districting would understandably be reluctant to exercise the supervisory power over the state that the Times, Places, and Manner Clause gives them. But congressional forfeiture of election reform does not blot out constitutional rights—and these the courts may and should protect. Such an assertion, in combination with the precedents which recognize the constitutional source of congressional voting rights in Article I, would have been sufficient to authorize judicial involvement. This conclusion would be further supported by exposition of the congressional authorization of original jurisdiction for federal district courts to hear any civil action

to redress the deprivation under color of any State law, statute, ordinance, regulation, custom or usage, or any right, privilege or immunity secured by the Constitution of the United States or by any act of Congress providing for equal rights of citizens or of all persons within the jurisdiction of the United States.[19]

Barely noting the above, Justice Black lay much of his emphasis on the intent of the framers. His essay on this subject led him to suggest that the drafters of Article I, in stating that congressmen are to be elected "by the People," could fairly have been taken to mean "one person, one vote." The view was sharply attacked by Justice Harlan in dissent. In addition to exposing the weaknesses of Black's treatise on the origins of Article I, Section 2, he argued impressively that the Times, Places, and Manner Clause was designed so that "the state legislatures, subject only to the ultimate control of Congress, could district as they chose." In Harlan's estimate, there was "no constitutional right at stake" in Wesberry's case. In spite of historical ambiguities, Justice Black put *Wesberry* v. *Sanders* on record as saying that "construed in its historical context, the command of Article I, Section 2 that Representatives be chosen 'by the People of the several States' means that as nearly as is practicable one man's vote in a congressional election is to be worth as much as another's."[20]

19. 42 U.S.C. 1343(3). Wesberry brought his civil action under 42 U.S.C. 1983, permitting equity suits for deprivations of rights secured by the Constitution.

20. Justice Clark, in a separate opinion, said that he would have dealt with the Georgia districting case, not on the historically hazardous grounds of Article I, but against the requirements of the Equal Protection Clause of the Four-

Districting as the Art of the Practicable

Webster's *Collegiate Dictionary* defines the term "practicable" as "capable of being put into practice or accomplished by available means." Differences among the federal courts in reviewing districting plans boil down to differences over the degree of equality that the legislatures decide is capable of accomplishment by available means and within judicially set limits. Cases in 1966 in Kansas and Texas illustrate that once the legislature's redistricting plan allowed a variation of no more than 10 percent from the average legislative district these federal courts were satisfied. The district court in Kansas reviewed a new plan for congressional seats in which the numbers represented in each area varied from +5.4 to −9.6 percent deviations from the state mean. The judges held that the revised Kansas map represented "a good faith effort to meet constitutional standards." The court explained that while mathematical perfection was not achieved, the goal was approached within permissible bounds "as nearly as the legislature in their good judgment believed to be practicable."[21] Likewise in Texas, a three-member federal bench judged valid a fresh congressional districting act in which the largest and the smallest constituencies each varied 9.7 percent from the state average.[22] In that case the tribunal noted that the legislature had set a 10 percent deviation standard for itself, and the resulting redistricting, which nearly over-reached the rule, sufficiently evidenced "a good faith effort to achieve substantial numerical equality, even though a one to three per cent deviation was theoretically attainable." In Texas, as in Kansas, the federal courts refused to identify the "practicable" with the theoretically possible. The implication was that it was not necessary literally to aim for equality but at best for something five to ten points removed. In the Texas case, Judge Noel observed that the state legislature's difficulties in redistricting were compounded by the fact that law-makers must adopt a plan "without chart or compass or any standard by which to gauge its end product except the population

---

teenth Amendment. The reason why Justice Black did not invoke that amendment has been a subject of speculation. His choice may well have represented a temporary compromise among members of the Court who were not yet prepared, as four months later eight of them were, to specify what the Fourteenth Amendment required of state legislatures engaged in reapportionment and districting; e.g., *Reynolds* v. *Sims*, 377 U.S. 533 (1964).

21. *Meeks* v. *Avery*, 251 F. Supp. 245 (Kan., 1966).

22. *Bush* v. *Martin*, 251 F. Supp. 484 (1966).

standard," and the latter's tolerances were uncertain. Legislatures were not alone. Equally without "chart or compass" were the federal courts commissioned on the front line of redistricting problems to pass on the validity of state statutes.

Without guidance from Congress, the percentage of deviation standards with which district courts experimented could be viewed as rules of thumb rather than requirements ensconced in federal law and equally applicable to all states. Judicial concessions to minimal departures from absolute mathematical equality appeared justified by statements in *Wesberry* which called for some flexibility. As the Supreme Court said in *Reynolds* v. *Sims*, "mathematical exactness or precision is hardly a workable constitutional requirement" because qualitative as well as quantitative factors affect a fair districting plan.[23] The *Reynolds* Court made this point (referring to state apportionment schemes) when Chief Justice Warren explained that "judicial scrutiny must be given to the *character* as well as to the *degree* of deviations from a strict constitutional basis," (emphasis added). What do these two aspects of representation mean?

The Degree of Deviation

Following *Wesberry*, federal district courts watched Congress closely for progress on legislatively set standards for population equality. In 1966, a three-judge court validated a revised Indiana plan under which "none of the districts varies from the ideal population figure [the average] by as much as 15 percent and only one by more than 10 percent."[24] The district court Opinion also noted that the 1966 plan measured up to the statutory equality standards then being considered by Congress. (Congressman Celler's bill would have set the outer limits of equality at 15 percent above and below the state's average district constituency.) Unfortunately for the court and legislature, however, H.R. 2836 was defeated by a series of crippling amendments.

In the late 1960s, congressional opponents of change could present

23. For the argument that contiguity and compactness, like population equality, can be reduced to quantitative measure, see testimony, James Weaver and Sidney Hess, Judiciary Subcommittee, *Hearings on Congressional Redistricting*, 88th Cong., 2d sess., 1964, pp. 76–105; and Weaver and Hess, "Nonpartisan Districting." Henry F. Kaiser, "An Objective Method for Establishing Legislative Districts," 10 *Midwest Journal of Political Science* 200 (May 1966).

24. *Grills* v. *Branigan*, 255 F. Supp. 155 (1966). Judge Holder, dissenting, thought it sufficiently demonstrated that partisan gerrymandering at Republican expense had inflated population inequalities.

strong arguments against adopting any statute to go into effect prior to the 1970 census because available social statistics were stale. Population figures dating back to 1960 were patently misleading as guidelines for rapidly changing cities and suburbs. The politics of redistricting was also considerably complicated by the fact that, after 1966, federal courts became increasingly strict in their application of the "one person, one vote" rule. The 1967 districting bill sponsored by Congressman Celler was correspondingly rigorous. It enjoyed serious consideration in both houses because "continued litigation underscores the urgency of Congress to declare its policy."[25] The conference committee version of Chairman Celler's H.R. 2508 set a rather stringent equality definition to go into effect in 1972 under the new federal census. In any state, the congressional district with the largest population "shall not exceed by more than 10 per centum the district with the smallest population. . . ." Notice that this 10 percent rule refers to the spread of variation between the largest and the smallest district as opposed to earlier proposals which measured variations above and below a state's average district. The pinch involved in tightening equality requirements may be appreciated when the Celler bill of 1967 is thought of as a rejection of the customary 15 percent standard in favor of what is virtually a 5 percent rule.[26]

Even without congressional help, redistricting after 1964 progressed at a steady pace spurred largely by litigation. By 1967, only eight states retained districts which could be condemned by the traditional 15 percent rule of thumb. On the other hand, only 12 states were securely within the limits of H.R. 2508 with its requirement of no more than a 10 percent spread between largest and smallest districts in a state.[27]

With respect to the degree of permissible inequality, the *Reynolds*

25. U.S. Congress, Senate, Judiciary Committee, *Congressional Redistricting Report*, 90th Cong., 1st sess., 1967, p. 3.

26. Actually, however, the new measure was framed in terms of a variation of 10 percent between the largest and smallest districts. Statistically this could work out in a two-district state such as South Dakota to a variation of 4.7 percent above and below the average district population. In a 41-district state such as New York, the 10 percent rule could apply to a theoretical 9.8 percent above average or to 8.8 percent below average.

27. The data is presented, as of June, 1967, in Appendix A (Congressional District Variations in All 50 States) and Appendix C (States Which Have Achieved a Maximum Variation of Less Than 10 percent) in the Minority Views, Senate Judiciary Committee, *Redistricting*, 90th Cong., 1st sess., 1967, pp. 21–22.

Court had noted that "an honest and good faith effort" must be made "to construct districts . . . as nearly of equal population as is practicable." This comment was followed by the rather ominous caution that because a state invariably has more state than federal legislative seats to distribute, "somewhat more flexibility may therefore be constitutionally permissible with respect to state legislative apportionment than in congressional districting." This caveat was partly clarified by the strict approach which the Supreme Court took to Indiana districting in 1967. That year, Congress again defaulted in setting districting standards, leaving the way open for an unrestricted review by the Supreme Court. By memorandum decision in 1967 (*Duddleston v. Grills*), the Supreme Court cut back on equality laxness by ordering a federal court in Indiana to reconsider its decision upholding a districting plan whereby only four districts varied more than six percent from the ideal.[28] (One was 12.8 percent under-represented.) The lower court was ordered to require of the state a more rigorous defense of existing inequalities in harmony with the comparable rule for state legislatures announced the same day in *Swann* v. *Adams* (see Chapter 8).[29] Again by *per curiam* decision, the Court dealt with a companion case from Missouri.[30] The high bench agreed with a lower federal court that Missouri's latest districting effort was constitutionally void. The state offered no acceptable defense for aggravating rather than alleviating maldistricting. For example, between an earlier scheme and that of 1965, boundaries for the under-represented First District (St. Louis City and County) were extended to include an additional 8,500 persons. Nevertheless, all districts were kept within 10.4 percent of the state average district population. Without offering explanatory opinions in either the Missouri or Indiana decisions of 1967, the Supreme Court issued two redistricting orders which apparently meant that even a 10 percent variation from a state's average district population is too large when it is not acceptably explained or defended.

In 1969, the Missouri case of *Kirkpatrick* v. *Preisler* returned to the Supreme Court.[31] There, Justice Brennan spoke for five members of the bench in using the case "to elucidate the 'as nearly as practicable' standard." The second *Kirkpatrick* case grew out of the state's response to the first. According to the Missouri redistricting plan of

28. *Duddleston v. Grills*, 385 U.S. 455 *per curiam* (1967).
29. *Swann v. Adams*, 385 U.S. 440 (1967).
30. *Kirkpatrick v. Preisler*, 385 U.S. 450 *per curiam* (1967).
31. *Kirkpatrick v. Preisler*, 394 U.S. 526 (1969).

1967, districts were permitted to range from 12,260 below to 13,542 persons above the average-sized district of 431,981. In percentage terms, the deviations from the average involved, at the least, a 3.13 per-cent under-representation for one congressional constituency compared to 2.83 percent over-representation elsewhere. While these departures from the average were small, the Supreme Court followed the district court in faulting the scheme on several grounds. Missouri used 1960 census figures for some districts, but arbitrarily abandoned them in others. The legislature rejected a redistricting plan submitted to it which provided for districts with even smaller variances. Finally, the plaintiffs demonstrated that the simple device of switching some counties from one district to another would have produced a plan much more nearly approaching population equality among Missouri's ten congressional districts.

In *Kirkpatrick*, Justice Brennan announced a rule of nation-wide significance when he said that no deviations from the "one man, one vote" principle, "no matter how small" are acceptable without strong justification. Brennan rejected Missouri's seven arguments advanced in support of the variances built into the act of 1967. (1) The General Assembly's attempt to take district interest groups into account was rejected as "antithetical to the basic premise of the constitutional command to provide equal representation for equal numbers of people." (2) The Court did not find "legally acceptable the argument that variances are justified as the necessary result from a state's attempt to avoid fragmenting political subdivisions by drawing congressional district lines along existing county, municipal, or other political subdivision boundaries." (3) Nor could "compactness" excuse inequality when only considerations of aesthetics were involved. "A State's preference for pleasingly shaped districts can hardly justify population variances." (4) A legislature may justify temporary inequalities in attempting to take into account projected population shifts. But this must be done by a "thoroughly documented" and "systematically" used set of projections and not, as in Missouri, on an *ad hoc* basis. (5) The state argued that some inequalities resulted from discounting large numbers of military or student personnel under a system in which eligible voters made up the representational base instead of the total population. The Court's chief objection on this score was the haphazard technique for making such adjustments. The presence of short-term residents was taken into account in the state's defense only where the Eighth District (St. Louis) was concerned. (6) Arguments invoking the "political realities of legislative interplay" were also set aside. Brennan wrote: "Problems created by partisan politics cannot justify an apportionment which does not otherwise pass constitutional muster."

Missouri's primary argument was that inequalities among congressional constituencies were so small that they should be considered excusably *de minimis* and for that reason not to require independent justification. In response, Justice Brennan took the important step of rejecting any discrete percentage figure for permissible variation:

We can see no nonarbitrary way to pick a cutoff point at which population variances suddenly become *de minimis*. Moreover, to consider a certain range of variances *de minimis* would encourage legislators to strive for that range rather than for equality as nearly as practicable. . . . [T]he command of Article I, Section 2, that States create congressional districts which provide equal representation for equal numbers of people permits only the limited population variances which are unavoidable despite a good-faith effort to achieve absolute equality, or for which justification is shown.

Justice Fortas wrote a concurring Opinion, objecting not to the result of the Missouri ruling, but to the way that the majority dealt with the contest. He thought it dangerous to require that all margin for error from "precise mathematical equality" be justified and then in the Court Opinion "to reject, *seriatim*, every type of justification that has been—possibly, every one that could be—advanced." Fortas, and Justice White who dissented, attempted to show that insistence on mathematical perfection does not make sense even on its own terms. For example, the Census Bureau concedes errors in its figures (of up to 20 percent for young adult male Negroes, to cite the sector of least reliable statistics). Justice Harlan, joined by Justice Stewart, in dissent, was sharply critical of the new ruling. "Whatever room remained under this Court's prior decisions for the free play of the political process in matters of reapportionment is now all but eliminated by today's *Draconian* judgments." Harlan thought that reliance on the single factor of population equality (encouraging disregard to traditional county lines and other historical factors) could subvert the quality of representation. "Even more than in the past, district lines are likely to be drawn to maximize the political advantage of the party temporarily dominant in public affairs."

The Character of Deviation

With respect to the character or quality of fairly defined congressional constituencies, the Supreme Court in *Reynolds* v. *Sims* had asserted: "*Wesberry* clearly established that the fundamental principle of representative government in this country is one of equal representation for equal numbers of people, without regard to race, sex, economic status or place of residence within a State." Aside from such offhand comments, the Supreme Court has shed little further light on the qualitative aspects of fair districting. In this dark corner of the law, gerrymandering comes into imprecise focus. The House Judiciary Committee considering Chairman Celler's H.R. 2508 in 1967 called for contiguous and compact districts. "Gerrymandering" was defined as districting "in an unnatural and unfair way" with the purpose of concentrating the voting power of disfavored groups in a few districts, or with the intent "to minimize or cancel out the voting strength of racial or political elements of the voting population."[32] In the Supreme Court decision of *Wright* v. *Rockefeller*, decided in 1964, Justice Black acted on behalf of seven members of the Court in sidestepping the task of defining gerrymandering in the light of the Constitution.[33] He ruled that a number of New York City voters (who complained of being racially segregated out of Manhattan's 17th congressional district) had failed to prove that the boundaries affecting them were drawn along racial lines. The Opinion of the Court provided no hint as to what the decision might have been had boundaries contrived to discriminate against Negroes and Puerto Ricans been proved. Thus the opportunity was not taken, as Justices Douglas and Goldberg in dissent thought it should be, to indicate a position on gerrymandering. The attempt to draw the lines of a congressman's bailiwick which adhere to population equality but which fail to set up compact and contiguous districts presents problems on the very frontiers of the law. Certainly political division perimeters which are manifestly charted along racially discriminatory lines are unconstitutional according to *Gomillion* v. *Lightfoot*.[34] The majority

32. In 1967, the Senate Judiciary Committee used the following definitions. Gerrymandering is the attempt: (a) to divide a territorial unit "into election districts in an unnatural and unfair way with the purpose of giving one political party an electoral minority in a large number of districts while concentrating the voting strength of the opposition in as few districts as possible"; (b) "to minimize or cancel out the voting strength of racial or political elements of the voting population." The latter quotation is from *Burns* v. *Richardson*, 384 U.S. 73, 89 (1965). Senate Judiciary Committee, *Redistricting*, 90th Cong., 1st sess., 1967, p. 4.

33. *Wright* v. *Rockefeller*, 376 U.S. 52 (1964). A similar result obtained in *Honeywood* v. *Rockefeller*, 214 F. Supp. 897. aff'd 376 U.S. 722 (1964).

34. *Gomillion* v. *Lightfoot*, 364 U.S. 339 (1960); see Chapter 4.

in *Wright* v. *Rockefeller* by no means denied that fact, as their holding turned rather on rules of evidence. The latter decision does illustrate, however, that it is difficult to prove the practical consequences of maldistricted and racially motivated representation schemes, apart from the arithmetical injustice of population disparities.

The lower courts have dealt inconsistently with popularly equal but "crazy-quilt" district boundaries where considerations other than race are concerned. Prior to *Kirkpatrick* v. *Preisler* in 1969, they sometimes did not hesitate to say that the Constitution does not take politics out of districting. A federal court in Kansas took the straightforward position in 1966 that "partisan political gerrymandering is not condemned as violative" of the Constitution.

In 1969, the Supreme Court reviewed New York's scheme of congressional districting in *Wells* v. *Rockefeller*.[35] David Wells, a member of the Liberal Party, charged that Assembly Democrats and Senate Republicans had taken advantage of their respective control of the two legislative chambers to strike a bargain by drawing district lines in order to protect incumbent congressmen. Two constitutional attacks were made on the resulting statute: The state law violates the "one-man, one-vote" principle of *Wesberry* v. *Sanders* (there was a 13.1 percent spread of deviation between the largest and smallest districts); and the statute represents a systematic and intentional partisan gerrymander violating Article I, Section 2 of the Constitution and the Fourteenth Amendment. In a brief Opinion, Justice Brennan was content to hold the plan void on the principles of the companion case of *Kirkpatrick* v. *Preisler*. The New York plan designated seven sections of the state as homogeneous regions, dividing each region into congressional districts of virtually identical population. The other ten districts were "groupings" of whole counties. Fatal to the plan was the fact that inter-regional inequalities were not defended as "unavoidable despite a good faith effort to achieve equality, or for which justification is shown." Accordingly, Brennan invalidated the plan and commented: "We do not reach . . . the merits of the attack upon the statute as a constitutionally impermissible gerrymander." In his *Kirkpatrick* dissent, Justice Harlan criticized the result in the New York case in compelling terms. He said:

The Court's exclusive concentration upon arithmetic blinds it to the realities of the political process, as the *Rockefeller* case makes so clear. The

35. *Wells* v. *Rockefeller*, 394 U.S. 542 (1969).

fact of the matter is that the rule of absolute equality is perfectly compatible with 'gerrymandering' of the worst sort. A computer may grind out district lines which can totally frustrate the popular will on an overwhelming number of critical issues. The legislature must do more than satisfy one-man, one-vote; it must create a structure which will in fact as well as theory be responsive to the sentiments of the community.

Wells v. *Rockefeller* and *Wright* v. *Rockefeller* suggest that a majority of the members of the Supreme Court are not prepared to take a strong stand on the gerrymander question. Until Congress or the Supreme Court address themselves to the problem of partisanly inspired misshapen districts, it remains open to question whether the Constitution requires (or even allows) the two traditional norms of contiguity and compactness as components of "practicable equality."

As for Congress, its default in laying down guidelines for fair districting has produced a costly decision-making vacuum. State legislatures, without "chart or compass" to guide them, may meet in expensive special sessions for districting purposes, but the courts retain the final say. Without congressional guidance, federal courts have required standards which are stricter than those which Congress might fairly set out. Here indeed is an ironic turn of events: "conservative" inertia in Congress has become responsible for litigation producing "liberal" court rulings at the grassroots level, decisions which by their strict emphasis on population equality take the very measure of political play out of districting which recalcitrant congressmen by their inaction had hoped to preserve. In this way, partisan control in the states of the districting process has become stalemated. Nevertheless, the states could regain the initiative in preparing for the 1970 census by following the lead of the Maryland and New York Constitutional Conventions. Although by 1968 both constitutions had been defeated by popular majorities on other issues, they similarly attempted to delete gross underhanded partisanship from the process of creating legislative districts. The eastern state proposals would have assigned both the reapportionment of the state legislature and the drawing of congressional districts after each decennial census to a bipartisan commission. Such a body cannot humanly be expected to be fully nonpartisan, but it can devote the necessary time and technical study to the array of districting proposals that would approach bipartisan fairness. Its specialized work can relieve the legislature of an inevitably disagreeable, usually time-consuming, and occasionally unwanted chore which they are not competent to handle objectively. If bipartisan districting boards could produce an approximate equality of representation, without partisan tricks and manipulations which might discourage party competition, they could contribute significantly to improvement in the quality of federal and state representation. By turning constructively to the intricate problems of fair and effective representation, they could remove districting from the litigation process where the quality of dialogue regarding representation is inhibited by the nay-saying powers of the judiciary.

10 Voting for the president "mediately by the people"

In *The Federalist* No. 68, Alexander Hamilton wrote that the framers of the Constitution sought a stable presidential selection process, a goal which was "peculiarly desirable to afford as little opportunity as possible to tumult and disorder." Nevertheless, the original plan of 1787 has given way to change, crisis, and controversy. Less than twenty years after the Philadelphia Convention disbanded, the need for change was recognized. On the basis of experience with party politics in the Jeffersonian election of 1800, sufficient support was mustered to alter by means of the Twelfth Amendment the original Electoral College arrangements of Article II. The constitutional crisis contained in the Electoral College system was poignantly illustrated in the selection of President Hayes. That episode in electoral misadventure brought Supreme Court members directly into presidential politics through the unique part which they played on the Electoral Commission of 1877.

Constitutional controversy over presidential elections, sporadically indicated by Supreme Court litigation, has been continual from the

1890s through the 1960s. Of course, law on the subject of presidential elections has undergone changes at several levels: party regulations and practices, state law, federal statutes, constitutional amendment, and constitutional litigation.[1] Virtually every component of the American electoral system is so affected; nevertheless, from local to federal elections, none has been so little the subject of litigious challenge or innovating decision by the Supreme Court as the process of presidential choice.[2]

CONSTITUTIONAL BACKGROUND

Today presidential electors, under the laws of 50 states, are picked by popular choice. The positions are usually filled by faithful political party workers nominated in party conventions, committees, or primaries. But in Article II of the Constitution, no mention of political parties is to be found. The drafting of Section 1 of this complicated measure which deals with electors was marked by protracted discussion and frequent evidence of frustration. The result was a compromise shrouded in vagueness.

When the Convention delegates first considered the mode of choosing a President, they discussed the most obvious alternatives: election by Congress or by the people.[3] The possibility of adopting a solution as simple as election by the people was precluded by apprehension about popular ignorance of the candidates. Also feared were the trappings of monarchy attending congressional choice (Gouverneur

1. For a complete survey of party regulations, state and federal statutes, constitutional provisions, and judicial rulings see *Nomination and Election of the President and Vice President of the United States, Including the Manner of Selecting Delegates to National Political Conventions* (Washington, D.C.: Government Printing Office, 1968). The exhaustive resumé was compiled, under the direction of Francis Valeo, Secretary of the Senate, by Richard D. Hupman, Senate Library, and Robert L. Tienken, Legislative Reference Service, Library of Congress. On political party reform, see Nelson Polsby and Aaron Wildavsky, *Presidential Elections* (2d ed.; New York: Charles Scribner's Sons, 1968), chap. 5.

2. See the formal model of constitutional innovation given by Glendon Schubert in his "The Rhetoric of Constitutional Change," 16 *Journal of Public Law* 15 (1967).

3. A fully annotated account may be found in Edward Dumbauld, *The Constitution of the United States* (Norman: University of Oklahoma Press, 1964), pp. 256–63. See also, Lucius Wilmerding, *The Electoral College* (New Brunswick: Rutgers University Press, 1958); Neal R. Peirce, *The People's President* (New York: Simon and Schuster, 1968).

Morris conjured a distasteful vision of a legislatively appointed executive in the role of a British Prime Minister) or the possible hegemony of large states in popular elections (to Oliver Ellsworth, "the matter of the sizes of the different states was unanswerable"). It was James Wilson who offered the outline of the scheme resembling the one later adopted. He thought that with the discarded alternatives behind them the idea of electing a President "mediately or immediately by the people" would find considerable support.

Details of Wilson's plan were worked out in the closed sessions of a Committee of Eleven. The group presented a two-step plan involving concessions to indirect popular representation and to equal voting strength among the states. First, the chief executive would be picked by electors "appointed" by each state and totaling the number of senators and representatives authorized to the state. The independent judgment of those honored as electors was to focus on the good of the people as a whole. To this end, federal *and* state attachments were to be transcended by forbidding federal office-holders to act as electors and by requiring that one of the two names placed on each elector's ballot would be that of a non-state resident. With independent judgment so shaped, a majority of the electors would be required for Electoral College selection of the President. It was foreseen that a majority behind one candidate would not easily materialize, and a plurality contest or one resulting in a tie between two majority vote-winners would generate the second step of the complex plan. At this stage, Congress would make a final decision. The presidential selection, Colonel Mason conjectured, would end up in the Senate 19 out of 20 times. The vote of the electors, therefore, would be in reality in the category of a popular nominating process favoring the populous states with their larger numbers of electors. But the final selection among the five "nominees" would be made through an undemocratic voting process in Congress where the smaller states would have equality with the larger ones. The last step of the process could distort the popular voice, but the first nominating step shaped the range of choice. The Constitution thus premised the presidential electoral process on the citizenry generally; the President was to be chosen "mediately by the people."

In the prototype scheme which became effective in March 1789, if the electoral vote were tied or resulted in no majority choice, the House was to ballot by states to make the final determination. In a plurality contest, the representatives were to decide on one among the leading five for the executive post. In any event, the runner-up was to become Vice President. It was this "double voting" procedure —a single balloting for two offices—which the Twelfth Amendment changed by setting up a separate election for Vice President in the Senate; however, the amendment invested the Senate with powers in electing the Vice President similar to those possessed by the House in electing the President. Thus it is possible under such circumstances that the two officers can be of differing parties corresponding to those of the chambers choosing them. The amendment did not change the language of the original provision in Article II regarding the count of the vote.

The election of 1800, which was not settled until congressional action in 1801, provides the clue to understanding why the double voting system of the Electoral College was changed.[4] Republican electors dominated the election and voted for Thomas Jefferson and Aaron Burr on the presumption that Jefferson would receive the presidency and Burr would become Vice President. The electoral ballots cast, however, made no discrimination between the offices, and Jefferson and Burr each received the same number of votes. Thus, the leader of the early Republicans and his personal rival Aaron Burr procedurally had equal access to the presidency. But, as Senator James Jackson of Georgia explained in the debates preceding the adoption of the Twelfth Amendment, "it was never intended to give them an equal chance." The majority tie that the election produced required final settlement in the House of Representatives. The House elected Jefferson but only after 36 ballots, nearly a week of intrigue, and an uncomfortable Republican reliance on the minority wishes of the Federalists led by Hamilton of New York and Bayard of Delaware.[5] Each state's representation arrived at its one vote by polling its members, and the candidate receiving the greatest number of votes of that state's representatives received the one full vote of the state. The deadlock of 1801 was finally broken when Vermont and Maryland Federalists agreed not to vote at all, thus allowing the Republicans in their delegations to elect Jefferson instead of Burr.

4. A rare but useful source on the Twelfth Amendment is Lolabel House, *A Study of the Twelfth Amendment of the Constitution of the United States* (Philadelphia: University of Pennsylvania Press, 1901).

5. See Henry Cabot Lodge (ed.), *Life and Letters of George Cabot* (Boston: Little, Brown and Co., 1877), George Cabot to Alexander Hamilton, p. 284. Equally conniving on the Republican side was John Taylor's estimate that the proposed Twelfth Amendment "would finally destroy the minority." 12 *Annals of Cong.* 482–86 (1803). Cf. Albert J. Beveridge, *The Life of John Marshall* (4 vols.; Boston: Houghton Mifflin Co., 1916–1919), pp. 11, 452–58; 532–47.

By 1804, victorious Republicans had eliminated ambiguity in Jefferson's quest for a second presidential term. The Twelfth Amendment was adopted two months before the election of 1804—another Jefferson victory. It provided that if no candidate for Vice President were to receive a majority among ballots expressly cast for that office, the Senate, voting by heads, was to make the selection. The Senate's option was restricted to a choice between the two most successful candidates for Vice President. A comparable Jeffersonian democratic advance was made in the choice of the President. The Twelfth Amendment restricted the discretion of the House in the event of a plurality or tie contest. Under these circumstances, representatives were to select a President, not (as Article II provided) from among the five, but from among the three closest to electoral victory, thereby amplifying the voice of the people. This minor electoral revision followed from changes at the state level. In 1800, 11 out of the 16 states appointed electors according to state legislative choice. But by 1804, 11 states extended to the voter the right to express a preference in the naming of electors.

Intraparty cohesion plus a democratizing spirit thus inspired enactment of the Twelfth Amendment at the dawn of the nineteenth century. It was a reform which reflected Republican dominance and the existing imbalance of national power in their favor. The dispatch with which the Twelfth Amendment was enacted vindicated the Jeffersonian belief that constitutional revision should be relatively frequent and responsive to political and social changes. Such was not to be the rule, however, as later nineteenth-century presidential elections pointed up idiosyncrasies (left untouched by the Twelfth Amendment) which came into greater prominence with a pattern of high voter turnout that carried into the twentieth century.

THE SUPREME COURT IN THE VOTE COUNT OF 1877

In his famous *Commentaries on American Law*, Chancellor Kent noted in the early nineteenth century that if ever the tranquillity of the United States is to be disturbed by crisis, "it will be upon this very subject of a choice of a President."[6] Among the most sensitive procedural problems that Kent studied was the question of whether the powers of Congress to count the votes of electors, provided by

6. James Kent, *Commentaries on American Law* (New York: O. Halstead, 1826), I, 255–56.

the Twelfth Amendment, include the authority to decide which electors had actually or lawfully been appointed? The first century of the existence of the Constitution witnessed four unsuccessful congressional attempts to establish machinery for deciding contested elections. Kent observed that the Constitution did not expressly declare by whom the electors' ballots are to be counted and recognized that "in the case of questionable votes and a closely contested election, this power may be all-important." It was the opinion of the author of the *Commentaries* that, in the presence of members of Congress acting as spectators, the President of the Senate should determine the results. Kent conceded that Congress could readily set the matter straight by legislation. But as a matter of fact, the House and Senate practice of voting on disputed presidential ballots rested for eighty years on no authority other than custom.

Between 1865 and 1876 the matter was settled by a temporary expedient known as Rule 22, empowering either chamber of Congress to reject disputed electoral votes.[7] In 1873 Senator Oliver Morton from Indiana argued that there was imminent danger to any country in which the rules for succession of its highest officer were not regularized and clear. He urged—in vain—that rule 22 should be made more than a temporary measure if crisis were to be avoided. In January 1875, the Democrats assumed control of the House of Representatives, and an apprehensive Republican Senate unilaterally repealed Rule 22. The Republicans feared that the Reconstruction resolution would permit their opponents to control the forthcoming presidential election. Conceivably, under Rule 22 Democrats could refuse to honor enough Republican electors to prevent any candidate from receiving a majority, resulting in the Democratic House selecting the President under the terms of the Twelfth Amendment. The abolition of the vote-count rule threw law and custom into confusion and the stage was set for the constitutional crisis of 1876. The nation faced the election of 1876 with no guidelines for resolving arguments over disputed electoral votes. The Republican Rutherford Hayes polled 4,036,572 votes, and his opponent, Samuel Tilden, polled 4,284,020. Nevertheless, neither candidate enjoyed an electoral majority because the allotment of 22 electoral votes remained in doubt in Florida, Louisiana, Oregon, and South Carolina.[8]

In the absence of Rule 22 and with Congress deadlocked on the

7. *Cong. Globe*, 38th Cong., 2d sess. (Feb. 6, 1865), I, 608.

8. An account of the election may be found in C. Vann Woodward, *Reunion and Reaction: The Compromise of 1877 and the End of Reconstruction* (New York: Doubleday, 1951).

disputed votes, opinion soon began to favor arbitration by a mixed commission to include five representatives, five senators, and five justices of the Supreme Court. The ten legislators and four of the justices were to be evenly divided between the two political parties. The all-important fifth justice was picked by his four colleagues. Justice David Davis, a political independent and maverick, was the anticipated choice. On January 25, 1877, Congress established the Electoral Commission. Simultaneously, with high drama and little prior notice, the Republican Illinois legislature elected Justice Davis to the United States Senate. Following this extraordinary maneuver, the New Jersey Republican, Justice Joseph Bradley, was elected to the board. Supreme Court members were Justices Clifford and Field, both Democrats, and three Republicans—Justices Miller, Strong, and Bradley. Hopeful observers reassured themselves that Supreme Court justices are "as free from bias as it is possible for men to be."[9] When it became evident that Bradley's vote favored, in every important instance, his fellow Republican Hayes, the prestige of the Justices greatly suffered. Soon afterwards Bradley penned: "The abuse heaped on me is almost beyond conception."[10]

Clearly the Court members had embarked on a perilous course in accepting the assignment to arbitrate an issue charged with the most explosive and immediate political consequences. Yet the Hayes-Tilden fiasco resulted in two positive and enduring consequences. On the one hand, Congress drew upon the experience of the Electoral Commission to provide for a partial remedy to future disputed contests with the Electoral Count Act of 1887.[11] (Interest in the issue was sustained over a decade during which the Republican Senate three times passed a vote-count bill which was persistently refused by a Democratic

9. "Current Topics," 15 *Albany Law Journal* 94 (1877). The sentiment was the basis for the proposed constitutional amendment to entrust electoral vote disputes to the Supreme Court. Failing in 1873 to emerge from the Senate Judiciary Committee, the idea had no chance of becoming the sixteenth amendment. *Cong. Globe*, 42d Cong., 3d sess. (Jan. 7, 1873), p. 368.

10. M. C. Klinkhamer, "Joseph P. Bradley: Private and Public Opinion of a Political Justice," 7 *University of Detroit Law Journal* 150, 168 (Mar. 1960).

11. As amended and codified, the Electoral Vote Count Act now specifies that, after the electors have cast their votes, the results are to be sent to the President of the Senate. (Act of Jan. 14, 1887, now codified as 3 U.S.C. 5 [see 1-21]; 3 U.S.C. 6-15.) Both houses gather in joint session on January 6, following the meeting of the electors. In the presence of the full Congress, the Vice President of the United States opens all the certificates containing the electoral votes. The ballots are called out and counted state by state, and the tally is announced by the presiding officer.

House.) On the other hand, the Supreme Court found two opportunities during the Chief Justiceship of Melville Fuller to deal authoritatively with issues reminiscent of the 1877 contest.

Among the contested electoral votes in the election of 1876 were four Democratic ballots, honored by a Florida circuit court in response to the old English *quo warranto* procedure initiated by Hayes electors. The decision was promptly unheld by the Florida Supreme Court. But in Justice Bradley's brief Opinion for the Commission majority (all Republicans), the state tribunal's ruling favorable to Tilden was rejected, and the Hayes electoral vote was accepted because "it was regularly certified to by the governor of the state."[12] Of uncertain impact was the argument heard by the Commission from William Evarts, counsel for the Florida Republicans. After awkwardly excepting present company, Evarts exclaimed that if "judicial intervention" in the electoral process were to become commonplace, then "at last government of the judges will have superseded the sovereignty of the people and there will be no cure, no recourse, but that which the children of Israel had: to pray for a king." Congress was more sanguine in the Electoral Vote Count Act of 1887 which prescribes that if a state establish any procedure "by judicial or other methods" for deciding Electoral College contests, that result is to be binding in the congressional count. In case of further disputes, written objections to a controversial vote are submitted to the presiding officer of the Senate, whereupon the two chambers separately pass on the question. Agreement of the houses is required for rejection, and disagreement results in the challenged vote being counted.

Participation of Supreme Court members on the Electoral Commission of 1877 sensitized its members to the need for clarification of certain constitutional aspects of presidential elections which were critical in Commission debates. These included the status of electors and the appointment power of the legislatures. The politics of the Commission's work was not less perplexing than the law. Of first importance was the fact that Hayes had to be awarded every contested vote to win. The Republican strategy therefore required soft-pedalling popular vote irregularities and emphasizing that Congress had no power to examine into the conditions of balloting. One justification offered for this view was that the Constitution did not make

12. U.S. Congress, *Proceedings of the Electoral Commission and of the Two Houses of Congress in Joint Meeting* (Washington, D.C.: Government Printing Office, 1877), p. 56. See L. Kinvin Worth, "Election Contests and the Electoral Vote," 65 *Dickenson Law Review* 321 (Mar. 1961).

electors federal officers but independent agents regulated only under state laws. By way of contrast, it was to the advantage of the Democrats to discredit through federal inquiry any state's choice of an elector; even an unresolved conflict on such votes could deprive Hayes or Tilden of an electoral majority and throw the presidential selection into the Democratic House. One result was that the traditional positions of the two parties was reversed, the Republicans using the rhetoric of states rights and the Democrats calling for increased federal supervision. In dispute after dispute, the Republican majority of the Commission took the position that they could not go behind the returns as authenticated by the election officials of the states, a tactic which resulted in Hayes' victory. Another politically important development that must be noted here, if only parenthetically, is that more than a temporary trade of party ideology resulted from the Commission's work. House Democrats agreed not to circumvent the electoral result because of assurances given to Democratic leaders that President Hayes would recall federal troops from their occupation of the South, the principal source of security for Reconstruction-era Negroes who voted Republican in large numbers.

SUPREME COURT LITIGATION FROM THE 1890s TO THE 1960s

In post-Reconstruction years, a "states' rights" perspective, carried over from the rationalizations of the Electoral Commission, informed the Supreme Court rulings touching on presidential elections. A decision involving the status of electors in 1890 and one clarifying the appointment power of the states in 1892 were of relatively little immediate importance. They did, however, set precedents for Supreme Court handling of presidential election litigation, and they established a pattern of deference to state supervision for which there were no major exceptions until 1968.

The States' Rights Cases of the 1890s

In 1890, the case of *In re Green* yielded the ruling that federal authority over presidential elections encompassed little more than congressional control of the election calendar. Surveying the relevant federal statutes of the time, Justice Gray said that Congress had not sought to interfere with the state appointment of electors and that, historically, Congress had not attempted to punish any fraud in popular voting for electors. In a key statement, Gray asserted that the lack of federal regulation was understandable because electors are "no more officers or agents of the United States than are members of the State legislature when acting as electors of Federal Senators."[13] Because Gray emphasized existing state functions to support his argument, the question of the future propriety of federal regulation of fraud in presidential elections concurrently with the states was not foreclosed by the ruling.

The case of *McPherson* v. *Blacker*, decided in 1892, combined with *In re Green*, further established the decentralized character of responsibility for presidential elections.[14] Prior to the Harrison-Cleveland election, Michigan electors were popularly chosen but under a modified district system drawn up along partisan lines.[15] The plan was the responsibility of the Michigan Democrats—the minority party in temporary possession of the legislature. They claimed to have acted under the Article II provision that "each State shall appoint, in such Manner as the Legislature thereof may direct, a Number of Electors, equal to the whole Number of Senators and Representatives to which the State may be entitled in the Congress." Their aim was to discard the established winner-take-all rule which they foresaw would favor the Republicans and to replace it with a sectionally based district system tailored to Democratic voting strength. Besides assigning one elector to each of the 12 congressional districts, two electors were elected at large. For partisan purposes, the state was divided into an eastern and a western section to which one elector-at-large was assigned. Michigan Republican nominees for presidential electors challenged the statute as being in conflict with the customary winner-take-all or unit-rule procedure. They concluded that selection by

13. *In re Green,* 134 U.S. 377 (1890). Curiously, Gray did not say, on the other hand, that electors were state officers. Only six years earlier, Justice Miller in *Ex parte Yarbrough* had evidenced a belief that electors are state officers. But to Miller, that did not imply a lack of federal authority over the control of violence and corruption in presidential elections; 110 U.S. 651 (1884). Cf. *United States* v. *Hartwell,* 6 Wall 385 (1868).

14. *McPherson* v. *Blacker,* 146 U.S. 1 (1892).

15. The state-adopted practice of giving all the electors to the party which wins the most popular votes—the unit rule or "general ticket system"—is a product of the early 1800s. In the election of 1804, five of the "popular election" states provided that electors should be chosen in districts similar to congressional districts. As experience with the plan accumulated, however, dominant parties in the legislatures soon realized that they could supply more electoral votes for their candidates, as well as prevent minority parties from representation, if the party with the most votes in the state were to win all the electors. By 1836, all the states had abandoned districting plans.

districts was not an appointment by the state (viewed as a legal unit) in the meaning of Article II. Chief Justice Fuller ruled to the contrary that custom, such as the practice that state electors vote together as a unit, has no legal standing when opposed by contrary practice authorized by the Constitution. Thus the legislature may go so far as to authorize the governor, the state's highest court, or any agent including voters divided by districts to appoint electors. The word "appoint," the Court asserted, conveys the "broadest power of determination." Further, the full Court rejected the contention that the allegedly inequitable districts violated voting rights by a lack of equal protection of the laws: "The object of the Fourteenth Amendment in respect to citizenship was to preserve equality of rights and to prevent discrimination as between citizens, but not to radically change the whole theory of the relations of the state and Federal governments to each other, and of both governments to the people."

The Problem of Federal "Police Power"

Despite the proposition—emphasized in *Green* and *McPherson*—that only the states have a specific grant of authority over the election of presidential electors, the Supreme Court in 1934 found an implied power in the Constitution conferring a degree of federal control over presidential elections. *Burroughs and Cannon* v. *United States*[16] involved two political committee officers convicted of conspiring in 1928 to evade the requirements of the Corrupt Practices Act as recently revised. They had agreed with each other not to file with the Clerk of the House of Representatives a statement of contributions and expenditures which they made to influence the presidential elections in two states. In sustaining their conviction and in speaking for the Court, Justice Sutherland acknowledged the premise of *In re Green* that presidential electors are not federal officers. Nevertheless, he said, "They exercise federal functions under, and discharge duties in virtue of authority conferred by the Federal Constitution." He reasoned that the federal government is possessed of the capacity to adopt all measures necessary to preserve its institutions from destruction. A half-century old dictum by Justice Miller in *Ex parte Yarbrough* was found both convincing and "enough to control the present case," inasmuch as it tested the validity of the Corrupt Practices Act of 1925 as applied to presidential elections. With approval, Miller's declaration was quoted:

16. *Burroughs and Cannon* v. *United States*, 290 U.S. 534 (1934); cf. *Walker* v. *United States*, 93 F.2d 383 (8th Cir., 1937); 303 U.S. 644 (1938) *cert. denied*.

That a government whose essential character is republican, whose executive head and legislative are both elective, whose most numerous and powerful branch of the legislature is elected by the people directly, has no power by appropriate laws to secure this election from the influence of violence, corruption and fraud, is a proposition so startling as to arrest attention.

Justice Sutherland succeeded in extending protection to the integrity of ballots cast in federal elections by employing a form of constitutional construction as effective and venerable as John Marshall's reasoning in *Marbury* v. *Madison*. The power of Congress to regulate congressional elections is founded on the *express* authority of the Times, Places, and Manner Clause. In *Burroughs*, the Necessary and Proper Clause was invoked as the *implied* authority sufficient to sustain the statute's regulation of presidential contests. Echoing Marshallian logic further, Sutherland went on to conclude: "The power of Congress to protect the election of the President and Vice President from corruption being clear, the choice of means is primarily for the judgment of Congress."

The net result of *Yarbrough* and *Burroughs* in combination was to underwrite a general federal police power over the entire field of federal elections. Of course, the invitation to occupy that field with a comprehensive federal code of election offenses and administrative machinery has generally been resisted by Congress. Nevertheless, the *Yarbrough-Burroughs* key does give constitutional entry to the traditional state preserve of presidential election control.

The Problem of the Faithless Elector

The transformation of the original plan of Article II into what has become a national popular election system has highlighted the problem of the faithless elector. Voting by presidential electors independently of their partisan promises to the electorate is relatively uncommon. But the strength of custom alone, a kind of unwritten amendment to the Constitution, explains the fact that until 1968, only eight of the 16,510 electoral votes cast were submitted contrary to "instructions." Litigation has not resolved the problem.

In 1944, groups of dissident Southern Democrats tried to block a fourth term for President Roosevelt with a short-lived movement to encourage electors to ballot for somebody other than FDR. In 1945, a repentant Alabama legislature attempted to require by statute that electors chosen on a party ticket support the candidates of their party's

choice at the national convention. But at the 1948 nominating meeting, half of the Alabama delegation walked out in response to the
addition of a civil rights plank to the Democratic Party platform. To
avoid embarrassment, the governor then asked the state Supreme
Court for an advisory opinion on the constitutionality of the three-
year-old statute which bound the Democratic electors to the Truman-
Barkley ticket.[17] The justices declared that by denying discretion to
the presidential electors the statute did not square with the intention
of the framers of Article II. Soon after the 1948 election, petitions
were filed with the United States Supreme Court to restrain Alabama
electors from voting, as they had told the electorate they would, for
the "Dixiecrat" candidates. The federal high bench twice refused a
hearing and the state's electoral votes were awarded to Senator Strom
Thurmond, the "Dixiecrat" nominee.[18]

In *Ray* v. *Blair*, decided in 1952, the Supreme Court upheld the
authority of the Alabama Democratic Executive Committee to require as a condition for party certification that prospective electors
pledge themselves to the national party's candidate.[19] The tribunal
reviewed the issuance of a court order requiring the party chairman
to certify Edmund Blair as an elector. He had qualified by winning
the primary election but had refused to pledge his ballot to the choice
of the Democratic party convention. Justice Reed, for the Supreme
Court, held that where a state authorized a political party to choose
its nominees for electors in a state-controlled party primary and to
fix the qualifications, it was not a violation of the Twelfth Amendment
for the party to require a pledge. It is important to emphasize that
Reed rendered the decision a hollow victory for the national Democrats by assuming that the pledge could not be legally enforced: it
merely represented a customary moral sanction in a new form.

As if to prove the point, this same pledge was taken and violated by
an Alabama Democratic elector who refused to vote for Adlai Steven-
son in 1956, preferring to give his vote to a home-state judge. The
situation in 1960 was one of even greater chaos. In the Alabama presidential primary that year, several candidates for electors acknowledged a pledge to John F. Kennedy, while others ran "unpledged."[20]

17. *Opinion of the Justices,* 34 So.2d 598 (1948).
18. *Folsom* v. *Albritton,* 335 U.S. 882 (1948); *Adcock* v. *Albritton,* 335 U.S.
882 (1948).
19. *Ray* v. *Blair,* 343 U.S. 214 (1952).
20. In 1964, a three-judge federal court upheld Mississippi's authority to provide by statute for unpledged electors of a national party on the ballot: *Gray* v.
Mississippi, 233 F. Supp. 139 (1964).

A number from each category were finally elected. The result was that in the November election voters obscured their choice when they pulled the party lever for the Democratic ticket and elected six unpledged and five pledged electors. How to tabulate the Alabama popular vote in the 1960 election under these circumstances remains a puzzle, but members of both political parties concede its implication. Democratic Senator Birch Bayh commented:

The standard procedure for recording the Alabama popular vote has been to credit Kennedy with 318,000 votes, the highest total received by a pledged elector. Under this method, however, most Alabama Democrats would have their popular votes counted twice—once for the Kennedy electors and once for the unpledged electors. In an attempt to correct this, some observers have made the following adjustment: five-elevenths of 324,050 is taken as Kennedy's popular vote and six-elevenths as the popular vote for the unpledged electors. This would leave Kennedy with 147,295 popular votes in Alabama, and would result in a nation-wide plurality for Nixon of 58,000. While the outcome of the election in the electoral college would remain the same, President Kennedy would have been a "minority" President.[21]

In 1968, federal legislators unsuccessfully attempted to deal with a North Carolina faithless elector by use of congressional sanctions. Dr. Lloyd Bailey, a North Carolina elector, was chosen in the November election to serve as an elector on a slate pledged to Richard Nixon and Spiro Agnew. Instead, Bailey announced after the popular election that he would cast his electoral ballot in December for George Wallace and Curtis LeMay. On January 6, 1969, Senator Edmund Muskie and Congressman James O'Hara registered a formal objection to Dr. Bailey's ballot under the Electoral Vote Count Act of 1887.[22] The effort to challenge his ballot as not "regularly given" failed to receive the necessary congressional support, thereby leaving untouched the impact of *Ray* v. *Blair;* only custom binds an elector to any pledge he may have made to his party or to the voters.

21. 113 *Cong. Rec.,* Senate 6525, 90th Cong., 1st sess., May 9, 1967. See also, from a Republican perspective, Thurston B. Morton, "Leadership Problems in the Opposition Party," in Paul T. David (ed.), *The Presidential Election and Transition, 1960–1961* (Washington, D.C.: The Brookings Institution, 1961), esp. pp. 141, 292–93. Cf. U.S. Congress, House, Judiciary Committee, *Hearings on Electoral College Reform,* Statement of Richard M. Scammon, 91st Cong., 1st sess., 1969, pp. 483–95.
22. 113 *Cong. Rec.,* Senate 15, 91st Cong., 1st sess. (Jan. 6, 1969), remarks of Senator Muskie. The Muskie-O'Hara objection to counting Bailey's vote was rejected 33–58. See 27 *Congressional Quarterly* 54–55, 143 (1969).

The Problem of Fair Access to the Ballot

The United States Supreme Court has never heard a case concerning a contested presidential primary election, though it had the opportunity to do so in 1963. When the Supreme Court denied *certiorari* in the case of *Stassen for President Citizens Committee* v. *Jordan*,[23] Justice Douglas wrote a dissent for himself, Chief Justice Warren, and Justice Goldberg. They thought that argument should have been heard and a decision rendered because "substantial federal rights" were arguably involved when California refused to accept the Stassen nominating petition. Douglas read the decision in *United States* v. *Classic* to mean that in federal elections, voting rights must be defined in terms of "free choice by the people" to extend to every step of the selection process. To Douglas, differing practices from state to state do not alter a broad federal guarantee. He reasoned that in California, constitutional rights in presidential elections stretch over four stages: the nominating petition, the primary, the party convention, and the general election. The guarantee of the "free choice of the people" extends to all these stages, he concluded.

By refusing to consider the merits of the complaint by the Stassen Committee, the Supreme Court left unqualified and unaffected an earlier ruling on nominating petitions. The discretionary power of the states to regulate access to the ballot through such petitions by minor party electors was the subject of the case of *MacDougal* v. *Green*.[24] The Illinois legislature passed a law requiring that a slate of electors nominated by a new and unrecognized political party must furnish, along with their application for placement on the November ballot, a popular petition. A list of 25,000 signatures was required, of which 200 were to be secured from each of any 50 of the 102 counties in the state. In suing Governor Green in 1948, the Progressive Party insisted that it was unfairly treated in its preparation for the presidential general election. The group pointed out that 13 percent of the population in the smallest counties under the law could place nominated electors of an unregistered party on a presidential ballot. At the same time, and allegedly in violation of the equal protection of the laws, 87 percent of the state's population in the 49 most populous counties could not. In a *per curiam* decision, five justices sustained the validity of the enactment. The Court did not concern itself with

23. *Stassen for President Citizens Committee* v. *Jordan*, 377 U.S. 914 (1963) cert. denied.

24. *MacDougal* v. *Green*, 335 U.S. 281 (1948).

the fact that the Progressive Party candidate, Henry Wallace, could not expect rural support because Progressives were largely concentrated in Chicago. Nevertheless, the majority of justices professed to be aware of hard-headed political realities. They agreed that "to assume that political power is a function exclusively of numbers is to disregard the practicalities of government." Justice Rutledge, in a separate Opinion, conceded the feasibility of judicially supplied relief for the Wallace partisans. But he stressed the nearness of the Court hearing to the election, with the consequent difficulties in preparing new ballots, and almost certain disfranchisement of absentee ballots. Justices Black, Douglas, and Murphy stood together in believing that the Illinois law amounted to a denial of the equal protection of the laws called for by the Fourteenth Amendment.

The Illinois statute involved in *MacDougal* was contested again in the 1968 election by independent candidates for the office of elector who supported Eugene McCarthy for President. Justice Douglas consigned the statute to legal repose and, in a brief opinion, over-ruled *MacDougal* in *Moore* v. *Ogilvie*.[25] The two cases were indistinguishable, but the results were diametrically opposed. Douglas said that the reason for this lay, not in increased urbanization in Illinois over the preceding twenty years, but in the intervening rulings of *Gray* v. *Sanders* and *Reynolds* v. *Sims*. In the Illinois presidential nominating formula, no less than in primary and general elections, "the idea that one group can be granted greater voting strength than another is hostile to the one-man, one-vote basis of our representative government." Justices Stewart and Harlan dissented on several scores, not the least of which was that the case was moot, the presidential election having taken place months earlier. They also faulted the majority for a "casual extension of the one-voter, one-vote slogan" to a past dispute where the litigants sued, not as voters, but as prospective candidates. (No mention was made of *Hadnott* v. *Amos*, the Voting Rights Act case which had also involved candidate litigants.) In addition to its significance for candidate-litigants, the *Moore* ruling carried other broad implications for political party operations. Justice Douglas, in words reminiscent of his *Stassen* dissent, declared in *Moore*: "All procedures used by a State as an integral part of the election process must pass muster against the charge of discrimination or of abridgment of the right to vote."

An equally innovative ruling growing out of the 1968 presidential

25. *Moore* v. *Ogilvie* 394 U.S. 814 (1969).

election was decided in *Williams* v. *Rhodes*.[26] Justice Black wrote the Opinion for six members of the Court. Its import was that, in spite of the broad language of Article II regarding legislative appointment of electors, a state is not completely unfettered in choosing whatever process it may wish for the designation of presidential electors. For the 1968 election, both George Wallace's American Independent Party and the Socialist Labor Party were barred from the ballot under Ohio election law. The state effectively foreclosed its presidential ballot to all but Nixon Republicans and Humphrey Democrats.[27] It did so by prohibiting write-in votes, by eliminating all independent candidates through a rule that nominees must enjoy the endorsement of a political party, and by defining "political party" in such a way as to exclude all but the two major parties.

Ohio conceded that the American Independent Party had met the petition requirement of 15 percent of the electorate to place named candidates on the ballot. But failing to meet the February 7, 1968 deadline, the Secretary of State denied the third party request for printed identification on the November ballot. Having demonstrated its numerical strength, the Wallaceites argued that the early deadline for filing and other burdens, including a party primary election conforming to detailed and rigorous standards, denied the party and identified voters of the state the equal protection of the laws. A three-judge court unanimously agreed with the contention but ruled in consequence only that the state must supply a space for write-in votes. Justice Black opened the Supreme Court review of the contest on appeal with a statement that the case raised a justiciable controversy under the Constitution and was not to be side-stepped by reference to the "political questions" doctrine (citing *McPherson* v. *Blacker*). He rested his rejection of the complex of Ohio laws on the grounds that,

26. *Williams* v. *Rhodes*, 393 U.S. 23 (1968).

27. Ohio law required a new party to obtain petitions signed by qualified electors totaling 15 percent of the number of ballots cast in the preceding gubernatorial election. Second, after the petition requirement was satisfied, a new party was required to elect a state central committee with two members from each congressional district and to set up county central committees for each county in the state. Third, at the primary election the new party must elect delegates and alternates to a national convention. Candidates for convention delegate and committeeman must not have voted as a member of a different party during the preceding four years. Fourth, the candidates for nomination in the primary would have to file petitions signed by "qualified electors" not linked with an established party. This, in effect, meant that the petitions would have to be signed by new party members who had not voted before. *Williams* v. *Rhodes*, 393 U.S. 23, note 1 (1969).

taken in combination, they "place burdens of two different, although overlapping, kinds of rights—the rights of individuals to associate for the advancement of political beliefs, and the right of qualified voters, regardless of their political persuasion, to cast their votes effectively." Black argued against Ohio's contentions that the avoidance of plurality winners, the development of party leadership proved by primary elections, and the promotion of a two-party system were not "compelling interests" of the state. He thought that, taken together, this web of election law did not rest on state interests sufficient to justify the burdens on the "right to form a party for the advancement of political goals."[28] Justice Douglas, in concurrence, reasoned that although it was true that the states may pick their electors through appointment rather than by popular election Ohio had chosen to rely on a popular vote. Having done so, the state could not burden the right to vote with the restrictive package of laws used. Justices Douglas and Harlan, writing in separate concurrences, thought it proper to grant declaratory relief to the Socialist Labor Party but in this they were alone. Chief Justice Warren, Justice Stewart, and Justice White each wrote separate dissents. The Chief Justice complained that neither the states nor the courts were given clear guidelines as to how they might regulate access to the ballot so as to show a causal link between legitimate state interests and at the same time to provide for orderly regulation of the conduct of presidential elections. The responsibility for disentangling the applicable constitutional principles for each of Ohio's laws was not met in the lower court as it should have been.[29] Nevertheless, Warren read the Court Opinion to mean that a State can, by reasonable regulation, condition ballot position upon at least three considerations—a substantial showing of voter interest in the candidate seeking a place on the ballot, a requirement that this interest be evidenced sometime prior to the election, and a party structure demonstrating some degree of political organization.

In his *Williams* Opinion, Justice Black said, "Concededly, the State does have an interest in attempting to see that the election winner be the choice of a majority of its voters. But to grant the State power to

28. The Court required Ohio to permit the Independent Party to remain on the ballot (in keeping with Justice Stewart's earlier order for the Sixth Circuit requiring that the Party's candidates be put on the ballot pending Supreme Court appeal). The Socialist Labor Party's request for the same treatment was denied because it failed to meet the petition requirements but most compellingly because its request for relief came too late for Ohio to provide still another set of ballots.

29. Citing the "electioneering" case of *Zwickler* v. *Koota*, 389 U.S. 241 (1967).

keep all political parties off the ballot until they have enough members to win would stifle the growth of all new parties. . . ." How the
states may promote their interest in majority choice has been left unresolved by the ruling of 1968. One result will be a strengthening of
the case of those who criticize the Electoral College for its operational
weaknesses in recording the popular choice.

The Problem of the Electoral College

It may now be asked whether the reapportionment and congressional districting cases of the 1960s suggest that the "one person, one
vote" rule should apply to presidential contests. As Chief Justice
Warren said in dissent in *Williams* v. *Rhodes*, "the advent of *Baker* v.
Carr and its progeny have substantially modified the constitutional
matrix in this area." No doubt, the winner-take-all approach which
all states have adopted in appointing their presidential electors distorts the effect of the popular vote. It amplifies the winner's gains and
effectively nullifies all minority votes within the individual states,
with results on the national scale comparable to the discredited vote-
juggling of the county-unit system at the state level. When the
Georgia county-unit system of voting in state wide and congressional
primary elections was reviewed on an Equal Protection challenge in
a federal district court, three judges agreed that there was a discernible point beyond which the awarding of the full county vote
to a plurality winner in a state-wide election became "invidious discrimination."[30] They said in this 1962 case, "no discrimination is
deemed to be invidious . . . if the disparity against any county is not in
excess of the disparity that exists as against any state in the most recent
electoral college allocation. . . ." The next year, when the case was
reviewed by the Supreme Court under the title of *Gray* v. *Sanders*,
the rule of giving the county vote as a unit to the local winner in
Georgia elections was voided. Justice Douglas, speaking for the majority of the Court, saw implicit in the Equal Protection Clause the
principle of "one person, one vote." He concluded by refusing to
sustain the county-unit system on analogy to the Electoral College,
explaining that the technique for selecting a President remains based
on a "conception of equality that belongs to a bygone day."

Of course, the dictum on changed notions of equality was only an
interpretive historical aside, carrying no legal weight by itself. But
with the "one person, one vote" rule which *Gray* v. *Sanders* helped
to incorporate into constitutional law, modern judicial notions of

30. *Sanders* v. *Gray*, 205 F. Supp. 158 (1962); *Gray* v. *Sanders*, 372 U.S. 368
(1963).

equality are nowhere more in evidence than in voting rights cases. Why should not judicial remedies vindicating equalized ballot rights be extended to presidential elections? In 1964, this question was being asked by such men as J. Harvey Williams of the American Good Government Society, James Kirby, Jr., then chief counsel for the Senate Constitutional Amendments Subcommittee, and John Gosnell, whose National Small Business Association ultimately came forward with $10,000 to support litigation. These men joined forces with Professor Robert Dixon of the George Washington University Law Center, Neal Peirce, political editor of the *Congressional Quarterly*, and Delaware Attorney General Buckson who offered his state's sponsorship for what these men shaped into an ingenious constitutional test case.[31]

Twelve states cast their lots with Delaware in 1966 in asking the United States Supreme Court to declare unconstitutional the technique of awarding a state's electoral votes as a unit to the winning ticket in the state. Invoking the Court's original jurisdiction to hear disputes between states, Delaware with its three electoral votes brought suit against New York with its 41 electoral votes, the District of Columbia (entitled to three votes since enactment of the Twenty-third Amendment), and other states. The feature of the existing system which appeared most vulnerable to constitutional attack and the one to which Delaware objected was the unit rule, the creation not of the Constitution but of state laws. More than a twice-told tale is the story of the way the states' winner-take-all method of awarding electoral votes adds to existing inequalities of the Electoral College to amplify the presidential vote of the eleven largest states, New York, California, Pennsylvania, Illinois, Ohio, Texas, Michigan, New Jersey, Florida, Massachusetts, and Indiana.[32] Thus in 1964 there were approximately 70.3 million popular votes cast in all, of which 42.6 million came from these eleven states. By a bare plurality in these states, about 21.4 million votes could have determined which candidate would receive their 268 electoral votes. Hypothetically then, less than 30 percent of the national electorate could have controlled the election because of their power over the largest blocs of electoral votes. In its brief for the Court, Delaware took the view that Supreme Court decisions since *Baker* v. *Carr* have been resulting in congressional and state legislative representation systems apportioned to represent all

31. The background of the case is fully discussed by Neal Peirce, "The Electoral College Goes to Court," 35 *The Reporter* 34 (Oct. 6, 1966).

32. See for example, Joseph Kallenbach, "Our Electoral College Gerrymander," 4 *Midwest Journal of Political Science* 162–91 (May 1960).

people on an equal basis. Since the under-representation of urban interests in these bodies is ending, "their compensating over-representation in presidential elections should correspondingly end."[33] Delaware's constitutional arguments were elaborated with a skillful mixture of legal and political analysis. Distilled to constitutional essentials, however, the state contended that

the state unit-vote laws deny the voting rights of minority voters within each state by totally cancelling their effects when the state's entire electoral vote is awarded to the winner of a bare plurality of the popular vote. This is an internal denial of equal protection which falls under the same "one person, one vote" principle which was fatal to Georgia's county unit system. This isolation of state minority voters leads to an external or interstate abridgment of fundamental rights to engage in national political activity because the state units combine nationally in a way which distorts, and possibly defeats, the popular will.

The argument was also pressed that such "compartmentalizing" of voters "offends the national due process requirement of the Fifth Amendment."

The thorniest area of the presidential "political thicket" which Delaware invited the Court to enter involved the problem of judicial standards and remedies. The Court could require the states to divide electoral votes so as to honor the value of all popular votes, based on a system of subdistricting the states or of dividing electoral votes proportionate to popular voting results. Not acknowledged by the Delaware brief were some of the political hazards of Supreme Court intervention along these lines. The involvement of Court members (albeit in different circumstances) in the outcome of the Hayes election of 1876 brought the prestige of the high bench into unusual jeopardy. The extremely controversial character of applying judicial standards to the weights and measures of presidential vote counts can be seen in Table 10–1. The table shows the results of the popular and Electoral College systems operating in elections from 1948 to 1968 compared to the hypothetical effects of the operation of either a proportional or a district system for these two elections. The proportional and districting plans used to devise the table rely on 1966 congressional proposals that were pending when Delaware brought its suit. That year Senator Mundt's district plan provided that electors would be selected by the votes of the people tabulated as one vote for each congressional district and two for each state-at-large. (One of

33. *Brief for the Plaintiff,* pp. 81–82, *Delaware* v. *New York,* Original No. 28, Filed July 20, 1966 in the Supreme Court of United States.

Table 10–1 *Comparison of Actual and Hypothetical Voting Systems in Presidential Elections, 1948–68**

	POPULAR VOTE		ELECTORAL COLLEGE		PROPORTIONAL SYSTEM		DISTRICTED SYSTEM	
	DEM.	REP.	DEM.	REP.	DEM.	REP.	DEM.	REP.
1948	24,105,695	21,969,170	303	189	257.8	221.4	292	187
1952	27,313,987	33,666,062	89	442	240.241	281.577	156	375
1956	26,027,983	35,579,190	74	457	227.228	296.667	116	413
1960	34,221,349	34,108,546	303	219	262.671	263.632	245	278
	34,050,341	34,108,546						
1964	43,128,956	27,177,873	486	52	320.042	213.593	466	72
1968	31,270,533	31,770,237	181	302	225.361	231.534	192	289

* Figures are adapted from legislative reference materials published in House Judiciary Committee, *Electoral College Reforms*, 91st Cong., 1st sess., 1969, pp. 976–87. In 1948, the popular vote for the States Rights Party was 1,169,021 (39 electoral votes); Progressive Party, 1,156,103 popular votes. In 1960, unpledged electors who voted for Senator Harry Byrd received 609,870 popular votes or 462,575 votes by the 6/11 formula applied to Alabama. The first and generally accepted popular vote total for Kennedy in 1960 credits him with the 318,303 votes which the most successful "loyalist" elector received in Alabama. But the confusing Democratic slate there also included six unpledged electors. By a different method of tabulation (giving 5/11 of the popular vote to Kennedy and 6/11 to the unpledged electors, Alabama having 11 electors in all), the second figure gives Kennedy a national popular vote total of 58,205 votes fewer than Mr. Nixon. In 1968, the American Independent Party received 9,897,141 popular votes and 46 electoral votes.

the initial supporters of the Delaware suit, the American Good Government Society, particularly favored the district plan.) The proportional plan, as urged in the Eighty-ninth Congress by Senator Saltonstall, would require that the electoral vote in each state be apportioned among the presidential candidates in accordance with the popular vote and that the electoral vote should be so divided figuring to three places beyond the decimal point.[34]

34. The *district plan* (S.J. Res. 12, 89th Cong., 1st sess.) also provided that, failing a majority for any candidate, the top three vote-getters would submit their fate to the choice of the Senate and House meeting jointly. The congressionally considered *proportional plan* would retain each state's electoral vote but divide it as described above. S.J. Res. 138 would require at least a 40 percent electoral vote to elect. A *direct election plan* (S.J. Res. 413) was considered the same session. It would retire the electoral vote altogether. The president and vice president would be elected by a plurality of at least 45 percent with a contingent plan for a congressional joint session to choose between the two tickets with the highest popular vote in case the 45 percent mark were not met.

Of course, the districting and proportional plans described above are not necessarily the same as those which the Court might require. Even so, the startling results for the 1960 election, with Nixon wins in two out of three systems, suggest the extraordinary delicacy of the problem and the inherent political explosiveness in any judicial solution. Close elections such as those of 1960 and 1968 demonstrate the clear need for a mathematically precise formula, something the Supreme Court has eschewed in voting rights cases generally. No Supreme Court ruling could eliminate the electoral vote. A decision which opted for a districted or proportionate division of electoral votes could promise only a partial solution to presidential voting inequities in a situation in which "half a loaf" might be worse than none.

Delaware's legal strategy recognized such hazards and suggested that the Court might wish to follow a remedial path, interim in nature, which would involve a ruling that each state's electoral votes must reasonably reflect the split of voter preferences within the state, and then leave it to Congress to enforce the Fourteenth Amendment requirement by devising an exact and uniform remedial plan.

In October 1966, the Supreme Court denied Delaware a hearing, thus side-stepping the entire problem and permitting it to fall by its own political weight into the lap of Congress.[35] The Supreme Court's original jurisdiction is wholly discretionary, and the Court's reasons for turning a deaf ear to the interstate contest can only be the subject of guesswork. As it turned out, however, the gauntlet laid down by Delaware which threatened to upset the existing presidential electoral system was an opening gambit rather than a final play, a signal to Congress to ready the foundation for a constitutional amendment which would bring presidential elections into harmony with the "one person, one vote" principle. The Delaware brief suggested that "the ultimate result" of judicial action "might be the submission of a proposed Constitutional Amendment for direct national election."

Even without judicial intervention, the "ultimate result" which Delaware sought by litigation was significantly furthered. After the state filed its brief with the Supreme Court, but before rejection of the complaint was published, Senator Birch Bayh, Chairman of the

---

35. *Delaware v. New York,* 385 U.S. 895 (1966). In 1967, a Mississippi Federal District Court dismissed a comparable challenge to the use of the unit rule for the state's electors. Authority for dismissal was rested on *Delaware v. New York* in *Penton v. Humphrey,* 264 F. Supp. 250 (1967). See also *Williams v. Virginia State Board of Elections,* 288 F. Supp. 622 (1968).

Senate Subcommittee on Constitutional Amendments, and Assistant Attorney General Ramsey Clark called upon the American Bar Association to examine the subject of electoral reform.

In February 1966, the ABA House of Delegates established a Commission on Electoral College Reform. The commission considered the operation of the presidential electoral system, including its many defects. The system permits a candidate with fewer popular votes than his opponent to be elected President, as when Hayes defeated Tilden in 1876. It allows the faithless elector to disregard the popular vote in casting his ballot in the Electoral College (*Ray* v. *Blair*). When no candidate receives a majority of the electoral votes, the election goes into the House of Representatives under the relatively undemocratic provisions of the Twelfth Amendment and Article II whereby each state has an equal vote regardless of population. Party competition has induced every state to adopt a unit rule whereby the winning candidate in a state receives all of its electoral votes. Access to the ballot is regulated variously among the states (*McPherson* v. *Blacker*), with results affecting not only minor parties, but sometimes disadvantaging major parties, e.g., Alabama Democrats in 1960. Because every state is allotted electoral votes according to its number of Representatives and Senators, there is a disparity between the weight of popular votes and the electoral power of every state.[36] Finally, the present system does not have a fool-proof method for tabulating the electoral vote, the Electoral Vote Count Act notwithstanding. In January 1967, the 15-member Electoral Commission published its conclusion that "the Electoral College method of electing a President of the United States is archaic, undemocratic, complex, ambiguous, indirect, and dangerous." According to Commission Chairman Robert Storey, members of the group had expressed preliminary views soon after their convening which revealed support for each of the traditional major reform proposals including the proportional, district, and direct election plans. Following extensive investigation and debate, however, a consensus was reached:

While there may be no perfect method of electing a President, we believe that direct, nationwide popular vote is the best of all possible methods. . . . The President is our highest nationally elected official. He occupies the most powerful office in the world. The problems and the issues with which

36. This point was not fully explored until the publication of the work of John Banzhaf in his "Reflections on the Electoral College, One Man, 3,312 Votes: A Mathematical Analysis," 13 *Villanova Law Review* 303 (Winter 1968).

he deals are largely national in character. It is only fitting that he be elected directly by the people.[37]

In a separate statement Chairman Storey commented: "In my opinion, direct election is an idea whose time has arrived." The natural evolution of the Constitution has been consistently in the direction of more reliance on the people: the abolition of property qualifications for voters, the popular election of Senators, women's suffrage, the granting of voting rights to Negroes, elimination of the poll tax, and the recent Supreme Court rulings requiring equal representation of voters in Congress and the state legislatures. Direct election of the President and Vice President would be a further fulfillment of this trend.

Prospects for changing presidential election techniques grow out of the fact that the complex fabric of American society and politics has changed during the 1960s. In 1956, Senator John F. Kennedy told Congress that he opposed substantial alteration of the Electoral College. He explained: "It is not only the unit vote for the presidency we are talking about, but a whole solar system of governmental power. If it is proposed to change the balance of power of one of the elements of the solar system, it is necessary to consider all the others." Since then, at least four prominent "elements of the solar system" have changed.[38]

1. Lower-voter-participation states, especially in the South, customarily guarded their strong interest in maintaining a guaranteed Electoral College vote in spite of the fact that the popular turnout on election day was sparse. Assessment of this interest must now be reviewed in the light of increasing Negro registration encouraged by private civil rights groups working at a new level of effectiveness under the Voting Rights Act of 1965 and related Supreme Court decisions.

2. Small states traditionally have clung to the advantage which the Electoral College system gave them in the form of electoral votes equal to the number of their senators and representatives. This has been offset, however, by the practice of giving all of a state's electoral

37. Commission on Electoral College Reform, *Electing the President* (Chicago: American Bar Association, 1967), pp. 4, 6.
38. Cf. House Judiciary Committee, *Electoral College Reform*, Statement by Prof. Alexander Bickel, 91st Cong., 1st sess., 1969, pp. 410–28.

votes to the winner of its popular balloting (no matter how small the plurality) which in turn has inclined party strategists to seek candidates and to direct campaigns with a view toward securing large industrial state support. Small states and one-party states have been largely disregarded in presidential contests. In response to this situation, the Electoral Commission noted, direct election proposals in recent years have been advanced by congressmen from both large *and* small states.

3. Reapportionment and congressional districting rulings by the Supreme Court following *Baker* v. *Carr* in 1962 have contributed substantially to checking the dominance of rural interests in state legislatures and in the House of Representatives. A changing balance of power along these lines undercuts the traditional argument that the advantages enjoyed by rural interests in legislatures is appropriately countered by the amplified voice of pivotal urbanized states. The Commission concluded that "direct election of the President would be in harmony with the prevailing philosophy of one person, one vote."

4. The two major political parties have traditionally been thought to have a vested concern in the winner-take-all unit rule used by every state. On a nationwide scale, it is conducive to two-party politics by limiting the effectiveness of votes for minority party candidates. The Electoral Commission reply on this score was that numerous factors within the American political system, "not the Electoral College alone, have worked to produce our two-party system." Moreover, the Commission's recommendation that a candidate should receive at least 40 percent of the popular vote to win would mean that "a group existing outside of either of the major parties would not be able to thrive in view of the certainty of defeat." The requirement of a run-off election between the two leading contenders in case no candidate obtained a 40 percent vote would also "have the tendency to limit the number of minor party candidates in the field. . . ."

Acting on the ABA recommendations, Republican and Democratic Congressmen allied themselves with Senator Birch Bayh to introduce a resolution to be considered by the Ninetieth Congress. It called for the adoption of a constitutional amendment that would provide for direct, nation-wide popular election of the President and Vice President and for a run-off election between the two top candidates if none of the contestants received at least 40 percent of the popular vote. Its other provisions which substantially embody Electoral Commission proposals are as follows:

1. Congress is to determine the time of the election.
2. The President and Vice President are to be voted for jointly.
3. The places and manner of holding the election are to be prescribed by the state legislatures, except that Congress may make or alter these regulations.
4. The voters in each state are to have the same qualifications as required for persons voting in that state for members of Congress, except that a state may adopt less restrictive residence requirements and except that Congress may adopt uniform residence and age requirements.
5. If, at the time for the official counting of the certified vote totals from the states, the winning presidential candidate is dead, the winning vice presidential candidate will be the President.
6. Congress may provide for the case of the death or withdrawal of a candidate before the election and for the death of both the winning presidential and the winning vice presidential candidate.[39]

According to Senator Bayh, the popular election of our two top national officers would not be a break with tradition. Rather it would be "a logical, realistic and proper continuation of this Nation's tradition and history—a tradition of continuous expansion of the franchise and equality in voting." Indeed, James Madison had said of presidential elections that "the people at large" provide the basis for choice which "was the fittest in itself." In relying on the archaic Electoral College provisions of the Constitution to provide a democratic result in presidential elections, the American voters have long depended on a talisman of questionable efficacy. The old machinery is geared for crisis and controversy. With the conditions that produced the Electoral College now nearly forgotten, the proposed Twenty-sixth Amendment stands ready to refute those who say that constitutional change is born of crisis alone.

39. S.J. Res. 2, 90th Cong., 1st sess., 1967; cf. S.J. Res. 1, 91st Cong., 1st sess., 1969.

II Nationalization of
the electoral process

That Americans have found many ways of transferring power from local to higher government units testifies to a dynamic system of federalism. Examples may be found in policy areas of national scope ranging from the regulation of commerce to the prohibition of sedition, by means as diverse as federal grants and preemption doctrines and by agencies of accommodation as far apart as political parties and federal courts. In the electoral process, not only trends in state law, but political party decisions, constitutional amendments, Supreme Court rulings, and congressional legislation have all led Americans to a more standard set of election laws and voting requirements. It is important to ask how we have come to a situation in the early 1970s in which virtually every election for public office is affected by both state and federal law—and where we go from here.

An understanding of the emergence of an increasingly unitary electoral system must advance along political as well as legal lines. The struggles for women's suffrage, black enfranchisement, abolition of the poll tax, and reapportionment are all historical commentaries on the direction of political change in the United States. In each of these movements, reformers found that when they were blocked at one level of government, they could gainfully seek another at which to advance their proposals. In the past century, the effective cutting edge of these movements has been at the national level (a point at which party competition is more continuous than at the state and local levels). Where the electoral process is concerned, however, nationalized politics rubs against the traditional legal grain because conducting elections and defining the scope of the franchise have generally been decentralized functions of state activity.

THE POLITICAL FRAMEWORK OF LEGAL CHANGE

The tension between federal authority and local control over the electoral process has been shaped significantly by the American party system and its adaptations to advancing modernization in many fields. Even before the Civil War, the process of democratization was afoot among state politicians who found it expedient to promote changes in the rules of the political game by increasing the number of participants.[1] Jacksonian Democrats frequently authored liberalized state franchise laws, enacting manhood suffrage or substituting tax-paying qualifications for property tests.[2] But the realignment of voters by party following liberalization of the suffrage remained sufficiently unclear to motivate both Democrats and Whigs to sponsor electoral reform at the state level.[3] The result was that in most American states before the Civil War, electoral law changes were the result of bipartisan efforts and a function of party and factional competition. Through the interplay of socioeconomic change and party politics, the opposition to suffrage reform on a nation-wide scale was first routed when the propertyless were brought into the electorate for political advantage.[4] By the mid-nineteenth century, adult manhood

1. William N. Chambers, *Political Parties in a New Nation* (New York: Oxford University Press, 1963).

2. Lee Benson, *The Concept of Jacksonian Democracy* (New York: Atheneum Press, 1964). A complete tabular summary was printed by the Commission on Civil Rights, *Report*, 1959, p. 24.

3. Richard McCormick, "Suffrage Classes and Party Alignments: A Study in Voter Behavior," 46 *Mississippi Valley Historical Review* 407 (Dec. 1959).

4. Chilton Williamson, *American Suffrage from Property to Democracy, 1760–1860* (Princeton: Princeton University Press, 1960). Cf. Alfred de Grazia, *Public and Republic* (New York: Alfred A. Knopf, 1951).

suffrage for all but Negroes and females virtually existed under the laws of the states. In 1832, Alexis de Tocqueville observed this process of democratization at work:

> The further electoral rights are extended, the greater is the need for extending them: for after each concession, the strength of democracy increases and its demands increase with its strength.[5]

The classic pattern of democratizing political parties, which act as brokers in the process of enfranchising more and more groups, has carried Jacksonian democracy into the twentieth century. De Tocqueville's diagnosis presently requires little reformulation except the notation that, since his day, the new demands stimulated by strengthened democracy have been carried outside political parties and state legislatures and into the constitutional amendment process, the courts, and Congress.

Historically, the reform of property and tax qualifications was effected with little reference to legal change at the national level. Yet, notwithstanding this experience with reform, resistance to electoral egalitarianism has generally been stronger at the level of local government than at the federal level. In the years following the Civil War, it was the Federal Constitution which proved the most significant vehicle for change. In the history of tinkering with the Constitution, about 5,700 suggestions for revision have been proposed. But the most successful have been those dealing with representation and voting. No less than seven amendments have served to advance federal standards for the electoral process.[6] Extension of the right to vote for

---

5. Alexis de Tocqueville, *Democracy in America* (New York: Vintage Books, 1955), I, pp. 56–57.

6. *United States Constitution*, Amend. XII (electoral college casting of ballots for executive); Amend. XIV, Sec. 1 (equal protection and due process of the law), Sec. 2 (federal sanction against states denying the right to vote); Amend. XV (denial of vote on account of race forbidden); Amend. XVII (popular election of senators); Amend. XIX (denial of vote on account of sex forbidden); Amend. XXIII (limited presidential right to vote extended to the District of Columbia); and Amend. XXIV (outlawing the poll tax in federal elections).

In the original Constitution of 1787, the following provisions are relevant. Art. I, Sec. 2, Cl. 1 (representatives chosen by state-qualified electors); Art. I Sec. 2, Cl. 3 (congressional apportionment); Art. I, Sec. 4, Cl. 1 (congressional authority to alter state election regulations); Art. I, Sec. 5, Cl. 1 (House and Senate as judges of respective elections, election returns, and membership); Art. II, Sec. 2 (the electoral college); and Art. IV, Sec. 4 (United States guarantee of republican government).

groups previously frustrated in their efforts to gain that right at the state level was accomplished at the federal level: Negroes (Fifteenth Amendment in 1870), women (Nineteenth Amendment in 1920), and the poor (Twenty-fourth Amendment in 1964). The net legal result has been that the introduction by gradual stages of universal suffrage has made the franchise a right of age, residence, and citizenship, and not one of property, race, sex, or occupation. The net political effect of universal suffrage in the United States is summarized in Table 11–1, which gives refined figures on the growing American electorate since the enactment of the Nineteenth Amendment.

The strenuous processes prescribed by Article V for constitutional amendment are themselves indicators of the consensus which exists at the national level on the desirability of expanding the representativeness of government and the lengths to which Americans will go in order to do so. The route generally taken to constitutional amendment requires the support of two-thirds of Congress and three-fourths of the state legislatures. Not surprisingly, then, since Reconstruction every successful amendment which affects the electoral process has enjoyed bipartisan support.

Enlargement of the franchise is one component of a larger social phenomenon which a contemporary sociologist, Talcott Parsons, has called "the inclusion process."[7] The history of inclusion of an ever larger portion of the population into the electorate may be viewed as a dynamic process of institutional adaptation by the major political parties. The growth of the electorate has enjoyed bi-partisan support, since doubt generally envelops the question of which party will be the lasting beneficiary of any given increment to the electorate and neither party wishes to let the other take full credit. The consequence of "the inclusion process" for the parties is that in addition to the sheer number of members, their structure, goals, and leadership recruitment may be changed. The parties establish roles and procedures useful in integrating diverse interests and in bargaining for goals and

7. Talcott Parsons, "Full Citizenship for the Negro American? A Sociological Problem," 94 *Daedalus* 1009 (Fall 1965). Elsewhere, Parsons elaborates a functional theory of voting de-emphasizing statistical studies in favor of stressing that elections operate so as to mobilize generalized support for leadership. The inferences of this perspective draw attention to the role of political leadership (or party "brokerage") in the electoral inclusion process. Talcott Parsons, " 'Voting' and Equilibrium of the American Political System," in Eugene Burdick and Arthur Brodbeck (eds.), *American Voting Behavior* (New York: Free Press, 1959).

Table 11-1   *The Expanding Franchise**

YEAR	ELIGIBLE POPULATION OF VOTING AGE	VOTE CAST FOR PRESIDENTIAL ELECTORS Number	Percent	VOTE CAST FOR U.S. REPRESENTATIVES Number	Percent
1920	60,581,000	26,748,000	44.2	25,080,000	41.4
1922	62,984,000	——	—	20,409,000	32.4
1924	65,597,000	29,086,000	44.3	26,884,000	41.0
1926	67,912,000	——	—	20,435,000	30.1
1928	70,362,000	36,812,000	52.3	33,906,000	48.2
1930	72,602,000	——	—	24,777,000	34.1
1932	75,048,000	39,732,000	52.9	37,657,000	50.2
1934	77,215,000	——	—	32,256,000	41.8
1936	79,375,000	45,643,000	57.5	42,886,000	54.0
1938	81,514,000	——	—	36,236,000	44.5
1940	83,512,000	49,891,000	59.7	46,951,000	56.2
1942	85,759,000	——	—	28,074,000	32.7
1944	89,517,000	47,969,000	53.6	45,103,000	50.4
1946	91,497,000	——	—	34,398,000	37.6
1948	94,470,000	48,691,000	51.5	45,933,000	48.6
1950	96,992,000	——	—	40,342,000	41.6
1952	99,016,000	61,551,000	62.2	57,571,000	58.1
1954	101,097,000	——	—	42,580,000	42.1
1956	103,625,000	62,027,000	59.9	58,426,000	56.4
1958	105,727,000	——	—	45,655,000	43.2
1960	107,949,000	68,839,000	63.8	64,133,000	59.4
1962	110,266,000	——	—	51,304,000	46.5
1964	113,931,000	70,644,000	62.0	66,044,000	58.0
1966	116,383,000	——	—	57,585,000	48.3
1968	120,006,000	73,211,562	61.0	66,109,209	55.1

* Published by the Congressional Quarterly Service, in *Politics in America 1945–1964*, p. 78. The population estimate for 1944 includes 4,342,000 members of the armed services serving abroad. The estimate for 1958 includes Alaska which voted for Representatives in November 1958, although it did not become a state until January 1959. Voting age is defined as resident population 21 years of age and older, except: 18 years and over in Georgia since 1944; 18 years and over in Kentucky since 1956; 19 years and over in Alaska; 20 years and over in Hawaii. The figures for 1966 are drawn from the *New York Times*, Nov. 13, 1966, p. 86 and Nov. 15, p. 36. The vote totals for 1968 were taken from 27 *Congressional Quarterly* 884 (Je. 1969).

resources for which those involved might otherwise compete in a mutually destructive manner. The newly enfranchised are encouraged at least partly to interpret their interests in terms of national political party objectives. But the reverse occurs as well. At the same time, there is a need for party flexibility to permit the redistribution of power and a shift in organization to accommodate the gradual entrance of new groups into the political process. Thus, the parties and the political system as a whole become more responsive to the enlarged electorate.

Four important present-day consequences for the federal government flow from this trend toward inclusion. All have to do with federal governmental responsiveness to a changing electorate. The first is that the enlargement of the franchise, together with social and economic change, has tended to reduce the dissimilarities between the cross-sections of state and regional electorates and such cross-sections of the national electorate as a whole. The Census Bureau statistics describe an increasingly unitary electorate.[8]

The second consequence is that the requirements of legitimacy allow for more national and uniform standards of voter qualification and electoral process. In the American political system, voting serves the function of legitimation, that is, as a means to determine which alternatives among leaders or courses of action will be accepted as legitimate and rightful by the entire citizenry. When the electorate and the manner of casting and counting votes differs from one part of the country to the other, the legitimacy of the outcome of various elections is thrown into question. In order to avoid a crisis of legitimacy, it becomes necessary to make qualifications and procedures more uniform so that they are acceptable to all (or at least to the dominant competitors for office and power).[9]

Third, the dynamic party competition for nation-wide support has brought about some nationalized standards of voter qualifications and

8. See "Estimated Characteristics of the Electorate, 1820–1960," in William H. Flanigan, *Political Behavior of the American Electorate* (Boston: Allyn and Bacon, Inc., 1968), pp. 10–12. Flanigan notes that, during the early years of the Republic, almost all voters resided in rural areas, the electorate becoming more urban over 150 years. The literacy rate of the electorate was high from the beginning, although the level of education was not. The rate of high-school graduates among the electorate has also risen rapidly since the nineteenth century. When Negroes were enfranchised after the Civil War, only about half of them had recently been slaves but the overwhelming majority were illiterate. The illiteracy rate among blacks has steadily declined and at present approaches the very low rate among whites. Naturalized citizens have never been a large proportion of the electorate and they are a decreasing feature of the electorate. See Bureau of the Census, "Characteristics of Persons of Voting Age, 1964–1968," Series P-20, No. 172, May 3, 1968.

9. Stein Rokkan, "Electoral Systems," 5 *International Encyclopedia of Social Science* 6–21, 9 (New York: Macmillan, 1968). See also Seymour Lipset, "Some Social Requisites of Democracy: Economic Development and Political Legitimacy," 53 *American Political Science Review* 69–105 (Mar. 1959).

representational legitimacy but has stimulated little demand for federal administration of elections. The same party competition which has generated equalized voter qualifications in the states has resisted repetition of the Reconstruction precedent, i.e., federal conduct of state and national elections. The reasons are many and do not end with high financial as well as administrative costs and with the resistance that may be expected because of vestiges of sectional bitterness over the unhappy experiment of the 1870s. The overriding explanation lies in the fact that, while standardization of voter qualifications and some electoral procedures support party competition, unitary control of the electoral process could too obviously threaten competition. Opportunities for abuse seem inherent in a system of centralized administration. The specter of manipulation from a single party source reinforces the existing tradition of decentralized administration. Centralized administration of all elections is seen as dysfunctional to party competition, whereas standardization of various electoral procedures and voter qualifications supports party competition.

Fourth, the parties are not equipped to handle completely the adjustment of rights and demands which must accompany "the inclusion process." Courts become involved as well. Their role has been to oversee the definition and realization of the rights of political participation which crystalize at two main points in modern American politics. One is the franchise; the other is the right to attempt to influence policy, starting with the rights of free speech and petition but extending to the sensitive areas of organizing for political purposes and lobbying.[10]

THE WARREN COURT AND THE ELECTORAL PROCESS

In 1962, Roy Wilkins, national director of the NAACP, expressed the view that his organization had come to look to federal courts for sympathetic treatment of political and civil rights. He said that, especially since the 1954 school desegregation case of *Brown* v. *Board of Education*, people from a number of states had requested aid in challenging local statutes, such as franchise tax provisions, which impaired constitutional rights.[11] The tide of such legal claims is reflected in

10. Parsons, "Full Citizenship," p. 1017. See generally, Samuel Krislov, *The Supreme Court and Political Rights* (New York: Free Press, 1967).
11. Wilkins Testimony, *Gray Record*, p. 307.

Table 11–2, which displays the swelling volume of civil and political rights cases. It enumerates all private civil rights suits commenced in federal district courts and the number of civil rights cases in which the United States served as plaintiff in a civil rights criminal or civil action. Notice the plateau of private litigation between 1948 and 1954, averaging 173 cases per year, followed between 1954 and 1961 by a generally rising slope until 1962, when apportionment litigation and the civil rights movement combined to generate a sharply increased constitutional rights docket (with some assistance from the Justice Department acting under both the Civil Rights Acts of 1957 and 1960 and the vestiges of Reconstruction Acts of 1870 and 1871). The figures for both private suits and government initiated actions for the years 1962 to 1968 show an unprecedented upgrade.

Table 11–2   *United States Government and Private Civil Rights Suits Commenced in United States District Courts, 1947–68**

YEAR	NO. OF PRIVATE SUITS	NO. OF GOVERNMENT SUITS
1947	92	10
1948	168	13
1949	159	22
1950	192	18
1951	158	16
1952	189	15
1953	149	24
1954	199	n.a.
1955	221	20
1956	275	20
1957	245	n.a.
1958	242	7
1959	280	3
1960	316	12
1961	270	13
1962	357	29
1963	424	53
1964	709	34
1965	994	40
1966	1,154	60
1967	1,006	106
1968	2,180	120

* Compiled from data published by the Judicial Conference of the United States, *Annual Report of the Administrative Office of the United States Courts* (Washington, D.C.: Government Printing Office, 1947–1969). See generally Table C2. The notation "n.a." indicates figures not available.

Allowing for a one to three year delay in the appeals process, it is not surprising that the Supreme Court's case-load of civil and political rights disputes should be heavy in the years from 1959 to 1969. In that decade, the Supreme Court has done more to extend voting and electoral process rights than during any other period in American history. In those years, the justices ruled, in constitutional terms, on the drawing of constituency boundaries;[12] on the apportionment of representatives at every level of government;[13] on racial discrimination where the political rights of voters are concerned[14] and on invidious discrimination where the rights of candidates are involved;[15] on state-set voter qualifications;[16] on electioneering practices;[17] and on the procedural fairness of Civil Rights Commission hearings regarding the state-conduct of elections.[18] These developments are registered in Table 11–3, which identifies 40 Supreme Court decisions in which a full Opinion of the Court was delivered affecting some aspect of the electoral process.

Before discussing specific cases which have contributed to the

12. Relevant cases, as identified on Table 11–3 are those with full opinions, *Gomillion v. Lightfoot*, 364 U.S. 399 (1960); *Wright v. Rockefeller*, 372 U.S. 52 (1964); *Fortson v. Dorsey*, 379 U.S. 433 (1965); *Wells v. Rockefeller*, 394 U.S. 542 (1969).

13. *Baker v. Carr*, 369 U.S. 186 (1962); *Gray v. Sanders*, 372 U.S. 368 (1963); *Wesberry v. Sanders*, 376 U.S. 1 (1964); *Reynolds v. Sims*, 377 U.S. 533 (1964); *Maryland Committee for Fair Representation v. Tawes*, 377 U. S. 656 (1964); *Davis v. Mann*, 377 U.S. 678 (1966); *WMCA v. Lomenzo*, 377 U.S. 633 (1964); *Lucas v. Colorado General Assembly*, 377 U.S. 713 (1964); *Burns v. Richardson*, 384 U.S. 73 (1966); *Swann v. Adams*, 385 U.S. 440 (1967); *Sailors v. Kent County Board of Education*, 387 U.S. 105 (1967); *Dusch v. Davis*, 387 U.S. 112 (1967); *Avery v. Midland County*, 390 U.S. 474 (1968); *Kirkpatrick v. Preisler*, 394 U.S. 526 (1969).

14. *United States v. Raines*, 362 U.S. 17 (1960); *United States v. Louisiana*, 380 U.S. 145 (1965); *United States v. Mississippi*, 380 U.S. 128 (1965); *South Carolina v. Katzenbach*, 383 U.S. 301 (1965); *Allen v. Virginia Board of Elections*, 393 U.S. 544 (1969).

15. *Anderson v. Martin*, 375 U.S. 394 (1964); *Bond v. Floyd*, 385 U.S. 116 (1966); *Fortson v. Morris*, 385 U.S. 231 (1966); *Williams v. Rhodes*, 393 U.S. 23 (1968); *Hadnott v. Amos*, 394 U.S. 358 (1969); *Powell v. McCormack*, 395 U.S. 486 (1969).

16. *Lassiter v. Northampton County Board of Elections*, 360 U.S. 45 (1959); *Harman v. Forssenius*, 380 U.S. 528 (1965); *Carrington v. Rash*, 380 U.S. 89 (1965); *Katzenbach v. Morgan*, 384 U.S. 641 (1966); *Harper v. Virginia Board of Elections*, 383 U.S. 663 (1966); *Kramer v. Union Free School District*, 395 U.S. 621 (1969).

17. *Mills v. Alabama*, 384 U.S. 214 (1966).

18. *Hanna v. Larche*, 363 U.S. 420 (1960).

Table 11-3 *Supreme Court Votes in Electoral Process Cases, 1959–69*

CASE TITLE	YEAR	TYPE	N.S.	VOTE	Warr.	Doug.	Bren.	Black	Wtkr.	Clar.	Stew.	Fran.	Harl.
Lassiter v. Northampton	'59	E	—	0–9	u	U	u	u	u	u	u	u	u	u
U.S. v. Raines	'60	R	+	9–0	f	f	F	f	f	f	f	f	f	f
Hanna v. Larche	'60	E	+	2–7	U	f	u	f	u	u	u	u	U	u
Gomillion v. Lightfoot	'60	R	+	9–0	f	f	f	f	fb	f	f	F	f	f
Cumulative Total f			3		2	3	2	3	2	2	2	2	2
u			1		2	1	2	1	2	2	2	2	2
Baker v. Carr	'62	A	+	6–2	f	fb	F	f	White o	f	f	u Gold.	u
Gray v. Sanders	'63	A	+	8–1	f	F	f	f	f	f	f	f	u
Anderson v. Martin	'64	R	+	9–0	f	f	f	f	f	F	f	f	f
Wright v. Rockefeller	'64	A	—	2–7	u	f	u	U	u	u	u	f	u
Wesberry v. Sanders	'64	A	+	8–1	fb	fb	fb	FB	fb	fn	fn	fb	u
Reynolds v. Sims	'64	A	+	8–1	FB	fb	fb	fb	fb	fn	fn	fb	f
Roman v. Sincock	'64	A	+	8–1	FB	fb	fb	fb	fb	fn	fn	fb	u
Md. Ctee v. Tawes	'64	A	+	8–1	FB	fb	fb	fb	fb	fn	fn	fb	u
Mann v. Davis	'64	A	+	8–1	FB	fb	fb	fb	fb	fn	fn	fb	u
WMCA v. Lomenzo	'64	A	+	8–1	FB	fb	fb	fb	fb	fn	fn	fb	u
Lucas v. Assembly	'64	A	+	8–1	FB	fb	fb	fb	fb	fn	fn	fb	u
Harman v. Forssenius	'64	E	+	9–0	F	f	f	f	f	f	F	f	f
Carrington v. Rash	'65	E	+	7–1	o	f	f	f	f	u	u	u	u
Fortson v. Dorsey	'65	A	—	1–8	u	U	U	u	u	f	f	f	u
Louisiana v. U.S.	'65	R	+	9–0	f	f	F	u	f	f	u	u	f
U.S. v. Mississippi	'65	R	+	9–0	f	f	f	F	f	f	f	f	f
Cumulative Total f			17		15	19	16	17	13	16	16	14	6
u			3		4	1	4	3	2	4	4	1	14

Table 11-3—continued Supreme Court Votes in Electoral Process Cases, 1959–69

CASE TITLE	YEAR	TYPE	N.S.	VOTE	Warr.	Doug.	Bren.	Black	White	Clar.	Stew.	Fort.	Harl.
So. Car. v. Katzenbach	'66	R	+	9–0	FB	fb	fb	f	fb	fb	fb	fb	fb
Katzenbach v. Morgan	'66	E	+	7–2	f	f	F	f	f	f	u	f	u
Mills v. Alabama	'66	E	+	9–0	fb	fb	FB	fb	fb	fb	fb	fb	fn
Harper v. Virginia	'66	E	–	6–3	f	F	f	u	f	f	u	f	u
Burns v. Richardson	'66	A	+	0–8	u	u	U	u	u	u	u	u	u
Bond v. Floyd	'66	E	+	9–0	F	f	f	f	f	f	f	f	f
Fortson v. Morris	'66	E	–	4–5	f	f	f	U	f	f	u	f	u
Swann v. Adams	'67	A	+	7–2	u	U	u	f	F	u	u	f	u
Sailors v. Board	'67	A	–	0–9	u	U	u	u	u	u	u	u	u
Dusch v. Davis	'67	A	–	0–9	u	U	u	u	u	u	u	u	u
Cumulative Total f			23		22	26	23	22	20	22	19	7	9
u			7		7	4	7	8	5	8	11	2	21
										Mars.			
Avery v. Midland	'68	A	+	5–3	fb	fb	fb	fb	FB	o	u	u	u
Williams v. Rhodes	'68	E	+	6–3	u	fb	f	F	u	f	u	f	fn
Hadnott v. Amos	'69	R	+	6–2	f	F	f	o	f	f	u	f	f
Allen v. Board of Elect.	'69	R	+	8–1	F	fb	f	u	u	fb	f	f	fn
Kirkpatrick v. Preisler	'69	A	+	6–3	fb	fb	FB	fb	f	fb	u	fn	u
Wells v. Rockefeller	'69	A	+	6–3	fb	fb	FB	fb	u	fb	u	fn	u
Moore v. Ogilvie	'69	E	+	7–2	f	F	f	f	f	f	f	o	u
Gaston County v. U.S.	'69	R	+	7–1	F	f	f	u	f	f	f	o	F
Kramer v. Union Free School	'69	E	+	5–3	F	f	f	u	u	f	u	u	u
Powell v. McCormack	'69	E	+	7–1	F	U	f	f	f	f	u	o	f
Cumulative Total f			33		31	36	33	28	24	9	21	13	14
u			7		8	4	7	11	11	0	19	3	26

standardization of electoral requirements, it is appropriate to take advantage of the panoramic view of the decade of Warren Court decisions presented in the table. Three types of cases are tabulated in which constitutional issues were adjudicated in the areas of districting and apportionment (18 cases marked "A" on the table), racial discrimination (nine cases marked "R"), and miscellaneous voter qualification and electoral process problems (13 cases marked "E"). The table itemizes the cases chronologically from top to bottom and takes account of the changing membership of the Court. It reports the decisions among the justices on each case, and it gives cumulative totals of the votes cast. Unanimous rulings are rare except in race-related disputes; this result is in harmony with the cohesive Warren Court treatment of racial discrimination in areas other than voting. Only three of the districting and apportionment decisions were unanimously decided (*Burns* v. *Richardson*, *Sailors* v. *Board*, and *Dusch* v. *Davis*), and each of these yielded a ruling unfavorable to the persons claiming a political right. Of the 13 electoral process decisions, three received the full support of the bench—*Harman* v. *Forssenius*, *Mills* v. *Alabama*, and *Bond* v. *Floyd*—and of these the latter two involved sensitive First Amendment, free-expression issues.

In the table, the vote of each justice is recorded as being favorable (f) or unfavorable (u) to the political or civil rights claim asserted. These ratings are not intended to imply that the litigant asserting that his rights were infringed was necessarily correct. In some instances where different grounds were advanced by a member of the Court for favoring the asserted right, "fb" registers a favorable vote on broad grounds and "fn" a favorable vote on narrow grounds. The vote of the author of the Opinion of the Court is entered on the table in a capital letter. Where a justice did not participate, a notation of "o" is made. In the column entitled Nationalized Standards ("N.S."), a simple rating is given based on whether or not the majority's ruling tends to advance a single national standard (+) where one may previously not have existed or to avoid requiring uniformity and therefore to sustain continued diversity (−) of electoral operations among the states. On this basis 33 rulings indicate standardization (82 percent of the 40 decisions), while only seven tolerate diversity.

Table 11–4 makes use of Guttman scaling to supply a precise description of the relative favorableness of individual justices to voting rights pleas and efforts to liberalize the application of the Constitution to the electoral process. The cumulative scaling technique for reporting judicial behavior focuses on non-unanimous cases for purposes of

Table 11-4 Cumulative Scaling of Non-Unanimous Cases from 1963-69 by Justices*

Legend:
+ = favorable
− = unfavorable
O = non-participant
• = not on Court

Case numbers and titles (column headers):

1. Allen v. Board
2. Wesberry v. Sanders
3. Reynolds v. Sims
4. Roman v. Sincock
5. Md. Cttee. v. Tawes
6. Mann v. Davis
7. WMCA v. Lomenzo
8. Lucas v. Assembly
9. Gray v. Sanders
10. Carrington v. Rash
11. Gaston County v. U.S.
12. Powell v. McCormack
13. Moore v. Ogilvie
14. Swann v. Adams
15. Katzenbach v. Morgan
16. Hadnott v. Amos
17. Harper v. Va.
18. Wells v. Rockefeller
19. Kirkpatrick v. Preisler
20. Williams v. Rhodes
21. Avery v. Midland
22. Kramer v. Union
23. Fortson v. Morris
24. Wright v. Rockefeller
25. Fortson v. Dorsey

CASE NO.	1	2	3	4	5	6	7	8	9	10	11	12	13	14	15	16	17	18	19	20	21	22	23	24	25	VOTE TOTAL PER JUDGE	SCALE POSITION	SCALE SCORE
DOUGLAS	+	+	+	+	+	+	+	+	+	+	+	+	+	+	+	+	+	+	+	+	+	+	+	+	+	25-0	25	+1.00
GOLDBERG	•	+	+	+	+	+	+	+	+	+	•	•	•	•	•	•	•	•	•	•	•	•	+	+	−	11-1	24	+.92
BRENNAN	+	+	+	+	+	+	+	+	+	+	+	+	+	+	+	+	+	+	+	+	+	+	+	−	−	23-2	23	+.84
WARREN	+	+	+	+	+	+	+	+	+	O	+	+	+	+	+	+	+	+	+	+	+	+	−	−	−	21-3	22	+.76
FORTAS	+	•	•	•	•	•	•	•	•	•	•	+	+	+	+	•	+	•	•	+	+	+	−	•	•	9-1	22	+.76
MARSHALL	+	•	•	•	•	•	•	•	•	•	+	+	+	+	•	+	•	+	+	+	O	O	•	•	•	9-0	22	+.76
WHITE	+	+	+	+	+	+	+	+	+	+	+	+	+	+	+	+	+	+	−	−	−	−	−	−	−	18-7	18	+.44
BLACK	−	+	+	+	+	+	+	+	+	+	+	+	+	+	+	O	+	+	+	−	−	−	−	−	−	17-7	18	+.44
CLARK	•	+	+	+	+	+	+	+	+	+	•	•	•	+	+	•	+	•	•	•	•	•	−	−	−	12-3	17	+.36
STEWART	+	+	+	+	+	+	+	+	+	+	+	−	−	−	−	−	−	−	−	−	−	−	−	−	−	11-14	11	−.12
HARLAN	+	+	+	−	−	−	−	−	−	−	−	−	−	−	−	+	+	−	−	−	−	−	−	−	−	5-20	3	−.90
vote	8-1	8-1	8-1	8-1	8-1	8-1	8-1	8-1	8-1	7-1	7-1	7-1	7-2	7-2	7-2	6-2	6-3	6-3	6-3	6-3	5-3	5-3	5-4	2-7	1-8			

CR = .93
CS = .72

* On the utility of cumulative scaling, see Glendon Schubert, "Behavioral Research in Public Law," 57 American Political Science Review 433 (June 1963), and Joseph Tanenhaus, "The Cumulative Scaling of Judicial Decisions," 79 Harvard Law Review 1583 (June 1966). "CR" refers to the coefficient of reproducibility and "CS" to the coefficient of scalability.

assessing the "liberalness" of each judge relative to his colleagues in closely contested cases. As expected, Justices Douglas, Goldberg, Brennan, Chief Justice Warren, and Justices Fortas and Marshall rank in the most liberal positions (with scale scores of over +.50), while Justices Stewart and Harlan have maintained consistently "conservative" positions in electoral process cases.

Before reviewing some of the more important cases of the last decade, it should be noted that the Warren Court has hardly been writing on a clean slate in directing its attention to the electoral process. No matter what the cause of debasement to the vote, myriad rulings have made clear that it is proper for the Court to look closely where a statute affects the right to vote. Where voting in federal elections was concerned, precedents from *Ex parte Yarbrough*[19] in 1884 to *Burroughs and Cannon* v. *United States*[20] in 1934 could be cited to identify a general federal police power over the entire field of federal elections (though it has never been fully exercised).

Generally, the federal government was placed on record as the enemy of racial and other arbitrary barriers to the exercise of the elective franchise. In 1950, Justice Douglas observed with Justice Black in *South* v. *Peters*[21] that Supreme Court rulings, including "our primary [election] cases since *Nixon* v. *Herndon* . . . have insisted that where there is voting there can be equality." The fact that Justice Douglas spoke in dissent suggests that reasonable men could disagree with his suggested application of the Equal Protection Clause to the arcane workings of the Georgia county-unit system of voting in state-wide elections for public officials. But his retrospective words did point to an important *fait accompli:* the Supreme Court's primary election cases had by 1950 yielded a new and flexible notion of federal safeguards in the electoral process.[22]

19. In *Ex parte Yarbrough,* Justice Miller identified the Times, Places, and Manner Clause of Article I, Sec. 4 as supplying the *express* authority for federal regulations against interference, intimidation, or fraud in congressional elections; 110 U.S. 651 (1884).

20. In *Burroughs,* involving the application of the Corrupt Practices Act of 1925 to presidential elections, Justice Sutherland relied on the Necessary and Proper Clause for the *implied* authority sufficient to confer a degree of federal control over the popular vote in elections for the President; 290 U.S. 534 (1934).

21. *South* v. *Peters,* 339 U.S. 276, Douglas and Black dissenting, at 281 (1950); cf. *Gray* v. *Sanders,* 372 U.S. 368 (1963).

22. *Nixon* v. *Herndon,* 273 U.S. 536 (1927); *Nixon* v. *Condon,* 286 U.S. 73 (1932); *United States* v. *Classic,* 313 U.S. 299 (1941); *Smith* v. *Allwright,* 321 U.S. 649 (1944); *Terry* v. *Adams,* 345 U.S. 461 (1953).

It is not too early to suggest that Supreme Court decisions, especially since 1958, have given impetus to the nationalization of the electoral process. This is not to deny that decentralized administration and control of local, state, and federal elections is a permanent feature of the American electoral process; rather it is to state that, increasingly, the conduct of every election proceeds within the limitations of federal guidelines.

The nationally standardized requirements which the Court has called for from case to case involve quite different types of prescriptions and proscriptions. Disparate constitutional provisions have come into play in the decisions itemized on Table 11–3, but by far the most potent constitutional instrument for change has been the Fourteenth Amendment. Its utility has been proved in the three areas of districting, racial discrimination, and electoral process cases. In the discussion that follows, a summary statement will be offered concerning the nationalization of the electoral process as evidenced in each of these three areas.

1. *Uniform standards of voting equality are emerging in districting and apportionment cases for elections at every level.* The Supreme Court opened the courthouse door when it ruled in *Baker* v. *Carr* that a claim of denial of equal protection by malapportionment presents a justifiable right to relief. In 1964, although the Court refused to set mathematical guidelines, it did hold that the Equal Protection Clause required that both houses of a state legislature be apportioned on a population basis.[23] *Wesberry* v. *Sanders* carried the population equality principle into congressional districting (under Article I, Section 2).[24] *Kirkpatrick* v. *Preisler* broke new ground for congressional districting standards by requiring the states to aim for absolute equality and not some arbitrary zone of acceptability.[25] *Avery* v. *Midland County* brought the "one man, one vote" principle to bear upon local units which exercise "general governmental powers" and involve the election of officials by districts.[26] So long as the Court remains engaged in the delicate post-*Reynolds* task of setting voter equality in workable order, it appears to prefer avoiding a fixed position on other, though clearly related, electoral problems. These include a consideration of the effect on constitutional rights of gerrymandering, multi-

23. *Baker* v. *Carr*, 369 U.S. 186 (1962); *Reynolds* v. *Sims*, 377 U.S. 533 (1964).
24. *Wesberry* v. *Sanders*, 376 U.S. 1 (1964).
25. *Kirkpatrick* v. *Preisler*, 394 U.S. 526 (1969); *Wells* v. *Rockefeller*, 394 U.S. 542 (1969).
26. *Avery* v. *Midland*, 390 U.S. 474 (1968).

member districting, and the shifting of representation from a basis of the whole population to eligible voters only.

2. *Vintage state-action doctrines have been removed as bars to federal protection of voters and registration workers against interference or intimidation by private individuals.* In *United States* v. *Guest*, dealing with the shotgun slaying of a black teacher by six private citizens in Georgia, the Court said that the involvement of the state need not be either exclusive or direct in order to bring federal protective statutes under the Fourteenth Amendment into operation.[27] A majority of the members of the Court in concurrence expressed the view that Section 5 of the Fourteenth Amendment "empowers Congress to enact laws punishing *all* conspiracies to interfere with the exercise of Fourteenth Amendment rights, whether or not state officers or others acting under the color of state law are implicated in the conspiracy." One result was the civil rights protection provisions of the Civil Rights Act of 1968. It avoids being "void for vagueness" by identifying clearly the rights marked out for federal protection. Voting is included, along with education, housing, employment, jury service, and travel. Among other things, Section 245 of the *United States Code* (Title 18) now applies criminal sanctions against "whoever, whether or not acting under color of law," willfully injures, intimidates or interferes with any person in his attempt at "voting or qualifying to vote, qualifying or campaigning as a candidate for elective office, or qualifying or acting as a poll watcher, or any legally authorized election official, in any primary, special, or general election."

3. *The Supreme Court has read a Necessary and Proper Clause into the Fifteenth Amendment, thereby offering Congress a vast measure of authority.* In *South Carolina* v. *Katzenbach*, the Court affirmed congressional power to write "appropriate legislation" enforcing the Fifteenth Amendment ban against racial discrimination in effective use of the ballot.[28] Federal enforcement is governed by the same "basic test ... as in all cases concerning the express powers of Congress with relation to the reserved power of the States," namely the elastic test given by Chief Justice Marshall with regard to the Necessary and Proper Clause.[29] State requirements setting literacy or other prerequisites for voting, or even governing the regulation of political

27. *United States* v. *Guest*, 383 U.S. 745 (1966); *United States* v. *Price*, 383 U.S. 787 (1966).
28. *South Carolina* v. *Katzenbach*, 383 U.S. 301 (1965).
29. *McCulloch* v. *Maryland*, 4 Wheat. 316, 421 (1819).

candidacy for office, must yield to "appropriate" federal legislation designed to enforce the Fifteenth Amendment. Among states affected by the Voting Rights Act of 1965, state regulation of the electoral process may even be suspended when the state fails to comply with federal approval procedures. This was dramatically indicated in *Allen* v. *Virginia Board of Elections* and in the black candidates' case of *Hadnott* v. *Amos*.[30]

4. *Sharp inroads in the name of the Equal Protection Clause of the Fourteenth Amendment have been made into traditional state claims of exclusive control over voting qualifications.* In *Katzenbach* v. *Morgan*, the Supreme Court upheld a congressional effort to alter state literacy requirements where no element of race was concerned, but it did so solely to enforce the Fourteenth Amendment.[31] Though the Court itself had found in the *Lassiter* case that literacy tests by themselves do not violate Equal Protection guarantees, it allowed Congress to activate their enforcement by "appropriate legislation."[32] The Court deferred to the independent judgment of Congress in using its power to deal with the domain of Fourteenth Amendment rights. It was sufficient in the English literacy test case that the Court could "perceive a basis upon which Congress might predicate a judgment" that New York's test, which handicapped Spanish-speaking citizens in attaining the vote, deprived them of greater equality in public services.

The Court has also shown a willingness to void state voter qualifications without reference to federal statutes but solely on the grounds of conflict with the Equal Protection Clause. In *Harper* v. *Virginia State Board of Elections*, Justice Douglas' Opinion not only said that Virginia's poll tax for state elections was invalid, but that states must draw no lines which are inconsistent with the Equal Protection Clause of the Fourteenth Amendment, including distinctions based on wealth or payment of a fee.[33] Douglas asserted that the Court had come to see the right to vote as too fundamental to be burdened by the condition of fee-paying. Comparable logic was applied in *Carrington* v. *Rash* against a Texas bar to military personnel voting in the state when they had qualified under state residence and voting laws in every respect

30. *Allen* v. *Virginia Board of Elections*, 393 U.S. 544 (1969); *Hadnott* v. *Amos*, 394 U.S. 358 (1969).

31. *Katzenbach* v. *Morgan*, 384 U.S. 641 (1966).

32. *Lassiter* v. *Northampton Election Board*, 360 U.S. 45 (1959).

33. *Harper* v. *Virginia State Board of Election*, 383 U.S. 663 (1966); cf. *Harman* v. *Forssenius*, 380 U.S. 528 (1965).

save being civilians.[34] A New York voter qualification statute was voided on Equal Protection grounds in 1969 in *Kramer* v. *Union Free School District.*[35] For five members of the Court, Chief Justice Warren condemned the selective provisions of the law which provided that residents who were otherwise eligible to vote in state and federal elections may vote in certain annual school district elections only if they own or lease taxable real property within the district or are parents of children enrolled in the local public school. Against the dissents of Justices Stewart, Black, and Harlan, the Chief Justice reasoned that "any unjustified discrimination in determining who may participate in political affairs or in the selection of public officials undermines the legitimacy of representative government."

5. *The free speech and press guarantees of the First Amendment limit the authority of the states to regulate "electioneering."* In *Mills* v. *Alabama* in 1966, the Supreme Court ruled that no test of reasonableness could save a state law from invalidation as a violation of the First Amendment when that law made it a crime for a newspaper editor to do no more than urge people to vote one way or another in a publicly held election.[36] Justice Black for a unanimous Court struck down the prosecution of a newspaper editor for disobeying the Alabama Corrupt Practices Act. The law made it illegal to solicit votes for or against any election proposition on the day for voting. Mills' paper published an election-day editorial urging a vote to replace the city commission form of government in Birmingham with a mayor-council arrangement. Justice Black acknowledged that the state's rationale for the statute was to protect the public from last-minute charges which could not be answered. Yet, Black said, the state law left people free to hurl their campaign charges up to the last minute of the day before election and then made it a crime to answer those last-minute charges on election day, the only time they could be effectively answered.

6. *The Equal Protection Clause of the Fourteenth Amendment and the right of assembly guaranteed in the First Amendment impose limitations upon a state legislature's freedom to restrict political parties in their access to the ballot.* In 1968, the Supreme Court gave its first

34. *Carrington* v. *Rash*, 380 U.S. 89 (1965).

35. *Kramer* v. *Union Free School District*, 395 U.S. 621 (1969). See also *McDonald* v. *Board of Election Commissioners of Chicago*, 394 U.S. 802 (1969) *per curiam*, regarding absentee ballot regulations; *Cipriano* v. *City of Houma*, 395 U.S. 701 (1969) *per curiam*, condemning the exclusion of non-property-taxpayers from voting on municipal utility revenue bonds.

36. *Mills* v. *Alabama*, 384 U.S. 214 (1966).

clear indication that the power of the states under Article II, Section
1 to select presidential electors is subject to the limitations of the
Fourteenth Amendment. In *Williams* v. *Rhodes*, Justice Black spoke
for six members of the Court in voiding the Ohio election laws that
had barred George Wallace's American Independent Party (as well
as the Socialist Labor Party) from the presidential ballot.[37] Ohio had
argued that presidential election provisions of the Constitution give
each state unlimited power to determine how it will choose electors.
Further, Ohio asserted an interest in promoting a two-party system,
in seeing that the winner of the popular vote be chosen by a clear
majority of its voters, and in specifying that parties demonstrate
established organization and popular support. To this end, Ohio outlawed independent candidates from its ballot. State law said that
endorsing parties must establish a network of county and state central committees and that such parties should rely on national nominations. For six members of the Court, Justice Black asserted that the
state's role in presidential elections, though extensive, must yield to
the First and Fourteenth Amendments. Once Ohio provided for a
popular vote, it could not debase the right of franchise by unfairly
barring from the ballot the candidates of third parties. Chief Justice
Warren lamented the hurried review (seven days of consideration)
given *Williams* v. *Rhodes* and noted that Justice Black's rationale,
based both on the Equal Protection Clause and the First Amendment
guarantee of freedom of association, would apply to all elections—
national, state, and local. "I think it fair to say," he wrote, "that the
ramifications of our decision today may be comparable to those of
Baker v. *Carr*, a case we deliberated for nearly a year."

Williams v. *Rhodes* notwithstanding, Supreme Court forays into
the "political thicket" have generally been marked by unhurried de-
liberation. Recent rulings supporting the six propositions identified
above indicate the Supreme Court's sense of responsibility for keeping open the channels for change inherent in democratic political
processes. In the last decade, the Court has been careful about staking
out federal claims for supervisory control of the electoral process.
From the Court's point of view, dealing with districting, discrimination, and electoral process cases has been something less than an exercise in self-aggrandizement. For example, many problems involving
broad social and political issues, including electoral process disputes,
might be removed from federal court dockets if *Baker* v. *Carr* and its

---

37. *Williams* v. *Rhodes*, 393 U.S. 23 (1968).

progeny result in making state officials more responsive to expanded constituencies. If not, the Warren Court has opened the door to congressional remedies. A review of the propositions advanced on the preceding pages suggests that in several electoral process areas, the Supreme Court has virtually invited Congress to follow the judge-blazed federalization path. Short of compromising judicially defined First Amendment rights and constitutional voting rights where race and fair representation are concerned, there appear to be few barriers left standing to impede Congress from doing what it thinks appropriate to enforce equal protection guarantees applicable to the conduct of any election. Under the Times, Places, and Manner Clause and the Fourteenth and Fifteenth Amendments, Congress could even remedy a state practice not condemned by the Court or, of its own accord, strike down a state voting requirement which it judges to be invidiously discriminatory. For example, if Congress can make a conclusive legislative finding that the ability to read and write English instead of Spanish is constitutionally irrelevant to an American citizen's casting of a ballot, then a determination that all literacy tests hinder the "equal protection of the laws" might be equally conclusive. Perhaps Congress could even make a similar finding regarding the denial of the vote to eighteen-year-olds, since they are subject to taxes and military service.

CONGRESS AND THE ELECTORAL PROCESS

In the light of the nationalization of the electoral process, no analysis of the Supreme Court's role in the process would be complete without discussion of the relative role of Congress in determining the content of demands for electoral reform. The Supreme Court has opened the constitutional door for Congress to give the national leadership it has hitherto avoided in setting selected uniform standards for the electoral process. Whether Congress is politically or temperamentally prepared to nationalize the rules of electoral operations is quite another question. Since the end of the Reconstruction Period, congressional interest in setting selected uniform standards for the electoral process has lagged behind Supreme Court leadership. Civil rights legislation since 1957, however, indicates a changing congressional temper. In addition, an increasing number of federal governmental agencies and commissions concerned directly or indirectly with the electoral process have been developed, and they stimulate or carry policy recommendations forward to Congress.[38] Particularly since 1961, various judiciary and elections subcommittees of Congress have been presented with an unprecedented flood of federal election law proposals, symptomatic of the needs of a nation becoming increasingly unitary. In the wake of the 1960 presidential election, it appeared that short-term interest in legislative changes was spurred by the combination of a new Administration's reforming zeal and the opposition's concern with alleged voting irregularities and with the need to scrutinize campaign funds. However, a larger perspective on the volume and variety of regulatory proposals from Congress to Congress during the 1960s must take account of technological and economic changes developing at a pace so rapid as to revolutionize campaign techniques and to make obsolete the traditional mélange of poorly meshed federal and state laws on national elections.

In spite of the fact that federal election-law proposals failed to receive sympathetic treatment in the House in 1961, momentum for

38. Federal government units which contribute to the security of voting rights or which are concerned with the electoral process have proliferated. They include committees on constitutional rights and on elections in both houses of Congress. The President's Committee on Civil Rights was succeeded by the U.S. Commission on Civil Rights. (See *Report of the United States Commission on Civil Rights*, 1959, Part I, *Voting*; *Voting* [1961]; *Voting in Mississippi* [1965]; *The Voting Rights Act, The First Months* [1965]; *The Voting Rights Act of 1965* [1965]; *Law Enforcement, A Report on Equal Protection in the South* [1965]; *Political Participation* [1968].) The President's Committee on Campaign Expenditures (*Financing Presidential Campaigns* [1962]) and the President's Commission on Registration and Voting Participation (*Report*, 1963) were both temporary panels under President Kennedy. The Commission on Political Activities of Government Personnel served for two years under President Johnson (*Report*, 1968). More long-lived is the responsibility of the Bureau of the Census for maintaining voting statistics. Occasionally doing work touching on voting rights disputes is the Community Relations Service with its race-relations "diplomatic corps." More directly relevant to enforcement is the work of the Office of Hearing Examiners of the Civil Service Commission involved in administering the Voting Rights Act of 1965. Voting Rights Examiners are under the direction of the Attorney General who is also responsible for deploying United States marshals and using the Federal Bureau of Investigation, occasionally brought into electoral investigations. The Justice Department discharges its duties under the civil rights laws through the Civil Rights Division. The Criminal Division maintains jurisdiction in election frauds and Hatch Act matters. The Civil Rights Commission and the Civil Rights Division of the Justice Department, although not always in policy agreement, have been particularly instrumental in developing the voting provisions of the Civil Rights Acts of 1960 and 1964, the Voting Rights Act of 1965, and the civil rights protection provisions of the Civil Rights Act of 1968.

reform was sustained by President Kennedy's bipartisan Commission on Campaign Expenditures. The report of the President's commission was published in 1962 with recommendations which were endorsed by Presidents Eisenhower and Truman.[39] The commission urged encouragement (largely by tax incentives) of unlimited contributions for bipartisan political activities. This recommendation was grounded on a faith in disclosure as a contribution-policing technique and on the assumption that giving money to one's political party could be viewed on a level with voting as a form of civic participation. Also suggested was a repeal of the easily-evaded ceilings on federal campaign expenditures in favor of renewed emphasis on an effective accounting for receipts and outlays by all political committees. With respect to Taft-Hartley prohibitions on corporate and union partisan spending, the report recommended that the continued equal legislative treatment of business and labor with respect to political contributions be maintained.[40] The proposals and findings of the campaign commission, in addition to a series of related and outstanding studies by scholars such as Stanley Kelley and Alexander Heard, did more to delineate the issues of presidential campaigning in the 1960s and to mark out the alternatives in a continuing debate on election law reform than to generate legislation.[41] As Senator Cannon conceded in 1967, "Congress after Congress has attempted to rewrite the Federal election laws, but without much success."[42]

39. President's Commission on Campaign Expenditures, *Financing Presidential Campaigns* (Washington, D.C.: Government Printing Office, 1962).

40. A complete statutory history and compilation of Taft-Hartley, Corrupt Practices, and Hatch Act provisions relating to federal elections may be found in U.S. Congress, Senate, Subcommittee on Privileges and Elections, *Federal Corrupt Practices and Political Activities*, Document No. 68, 88th Cong., 2d sess., 1964 (available from the Government Printing Office).

41. Stanley Kelley, Jr., *Political Campaigning* (Washington, D.C.: The Brookings Institution, 1960). Alexander Heard, *The Costs of Democracy* (Garden City, New Jersey: Doubleday, 1962).

42. An exception was the Presidential Election Campaign Fund Act of 1966. Hastily enacted in the closing hours of the Eighty-ninth Congress, it permitted taxpayers to designate one dollar of their income tax for expenses of the next presidential election campaign. "Major parties" which polled 15 million or more votes in the last presidential elections would divide contributions evenly. For each, actual expenses would be met and no more, *or* one dollar times the number of votes above 10 million, whichever were lower. A "minor party" which polled between 5 and 15 million votes would receive one dollar for each vote above 5 million. Only such expenses as were already incurred would be subsidized under the supervision of the General Accounting Office. The law, which would give immense new power to the federal government over the local parties, was repealed in 1967; 113 *Congressional Record* (4/13/1967).

President Kennedy's appointment of a Commission on Registration and Voting Participation also contributed to the widening scope of debate over federal election law. Indeed, something of the range of legislatively federalized elections standards, aside from race-related matters, is suggested by the commission's report, published in 1963. Its recommendations are addressed to the states, and the commissioners realistically assumed the continued administration of elections by state and local officials. Nevertheless, it is instructive to read through the score of proposals which were made and to note those which, in the years 1964–68, have come under congressional consideration for enactment as uniform national standards. Of the 21 electoral standards advanced, over half (those starred in the following list) have become the subject of proposed federal legislation, congressional inquiry, or federal action within six years of the report's publication.

In the listing which follows, parenthetical reference is made to only the most prominent examples of expressed federal concern or national action.[43]

1. Each state should create a commission on registration and voting participation or utilize some other existing state machinery to survey in detail its election law and practices.

*2. Voter registration should be easily accessible to all citizens (H.R. 8176 would make pertinent "recommendations" to states. 90th Congress.)

3. State residence requirements should not exceed six months.

4. Local residence requirements should not exceed 30 days.

*5. New state residents should be allowed to vote for the President (S. 1881 [90th Congress] proposes such a requirement).

6. Voter registration should extend as close to election day as possible and should not end more than three or four weeks before election day.

7. Voter lists should be kept current.

8. No citizen's registration should be cancelled for failure to vote in any period of less than four years.

*9. Voter registration lists should be used only for electoral purposes (S. 1026 would require the use of voting rolls for the random selection of all juries. 90th Congress).

*10. States should provide absentee registration for voters who cannot register in person (H.R. 8176 [90th Congress] so recommends for overseas citizens).

---

43. *Report of the President's Commission on Registration and Voting Participation* (Washington, D.C.: Government Printing Office, 1963), pp. 3–4.

*11. Literacy tests should not be a prerequisite for voting (Civil Rights Act of 1964 and Voting Rights Act of 1965).

*12. Election day should be proclaimed a national day of "Dedication to Our American Democracy" (S. 2111 [90th Congress] would make presidential election day a legal holiday).

13. Polling places should be so equipped to eliminate long waiting periods.

*14. Polling places should be open throughout the day and remain open until at least 9 P.M. (H.R. 2 [90th Congress] would require a uniform closing time for polling places in presidential elections).

*15. The states should provide every possible protection against election fraud (a study of electoral fraud irrespective of racial discrimination by the Civil Rights Commission is authorized by the Civil Rights Act of 1964).

*16. Candidacy should be open to all (see Civil Rights Commission recommendations regarding federal protection of rights of candidates and dissemination of information regarding candidacy qualifications, Commission on Civil Rights, *Political Participation*, 1968).

*17. The right to vote should be extended to those living on federal reservations (S. 1581 [90th Congress] would facilitate the necessary federal-state cooperation).

*18. Absentee voting by mail should be allowed for all who are absent from home on primary or general election day (S. 1881 [90th Congress] so provides).

*19. The poll tax as a voting qualification should be eliminated (the Twenty-fourth Amendment supplemented by *Harper* v. *Virginia* and the Voting Rights Act of 1965).

20. Each state should keep informed on other states' practices and innovations in election administration.

*21. Voting by persons 18 years of age should be considered by the states (S.J. Res. 8 [90th Congress] seeks to lower the voting age to 18 by constitutional amendment).

With respect to the last-mentioned standard, it might be noted that abolition of the electoral college, recently regarded with renewed interest, could induce states to compete for larger popular electorates by lowering age qualifications. Under these circumstances, the necessity for a uniform national standard could become inescapable. It could materialize in one of two ways. First, a uniform and democratic suffrage could be attained by a positive statement of federal responsibility incorporated in a constitutional amendment similar to the following: Section 1. Every citizen of the United States of the age of eighteen years or older who has resided in any State or Territory six months and in the voting precinct 30 days, immediately before offering to vote, shall be entitled to vote at any primary election or other election therein, in which candidates for any public office are nominated or elected, except that the right to vote shall not extend to persons in confinement for crimes nor to persons adjudicated unsound of mind. Section 2. Congress shall have power to enforce this Article by appropriate legislation.[44]

Second, if the constitutional amendment route to nationalized standards is not followed, a line of federal statutory development that would probably parallel the expansion of federal regulation of commerce would be the likely alternative. After a period of litigation challenging each new incursion, all concerned would finally demur to the proposition that the question of whether local regulation should be preserved is more a matter of policy for Congress than a question of law for the courts.

Building on the recommendations and findings of the two presidential commissions concerned with campaign financing and voting participation, President Johnson in 1967 called for comprehensive reform and a new set of nationalized standards to apply to federal elections. His message to Congress—"The Political Process in America"—included a five-point program designed, as he put it, to

Reform our campaign financing laws to assure full disclosure of contributions and expenses, to place realistic limits on contributions, and to remove the meaningless and ineffective ceilings on campaign expenditures.

Provide a system of public financing for Presidential election campaigns.

Broaden the base of public support for election campaigns, by exploring ways to encourage and stimulate small contributions.

Close the loopholes in the Federal laws regulating lobbying.

Assure the right to vote for millions of Americans who change their residence.[45]

44. The text of this amendment proposal is a modification of the suggested constitutional change urged and fully explored by Dudley McGovney, *The American Suffrage Medley* (Chicago: University of Chicago Press, 1949), Chapter IX.

45. The President's Message to Congress on May 25, 1967, entitled "The Political Process in America," was reprinted by the Senate Committee on Rules and Administration, *Hearings on Federal Election Reform*, 90th Cong., 1st sess., 1967, pp. 3–10.

Reforms such as these are workable if they move with the grain of dominant patterns of political forces and social and economic facts. The proposals on campaign financing, for example, take into account that modern technology makes possible a national presidential contest marked by expensive jet-age campaigning from Florida to Alaska and from Maine to Hawaii, by telethons costing hundreds of thousands of dollars, by costly specialists and advisors, by nation wide intelligence networks, and by the inclination of each of the political parties to assume above all that defeat is the highest price it can pay. The proposal for uniform residency requirements in presidential elections recognizes that citizen mobility in the 1960s has generated a disfranchised group that rivals, if it does not surpass, historical groups of otherwise qualified but voteless Negroes. In the single year, 1965–66, changes of residence from one state to another were made by 6,263,000 Americans.[46] Large numbers of persons so endangering their votes by moving from one jurisdiction to another constitute an imposing political problem. The traditional justification for state residence prerequisites ranging from six months to two years originally lay in the need for familiarity with local politics and problems. But American voters at home, abroad, or on the move can familiarize themselves with the national issues of presidential campaigns. In the English literacy test case of *Katzenbach* v. *Morgan*, the Supreme Court supplied Congress with the constitutional underpinnings sufficient for it to remedy the discrimination faced by mobile Americans whose travel bars them from voting in presidential elections. The impact of this problem has been enough to stimulate reform efforts at both the state and federal levels.[47] In 1962, the National Conference of Commissioners on Uniform State Law proposed a remedy in a model statute

46. Current Population Report No. 156, "Mobility of the Population of the United States from March 1965 to March 1966," (Washington, D.C.: Department of Commerce, Bureau of the Census, 1966), p. 20. A meticulous reworking of 1960 mobility data by William G. Andrews indicated that 5.4 million adult Americans were barred from voting by residence requirements, William G. Andrews, "American Voting Participation," 19 *Western Political Quarterly* 639–52 (Dec. 1966).

47. The Federal Voting Assistance Act of 1955 (5 U.S.C. 2171) replaced the Soldiers Voting Act of 1942. The 1955 version provides for a simple, uniform federal post card application procedure for absentee registration and voting by members of the Armed Forces, their dependents, and civilian government employees abroad. In 1967, Congressman Brademas asked for revision (H.R. 8176) in the Act of 1955 to make it applicable to all Americans temporarily abroad. His bill would follow the Voting Assistance Act in permitting states to accept or reject its recommendations.

which they urged the states to adopt. It applies only to new residents and to presidential elections. With built-in reservations to protect against double voting, the act grants a waiver from existing residence requirements to otherwise qualified state newcomers who wish to vote in an upcoming presidential election.[48] When the proposal for a similar requirement under federal law was made by the President in 1967, enough states had already adopted the model state statute so that changes in less than half of the states would be required to bring about uniformity. The federal law thus would have the effect of hastening a reforming tendency already in motion for a problem that is fundamentally interstate in character.

The increasing volume of federal statutory proposals which have busied Congress in the last decade have focused chiefly on presidential and congressional elections (except where Congress sought to remedy racial discrimination in all elections under civil rights legislation). Some proposals have been advanced as recommendations to the states. How long such federal self-restraint will prevail will depend upon such factors as the changing social and technological realities of the political system, on changing party structures, and on the effectiveness of local governmental representation. Inhibitions on the nationalization of the electoral process now depend little upon constitutionally imposed limitations. If the litigation process is to recede from the center of the electoral arena it has occupied for ten years, it will probably take its exit only because it has given way to legislation, to changing patterns of party competition and party discipline, or—less happily—to irresponsible extra-legal procedures.

EPILOGUE

Congressional entry into the field of electoral regulation does not necessarily mean that the litigation phase of influencing voting rights

48. See Note, "Elections: Qualifications of Voters, Residency Requirements Reduced for Voting in Presidential Elections," 77 *Harvard Law Review* 574 (Jan. 1964). In 1967, three scholars showed the strong correlation between the stringency of residence requirements and voter turnout. They concluded that "registration requirements are a more effective deterrent to voting than anything that normally operates to deter citizens from voting once they have been registered, at least in presidential elections." Stanley Kelley, Jr., Richard E. Ayres, and William G. Bowen, "Registration and Voting: Putting First Things First," 61 *American Political Science Review* 359, 362 (June 1967). See also *Drueding* v. *Devlin*, 234 F. Supp. 721 (1964), *aff'd.*, 380 U.S. 120 (1965).

policy is drawing to a close. Table 11–5 reports on the volume of electoral litigation in federal courts over a 20-year period. Since unreported cases and state court litigation are not reflected in these figures, the count should be considered conservative. Not unexpectedly, the volume of litigation in each category is sharply rising with no end apparently in view. The three-year increments used in the table conceal the fact that both reapportionment and race-related cases appeared to reach their crescendo of volume in the lower federal courts in 1965 (with a year's lag in the "peak out" of the Supreme Court docket in 1966). All categories of cases marginally declined in the "off year" of 1967, but the major election year of 1968 raised a host of simple as well as sophisticated election law contests in the courts.

Table 11–5   *Voting and Election Litigation Raising Constitutional Questions in Federal Courts, 1946–66**

YEARS	APPORTIONMENT & DISTRICTING		RACE-RELATED		MISCELLANEOUS	
	Fed Ct.	Sup. Ct.	Fed Ct.	Sup. Ct.	Fed Ct.	Sup. Ct.
1946–48	1	3	6	—	4	4
1949–51	7	2	9	2	3	1
1952–54	—	3	5	3	2	1
1955–57	6	2	10	—	3	—
1958–60	11	2	10	—	3	—
1961–63	60	3	50	3	8	1
1964–66	103	30	106	12	15	9
TOTALS	188	45	196	20	38	16

* Federal court rulings include those of district and appeals courts. Supreme Court decisions include significant *per curiam* rulings and memorandum affirmations. The appeals process makes for some duplicate counting. Apportionment cases include congressional districting decisions. The category on race encompasses Twenty-fourth, Fifteenth, and Fourteenth Amendment cases, including Section 2 tests of the congressional representation sanction for racial discrimination. The miscellany column embraces Electoral College disputes, nomination petition challenges, county unit rulings, corrupt practices litigation where constitutional questions were raised, residence requirements under the Equal Protection Clause, and a variety of other electoral process disputes affected by the Federal Constitution.

It remains to be seen whether the volume of litigious activity in the race and reapportionment areas will involve a decline. The 1970 census will predictably bring both a resurgence of districting cases and a series of Voting Rights Act suits for states where registration figures by race indicate an end of examiner programs (under Section 4b).

Certainly the struggles for effective Negro and urban balloting are not finished movements. Gains will have to be consolidated in both areas. The new phenomenon of black-power politics on the one hand, and the old problem of gerrymandering on the other, may generate litigious contests of unforeseeable varieties.

The powerful legal engine that has carried the racial minorities and urban majorities movements along has been the constitutionally based voting right. It may be that this legal claim will appear to be comparatively exhausted by the early 1970s when a majority of Negroes in each state are securely registered to vote and after census figures have been translated into fair reapportionment. Traditional constitutional voting rights cases, with their emphasis on ballot-casting and voting equality, have already spawned a second generation of disputes where the emphasis scores the qualitative factors of the environment in which voting rights can be meaningfully exercised. Increasing in number are suits which point constitutional queries at the electoral process where voting rights are not precisely at stake. Relevant problems touching on race involve free expression in southern campaigning and the seating of black legislators such as Julian Bond and Adam Clayton Powell. Relevant problems touching on reapportionment involve partisan districting where voting equality is satisfied, multimember districting, and the structure and procedures of representational bodies. Sensitive to some features of this development, the Civil Rights Commission in 1967 took steps to launch a study of the electoral process in southern states to include such diverse topics as the use of voting machines and the procedures involved in filing for candidacy. The commission also made preparations to act for the first time on its statutory authorization of 1964 to study vote fraud practices irrespective of race or of voting rights as traditionally defined.

The constitutional benchmarks of the 1970s may well take the Supreme Court further into the hinterland of the electoral process. Litigation trends statistically described are not enough to sustain this judgment. Litigation itself reflects changing patterns of felt social needs growing out of subtle shifts in popularly held values and material-technological advances. Some prospectively focused examples follow. (1) An accelerated diffusion of middle class values concerning civic participation—"I want to help decide," "I want to be heard"—may be translated into civil suits challenging electoral process techniques which ignite an "I've been cheated" feeling. (2) On the demographic side, the prediction of the *Congressional Quarterly* that by 1970 Negroes will make up 40 percent or more of the population in 14 of the nation's major cities should alert citizens to racial gerrymandering.[49] (3) The growing megalopolises of an increasingly urbanized America can be expected to generate needs which will transcend state boundaries and thereby challenge traditional representational institutions. (4) Mass media technologies have already changed the style of politics and have given the advantage to the candidate who can afford the widest television coverage. Coping with this problem (as Congress tried to do with the Presidential Election Campaign Fund Act of 1966) by supplying government subsidies to candidates, may raise due process and equal protection problems for minor parties seeking an equitable share of public finance. (5) Increased mobility among Americans has already made onerous the diversity of residence requirements for voting among the states. (6) Communications and electronic advances have opened new possibilities for registration practices. In 1967, while it was still under the sanctions of the Voting Rights Act, South Carolina became the first state to spell obsolescence for local voting registration boards by switching to a fully computerized, color blind, and central registration system. This forward step illustrates one way whereby a technocratic society may become increasingly unitary. At the same time, it must be recognized that these technologies also multiply the possibilities for centralized manipulation of the electoral process. Communications advances have opened new possibilities for sampling voter preferences, but the electoral process itself may become devaluated by the increased frequency of public opinion polls. (7) What is more, the stakes of the electoral process may be expected to be raised. If, as Martin Shubik has suggested, individual, corporate, and government control of "assets and decisions" are distributed during the late 1960s roughly a third, a third, and a third, and if, as appears to be the case, the trend is in the direction of a larger share for government, then Americans will be increasingly involved in substituting the political process for the economic allocation process.[50] As government agencies replace the market in making decisions that affect more and more lives, interest groups may become more fractious in seeking to influence public policy and the closely related control mechanisms of the electoral process.

Changes such as those mentioned above hardly suggest the prognosis that litigation will disappear from the political process. It is

49. *Congressional Quarterly*, Aug. 26, 1966, p. 1860.
50. Martin Shubik, Working Session Transcript, "Toward the Year 2000," 96 *Daedalus* 684, 690 (Summer 1967).

tempting to speculate that litigation in the field of public law will increasingly focus on novel problems of the electoral process. Be that as it may, one prospect is certainly clear. If the politics of a technocratic society paced by sharpened competition can long endure within the framework of democratic accountability to the electorate, the achievement will in no small measure be attributable to the legacy of constitutional voting rights marked out for protection by the Supreme Court.

List of Tables

Index of Cases

Index

THE JOHNS HOPKINS PRESS

Designed by James C. Wageman

*Composed in Janson text and display
by Service Typographers, Inc.*

*Printed on 60 lb. Perkins and Squier R
by The Murray Printing Company*

*bound in Bancroft Arrextox
by The Colonial Press, Inc.*